LEABHARLANNA CHONTAE FHINE GALL
FINGAL COUNTY LIBRARIES

Store

Items should be returned on or before the date due
below. Items may be renewed by person, writing,
telephone or by accessing the online catalogue on
Fingal Libraries' website. To renew give the barcode
ticket number and PIN number if using online catalogue. Fines
are charged on overdue items and will include postage incurred
in recovery. Damage to, or loss of items will be charged to the
borrower

Date Due	Date Due	Date Due
02 FEB 10		
08 MAR 10		
23. JUL 11	08. NOV 13	
	10 NOV 14	
20. JUL 12	08. JUN 17.	
10. APR 13		
05.		

Joseph O'Connor was born in Dublin. Among his books are the novels *Cowboys And Indians* (shortlisted for the Whitbread Prize), *Desperadoes*, *The Salesman* and *Inishowen*, a collection of short stories *True Believers*, and *Sweet Liberty: Travels in Irish America*. His novel *Star of the Sea* was an international bestseller, selling more than 1 million copies and winning an American Library Association Award, the Nielsen-Bookscan Golden Book Award, the Irish Post Award for Fiction, France's Prix Millepages, and the Prix Littéraire Européen Zepter for best European novel of the year. It has been published in thirty-six languages. Its sequel *Redemption Falls* received rave reviews internationally. *The Guardian* pronounced it 'a major work of modern fiction from an astonishingly accomplished writer'. He has also written stage-plays, including the award-winning *Red Roses and Petrol*, and he broadcasts a popular weekly diary on RTÉ Radio One's *Drivetime With Mary Wilson*. He is the 2010 Harman Visiting Professor of Creative Writing at Baruch College, City University of New York.

ALSO BY JOSEPH O'CONNOR

Novels
Cowboys and Indians
Desperadoes
The Salesman
Inishowen
Star of the Sea
Redemption Falls

Short Stories/Novella
True Believers
The Comedian
What Might Have Been

Non-Fiction
Even the Olives are Bleeding: The Life and Times
of Charles Donnelly
Sweet Liberty: Travels in Irish America
The Secret World of the Irish Male
The Irish Male at Home and Abroad
The Last of the Irish Males

Stageplays
Red Roses and Petrol
The Weeping of Angels
True Believers (adaptation)
Handel's Crossing

Screenplays
A Stone of the Heart
The Long Way Home
Ailsa

Editor
Yeats is Dead! A Novel by Fifteen Irish Writers for Amnesty
International

The Irish Male

His Greatest Hits

JOSEPH O'CONNOR

NEW
ISLAND

THE IRISH MALE – HIS GREATEST HITS
First published 2009
by New Island
2 Brookside
Dundrum Road
Dublin 14
www.newisland.ie

ISBN 978-1-84840-037-5

Book design by Claire Rourke

Printed in Ireland by ColourBooks

New Island received financial assistance from The Arts Council (An Chomhairle Ealaíon), Dublin, Ireland

10 9 8 7 6 5 4 3 2 1

Probably the only place where a man can feel really secure is in a maximum security prison, except for the imminent threat of release.

Germaine Greer, *The Female Eunuch*, 1970

Contents

RTÉ *Drivetime* Radio Diaries

Afterword

Introduction
Wanda and Me - A Brief History

The Secret World of the Irish Male was published in 1994, when dinosaurs still roamed the earth. (The book features a chapter about this funny new thing called 'the internet' and another on that cutting-edge item of modernity, the answering machine.) To my astonishment, it became an enormous bestseller in Ireland, largely because it contained a lengthy and light-hearted account, originally written over five weeks for the *Sunday Tribune*, of that year's World Cup finals in the USA. Vincent Browne was the editor of the *Tribune* at the time and it was his idea that I should go to America with Jack Charlton's Emerald Army. (I don't know if it was his idea that I should ever come back.) The other newspapers were sending their finest sportswriters, and the *Tribune* did too, but I think the notion of subjecting a total ignoramus on football matters to a baptism of beer at the World Cup appealed to the storyteller in Vincent. My brief was to write about the fans, not the matches per se, and it turned out to be the most enjoyable journalistic assignment I'd ever had. The book that resulted from the adventure was put together in roughly six weeks, with most of the editorial work, such as it was, carried out by my good friend Dermot Bolger, and I have to confess that its subsequent success unnerved me slightly. I felt I hadn't really written it. It had just arrived in some way. It reminded me of the children's story *The Elves and the Shoemaker*. I had awoken one morning to find *The Secret World of the Irish Male* on my workbench. Bolger, the elf, had created it.

It rapidly outsold the literary novels on which I had worked for years. Before long, it outsold all my previous books put together. I would turn up somewhere to give a reading from one of those hard-born novels, each taut and noble volume the result of endless nights of sweat and tears, and if the audience kindly indulged me, it was only a matter of time before someone would say, 'Now that's all very nice. Seriously. No, it is. But would you give us that funny stuff about what's-her-name in Disneyworld? About the rides and the mickeys? Now that is the business.' (The reference was to a particular sequence in *Secret World* in which I had described the doe-eyed incomprehension of a young woman Floridian tour-guide called Wanda as she faced a tsunami of Irish male double-entendres. She kept talking about the 'amazing rides' the pleasure-park featured, not realising her audience regarded her as one of them.) Anyhow, I'd suggest, 'I could read more of my novel, if you'd like? The sensitive bits about my childhood? The beautifully poetic and critically acclaimed outpourings of a wounded yet somehow unbroken soul?' There would be a strange sort of silence, punctuated by coughs and soft shufflings. 'Wanda!' someone would cry.

The *Secret World*'s sequel, *The Irish Male at Home and Abroad*, came in 1996, and a third instalment, *The Last of the Irish Males*, was born in 2002. The book you're reading now is effectively a compilation album comprising material from those three collections, together with a selection of the radio diaries I began to write in 2008, as the Celtic Tiger upped paws and skipped town. I was struck, when re-reading all the material, by how it could be read as a chronicle of change; but equally you could see it as something much less, or as something slightly more, or as both. I leave the verdict to the reader, who is always a wiser judge than the author. But I have enjoyed amassing the Book of Evidence.

I'm not sure that I always recognise the narrator of the *Irish Male* pages, with his wisecracks, lugubrious sarcasms, blissfully ignorant certainties, and his at times annoyingly puppyish desire to garner laughs. But he seems to have had a notably good time in his youth (a far better one than I had, the jammy little sod); and reading back over his archives, a lot of which are flagrantly unbelievable, made me smile and even chuckle from time to time. The idea that this dingbat is the author of *Star of the Sea* and *Redemption Falls* seems preposterous and frankly libellous. There were occasions when I wanted to slap him and others when I wanted to murder him. Once or twice I even wished I could put my arms around the poor nincompoop in a protectively avuncular manner, taking advantage of our physical closeness to discreetly whisper in his ear my fervent advice to shut up NOW. Certain other passages I found myself reading through the grid of my fingers. The very great Anthony Cronin says in his classic memoir *Dead as Doornails*, a book in which there is an awful lot of drinking and staying up late, that if anyone ever asks him what he did in his young years, he intends to reply, 'Not enough.' If the first three sections of the present volume are an accurate record of what I did in my own, my answer would be, 'Too much.'

Some of the people mentioned in the pieces have shuffled out of public view over the years, and some of the events in which they participated have been forgotten. But in assembling this selection, I've usually opted to allow the texts to remain pretty much as they first appeared. An occasional howler has been removed and a couple of thirteenth-century jokes have been subjected to euthanasia, but the compiler of any retrospective collection of written material must resist the temptation to re-polish. Amend the stuff too often and you're actually rewriting it, and since you're not the same person any more, you're not the same author either, which can result in a retrospective form of abashed self-delusion, an attempt to correct the record and make yourself appear cleverer than you were. Wise-after-the-event is easy; a monkey could do that. And the *Irish Male*, despite his table manners, ain't no monkey.

So these pieces were what they were, and they are as they are: sometimes derivative of the giants of comic writing who were among my heroes as a kid (Kingsley Amis, Dave Barry, Woody Allen, P.J. O'Rourke, Robert Klein, J.D. Salinger, Alexander Cockburn, Flann O'Brien, John Cooper Clarke, Hunter S.

Thompson, Gay Talese, Tom Wolfe, Tom Lehrer – and Anthony Cronin too), sometimes trying too hard, sometimes missing a trick, but I hope, here and there, still capable of raising a deserved laugh, an occasional tear, and no lawsuits. Every piece was written quickly, almost invariably against a deadline; indeed one section of my 1994 World Cup Diary was scarcely 'written' at all, having been composed over a public telephone in the vast car park of the Citrus Bowl Stadium, Orlando, to a sub-editor in the *Sunday Tribune* in Dublin. Ireland had just been beaten by Mexico under the cruel Floridian sunshine, and my report was required with urgency. I had a page of scrawled notes in one hand, a can of beer in the other, the phone uneasily cupped between shoulder and chin, and with the line crackling and buzzing and my pile of quarters rapidly disappearing, I managed to stay one sentence ahead of my scribbling listener. I should add that I was somewhat the worse for Mexico's national drink, which, alas, is the pollutant called tequila. Indeed I was approaching that particular stage of lachrymose drunkenness when one starts declaring love to passers-by. Trying to write a novel in a phonebooth under such intensities of pressure might lead to interesting results. Maybe I should give it a go.

Almost everything in this book was written because someone took a chance and commissioned it. I'm grateful to the *Sunday Tribune*, the *Sunday Independent*, the *Guardian*, *Esquire*, the *New York Times*, the London *Independent*, and to the many other publications where I've been given page-room over what it amazes me to realise is now twenty years as a writer. I've written novels, articles, poems, stage plays, film scripts, radio diaries, and the occasional rubber cheque, and I've been more unendingly fortunate than I could possibly have imagined when, as a teenager, I first hoped to make writing my profession. A writer needs luck and I've had more than my slice. To have stumbled into the authorship of the three *Irish Male* books and to have worked, as a result, with some of the best book people in Ireland, has been among the happiest accidents of all.

The radio diaries that comprise the book's fourth section were specially commissioned by producer Marian Richardson at RTÉ Radio One, for the daily news progamme *Drivetime With Mary Wilson*. (The broadcast versions can be heard at the programme's website, www.rte.ie/radio1/drivetime/.) When I was a teenager in the dismal Ireland of the 1970s and early 1980s, Marian used to present a weekly radio programme of traditional music, and was, along with John Peel and a young lout called Dave Fanning, one of the unmissable highlights of my week. She had then, and has still, one of the most gorgeous speaking voices imaginable, and it filled my boyish soul with melodies as sweet as those which she played on her programme. (All right, all right, I fancied her! It's a free country, isn't it?) To me, she and her colleagues embody all that is best in public service radio, one of the few uncomplicatedly great things we have in Ireland. Had anyone told me as a kid that one day I would be fortunate enough to be a minuscule part of it, I wouldn't have believed my luck. So my sincere gratitude and admiration to Marian and her fantastic team at *Drivetime*. To have had five minutes every Wednesday to talk to the listening public has been an honour. (Many a middle-aged Irish Male might like to give the nation a good dose of himself on a weekly basis. This one has certainly found it therapeutic.) And I thank Marian, not only for her matchless professionalism and warmth and kindliness, but for the hours of world-opening joy she brought to the life of a Dublin youngster who didn't have a whole lot of reasons to be joyful. Radio is a medium with an astounding reach. Your voice is in people's cars, in their kitchens as they prepare family meals, in shops, doctors' waiting rooms, student flats, the cabs of trucks, and if it is true, as I think it is, that every storyteller wants an audience, there's none finer than the one that lives in Irish Radio Land. And so I thank its listeners more than I can say for allowing me to gatecrash now and again. It's been an absolutely treasured privilege.

Some housekeeping remarks and other acknowledgements:
All the material in the first three sections was previously published in the *Irish Male* trilogy. A few short sections of the World Cup Diary had first lowered the tone of the *New York Times* and the London *Independent*, and 'The Emperor's New Clothes' had irreparably sullied the heretofore chic reputation of the international fashion magazine *Elle*. The poem 'Old Suitcase for Sale: No Offer Refused' was first published in *The Irish Times Magazine*, and I thank the magazine's editor Patsey Murphy.

My homeboy Anthony Glavin, who edited this book and helped to make the selection, is a prince, a scholar and a gentleman. A gifted writer too, he brought his immense skills to the task, and I thank him for his assiduousness and expertise.

I thank Edwin Higel and his excellent shipmates at New Island for seeing this collection and its three forebears into print. A special genuflection and rub of the relic must go to the Blessed Dermot Bolger, whose suggestion the first book was. I couldn't name every friend, colleague or loved one who ever gave me an idea for an article, but the guilty know who they are, and I thank them. However, some conspirators, alas, cannot be spared their place alongside me in the dock, for their complicity was so important in different ways, and so I hereby indict Ciara Considine, Jim Culleton, Michael Colgan, Declan Heeney, Noirín Hegarty, Cormac Kinsella, Sarah Moore, Colm Toíbín, Monica Casey, Bairbre Drury-Byrne, Peter Murtagh, Sarah Lehman, Amanda Ross, Adrienne Fleming, the late Lar Cassidy, Sarah Bannan at the Arts Council, Sinéad Mac Aodha at the Ireland Literature Exchange, Madeleine Keane, Miriam Donohoe, Philip King, the late Nuala O'Faolain, John Scally, John Spain, Dr Eimear O'Connor, my literary agent Carole Blake and her colleagues at Blake Friedmann in London, and my dear sons James and Marcus.

My wonderful father Sean O'Connor taught me to read, and I owe to him the fact that I ever wanted to be a writer. I thank him and my stepmother Viola for their loving solidarity. My late father-in-law, John Casey, was a beautiful man, and I think about him often with affection and much laughter. His grandsons have inherited his lovely way with a joke, as well as his quiet sense of mischief. After my novel *Star of the Sea* became a big bestseller in England, he loved telling people the story of how his car had one day broken down in Slough, where he had brought it to the nearest garage. Out of the workshop came the mechanic, with a grease-thumbed copy of my book in hand. 'You've made it in Slough,' John told me wryly. 'Who needs the Pulitzer Prize?'

Like most writers, I am never less than a paradisiacal joy to live with, as must be evident to any even semi-sober reader of these pages; but despite my perpetually angelic disposition and total lack of unreasonableness, I would still like to mention my beloved Anne-Marie Casey. She's the max, the bomb, and she got it goin' on, and as Austin Clarke puts it in his beautiful poem 'The Planter's Daughter', she's the Sunday in every week. She has probably ruined my career as an Irish memoirist by making me so happy, and for that – for everything, for more than I could ever say – I offer my adoring thanks.

My deepest gratitude, finally, to the readers my stuff has been blessed to find, and who have supported me, encouraged me, come on sometimes strange journeys with me, and given my work whatever reason it has to exist. We've been across the Atlantic on a famine ship, through the battlefields of the Civil War, to Nicaragua in the 1980s, through Disneyworld in the 1990s, through Ireland in the downturn, into Lord Archer's palatial bathroom, and God knows where we're going next. (Well actually I've a pretty good idea. And no, it isn't back to Wanda's for coffee.) I don't believe in art for art's sake, and in the end I can't get with any writer who does. I write for all sorts of reasons, most of which I don't understand, but the main one is to tell a story, hopefully to make a connection, by doing the thing I love best. As a teenager, I developed a secret crush on the

English language, and as I enthusiastically embrace my imminent midlife crisis (hurray!), I find, as does many a balding Irish male on the brink of anecdotage, that the hot flush from old flames still warms the cockles. I'd like to write better. It's either that or get leather trousers and a tattoo. So the fact that you're reading these words means a very great deal to me. Thank you. Thank you. Thank you.

Joseph O'Connor
June 2009

From
The Secret World
of the Irish Male
1994

My Difficult Childhood

I have never actually met anybody called Valentine, and I suspect there is a bloody good reason for this. Calling one's child after one of the more obscure saints – Boniface, say, or Begnet or Bede – I can actually understand. But calling one's child Valentine would bring back wistful memories to most people. What does Valentine's Day really mean? I'm thinking of the exuberant canter down to the letterbox on the morning of 14 February, the blood scuttling through the veins at top speed, the tongue flapping with anticipation, the nerves doing gymnastics, the exquisite agony of it all, only to be followed by disappointment, the bare doormat, the poignantly cardless climb back up to the scratcher, the placing of the head beneath the duvet, the agonised screeching of abusive epithets and the subsequent moistening of the pillowcase with tears so salty you could sprinkle them on chips. Calling one's child Valentine would be like calling it Disappointment. And Disappointment O'Connor would not be much of a name for a child, even though, no doubt, it would eventually get abbreviated to Dizzy O'Connor – and I've met one or two of those in my time, God only knows. Sappy O'Connor would be another possibility, I suppose.

Anyway, in the whole dismal cornucopia of abject anniversaries, foul festive frolics and rancid rejoicings, is there anything really worse than Saint Valentine's Day? Fresh from prising the shekels out of us for Christmas, the greetings card hucksters need a little extra just to keep them in the style to which they are accustomed, and, let's face it, desire is the most marketable concept there is.

When I was six I had a teacher called Miss Glennon. She was a very good teacher. She believed that there was more to early education than the repetitive chanting of ideologically suspect nursery rhymes and the digital manipulation of plasticine, and so, when Saint Valentine's Day came around one year, she made every boy and girl in the class write a Valentine card, complete with a poem. For those less creatively gifted students, Miss Glennon explained that it was acceptable to start off with the time-honoured couplet 'roses are red, violets are blue'. We got ten minutes. The completed cards were then placed in two piles at the top of the class, one for boys and one for girls. We each had to pick one at random, and read it aloud to the assembled unwashed.

At the time, I entertained an uneasy but quite fervent affection for Michele Killen, a tempestuous redhead who could play conkers like nobody's business, and whose pipe-cleaner men were the talk of Saint Joseph of Cluny School. Michele did not like me much. On one occasion she called me 'a weird little fecker', I recall, but, hey, it was kind of a Burton and Taylor thing. The card I picked out, however, came from a girl called Sheena whose hand I always had to hold whenever Miss Glennon took us on nature walks, which was a little too often for my liking.

Flushed with romantic excitement, I stood up at the top of the class that morning long ago and began to read out the words Sheena had written. They were, and here I quote in full, 'Roses are red, Violets are blue, I think you're horrible [sic] and you are like a poo.' I was shattered. Not only was the thought less than affectionate, but I mean, it didn't even bloody scan properly.

Every time I even think about it, I still blush to the colour of Ribena. Saint Valentine has an awful lot to answer for, in my book. In the unlikely event of my ever making it into paradise, be assured, I will certainly have a thing or two to say to him.

Another person from my difficult childhood I would like to meet, either in this life or the hereafter, is the famous and talented Australian entertainer, Mr Rolf 'Didgeridoo' Harris. You know, I actually used to like him a lot. When I was a nipper, the words of 'Tie Me Kangaroo Down Sport' were as important to me as the words of the 'Hail Holy Queen' were to other children.

I remember seeing his supreme Rolfness on the *Late Late Show* when I was a youngster. I think it was 1975. People had been on the show talking about Northern Ireland, about their lives and their sufferings, and about the deaths and maimings of their loved ones. It had been harrowing, to say the least. Rolf Harris had been listening to all of this in the wings, and he had been so moved that when he came on to perform he just broke down in tears in mid flow. It was an extraordinary sight, to a child. Rolf Harris simply stopped miming and took off his glasses and put his hands to his face and cried, while the tape of his disembodied voice singing 'Two Little Boys' continued to echo through the *Late Late Show* studio. It was one of the most important moments of my difficult childhood.

Yes, I had a spot in my heart for Rolf Harris. But the little antipodean cur has burnt his boats with me now. In 1993 he released a cover version of Led Zeppelin's song 'Stairway To Heaven'. It got to number nine in the charts, which is eloquent argument, if such were needed, that young people are not to be trusted. Anyway, if I ever get my mitts on him, Rolf Harris will certainly be crying again.

You see, 'Stairway to Heaven' is more than a song to me. The first girl who ever broke my heart did so while 'Stairway to Heaven' was playing in the background. I was a mere boy, and I was in the Connemara Gaeltacht one summer. She was a little older than me, and she was popularly reputed to know how to kiss people. When she kissed me, I became a little over-enthusiastic and my tongue got stuck in the brace on her teeth. It was agonisingly painful. It took me ten whole minutes to free myself. My eyes still moisten, in fact, whenever I hear Irish spoken. Sometimes people misinterpret this as national pride.

She was from Baldoyle and I was from Glenageary, which delightful Dublin suburbs are separated by a distance of perhaps a dozen miles. But a dozen miles is a veritable ocean when you're only a dozen years old, and anyway, immediately following her return to Baldoyle, the fickle and heartless little Jezebel seemed to suddenly remember that she had to play handball on a Wednesday after school – now *there's* a thought-provoking excuse – the very afternoon we had set aside for our secret and passionate trysts. She tried to let me down lightly but it was abundantly clear that the magic had just died. 'Stairway to Heaven' came on, as she gave me the big E. When the almost Yeatsian observation '*woarghh-oh, coz you know sometimes words have two meanings, unghg*' rang out of the jukebox, I told her I would never get over her. (By the way, if she's reading this now, I wasn't lying.)

But ah, that delicately descending A minor chord sequence with the bass part slithering down to F, then soaring with the grace of a young albatross back up to the final plaintive G, A minor. Every two-bit guitarist in the world can play it. It's banned in some guitar shops, because people play it so much.

It used to be the last song of the night at the Presentation College disco, Glasthule, where I first strutted my funky stuff. 'Prez', as it was known, was a pretty rough joint. They searched you outside for strong drink and offensive weapons and if you didn't have any, they didn't let you in. But 'Stairway to Heaven' reduced even the most hardened gurriers, savage boot boys and nefarious ne'er-do-wells to wide-eyed blubbing wrecks. I can still see it now, a great head-banging mass of denim and cheesecloth and existential angst.

You know the bit with Robert Plant plangently wailing '*woooohooooh, and it makes me wonder, woooh yeah*'? I mean, you can keep your Seamus Heaneys, *that's* deep. And what does Rolf Harris do? The heartless reprobate 'sings' this line – '*wooooh-oooh, and it makes me wonder'-* and then he quips, presumably to his backing group, 'and how does it affect you blokes?' It's blasphemy. It's sacrilege. It's like spitting in the face of the *Mona Lisa*. When the time of retribution comes, this backing group needn't bother whimpering to me that they were only obeying orders.

And the brilliant bit at the end? You know the bit that goes BLAM BLAM, *CHUNK*, BLAM BLAM, *CHUNK*, BLAM A BLAM A BLAM A BLAM A *CHUNK CHUNK*? *And as we wind on down the road...* Only the crowning glory, I mean the musical equivalent of the Sistine bloody Chapel ceiling, and Rolf leaves it shagging well out! God, it's like saying the Mass without bothering to have the consecration. It's pointless.

This is surely the worst period ever for popular music. When I was a teenager, people were embarrassed about liking Slade, The Sweet, Mud and Alvin Stardust. But these days, Alvin's 'Won't You Be My Cooka-Choo' seems like a Bach prelude and Mud's 'Tiger Feet' has all the brooding sexual magnetism of early Elvis. The charts are full of trite cover versions, and rich kiddies chanting about machine guns and the size of their penises over stupefyingly dull synthesizer beats. Me, I'm pining for Horslips. I'm missing Thin Lizzy. This is my past here, that Rolf Harris and his hell-spawned ilk are messing with. Hold me down, boys, till I strap on my air guitar. Rolf Harris, I'm coming after you, sucker. In my dreams, you are forever in the playground of Saint Joseph of Cluny School, Glenageary, and I am there too, giving you an eternal dead leg.

But dreams work strangely. One minute you are in Casablanca with Cindy Crawford, the next you are in Castlepollard with Michael Crawford. You never know what is going to happen in a dream. You never know what's going to happen in real life either, but some things you can be relatively confident about. The truth will always hurt, half your socks will always disappear in the washing machine and John Bruton in full flight will always be strangely reminiscent of Kermit the Frog in *The Muppet Show*.

One night recently I had a strange dream, one which I've had many times before. In this dream I am seventeen. My face is a sordid mess of oozing carbuncles and leaking pustules. I am about to do my Leaving Certificate maths exam. The *cigire*, a tall ungainly fellow with wings and a large yellow beak, is flapping up and down the aisle. Another teacher is sitting at the desk next to mine, laughing at me. I should explain that this dreamlike teacher is, or more accurately was, a real teacher, a kind-hearted priest who taught me once and has now passed on to what I hope will be a pleasant reward. If he's up there now I expect he's got the Jacuzzi, because Janey Mack, does he deserve it.

This poor holy man had been on the missions in Africa, and had regrettably gotten a chunk chawed out of him by some malevolent and toothsome insect. To recuperate, he had been sent home to Ireland to teach teenage boys. Wonderful, huh? Rampant malaria must have seemed almost cuddly compared to the suffering we put him through. Truly, we made his life such a purgatory that he must have often wished he was back on the banks of the Zambezi taking his chances with whatever vicious and carnivorous beastie might next come cantering wild-eyed and peckish out of the jungle. He was a thick-haired avuncular cove when he began to instruct us in second year. By the time we got to the Leaving Cert he was a gibbering basket case, bald as a billiard ball. He was thus given the affectionate nickname 'Penis Head'. In the end, I think that's what drove him over the edge. I used to imagine him looking at himself in the mirror while shaving every morning and hoarsely whispering, 'I don't really look like that, do I? I don't. No, I don't. I *couldn't*.'

Anyway, back to this dream. There I am in the hall, with poor old PH (RIP) munching his fingernails and mumbling incoherently about the Zulus, and I turn over the maths exam paper and begin to read. With cold horror, I realise that I cannot answer any of the questions. I have to sit and watch everyone else write. It is horrible. So horrible, indeed, that I always like having this dream, because it is so incredibly pleasant to wake up from.

My Leaving Certificate maths exam has haunted my nights for the last thirteen years. I was always desperate at maths. I could never understand it. Teenage life seemed so full of real problems that inventing artificial ones purely in order to solve them seemed utterly farcical. Why was it important to know how quickly a half-full train doing average speed would get to Limerick Junction via Portarlington when I could spend my days dreaming up witty things to murmur during the slowsets at Prez? ('Listen, Concepta, can I buy you a fizzy orange after "Freebird" or would you rather just have the money?') Even now, I only remember one mathematical fact. The square on the hypotenuse equals the sum of the squares of the other two sides. The other two sides of *what*, I never knew. (Smoked salmon, is it?)

Each and every June, Ireland is full of pressurised young people worrying about exams. They are important, of course, but one thing should be made clear. Exams examine your ability to do exams. They have nothing at all to do with education, and they're not worth going bananas over. If God must test us, Woody Allen quipped, I wish he'd give us a written. But God, if he exists, and if he is testing us at all, is doing so by continuous assessment. There will not be a *cigire* on the last day of judgement. No way. So what I want to know is this: if it's good enough for God, then, why, damn it all, couldn't it have been bloody well good enough for the civil service?

Anyway, in time, my difficult childhood ended, I grew up and out, and I started going to pop concerts instead of just listening to Mud records. It was a decision I was often to regret. What is this tragic madness that takes hold of the youth of Ireland? It is still beyond my understanding that every summer in our country young people trek off to Slane or some other sad little town to git on up, shake their booties, sink ankle deep into country muck and consume dubious hamburgers, some of which have prices as artificially pumped up as the cows from which they once came.

In the entire panoply of cultural tortures, is there anything really worse than the outdoor rock festival? I mean, yours truly is no party pooper. Be assured, yours truly has gotten down with the best of them, put my funk in numerous faces and agreed, quite fervently, that boogie nights are always the best in town. My own bootie has been shaken as thoroughly as James Bond's martini. But I draw the line at the rock festival. If there is a Hell being prepared for me somewhere – and I feel sure there is – it is an eternity of Lord Henry Mountcharles and his famous back garden.

I spent my teenage years going to rock festivals. I have seen the horror. I know what gives. You go down the country on a rattling coach, suffering from an appalling hangover. When you arrive in Slane/Thurles/Tramore, you realise that the locals have discovered the fine art of fleecing Van Morrison fans instead of sheep. You mortgage your as-yet-unborn first child to pay for a Coca Cola and begin the three mile trek over rough country to get to the venue. It is your luck to come across one of those festering Beelzebubs who masquerade as security staff. By the time you are granted admission, Sting is on stage, saying that we all godda, y'know, do a liddle bit more for the environment and animal rights. You feel you would be quite happy not to buy shoes made of animal skin, if only you could buy shoes made of *Sting's* skin, and that you just want to go home and back to bed, but you can't, because you're *having a good time*.

As Prince says in one of his songs, 'Dig, if you will, the picture'. There are 70,000 punters all being whipped into a quite advanced and dangerous state of sexual excitement by the throbbing primitive beat. All of them are very much the worse for strong drink. 35,000 of them are sitting on the shoulders of the other 35,000, waving instamatic cameras and plastic bottles of hooch in the air. The place is crawling with lost and screeching infants, savage dogs, arguing couples, plain-clothes members of the drug squad, stoned ravers in psychedelic shirts, Fine Gael TDs and recently released political prisoners trying to get their photographs into the newspapers. And Neil Young is on the stage now, yowling and wailing and falling about and thrashing his tuneless guitar – '*I wanna live, I wanna give, I've been a miner for a heart of gold*' – and the hippies think it's deep and people are trying to dance to this, although in truth you couldn't even do your shopping to it. And all around the edges of this vast and restless crowd, people are queuing up to evacuate their bowels in the nettle bushes. And you can't face this, so you go back, and you try to find your friends, but it's impossible, and it's getting terrifically hot now, and The Saw Doctors come on and everyone jumps up and down and roars and someone tramples on your toes. And there are long lines of punk rockers all puking and fighting and interfering with each other and sticking safety pins in their faces, and there are sunstroke victims having visions of the Blessed Virgin Mary, and there are Chris De Burgh fans having terrible fits, insanely screaming the words of 'Patricia The Stripper', and there are young fainting women being passed over the heads of the fevered crowd, and there are bottles of lager being passed through the crowd too, and parched punters down the back are gratefully swigging, only they don't realise the diehards up the front have finished their homebrew, and, not wanting to lose their places in the throng, have put those plastic bottles to a use that nature never intended, then turned and flung them into the sea of bodies. And your nose starts to bleed with tension, all over your shirt, and you look like the victim of a gang attack. And as one more fat once-relevant pop star in unwise trousers bounds out on stage and bellows, 'YEAH, WOAH, yeah, allRIGHT, SLANE you're BEAUTIFUL!! HOW YA DOIN'? I CAN'T HEAR YOU. Rock and ROLL, ALLRIGHT!!' you stop and realise that you may be young, but you're already pining for the time you can stay in of a summer afternoon and lie on the couch with a large gin and tonic and watch the bloody television, instead of going to rock concerts.

Of course, you have to be careful about relaxing too. It can be a very dangerous activity. One afternoon recently, I actually tried to do this. Relax, I mean. I wandered casually over to my parents' house with the intention of spending a few pleasant quiet hours with my loving brothers and sisters. An hour later, to drown out the noise of the roaring, I turned on the radio. A man from the Labour Party was on, talking about emigration and our young people.

He was in generous mood. He had no problem at all with the emigrants being given the vote, he said. I thought this was big of him, considering that the disastrous policies of the last Labour–Fine Gael government are what has most of them emigrants in the first place. Ah, the memories of my university days came flooding back.

The very socialist and progressive Labour Party was in government when I was in my second year in University. One of the really progressive things it wanted to do was to take the medical card away from students. OK, so I know that's not exactly the bombing of Guernica, but, hey, we were upset about it at the time. We were young, I suppose.

We all met in Trinity College. There was going to be an occupation. Our student union leader told us to be inconspicuous. Fifty of us took our bus fares, our banners and our bullhorns and we marched down to the Department of Health looking about as inconspicuous as the massed Serbian irregulars on a day trip to a mosque.

Once we had penetrated the minister's office, we all sat down on the shag pile and waited for something revolutionary to happen. I had taken along my cigarette lighter so that if anyone struck up a sudden chorus of 'We Shall Not Be Moved' or 'Blowing in the Wind', I could hold it up in the air and wave it meaningfully from side to side. I was very optimistic in those days.

After a while the police arrived. They were quite angry. They said they would 'do whatever was necessary' to get us out. They repeated the phrase a few times. We scoffed, heroically. We'd be here, we said, until all of our demands had been met. They asked what these demands were. There seemed to be a bit of confusion at this point. Personally, in addition to having Ireland immediately declared a 32-county socialist republic, I wanted to have a regular girlfriend and *Brideshead Revisited* repeated on a Monday night. Anyway, while we argued, the coppers left, no doubt happily reflecting on the fact that their monthly PAYE payments were helping to subsidise our youthful exuberance.

Their sergeant came in then, a nice big fellow from Cork. He parked his ample behind on the minister's desk. He told us that we were all very bright young people (which, incidentally, was questionable in a number of cases) and that we were very lucky to be getting an education (which, incidentally, was true). Then he asked us to leave. We told him to shag away off to hell, him and his fascist free-state, goose-stepping, imperialist paymasters. Well actually, I think we just said no. He shook his head sadly. He took off his cap. It was a terrifying sight, for some reason, a policeman taking off his cap.

OK, he sighed, there was one thing he wanted to say, before giving the order for us to be forcibly removed. The phrases 'give the order' and 'forcibly removed' were quite effective actually, now that I think of it. You could almost hear the sound of fifty pairs of buttocks being simultaneously clenched with anxiety.

He pointed a finger. 'If any of you are arrested today,' he breathed, 'you'll get a criminal record.' We greeted this threat with jeers and coarse whistles. 'And if you get a criminal record,' he continued, 'you will never get into America.' There followed a silence which can only be adequately described as stunned. 'Never,' he said, 'Never. Think it over.' He told us he would give us ten minutes to consider our options. He slipped from the room like a graceful phantom.

Reader, no water cannon was ever so effective. There was a stampede out of that office. There was dust coming out of the carpet. It was like the back door of a brothel during a raid.

I hung on with the hard core. At the time, I was going through that stage of adolescence known as virulent anti-

Americanism, so I didn't really care what would happen. What did happen was that two hefty guards carried me out and dumped me down on the steps so hard that I nearly shattered my spine. It was ten years ago. I've put on a bit of weight since. It would take the whole cast of *Hill Street Blues* to do the same job now.

Anyway, that sergeant understood something very important. He understood that our politicians are such embarrassing, dismal failures that emigration is an utterly ingrained part of the Irish psyche. Growing up in Dublin, you just expect emigration to happen to you, like puberty. In Chile the cops attach electrodes to your private parts. In Ireland they just tell you you'll never be able to emigrate. It works too. It's the biggest threat of them all.

The Birds and the Bees:
How to Fall in Love

Even before my difficult childhood had ended, I already knew that the most important thing I would learn in school was that almost everything I would learn in school would be utterly useless. When I was fifteen I knew the principal industries of the Ruhr Valley, the underlying causes of World War One and what Peig Sayers had for her dinner every day. Did even one minuscule titbit from this smorgasbord of knowledge ever come in handy in later life? Did it my buttocks. What I wanted to know when I was fifteen was the best way to chat up girls. That is what I still want to know.

It's something I have never been able to do. I have 'friends' who know how to do it and I loathe them with an almost religious intensity. You know the type. Relaxed easy manner, cheekbones you could hang a sombrero on, normal, well-adjusted men who've had their teeth capped, read three of the novels on the Booker Prize shortlist and once been to an opera directed by Jonathan bloody Miller. Vile unspeakable pondscum, in other words, but boy do they know how to get on – and indeed off – with women.

Last summer I was in New York, reading a copy of the *Village Voice* one day, when my eyes fell upon an advertisement for flirting classes. 'Huh,' I thought, 'I don't care if I can't chat anyone up, only a *really* sad pathetic person would ever do something as incredibly stupid as a flirting class.'

On the first night I was ten minutes late. By the time I arrived there were six men and seven women, all of them fidgeting, blushing, biting their fingernails, gnawing their lips, and all of them hoping too that by the end of the evening the lips they would be gnawing would be firmly attached to the face of somebody else. It was a hot Manhattan night and the sexual tension in that classroom was positively sparking. The air seemed drenched with pheromones. If you had inhaled suddenly you would have got pregnant with quads.

The teacher breezed into the room like a pop star arriving backstage at Wembley. Her name was Lucy. She was a wonderful gal, a vision in stretch lycra and black 501s. She made us feel that it was OK not to know how to flirt. It didn't necessarily mean that we weren't attractive, she confirmed (I have to say, I wasn't too crazy about that 'necessarily'), but it was an important skill to acquire. Most relationships, after all, began with a flirtation. My own usually began with an act of emotional hara-kiri, I reflected, but that was another story.

Lucy kicked off with a bit of guff on feeling good about ourselves in social situations. Dinner parties, for example. I ignored this. Dinner parties, after all, are not there to make us feel good about ourselves. Dinner parties are there to remind us that God does exist and that he hates us. And anyway, if we were the kind of people who felt good about ourselves at dinner parties, then why the fuck weren't we at one, rather than forking out good hard-earned spondulix to sit in a stuffy classroom reeking of testosterone and sexual panic and trying to look like we were only here because we wanted to write an article.

Things improved when we got down to the specifics. Step one: Basic Flirtation. Lucy said you had to look the desired person in the eye. You had to smile and use the person's name. You had to pay compliments and, if at all humanly possible, touch the person. Not run your mitts all over them, of course, just 'lightly brush' against them, preferably while 'sharing a joke'. A joke came thundering into my mind. What's the difference between a raw egg and a good ride? You can beat a raw egg. Perhaps that was not the kind of joke you would share with a total stranger. Above all, Lucy said, you had to ask questions. So far so good, I felt. I like asking people questions anyway; it is a very good way to stop people asking questions about you.

Next stage was Getting That Date. Lucy said she would give us her secret weapon. The hormonal activity in the room seemed suddenly to surge. She leaned forward. 'Little pauses,' Lucy whispered.

Basically, the gist was that we were not supposed to go blundering in, grinning 'howarya petal? Fancy a tequila sunrise or what?' We were supposed to 'insert a little pause'.

Lucy showed us what she meant. I was selected as guinea pig. She came over, sat down and gazed into my face, touching my wrist with just the right degree of pressure. My God, if there was one thing this woman understood, it was gravitational pull. She smiled. She moved her hair gently away from her sparkling eyes. She was so close now that I could smell her musky perfume. The class inhaled, en masse. I felt my palms moisten.

'Listen Joe,' she beamed, 'Do you, uh, want to have a drink with me sometime?'

The class exhaled and almost burst into applause. 'Are turkeys fucking nervous in November, Lucy?' I thought, silently. 'I see what you mean,' I said.

'Now you try it,' she grinned.

We broke into pairs and I got Alison, a very nice legal secretary from the Bronx. I noticed that on the name badge she was wearing she had drawn a little smiley face where the dot over the 'i' in her name should have been, but that apart, things were looking up. 'Now,' Lucy said, in the cool tone of voice used by brain surgeons who are just about to go into someone's cranium with a revved-up Black and Decker, 'Look into the eyes.' I peered into Alison's pupils as though she were Dan Quayle and I was trying to find measurable evidence of human life.

'OK, people,' Lucy urged, 'now smile, speak, and *insert that pause.*'

I could feel the sweat trickling down my back. 'Emmm,' I grinned, maniacally, 'you, uh, want to have a drink with me sometime?'

Alison laughed so hard that a ball of snot came shooting out of her nose with the force of an Exocet missile. I wondered whether this was my opportunity to 'brush lightly' against her by offering her a tissue, or, at the very least, the back of my sleeve.

'Use Alison's name, Joe,' Lucy chuckled, throatily. 'You've inserted, but you haven't used her name yet.' I conceded that this had indeed been an error of some magnitude.

I tried again. 'Urgh, Alison, you, um, want to have a drink some time, hrnmgh?' The entire class collapsed into a frenzy of tittering. It was dreadful. You could have eliminated the national debt of a small third-world country with the amount of money these people had spent on psychotherapy. Yet here they were, control freaks, social inadequates and tragic misfits all, weeping tears of laughter, slapping not only their own thighs but each other's also. It was very unfair, I felt.

I attempted it once more. 'Urff, Alison, I dunno, you hmmmm, wanna go...?' People were practically on the floor now. Bill, a very pleasant chap from Queens, had to get up and leave the room, shaking uncontrollably, hankie clasped to his frantically guffawing gob. I just couldn't figure it out. Every time I asked Alison if she wanted to have a drink, I sounded like I was already pissed. It was a hopeless situation. My little pauses were yawning chasms of existential angst.

Outside, later, fourteen of us stood on the sidewalk. We all agreed, quite dishonestly in my view, that it had been 'a lot of fun', but that some of us would have to work harder than others. We said our goodbyes and went to leave. I walked a block with Alison and Bill in nervous silence. Then, very suddenly, Bill stopped and slapped himself on the forehead, as though swatting some particularly virulent breed of mosquito.

'Urm, Alison?' he said. 'Hey I just thought, I'm like, going uptown. You, er, wanna share a taxi?'

She turned, the pale pink haze of the streetlight caressing the side of her angelic face. She reached out and touched his wrist. 'Uh, yeah, Bill,' she smiled. 'Yeah. That'd be really neat.'

'Errmm?' I ejaculated, hopefully, 'urrfmfgh?' But, tragically, too late. The taxi pulled up and in an instant they were gone.

And as I stood on the pavement alone, watching their yellow cab roar off into the sultry heat of the Manhattan night, I couldn't help but reflect that when dealing with women, it is a truly wonderful thing to have had an education.

This was a thought that had occurred to me many times before, of course, particularly in my student days. I should explain that in my home town of Dublin, in the grounds of Trinity College, a near-legendary event called the Trinity Ball is held every year. Although officially only open to students at that marvellously appointed inner-city university, it is actually attended by large numbers of students from other establishments, including my own fair and glorious alma mater, University College Dublin.

Anyway, the Trinity Ball begins at midnight and ends with a huge outdoor disco at dawn the following morning. During this time, attending students are expected to get togged up in formal gear, get drunk, get stoned, and, perhaps most importantly, get off vigorously with the person they came with, or, failing that, whoever else they can lay their hands on. Well, hey, it didn't actually say that on the tickets, but that was certainly my understanding. It was, without a doubt, the worst evening of my entire life.

The woman I went with was a lithe creature with blonde hair, a stunning smile and legs that seemed to go all the way up to her neatly coiffured armpits. When I tell you that she had something of the startled deer about her, I do not mean that she had antlers or anything. Rather, her eyes, when she turned suddenly to look at you, were just mesmerisingly cute. If bodaciousness was a commodity covered by the GATT talks, she would have been responsible for Ireland coming up with a very considerable surplus. She was a stunner. She was the princess of Babelonia. I would with equanimity have consumed a large portion of *pommes frites* out of her intimate undergarments.

I was highly surprised that she had agreed to go with me to the ball, because I knew that I was not at all her type. She tended to bestow her favours on aspiring rockstars, Keanu Reeves look-alikes, men with silky skin and broad shoulders and a total lack of musical talent. I don't know now why I asked her, but somehow I did, and to my astonishment she agreed.

However, at the pre-ball party which our mutual friends had thrown, I began to intuit that the evening was not going to end in the shattering banquet of mutual carnal fulfilment which I had had in mind. It was the small things really. The look of cold horror that came over her face when she saw my hired evening suit, its stained lapels flapping like the wings of a deranged angel. The way she vomited up her twiglets with the force of a broken-down fruit machine when I tried to hold her hand in the kitchen. I dealt with my teenage nervousness by drinking an entire bowl of rum punch, smoking several joints and trying to snog somebody else upstairs in the toilet.

I was very drunk by the time the fleet of taxis arrived to convey us all into town, and, for some reason, my date did not seem to want to sit beside me. In fact, it was only with considerable effort that I managed to dissuade her from strapping herself to the roof-rack, or following us in on the bus.

We stood in the queue outside Trinity for half an hour, during which time we did not exchange one single word. Well, I think I tried out my favourite joke. Once upon a time there were three bears. Now there's bloody millions of them. Astonishingly, she didn't even titter. Once in, I got even more drunk and I fell asleep on the floor of the Examination Hall, where, as I recall, The Pogues were playing; a difficult band to fall asleep to. When I woke up, my head was hammering, my left shoe and sock were missing and there was a large muddy footprint on the front of my tuxedo. For some reason I have never been able to figure out, my date was gone. I searched the room, elbowing my way through the perspiring swarm of diddley-eying Trinity students, but she was nowhere to be seen.

I sought her in the bar and the restaurant, on the rugby pitch and in the Arts Block. I got the security men to broadcast a message over the intercom. I lurched up and down the quad, trying to describe her to total strangers, most of whom laughed, jeered or pelted me with water-inflated condoms. One of them tried to piss on me. Unmentionable rustlings were going on in the bushes, where the spirit of Saint Valentine was being vigorously commemorated al fresco. Such was my total stupidity, my drunkenness and immaturity that I actually managed to persuade myself it had all been a *misunderstanding*; that my love would fall into my arms just the moment I found her, before leading me gratefully into the shrubbery by my dickey-bow. Oh, the terrible thing that is young male self-delusion. I bellowed out her name like a foghorn, or a snog-horn. But no trace of my punk-rock Cinderella.

I finally caught up with her at the dawn disco, at seven thirty in the morning. It was very cold, a light rain was falling, and she was efficiently snogging the gob off my best friend's brother. She had her hand up the back of his shirt, I noticed. Had she been sucking his face any harder his skin would have simply peeled away in her mouth. I turned around and shambled all the way home, where I collapsed on my bed, took off my tuxedo, lit my last cigarette and cried myself into oblivion.

Fun, I think it is called. I remember my kind and gentle stepmother consoling me at the time, saying that relationships become easier the older you get. Little did I know how spectacularly untrue that was. Love is never easy. Getting into it is almost impossible and getting out of it is even harder. I remember once having a relationship with this crazed woman who really didn't like me very much. Things were kind of tense between us. In fact, things got so tense that it often felt that our relationship was being directed by Alfred Hitchcock.

I had cause to reflect on all this recently, while having dinner with a close woman friend. It was one of those upmarket restaurants where there is a wafer-thin sliver of kumquat in the water jug and the waiter insists that you call him Serge, when, really, you would much rather call him waiter. And the subject turned, as for some reason it often does when you eat polenta, to love.

This woman is going out with a prize bozo, who possesses the brains of a piece of toast, the charm of Margaret Thatcher and the looks of Rod Steiger. He is an aspiring actor, actually, and his performances are not so much wooden as finest mahogany. 'I haven't got the guts to finish with him,' my friend said to me, 'I'll break his heart.' I sat there nodding sympathetically, hoovering up lengths of spaghetti into my gob as discreetly as possible, and reflecting that it wasn't dreamboat's heart that needed breaking, so much as his coccyx, when suddenly, a very simple solution occurred to me. 'I'll do it,' I said. 'I'll finish it for you.'

I am now prepared to extend this new service to the readers of this book. 'AN IRISH MALE DUMP-THE-CHUMP PROMOTION!' Here's how it works. You send me your hard-earned shekels, and I do your dirty work for you. Simple or what? For ten pounds plus VAT you get the basic service. I ring up the mistreating brain-dead sap you used to be sad enough to snog and tell them they can shag away off and die because you are fed up wandering about with WELCOME on your back. You don't want them any more. Furthermore, actually, you never *did* really want them. If the survival of the entire human race depended on you having sex with them just one last time, for about thirty seconds, and for a billion pounds afterwards, you would say no, you scum-sucking sweaty-buttocked foul-breathed bandy-legged bollocks.

For thirty pounds, we can go a little upmarket. I will turn up on their doorstep masquerading as an elder of the Mormon church, invite myself in for coffee, and say, 'Listen .... (your name here) really does like you a lot, an *awful* lot, straight up, but he/she just doesn't like you *in that special way*.' I will then dry their weeping eyes with a Kleenex, wipe their nose on my newly laundered sleeve and tell them not to worry about it, because while there may admittedly be not too many more fish in the sea, post-Sellafield, there are certainly plenty more poison-spitting snakes in the cesspit.

After that, it does start to get a bit pricey. But worth it. Spare yourself all the guilt, the recrimination, the tears and accusations, the ripped-up lovey-dovey photographs of you and your formerly better half sharing pina coladas on a balcony somewhere, returned to you in a re-useable envelope with the word 'bastard' inserted between your first name and your second. Avoid the cute little fluffy toy rabbit wearing the 'Gee, I weally wuv you cos you're such a cuddlesome funny bunny' T-shirt that you gave her/him last Valentine's Day being anonymously delivered back to your place of work in a shoebox with a stake through its heart, its eyes gouged out, its ears hacked off and inserted into its anal cleft and a rather unattractive heart-shaped scorch-mark where its leporid genitalia should be. It's simple. You just pay me, and I take the rap.

There are several optional extras of course. For twenty pounds, I am prepared to say you have some dreadfully infectious venereal disease that will surely rot the very fundament off anyone misfortunate enough to come within a donkey's bray of you. For thirty, I will tell them you are a Spurs supporter or a secret born-again Christian. For fifty, I will say you once owned a copy of 'Shang A Lang' by The Bay City Rollers, and were secretly and erotically fixated on drummer Derek Longmuir.

I will, however, have to ask for danger money if you expect me to use corny lines. You're just not good enough for them? A tenner surtax. You're coming out of quite a long relationship in which you were deeply hurt and you're just, you know, not ready for that kind of serious commitment again yet? Twenty. You don't really know what's wrong but it's all down to your difficult childhood and the fact that you didn't get enough hugs from your parents – a particular favourite of my own, I must say – thirty-five. And then there's the deluxe service.

For one hundred and ninety-five pounds, I will take your partner out to supper in a fancy joint, ply them with veal's throats, pheasant's tongues and vintage champagne, flirt like Zsa Zsa Gabor, discourse at length on W. H. Auden (or any major twentieth-century poet of your choice – January is a special Pablo Neruda month), make them feel great about themselves, tell them how beautiful and intelligent they are (even – perhaps *especially* – if they are stupid and ugly enough to turn water sour, which, let's face it, they probably are, otherwise you wouldn't be in need of this service), cackle maniacally at their abysmal jokes, then slowly, inexorably bring the subject around to *you*. I will explain with tenderness and sensitivity that, hey, it's so *so* tragic, but the magic just slipped right away while you weren't looking. Still, I shall say, it was a beautiful thing while it lasted, and you feel that you're not so much closing a door on your love as sealing a perfectly wonderful memory in the emotional aspic of the past. The hankies with which I mop your now ex-beloved's tears will be of finest hand-spun Chinese silk. The shoulders of my jacket, into which the broken-hearted dumpee may plunge her or his wailing and hysterically snivelling chops will be efficiently padded. The songs I gently croon as I take hold of your trashed darling-no-more's screeching face and slap, *slap*, slap again to calm them down will be purest Manilow. Go on. Christmas is coming. You know it makes sense. Dump that chump.

It's not that I want to be cynical. If you have met the right person, you should do the right thing, and marry them immediately. In fact, two good friends of mine who have been going out together – and, worse, God help us all, quite frequently staying in together and refusing to answer the telephone – told their families recently that they were going to get married soon. (Happily enough, to each other.) I was pleased to hear this news, because I am a great believer in the institution of marriage, and I can hardly wait to get married myself. In fact, I intend to do so as often as possible. Not that I am a romantic or anything. It is just that if I am going to get fat, disillusioned and sad anyway, I am bloody well taking somebody with me.

We talked for a while about their impending nuptials, my friends and myself. I am to be a witness on the happy occasion. I dislike the word witness, really, for its unpleasant legal overtones. I mean, you could just as easily be a witness at somebody's divorce as their marriage. And am I to be a witness for the prosecution or the defence? I think I should be told.

I am to make a speech on the glorious day, and I was instructed by the bride-to-be not to use the ideologically tainted words 'wedding' or 'marriage' in this speech. We finally settled on the 'bonding', which phrase I am not particularly happy about, as I feel it conjures up agonising and highly embarrassing scenes involving superglue, crowbars, teams of strong men and large tubs of axle grease. But who am I to disappoint a blushing bride? Bonding it is.

Marriage has not been very fashionable in ultra-liberal circles for some time. I lived in London for some years, and in certain parts of that right-on, politically correct city, if you happened to let slip at a dinner party that you were thinking of getting married, people tended to peer at you as though you had just piercingly farted during the funeral of a prominent member of the ANC. There then ensued a turgid lecture from some scrawny polo-neck-wearing part-time poet about just how preposterously conventional and middle-class marriage was, immediately before the hostess brought in the desiccated kiwi fruit for dessert.

I cannot figure out why marriage has such a bad press. It is a romantic and idealistic institution, but surely we need more romance in this lonely world. Yes, I know some marriages sadly do not work out. But governments do not work out either, from time to time, and we do not pooh-pooh the general idea of parliamentary democracy as a result. We do not demolish Dáil Éireann, for instance, just because of the existence of Sean Haughey, formidable argument though he may be for direct rule from Mars. And yes, on paper, marriage makes very little sense. How in the name of God are you supposed to find the one person you can love for the rest of your life, and go on loving them and putting up with their weird antics, cranky opinions and off-putting personal habits? How are you supposed to perpetually cleave to this one special soulmate, even in the event that some balmy night, just after you have enjoyed frenzied connubial congress, she may sigh deeply, light up a fag, rest her head on your breast and languidly confide that she feels Daniel O'Donnell isn't actually *that* bad, y'know, if you really listen to the words of 'Whatever Happened to Old Fashioned Love'?

The idea that marriage provides security is incorrect. But insecurity is the whole point of matrimony. You may think you are certain of your feelings, yet marriage at its most essential is the emotional equivalent of jumping out of an airplane not knowing whether the bundle so firmly strapped to your back contains a parachute or a grand piano. I've never been spliced myself, but I can understand how some folks find it more exciting to plummet through midair thinking 'so far, so good' than to sit in the cockpit, fly the plane and admire the scenery below.

Not that I'm necessarily recommending marriage for everybody. Different strokes, as the conservative MP exclaimed in the massage parlour. I spoke to another pal about the subject recently. The unhappy chap is knocking about with a woman who wants to marry him, but he does not share her desire. (In conversation, he often refers to his unfortunately intense beloved by the pseudonym Wanda, which, he says, stands for 'What? Another Neurotic Disaster? Absolutely!' 'It's awful,' he sighed, 'Wanda's gone and bought herself a year's subscription to *Bride-To-Be Magazine*.' His face took on the length of a fortnight's holiday in Termonfeckin. 'Well, look,' I suggested, 'her birthday's coming up. You could always extend it to five years as a present.' He looked at me blankly, then. And for one awful moment, I felt sure he thought I was serious.

Money

My financial life is an utter disaster. The rest of my life –
emotional, political, psycho-sexual etc – is merely a cataclysmic
misery. But the money end of things, now that is serious. My
problem is that I have pretty much the same economic planning
ability as El Salvador. My tax is a mess. My invoices are a
veritable Gordian knot of confusion, grief and disorganisation. I
feel these days like a very large flamingo. No matter what way I
turn, there is always a very large bill.

I am broke as the Ten Commandments. I am skint as a pox
doctor's clerk. Church mice come up to me in the street and
offer me their spare change. My creditors are hounding me. My
cash card has been swallowed up more often than a potent
tranquilliser in suburbia. My credit card has been declined more
forcefully than the offer of a brisk no-questions-asked shag at a
nuns' convention. The bottom line of my telephone bill looks
like a telephone *number*. When I was a wide-eyed and credulous
nipper, they used to tell us in maths class that you could not
multiply infinity by two. Well, they were wrong. I've seen it
done; the answer is written on the bottom line of my phone bill.

Recently I went to see an accountant. After I had finished
weeping and gnashing not only my own teeth, but also my
grandmother's dentures, which I had specifically borrowed for
the occasion, the accountant talked me in off the ledge, sponged
me down and explained calmly that as a self-employed person I
could claim various expenses against my tax. I had recently

bought a word processor, for instance, and I could claim for that, and for part of my telephone bill also, once I had the receipts. Receipts were the key to human happiness, she seemed to feel. Receipts were everything. The answer to the speculative question, *tsch*, life, what's it all about, eh?, was 'receipts'. On the Last Day of Judgement, when we are all queuing up at the pearly gates, Saint Peter will not be asking for lists of prayers fervently said or good and charitable works piously performed or fleshly temptations successfully avoided, but, rather, for our VAT returns, our national insurance numbers and, above all, our receipts.

'Receipts?' I guffawed. 'What? Them annoying little bits of paper you get when you buy something? Heck, I just chuck them in the bin. Is that not what everyone does, no?'

My accountant tittered with the air of a woman beginning to suspect the presence of a hidden camera in an ante-room. 'You're having me on,' she said.

'*Au contraire*,' I replied. She went a bit quiet.

'Receipts?' I scoffed, 'Don't make me laugh. Into the garbage with them, faster than a hot snot from a headbanger's nose.'

She peered at me at this point, as though I had just broken wind.

'Your cheque stubs, then,' she said, her face paling to the colour of cream cheese. 'Surely to God man, you keep your cheque stubs.'

'Well,' I said, 'not exactly.' I told her I threw my cheque stubs away, and in any case I rarely filled them in, because the only time I ever actually wrote a cheque was when I was half-plastered at three a.m. in some subterranean fleshpot and gagging for another bottle of Moroccan Beaujolais before doing the funky chicken with some inebriated and dribbling psychopath.

'But your bills,' she gasped. 'You have your bills, though. You wouldn't throw *them* in the bin, surely to the Sacred Heart?'

'Er, yeah, Marie,' I explained. 'You see, when I get a bill I write a cheque. Then I throw the bill away. This means the bill is gone, and I can start my life all over again with a clean slate.'

I tried to explain that as a lapsed Roman Catholic, paying a bill was the fiscal equivalent of going to confession for me. Paying a bill was a process of self-purgation, and just as a forgiven sinner wants to forget all about his past wickedness, a bill-payer does not want to be reminded of long-gone and only faintly remembered pleasures. But she didn't seem to understand.

Learning to Say You're Sorry

There is a man in New York called Mr Apology. He is a carpenter by trade, but when he is not knocking out sturdy chairs and attractive coffee tables, Mr Apology is providing another useful public service. He is turning himself into the conscience of America.

The deal is that you call Mr Apology's phone number and tell his answering machine your darkest secret. It's very simple. You ring the machine and let it all out. It can be serious or trivial, whatever you like. Your time is unlimited. Other people then call in and hear the tape of you getting it off your chest. You can call back and hear their recorded advice, if you like, but it's up to you. (Mr Apology makes no money out of this, by the way.)

I rang Mr Apology myself recently, and I must say it was the most fascinating half hour I've spent on the telephone in years. The recording first cautions, 'If you wish to confess to a major crime, please call again from a public telephone, as the police may try to trace your call.' There then follows as much public breast-beating as you can possibly take. Fraud, theft, bestiality, gluttony, sloth, it is all marvellous stuff. One man who works in a well-known hamburger chain confessed to regularly 'dicking the French fries', whatever that may mean. (Philip Roth, in *Portnoy's Complaint*, writes about masturbating with a large chunk of liver, 'I fucked my family's dinner!') Another apologist felt guilty for having regular *and* consensual sex with his adult sister ('I guess we're just, y'know, closer than other brothers and sisters'). Another man was bragging, rather than apologising, for having slept with many of his clients' wives. I had fully intended to leave a confession myself, but my own sins were not half as interesting as those of the other callers. And then something occurred to me. Not one of these apologies sounded genuine. The callers were real all right, but I felt that they had invented their wrongdoings. Which was even more fascinating in a way.

Still, one thing the Roman Catholic Church and the West Midlands Serious Crime Squad have in common – well, one of many things actually – is the shrewd professional understanding that, given the right circumstances, people will always want to confess, whether guilty or not. This fact can get you into big trouble. The American writer Tobias Wolff has a salutary tale about an encounter he once had with a fellow author, the late Raymond Carver. In the middle of a pleasant evening, Carver suddenly broke down and told Wolff he had been an alcoholic for years. After Wolff had sympathised and bucked him up, a strange thing happened. 'Listen Ray,' he found himself saying, 'I've got something to tell you.'

'Jesus, Toby, of course,' Carver replied. 'What? What is it?' Wolff hung his head in shame. 'This isn't something I want people to know about. But Ray, I used to be a heroin addict.'

'I couldn't stop myself,' poor Wolff tells us. 'Ray's surprise and horror were even greater than my own, and I found them bracing, inspirational. What I know about heroin can be engraved on the head of a pin. So I improvised. I let my invention run riot over Ray's credulity until I was satisfied that I had topped him… I made him promise once again not to tell anyone.'

Wolff brooded for weeks, until the next time he saw Carver. He told him there was something he should know. 'What's that, Toby?' Carver asked, no doubt in eager expectation of being regaled by further lurid tales of 'horse', 'chasing the dragon' and 'heavy vibes'. Wolff confessed that he had never taken heroin in his life, and that he had no explanation for inventing such a yarn. Carver was gobsmacked. The two sat in silence for some minutes, Wolff feeling extremely guilty for having deceived his old friend. But the lie wasn't the problem. Eventually, shame-faced, Carver made a confession of his own. He had 'told a few people'. Actually, he said, he had told everyone he knew. 'But Toby,' he pleaded in mitigation, 'I swore them all to secrecy.'

'From that day on,' Wolff recalls, 'we never spoke of it. But now and then other people, some of them complete strangers, have given me cryptic words of sympathy and encouragement.'

Confession is a very dangerous activity, you see. Guilty readers take note and be warned.

On a Dark Desert Highway: The Role of the Publicity Tour in Modern Irish Fiction

I had a novel published in the spring of 1994. It was called *Desperadoes*. With hindsight, the name may have been a mistake. Two years of telling people the title of your new book, only to have them go, 'Oh really, you're an Eagles fan, yeah? Always liked that "Hotel California" myself.'

You have slaved away for years crafting this noble, intelligent and perceptive tome, only to have it sullied by comparison with a tawdry so-called 'song' by Southern California's answer to The Osmond Brothers. You have spent all that time virtually alone, writing. But now, suddenly, you have to go public. Now, you have to talk about it. Now, you have to do an author tour.

You arrive in the first town. Your publishers have mistakenly put you up in a sensationally expensive hotel, thinking you were somebody else. It is the kind of hotel where they knock on the door every fifteen minutes and come in to turn down the bedsheets. You are not used to this. The kind of hotel you usually stay in, they knock on the door every fifteen minutes and shout, 'Time's up, Mac.'

But you begin to feel good about yourself. Hey, you're a real author now. You've made it! You strut around the enormous bathroom like a black polo-necked peacock, opening and sniffing the miniature plastic bottles of hair tonic, shoe polish and hand cream. You sniff so hard that you begin to hallucinate. The room pulses and vibrates in the manner of early Led Zeppelin videos, or the beginnings of flashbacks in Australian soap operas. But you're feeling cocky. All that hard work was worth it. You should really go home right now, while you're still feeling good. But you don't. You make the mistake of turning up to do your reading.

Nothing in life brings you back to reality like arriving at a bookshop in a rainy Northern English town to find the pallid and overworked staff trying to spread out and look like a crowd.

If you are very lucky, there will be about thirty people at a reading. Perhaps ten will have come to hear you read, and, miracle of miracles, to buy your book. But ten of the others will have come to shuffle up to you before the reading begins and explain frankly how they read your last book and thought it a smouldering mound of dogshite, how they are all writing much more interesting books themselves, and how, in point of fact, they would not buy your new book even if somebody threatened them with a Kalashnikov. Of the remaining punters, four will be distant cousins who live in this God-forsaken locality, begrudgingly press-ganged into turning up by their parents, who have threatened to disinherit them otherwise. You will not have seen them since you were seven, when you gave one of them a severe Chinese burn for saying your mother had a moustache. There will be two postgraduate English literature students from the local university down at the back, loudly swopping epigrams from the complete works of Michel Foucault. And there will be at least one amiable schizophrenic who has wandered in for the free glass of Liebfraumilch and a tepid sausage roll.

You stand about for a few minutes feeling nervous. You attempt small talk with the manager and his underpaid staff. If you are Irish, as I am, the small talk will invariably be about how well Roddy Doyle is doing. 'Oh yeah,' the manager will laugh, 'we had Roddy here last May and they were hanging out of the rafters. We turned three hundred people away.' You sweat like a sodden sponge. You swig from a bottle of warm Harp. You light up a cigarette, forgetting that you're in a bookshop, so you're not allowed to smoke. You stub your cigarette out in an empty beer bottle. Moments later, you forget that you have done this, and you take a big reassuring slug from the beer bottle. You chunder all over the cash register.

Nobody has a tissue. So you absent-mindedly rip pages out of big thick books like the Bible. When the mop-up is finished, the manager sighs and says you would have got a much better crowd if it wasn't for The Match, or The Weather, or The Time Of Year, of The Fact That *Brookside* Is On Tonight. What he really means is that you would have got a much better crowd if you were Roddy Doyle. You feel people's eyes glaring at you, and then glaring at the life-size poster of you which has been sellotaped to the wall behind the wonky lectern where you are going to read. In the photo you are slim, smiling, relaxed, groomed and then thoroughly airbrushed just to be on the safe side. In real life, you are overweight, tired, tense, messy, grinning like a botched brain-surgery case. You cut yourself shaving earlier, so a crimson hunk of toilet paper is dangling from your double chin. You couldn't get the trouser press in your room to work, so your chinos look like you recently had sex without taking them off. The manager introduces you. 'Joe will be reading from his new novel, *Desperadoes*.' Then he grins, broadly. 'Hope all the Eagles fans are in tonight.' You stand up and begin to read.

The till bleeps and jingles all the way through your reading. All the jokes on which you worked so hard fall utterly flat. As if to compensate for this, people laugh at the tender moments with such ferocity that you fear they will rupture themselves. Then, just as you get to the particularly poignant bit about Granny dying with the cute little puppy the orphan gave her in her arms, the schizophrenic stands up, drops his trousers, starts going on about being followed by the government and begins to masturbate vigorously. Glancing up, you notice that the manager is gnawing his lip now. His own lip, that is. Not the schizophrenic's lip.

You finish the reading and sit down to a torrential trickle of applause. Then, the worst part. The manager says there is time for a few questions. Total silence. 'Come on,' he urges, 'don't be shy.' Coughs. Nervous titters. One solitary piercing fart from your second cousin. Silence again. If you cracked your knuckles, the resulting sound would seem like a burst of rifle fire.

Back in the hotel you eat all the peanuts in the minibar. This makes you unbelievably thirsty, so you start drinking. You fall into a coma and wake up at dawn on the bathroom floor, singing 'Drop Kick Me Jesus Through the Goalposts of Life', with the plastic bottle of body lotion in your mouth and the disposable shower cap on your head. The hotel manager is knocking on the door, wondering what the commotion is about. You invite him in for a drink. He is cross. He tells you he would like you to check out. You don't understand. You grab him by the lapels. You can check out any time you like, you tell him, but, woah, you can never leave.

The Road to God Knows Where:
An Irish World Cup Diary

Wednesday, 15 June 1994, 7.20 a.m., Dublin Airport: I am shattered. I only finished my packing at three this morning. Now I am here in the check-in queue, so tired that I would quite cheerfully swop my plane ticket, my hotel voucher and my Category A tickets for all three World Cup round-one matches for a dark room, clean sheets and half an hour's shut-eye. The queue is enormous. I am surrounded by a group of six or seven middle-aged men wearing Republic of Ireland jerseys, green slacks, green denim jackets, green runners, enormous green sombreros speckled with shamrocks and harps, stars-and-stripes patterned dicky bows. They are carrying tricolour flags and rolled-up banners. One of them is applying green, white and orange make-up to his cheeks, squinting and pulling faces in a small mirror, smouldering fag stuck to his lower lip. 'You don't think that's a bit much, do you?' one guys asks, 'They're after sayin' on the news the customs fellas wouldn't let you in if you had that stuff on your face.' The make-up man turns to him. 'Don't be such a bleedin' daisy,' he says.

7.40 a.m.: A middle-aged man in an Ireland T-shirt is sitting in the airport bar eating a large greasy breakfast of black pudding, white pudding, beans, sausages, rashers and fried eggs. He is also swigging from a pint of Guinness. I gaze at him for some time, astonished that he could actually consume something like that at this hour of the morning. He catches my eye, raises a forkful of beans to his mouth, winks and swallows. 'Keep it country,' he says. I take this as an invitation to sit down and talk to him. He is from Mallow, County Cork, and he is going over to the World Cup, and to stay with his brother who lives in Queens. He hasn't seen his brother for seven years. He has a nephew over there who he's never met. 'It'll be brilliant,' he says. 'I'm not that bothered about the football actually, but I just can't wait to see him again.'

8.10 a.m.: We get on the plane and take our seats. I watch the fans filing on. There are a lot of men, of course, of all ages, all wearing green shirts, but there are a good few women too, and loads of teenagers and children, some of them quite young. One man swaggers down the aisle with a sleeping toddler in his arms. Father and son are dressed in identical green soccer shirts. A boy of sixteen or so clambers on, wrapped in a tricolour. His mother and father follow him, also wrapped in tricolours. Everyone looks wide-eyed with excitement.

8.30 a.m.: The captain comes on the radio and announces that there's going to be a delay of an hour. 'I know you need this news like a moose needs a hatstand,' he quips, 'but once we get up there, we'll do our best to pedal a bit harder than usual.' His name is Terry, he tells us, and we're to feel free to ask him anything we like. For some reason, I am not sure I feel confident being flown across the Atlantic by a man called Terry. Irrational, I know. But there it is.

9.20 a.m.: The plane takes off for the short flight to Shannon. I get chatting to the chap beside me. He, his five year-old son, his father and father-in-law are all going to the World Cup. 'It's expensive, but it's the chance of a lifetime,' he says, 'It's a special memory we'll always have together.' We land at Shannon, get off and shuffle into the transit lounge. More delay. The fans converge on the bar. It is very early in the morning, but the chanting and singing – 'Oooh Ahh Paul McGrath' and 'You'll Never Beat the Irish' – has already started. 'You'll certainly never beat the Irish to the feckin' bar,' one man says.

11.30 a.m.: All safely back on board, Captain Terry revs up, puts his foot down and soon gets us airborne. There is an almighty cheer as the plane soars into the clear sky. Terry, who is English, comes on to the intercom and expresses the hope that Ireland do well in the World Cup. A new chant begins. 'England Aren't In It. England Aren't In It.'

12.00 p.m.: I go down the back for a smoke and find myself sitting beside a nine-year-old child, my worst nightmare on a long flight. He is very self-confident too, which makes it worse. 'I'm going to America,' he says. I contemplate telling him that he's on the wrong plane, and that he's actually going to Siberia, but his parents are sitting just across the aisle. 'Ireland are cool,' he says, 'aren't they?' I agree that Ireland are cool. 'I have a girlfriend,' he says, 'and I'm going to marry her when I grow up.' I offer heartiest congratulations. 'I kiss her,' he says, 'I kiss her and everything.' I say I think he's a bit young to be kissing girls. 'I am not,' he says, 'you put your tongue in their mouths but you don't swop spits.' I suddenly realise what I've been doing wrong all these years. Down the back the fans are chanting 'Irela-hand, Ire-lahand, Ire-lahand.' 'Do you kiss girls?' the kid says. I ignore him. 'DO YOU KISS GIRLS?' he shrieks. 'Not as often as you do,' I say. 'I bet you do,' he sniggers, his little voice gurgling with malevolent pleasure, 'can I try on your glasses, fatso?' It is going to be a very long flight.

1.30 p.m.: Somewhere over Newfoundland. The in-flight video is showing highlights from the Republic's qualifying match against Northern Ireland. The Alan McLoughlin goal sends an electric shiver of pleasure up everyone's spine, particularly, no doubt, the spine of the manager of the travel agency which organised today's flight, who owes Alan McLoughlin a very great deal indeed. Every time the score is shown again in slow motion, there is another cheer from the passengers. After the fifth time, the hostesses are cheering too.

2.30 p.m.: We land at Newark Airport and clear customs. The fans are looking more than a little bedraggled after their long day. But they are still singing. 'Olé, Olé, Olé, USA, USA, USA.' On the hotel bus I get talking to a Dublin solicitor who is here with three other solicitors. I tell him I am a journalist. 'You're not to write anything horrible about solicitors,' he says. As if I would. (Q: What do you call seven hundred solicitors at the bottom of the sea. A: A bloody good start. Q: How many solicitors does it take to change a lightbulb? A: Are you paying with Visa or American Express? Q: What do solicitors use for contraception? A: Their personalities.)

7.00 p.m.: The hotel bar. I am having a drink with a group of fans. 'Showered, shaved, and sheepshagged,' as one of them puts it, they are ready for a good time. The problem of the lack of tickets for the Italy game is being keenly discussed. A huge number of supporters do not have tickets for any of the games. A chap from Galway gives me a phone number he has for a tout. Out of interest, I go to the lobby, ring the number and ask about prices for Ireland versus Italy. 'That's the hottest ticket in town, mac,' the tout says, 'I got four real nice seats together, two thousand bucks.' 'That would be for the four?' I say. He whimpers with derisive laughter. 'What are you, buddy, crazy? That would be each.' I put the phone down, canter into the jacks and take my tickets out of my underwear, where they are being kept for safe keeping. Even if I am mugged, I figure, nobody is going to examine the contents of my boxer shorts. I look at my tickets. I touch them. For one moment, I am tempted to sell my tickets for two thousand dollars each, watch the match on the television in my room and write up the piece pretending that I was there. Journalistic ethics get the better of me. And anyway, the television in my room is not working. I fold up my tickets, stuff them down my trousers and go back to the bar. A man from Meath is standing on a chair singing 'Boolavogue'. When he gets to the line 'one more fight for the green again', the roof nearly lifts off with applause.

10.30 p.m.: The Stephen's Green Pub, Queens. The walls of this friendly bar are plastered with black-and-white stills of great

Irish football games from the last few years. The crowd are young, Irish, working class, sharply dressed. They are out for a good time; spending money like it is going out of fashion. Ireland being in the World Cup here in America is 'the best thing that ever happened to me,' one guy says. 'It's absolute magic.' He has been over here working in New York as a furniture remover for eight years, he says, the money is great but the work is hard. 'You'd need two hearts sometimes to do it,' he says, because the loads he has to lift are so heavy. The crack is mighty in New York, but you'd miss home, Letterkenny, County Donegal. Two lads from Finglas tell me that the trip has cost them so much they won't have another holiday for years. But they don't care. 'It'd be great if we do well,' one says, 'but it's great to be here anyway. Christ, what a place.' The jukebox is on loud, playing The Cranberries, U2, Thin Lizzy and The Horslips. Pints of Guinness are passed from the bar, over people's heads, through the crowd. People are dancing around in rings, stamping their feet, holding hands, singing along to the music. One of the Finglas lads fancies a girl who is sitting with her friends on the far side of the room. He keeps smiling at her. She is wearing an Ireland Jersey with the word 'KEANE' printed on the back. He says he wonders is she. Keen. She keeps bending forward to talk to her friends, then laughing uproariously before glancing back at him. 'Give it a lash,' his friend says. He finishes his pint, strolls over, sits down with her and her friends. Half an hour later they are slowdancing to 'I Useta Love Her' by The Saw Doctors. A difficult thing to do. His friend turns to me. 'Funny old game right enough,' he says, and we order tequila slammers.

2.30 a.m.: As the cab moves across the Queensboro Bridge, the millions of lights in the windows of the Manhattan skyscrapers glimmer and sparkle through the darkness. The sight looks like the most magical thing on earth. 'Noo Yawk,' the driver says, 'everyone thinks it's, hey, like this really romantic place, but actually, there's more weirdos per square inch of New York than anywhere else in the world, buddy, except maybe

Russia.' The Empire State appears in the distance, shimmering with pale red and blue light. Rain starts to fall on the empty avenue. 'Still,' the driver sighs, 'I suppose ya gotta dream a liddle, and I guess it's a great place for dreamin'. Now that's the funny thing see, about Noo Yawk, cuz sometimes it's so beauootiful, you lose your concentration, see, where ya just drift away in a second, ya know what I'm sayin'?'

'Huh?' I say.

3.00 a.m.: Slim's All Night Diner, Second Avenue. I am reading tomorrow morning's newspaper. Most Americans know nothing at all about soccer, and there is an article explaining the rules in endearingly simple terms. A tackle is 'when one player tries to get the ball from another'. A throw-in is 'when a player throws the ball into the field of play'. The goalkeeper is 'the only player who is allowed to use his hands'. What exactly the goalkeeper is allowed to use his hands for is not explained. It is now the early hours of 16 June, Bloomsday. I remember a story about James Joyce. A young fan once asked if he could shake the hand that wrote *Ulysses*. 'You can,' Joyce said, 'but remember, it's done a lot of other things too.' If anyone ever asks Packie Bonner to shake the hand that saved the Romanian penalty in Italia '90, I hope he says the same thing.

Thursday, 16 June, 10.00 a.m.: A crowd of badly hungover fans are having breakfast in a diner on Second Avenue. They are clearly finding it difficult to deal with the complexities of American food. One of them asks for a bacon sandwich. The waitress says, 'what kinda bread? We got rye, brown, sodabread, white, bagels, black bread, rolls, Italian heros.' He says he'll have an Italian hero. This gets quite a response from his pals. By the time they've finished slagging him off, his breakfast has been brought to the table. The plate contains a mound of food, french fries, pickles, various kinds of lettuce. It looks like something out of the Amazon rainforest. He gapes at it, open-mouthed. 'Does your one want me to eat this?' he says, 'or put shagging Moss Peat on it?'

1.00 p.m.: The temperature is now almost a hundred degrees, and New York is bathed in a sticky and oppressive humidity. It is hotter here today than it is down in Orlando. It's too hot to walk around much, so the fans are sitting in the air-conditioned hotel lobby, smoking and drinking and talking about Saturday's game. Everyone hopes the weather will cool off, but someone says the forecast doesn't look great. There's no news at all in the papers about the Ireland team, hardly anything about the whole tournament. People are ringing up their friends and relations back in Ireland to get news about the team. Another busload of supporters arrives from the airport. 'Jayzsus, I'm dyin',' one of them says, as he drops his cases and takes off his soaked jacket. 'If it gets any hotter we'll be carried home in bottles.'

8.00 p.m.: Go out for drinks with a crowd of boisterous Australian Ireland fans who have just arrived at the hotel. Jill from Sydney tells me that the trip cost her and her boyfriend $10,000, but they don't care. (Her boyfriend is already almost comatose with alcohol.) They've been saving for months to come and see Ireland play. The Australians are delighted that England have not qualified. They consume a lot of beer and tell Pom jokes to the Irish supporters they meet. 'Where do you hide a Pommie's bar of soap?' 'Under his facecloth.' 'What's the difference between a Pom and a jumbo jet?' 'A jumbo jet stops whining when it lands at Sydney Airport.'

2.00 a.m.: Friday morning: Go to bed slightly the worse for drink and dream of James Joyce heading in a corner against the Italians.

Friday, 17 June, 8.00 a.m.: Wake up feeling like my brain has turned into spaghetti. Something bit me in the middle of the night. A bloody cockroach no doubt. I have a spot on the end of my nose the size of The Bronx and twice as unpleasant. The bags under my eyes could be packed. I plaster myself with mosquito cream and suntan lotion and go down to breakfast, looking like a turkey that's about to be put into an oven. The Australians are already on the beer. One of them is singing 'Pommie dingbats stuck at home, doo-dah, doo-dah'. A gang of Ireland fans wander in, wearing giant inflatable green plastic hands and green skiing goggles. The Australians cheer and order beers for everyone. 'Hey spotnose,' Jill's boyfriend calls, 'you wanna lager?' Everyone laughs at the carbuncle on my schnozz. One of the Ozzies says I should dye it green for Jack and the lads, only then, as he points out, 'it would look like a flamin' great snot, wouldn't it?' This seems to go down very well indeed. I sit down and order a coffee. The waitress asks if I want milk. 'Just a spot,' another Antipodean titters. For an instant, I find myself hoping that Ireland get hammered, because I'm not sure I can take more than two weeks of this.

Saturday, 18 June: We play Italy. The rest is a bit of a blank.

Sunday, 19 June: On the morning after the Italy game I wake up at about seven. I am still wearing my clothes – at least, I think they are my clothes, although they don't seem to fit me too well. My head is pounding like the Kilfenora Ceilidh band on ecstasy. My throat is sore. My mouth feels like Oliver Reed died in it. The sheets, when I roll over, are full of loose change, crumpled beermats and segments of soggy lukewarm pepperoni pizza. I lurch out of the bed, crawl across the shag pile like some sort of semi-comatose and inebriated slug and gaze at myself in the mirror. The sight that greets me is pretty scary.

My eyes are pink as a teddyboy's socks. My lips and teeth are stained black from Guinness. My skin is light green in hue. I look like an alien out of one of the more convincing episodes of *Star Trek*. I try my best to hose and heave my ruined mug into some kind of order, but I have the distinct and uneasy feeling that today is going to be a bad hair day. Someone spilled a pint over my head last night. I can't remember why or where. All I can remember is this big thick English plankbrain in a Fifth Avenue bar, getting on my nerves. I think I remember saying he was so bleeding stupid he thought a quarterback was some kind of refund deal. And all I can remember then is being in an all-night diner with people from Kerry and trying to dry my hair on the Books section of the early city edition of the *Sunday New York Times*. This strategy obviously did not work. My hair is now so dishevelled that I look like Carlos Valderamma in National Health Service spectacles.

I stagger out of my room and into the lift, still wearing the clothes I sat through the match in, went out afterwards in, got plastered in and slept in. I smell like a putrefying yak. Every time the lift stops, more people get into it. It is an odd sight, an elevator full of people all politely coughing and examining their fingernails and softly whistling 'Olé, Olé, Olé' and trying desperately not to inhale through their nostrils. On the fourth floor, two of the Australian Irish fans get in, grinning pleasantly. Jim is wearing no shirt, no socks, no shoes, and a pair of shorts so tight that you can almost read the dates on the coins in his pockets. Debs is wearing a minuscule green bikini. Don't you just love Australia? After only a moment, Jim turns around, holding his nose between his index finger and his thumb. 'Aw, blow me backwards,' he groans, 'what crawled up someone's bum and died, mates?' This does a little to break the tension.

Down in the lobby, the scene is like something from the last days of the Weimar Republic. There are empty bottles, pyramids of cans, overflowing ashtrays, upturned potplants, and there are Irish fans sprawled everywhere, looking so banjaxed and bedraggled that I cannot figure out whether they have only just scuttled out of the scratcher this minute, or whether they have been up all night. A man with a pair of underpants on his face is lying under the grand piano. He is rolled up in a tricolour flag, so that he looks for all the world like some class of Hibernian mummy. It is a sight to gladden the heart of Patrick Pearse. A young couple are wrapped around each other on the bar sofa, open-mouthed, both snoring like motorbikes. A trio of middle-aged men are sitting on the floor, playing cards for dollar bills.

One of them suddenly staggers to his feet, punches the air and bellows, 'Come on Lads, Let's Go, You'll Never Beat the Irish. You'll Nev...' There is silence, punctuated only by a solitary piercing fart and a few weary mutters of 'ah, shut your feckin' gob, you great eejit.'

I cannot find the woman from the travel agency. I sleepwalk back up to my room and sit on the bed, wondering how it is possible to feel this woeful and still be alive. I light a cigarette and count the coins in my sheets. There's almost enough for a tequila sunrise. I cheer up. I extract a piece of the pizza from under my pillow and eat it. I ring down to the lobby. They manage to find the tour guide. I remind her that I will be staying in New York for an extra day, and will join up with the tour tomorrow in Orlando. I sleep. I wake up ten hours later, finish the pizza, sleep again. We beat them one–nil, I ponder as I munch. How sweet are the spoils of victory.

Monday, 20 June, New York: I wake up feeling a lot better. The minibus arrives at the hotel to take me to the airport. 'Are you JFK?' I ask the driver. 'What, I look like the back of my brainbox is blown away?' he quips. I am the only passenger on the trip. The driver, Duane, tells jokes all the way. 'These two bags of sick walk into a bar, see, and they order a beer, and then one of them says to the other one, gee, I'm feelin' real sentimental, cos I was brought up around here. Ya geddit, buddy? Brought up, see? They're, like, bags of sick, OK? HAHAHAHAHA.' He has a laugh like a machine gun.

We arrive at JFK and I get on the plane. I get talking to a very nice Mexican woman who is coming to Orlando to meet her boyfriend for the Ireland match.

We land at Orlando airport and I ask the taxi driver to take me to the hotel into which I have been booked by my travel agent. This is the Howard Johnson Plaza Hotel on International Drive. The taxi driver explains that he cannot do this, as the Howard Johnson Plaza Hotel on International Drive was actually demolished a month ago and is now a very nice parking lot.

I consider my position. Here I am in Orlando, a town where I know nobody at all, without a hotel to stay in, having lost the four hundred odd (very odd) fans I am here to write about, and thus, in point of fact, having lost all reason for being here in a professional capacity. I can feel my duty to *Sunday Tribune* readers being severely compromised. I can also feel a very promising expense account about to go up in smoke. Hmmm.

In a dazzling flash of Pilgeresque bravery under fire, I get a taxi to another hotel, check if they have air conditioning and minibars and then, with no thought at all for my own personal safety, book in. By a stroke of the most pure unexpurgated luck, this turns out to be the hotel where most of my group of fans are staying. There are tearful reunions. I never thought I would end up having tearful reunions with men called Hatcho, Bullso, Whacko, Bowso, Scazzo and Mazzo, but, hey, it's a guy thing. It occurs to me, as I say hello again to Liffo, Meerto, Leppo and Bongo, that the Irish team have more fans whose names end in 'o' than the Italians and Mexicans put together. I consider trying to come up with a name ending in 'o' for myself. Under pressure, 'Potato' is the best I can do. If I were Dan Quayle, I console myself, I could not even do that much.

I retire early, leaving the lads merrily emptying the bar. I am overjoyed to discover that there is a karaoke lounge directly beneath my bedroom. The fans are loudly singing hit songs and inserting the word 'Ireland' into them at every opportunity. The recent Whitney Houston smash thus becomes:

And *Eye-ee-eye-eer-land wheel always love yew*
Ireland, Ireland
Wheel always love yew
Ireland, Irela-ha-hand.

As the night wears on, the songs become even more thought-provoking. 'Why, Why, Why, Delilah' becomes 'Why, Why, Why, Schillachi'. 'Sexual Healin'' mutates into 'Sexual Ronnie

Whelan', and then, rather effectively, into 'Sexual Terry Phelan'. The high point of the evening, for me, is when my dear sister Sinéad's poignant lament 'Nothing Compares 2 U' is sublimely reinterpreted as 'Nothing Compares 2 Phil Babb'.

After several hours of this, I fall into a fitful and flickering slumber. I wake up gibbering at some unearthly hour, with a roaring noise in my ear and no idea where in the name of God I am. After a moment or two I become aware that the roaring noise is actually the undeniable – if at this stage tediously unoriginal – sentiment, 'One Packie Bonner, There's Only One Packie Bonner, One Packie Bonner, There's Only One Packie Bonner, One…' being sung in the corridor outside.

This full-blooded testimony to the quite phenomenal singularity of Mrs Bonner's baby boy continues unabated for some time. Then, suddenly, from somewhere down the corridor, an unmerciful screech splits the air. 'IF YOUZE DON'T SHUT YIZZER FOOKIN' BEAKS I'LL COME OUT THERE AND I'LL DANCE THE WHOLE FOOKIN' LORRA YEZ INTO THE BLEEDIN' CARPET, YIZ SHOWER OF FOOKIN' BOLLIXES.'

Astonishingly, this seems to work. There is silence, then muffled goodnights, whispered adieux and one softly hissed, 'I suppose a ride'd be owa the question, Lippo, wha'?'

Tuesday, 21 June, afternoon: A colleague, David Modell from the London *Independent* magazine, who has been travelling with the same group of fans as myself, manages to find me. I am glad to see him. It is rather nice to talk to someone whose name does not end in 'o', although I do find myself beginning to refer to him from now on as either Davo or Moddo.

He tells me what happened to the fans on Sunday. Having been delayed for five hours at the hotel, they were bussed out to JFK, then delayed for six more hours with no food and precious little drink before getting on a flight that landed at the wrong airport. 'It got a bit ugly,' Davo says. 'Security had to be called in.'

Tuesday night: Davo and myself go for what is called in vulgar circles a good nosebag in a posh French restaurant in downtown Orlando – posh, in America, meaning the waiters don't tell you their names – and then on to an Irish Bar on Church Street, where we skull pints, talk to the fans and listen to hopeless Irish-American singers doing toe-curling impressions of Christy Moore. One of the singers says he'd like to dedicate this next song to The Cranberries, 'who had to go away to be recognised.' I reflect on the fact that my only problem with The Cranberries is that they haven't actually gone far enough away, in my book.

Wednesday, 22 June: I am getting World Cup Fever. I do not mean excitement, I mean getting sick. I am coughing and sneezing, my eyes are watering. This is being caused by my wandering about downtown Orlando in ninety-degree heat for hours, sweating like a sow in a sauna, and then going into a shop or bar where the air conditioning would freeze the bejapers off a brass monkey. I go to the chemist and buy as many medicaments as I legally can. The chemist tells me the Irish fans have been stocking up on suntan lotion, a little too late. She has seen several cases of sunstroke already. One balding man had 'the top of his poor head plumb near burned offa him'. She feels the Irish don't understand just how dangerous the sun can be. 'If you're gonna do somethin' useful,' she says, 'you tell those fellers to get a hat if they don't wanna make scrambled eggs outa their brains.'

Wednesday afternoon: In a daring Kate Adie-like raid on the outdoor heated swimming pool, I run into an Irish supporter called Brian O'Byrne, who has been running into a lot of people lately. Mr O'Byrne is one of the two Irish fans who cantered gleefully onto the pitch following the Italy–Ireland game, only to be so enthusiastically welcomed by the fun-loving and generous-spirited goose-steppers of the New Jersey Combined Police and Rugby Tackle Department. It turns out that Mr O'Byrne is a successful young actor who is currently appearing on Broadway, and although I must confess that I can often see a compelling argument for successful young actors being placed in handcuffs and then vigorously beaten (preferably in front of a large crowd), in his case I must say, I would have made an exception. He is a very nice mannerly fellow, who, as he puts it, 'just got a bit carried away by the fun'. Sadly, as we all saw, he also got carried away by the revolting rozzers and was later charged with the wonderful offence, 'tumultuous behaviour for no apparent reason.' That's the bit that annoys him. 'It was one–nil,' he gasps. 'What do they mean, no apparent reason?'

Anyway, Mr O'Byrne describes to me being concussed and regaining consciousness a few moments later, only to find Jack Charlton standing there in all his glory, interceding with the coppers on his behalf. 'I wasn't sure it was Jack at first,' he says, 'but then I saw his hair flapping in the breeze, and I mean, nobody has hair that flaps in the breeze the way Jack's does.' Poor Mr O'Byrne will certainly remember the Ireland–Italy game.

Some of the other fans have mixed feelings about Mr O'Byrne and his pitch invasion. They tend to shake their heads, sigh dolefully and say that Mr O'Byrne 'let Jackie's army down', or that he 'gave the wrong impression of Ireland'. They usually say this immediately before donning overlarge green goggles, inflating enormous plastic shamrocks, daubing each other with tricolour make-up and marching in formation down to the pub to get absolutely ossified again, all the time talking about how 'disciplined' and 'ordered' they are. Most of the Irish fans over here are very nice people, a joy to be with. A small minority of them are adult boyscouts, the most almighty effing pains you ever met in your natural life.

Thursday, 23 June: Orlando – the name of a city and not the name of an Irish soccer fan – is practically owned by the Disney corporation. Hence today, against my better judgement, I trot along to Disneyworld's Magic Kingdom with a group of Irish supporters. Now, dear diary, I do not know if you have ever spent much time in the company of a large group of Irish men who are far away from home, in a hot climate, with only a large group of stuffed animals for company, but if you haven't, then take my advice. Don't. Ever. And if you have, why, then you will know what a surreal experience it is.

The first bizarre thing about Disneyworld is that each of the car parks is named after one of the Seven Dwarfs. There is Bashful, Sleepy, Grumpy, Dopey and so on. Thus, when you get on the little commuter train that whisks you into the park, a grown adult has to call out, over the intercom, 'now arriving at Happy, all passengers for Happy and Dopey, next stop Grumpy, hold tight now.' For some reason, I find this amazingly funny. We amuse ourselves by thinking up new dwarf names, Sleazy, Sarky, Horny and Crappy being my favourites.

Once in to the park, we decide to go on the boat cruise through 'Small World'. There is a sign over the entrance to the tunnel. 'Welcome to the happiest little cruise in the world', it says. Reading this, I feel like indulging in the almightiest little puke in the world, which phrase, conveniently enough, also describes the six-year-old child sitting beside me. He is humming to himself as he trails his little hand in the water. I utter a silent fervent prayer that alligators are native to this part of Florida.

Halfway through the tunnel, a party of Mexican fans are sighted in a neighbouring boat. The chant begins straight away. 'You'll Never Beat the Irish, You'll Never Beat the Irish.' The Mexicans chant back at us, waving their fists and cursing in Spanish. One of them holds out his right hand, pistol fashion, and begins roaring, 'bangbang, bangbang'. While all this is going on, Mickey Mouse, Goofy, Pluto and Snow White are standing on the far bank of the pond, dancing up and down, blowing us kisses, waving their hands in the air, and singing 'Hi Ho, Hi Ho, It's off to work we go'. The fans join in. 'With buckets and spades and hand grenades, hi ho, hi ho, hi ho.'

Outside again, our tour guide Wanda is waiting for us. Wanda is a very nice young woman from Kissimee. 'There's some rully good rides here at The Magic Kingdom,' she says, to a chorus of snuffles and titters. 'We have big rides, small rides, scary rides, happy rides, whatever kind of ride you like you can find here at The Magic Kingdom.' One fan is falling about the place now and another – Crocko by name – is laughing his bloody dentures out. Wanda must be wondering what it is she is saying that has all these grown men nearly widdling with laughter. But, true professional that she is, she continues.

'Er...some of the rides have been here for a long time, but other rides are new, and here at Disney we're constantly looking at ways to make rides more exciting.' The fans are slapping their thighs and guffawing at this stage. One usually quiet man from Laois is actually honking with laughter, throwing his ponderous head back and honking like a great big white-legged hysterical mallard duck. Honko, I'm going to call him from now on.

'What's so funny?' Wanda says.

'Nothing, Wanda,' Honko replies.

'No, c'mon,' she says. 'Am I, like, saying something funny?'

'Not at all Wanda, you're grand, sweetheart. And c'mere, tellus, do you like the odd ride yourself, Wanda?'

'Oh yes, of course.'

'And how many rides would you have a day?'

'Oh, I dunno, three or four I guess. Depends how much spare time I get.'

Well, at this stage several of the fans have to go and sit down in the shade, or pour water over themselves, so frantic are their cackles. Some are actually sobbing with laughter. Donald Duck wanders over to one of them and begins gently to peck him on the head with his enormous yellow beak. 'Go away, ye big feathery fairy,' the fan says. A hearty chant soon begins, the scheme of which is based on the considerable rhyming potential of the words Donald Duck. What a talent for poetry the Irish have! Seamus Heaney would have been proud.

Things are about to get even worse, however. An enormous structure depicting Mickey Mouse is pointed out on the horizon. Wanda tells us, her voice fairly brimming over with pride, 'and guys, you know what, that's the largest self-supporting Mickey in the whole of the United States.'

Well, I don't think I have to describe the communal reaction, really. It is as though the entire party has been blasted with laughing gas. Several of the supporters will need medical attention soon.

'Oh, there are other Mickeys,' Wanda sniffs, dismissively. 'There's a rully big Mickey in California, of course, and there are some rully large Mickeys in some of the other states, and a big old Mickey over there in Eurodisney. But I gotta tell you, we're real proud of our superb superbig Mickey that we got down here in Florida.'

The sun is blazing hot now, and the white stone floor seems to be sucking the heat into itself. Tears of laughter are spilling down the faces of my companions. The Seven Dwarfs saunter past us, pursued by the Mad Hatter, the Wicked Witch of the West, the Queen of Hearts and various assorted fluffy tigers holding hands. The fans are chanting again now. 'You'll never beat the Irish. You'll never beat the Irish.' If Wanda smiles any harder, her eyebrows will disappear into her hairline. I close my eyes. I try to imagine just how much money you would have to spend on drugs to achieve this weird a feeling.

Friday, 24 June: Match day is here at last! This is very good, because Orlando is the most boring place in the world, and if you did not have the football to go to, you'd end up trying to drown yourself in the swimming pool just to kill a bit of time.

The Orlando city authorities have made a bit of a hames of the traffic arrangements. We leave the hotel in a rattling little coach at 9.30 a.m. and arrive almost two hours later, sweaty, dejected and part-broiled, at the Citrus Bowl. There, we are invited to shell out thirty bucks for lurid baseball hats, forty or fifty for ghastly souvenir T-shirts that somehow you know you will wash just once before they shrink in your machine to the size of a J-cloth.

The roofless stadium is completely exposed to the midday sun, and it is incredibly hot. The Mexican fans are a lot more in evidence today than the Italians were at the weekend. The teams troop out into the baking heat, the Mexicans in green, our boys in white. Jorge Campos, the Mexican goalie, is wearing a rather fetching cape-like number in orange, green, yellow and red. He looks like a part-time superhero, and, indeed, would not be out of place on one of the rides at Disneyland. 'Ye bleedin' Christmas tree, yeh,' shouts one of the fans behind me. 'You're only a feckin' prettyboy.' Another one roars, 'Jorge Campos, the day-glo Dago.'

The match starts well for Ireland. Staunton attacks down the left-hand side. The Irish fans start humming the theme tune of the Laurel and Hardy films. This, I am told, is because Steve Staunton looks like Stan Laurel, which I really don't think he does. But anyway. In the twenty-fifth minute, Irwin is booked for wasting time. 'Referee, you're a tosser,' screams the Liverpool man behind me to Swiss Mr Roethlisburger. 'You're a bleedin' Barclays Banker, you are, you're a shaggin' hand shandy merchant, ref.' Further imaginative opinions are widely expressed regarding auto-erotic activities chez Roethlisburger. Two minutes later Roy Keane narrowly avoids featuring in the little black book when he gamely puts the studs into one of the Mexicanos. I see a banner on the far side of the pitch. TOMMY COYNE, SHARPER THAN JIMMY HILL'S CHIN.

Just my luck, the man seated to my left turns out to be a statistic fiend. He tells me that Mexico scored 39 goals in their 12 qualifying games, and then he looks at me with a profound stare. 'You'll Never Beat the Irish', we sing, 'You'll Never Beat the Irish'. Four minutes later, Luis Garcia rockets the ball from outside the area past Bonner's outstretched right hand. That shuts us all up, I can tell you.

The half-time break is depressing. Everyone around me is quiet. The statistics man takes a mint from his pocket, puts it in his mouth and sucks it. The thermometer on the stadium wall says that the pitch temperature is 110 degrees Fahrneheit. Everyone else is losing gallons of body fluid every minute, but Mr Statistics looks like he has never sweated in his life.

We start the second half positively. Campos comes under severe pressure from Tommy Coyne. Mr Statistics is at it again. He leans over and breathes a mouthful of mint at me. Ireland have only ever scored three World Cup goals in six matches, he goes, with the air of a medieval mystic announcing the meaning of life. I wish he would stop talking. Every time he opens his beak Mexico get the ball and nearly score. 'Ah, we're finished,' he says, leaning back and folding his arms. 'I'm telling you, the goose is cooked now, my son. We'd be as well to go on home.'

Garcia slithers into a brilliant position and narrowly misses, his shot just curling away from the post. Mr Statistics seems almost pleased. 'What did I say?' he barks at me. 'I told you, didn't I? We're washed up.' He does have a point, I must say. We are 51 minutes into the game and bloody fortunate not to be two goals down.

Shortly after this, Campos is booked for time-wasting, which cheers us all up no end. Terrible slurs of a politically incorrect nature are cast on Campos, on Señor Campos senior, on his good lady wife, on all of Campos's female siblings, on the family pet mongrel, and, indeed, on the entire Mexican nation. Suggestions are made as to what a person could most usefully do with a sombrero, and, suffice it to say, they do not involve the Mexican hat dance. Unfortunately, Campos then saves a John Sheridan shot, which puts the mockers on us again.

It is getting even hotter now. Garcia jostles Roy Keane, who turns and growls and looks as though he's just about ready to batter seven shades of guacamole out of him. 'Go on Roy,' shouts the Liverpool man, 'give the little spic a good kicking for himself. *Go on, Roy, rip his greasy head off.*'

A halt is called to our fun when, in the sixty-fifth minute, disaster strikes. Garcia scores again, this time blasting it in from the edge of the box. 'That's it,' says Mr Statistics, 'I knew that was going to happen. I told you, didn't I?'

Down on the touchline a row seems to be brewing between John Aldridge, who wants to come on, and one of the FIFA officials, who is preventing him from doing so. Aldridge seems to be pushing the official and roaring at him. 'Put the shagging boot into him, John,' Mr Liverpool roars. 'Get stuck in there, son.' 'That's not the way at all,' says Mr Statistics. 'Send him home to Dagoland in a coffin,' suggests the Liverpool man. 'Rip his lungs out.' Aldridge and McAteer come on, but things are falling apart for Ireland. Phelan gets booked. He and Irwin will both miss the Norway game. 'We may as well go home now,' sighs Mr Statistics. 'There's no point really, not without those two.'

Garcia continues to be absolutely tireless, lobbing in shots from all angles, while our players are beginning to look like sponges which have been squeezed too hard. Then, suddenly, in the eighty-third minute, Aldridge bullets in a brilliant header, which bounces right on the line before ending up in the back of the net.

'WAAHHAAYYYYYYY' cries the man behind me. 'YESSSSSSSS' roar the rest of the crowd. We jump up and down and hug each other, 'YESSSSSSSSSS, YESSSSSSS, YESSSS.' 'You know?' says Mr Statistics, calmly unwrapping another glacier mint. 'That's actually John Aldridge's fourteenth goal for Ireland.'

Everyone is standing up and roaring now. For some endearing cultural reason or another, Mr Liverpool is leading a chorus of 'Are You Watching, England?' (The answer, presumably, being 'yes, and we're enjoying every minute of your crushing defeat, sad Scouse loser.') Even Mr Statistics shuffles to his feet and cries feebly, 'Come on, boys.' I say I think it's too late. There's only a few minutes to go; there's no way we can score. 'Actually, you're wrong there,' says Mr Statistics. 'You see, in seven of the seventeen games played so far in USA '94, crucial goals have been scored in the last five minutes.'

I make up my mind that if he opens his mouth just once more I will kill him myself, with my bare hands, and then happily skip to the electric chair feeling I've accomplished something useful in my life.

The game boils to a frantic climax. Ireland try to press forward, but the players are absolutely shagged out. The Liverpool man is chanting 'You'll Never Beat the Irish', which, at this stage, sounds profoundly optimistic. In the last minute, Campos stops a thunderbolt of a shot from bleach-blond Andy Townsend. One minute of injury time. Then two. Mr Roethlisburger looks at his watch, blows his whistle and poops our party, bigtime. We've been hammered. We sink back into our seats, groaning and cursing. 'That was quite a lot of injury time, wasn't it?' says Mr Statistics. 'Third highest amount in the whole tournament so far actually. Quite remarkable. Anyway, bye then, I'm off. Best to get out early if you want to get a bus, you know, Cheerio.' He stands up and leaves his seat and climbs down the big steps towards the exits. Myself and the Liverpool man catch each other's eye. 'Tosser,' the Liverpool man says. I cannot help but agree.

Saturday, 25 June, New York: Here in America, soccer is having some problems. The massive public indifference to the World Cup is pretty astonishing, especially when back home in Ireland the very leaves on the trees are discussing pennos, volleys and Jack Charlton's intriguingly postmodern ads for Shredded Wheat. It is very strange. A survey in last Thursday's *New York Times* reported that 71 per cent of Americans do not even know that the World Cup finals are being played in their country. In another poll, taken just after the draw for the tournament, soccer turned out to be a mere sixty-seventh in terms of national popularity. It came in behind rock-climbing, log-splitting and tractor-pulling, and, indeed, was only marginally more popular

than the ideologically suspect sport of 'dwarf-throwing'. Don't
you just love Americans? When asked to explain the rules of
soccer, 12 per cent said that it was played with racquets and a
noble 6 per cent told pollsters that it was played underwater,
which, I suppose, at least gives a new meaning to the phrase
'diving tackle'. What a wonderful country!

When the World Cup draw was announced in December
1991 I was here in New York, and it received no coverage at all
on American television and hardly any in the newspapers. Since
then, things have not improved much. NBC are only
broadcasting nine games live (out of a total of 51). Even pay-per-
view cable television is showing only 21 matches. The problem is
that FIFA refused to bend to American television's demands that
matches be interrupted every four minutes for commercials.
Baseball and American football, being long and spectacularly
dull games that go on for hours at a time, are extremely
advertising-friendly. Indeed the only good reason for watching
baseball on television is that you get to see a lot of really good
adverts. (My current favourite is for a little plastic device which
humanely traps cockroaches: 'Get your family a cockroach
motel NOW. They check in, yes, but they never check out!')

Somehow, FIFA said no to the idea of blistering power-
headers, blinding runs down the wing and spectacular diving
saves being interrupted by the cockroach motel. Other fine ideas
for giving soccer a more American flavour included making the
goalposts bigger to allow more goals to be scored (I love that
one. Let's have goalposts fifty feet wide, for God's sake), getting
rid of the offside rule, and making draws illegal. (This last
measure would have been achieved by the adding on of an
unlimited period of extra time. No doubt, if introduced, it
would have meant that many of Ireland's games would have
lasted as long as the Hundred Years War.)

You can walk the streets of New York without seeing any
evidence whatsoever that football's greatest and most compelling
ritual has kicked off in this country. There is not a poster, a flag

or a banner to be seen, nor a chorus of 'Olé, Olé, Olé' to be heard unless you actively seek it out and go trawling around the Irish or Italian bars. Last night I asked a New York taxi driver who he intended to support in the World Cup, 'Oh, the Rangers,' he shrugged meaning one of New York's ice-hockey teams. Another New Yorker I met in the course of my ramblings opined that soccer was 'one of those Commie European games for faggots and Nazis.'

All of this is a shame because the United States actually has a proud history in the beautiful game. Consider, for example, that the land of the free actually took part in the very first World Cup, held in Uruguay in 1930, and even reached the semi-finals on that occasion, before being narrowly beaten 6–1 by Argentina. The match is affectionately remembered not for its scoreline, but for an intriguing incident which took place when the referee called a foul against one of the Yanks, and the team's doctor scuttled onto the turf to give out, tripped, dropped his box of medicinal aids, shattered a bottle of chloroform and was knocked out cold by the ensuing fumes. He ended up being carried off unconscious, thus adding greatly to the general gaiety of the crowd. The poor fellow took months to recover. (He was obviously not a Charlton Athletic supporter, as I am myself. I can tell you, a couple of Saturday afternoons watching those guys, and chloroform poisoning begins to seem almost invigorating.)

Tuesday, 28 June, New York: Up very early to get the bus out to Meadowlands for the Norway game. As usual, the coach is full of boisterous fans wearing emerald-green boxer shorts, shamrock-patterned T-shirts and tricolour face paint, and carrying all kinds of inflatable green objects, from crocodiles to overlarge plastic hands to giant beer bottles. (How good it is to know that somewhere in Ireland a large factory, on a massive IDA grant, is churning out enormous green blow-up alligators.)

This morning, however, one of the fans also has a large

rubber inflatable woman in the seat beside him, spray-painted green from head to toe. I should point out to morally sensitive readers that the large inflatable woman is not naked or anything. No, she is wearing a stars and stripes patterned bra, a tight pair of khaki cycling shorts and a hideous baseball cap with GIVE IT A LASH JACK printed on the front. For some amazing reason or another, the only seat left on the entire coach is beside this guy and his pneumatic companion, so I am forced to squeeze in there, elbowing her in the ribs as I do so. I feel like a right gooseberry.

The chap informs me that he purchased his latex lovebird in one of the sex shops on Times Square the other day, specially for today's game, and painted her in his room last night. She cost a hundred dollars, he says, but she was worth every penny. 'She's anatomically correct, yeh know,' he confides to me, his eyes wide. She certainly doesn't look it to me, I must say, but I have no intention whatsoever of asking for proof. 'D'ya like her anyway?' he asks. I answer candidly that whatever about her anatomical correctness she does certainly seem to have more personality than some of the other people I've met on the trip. 'She's a petal,' he says. 'She's a little dote, aren't you love?' She does not reply. 'We're a bit shy in front of strangers,' he explains.

He takes a pair of large mirrored sunglasses from his breast pocket and slips them on. Slips them on to the doll, I mean, not onto himself. 'Now love,' he says, 'there y'are, sure yeh don't want to be bloinded be the sun.' It is nine o'clock in the morning. I am on a bus to New Jersey, and I am sitting beside a man who is having a fond conversation with a giant green inflatable sex toy. Oh, the glamour of journalism. 'I'm goneta call her Shee-Shee, he says, 'because she remoinds me of Síle de Valera.'

The drive to New Jersey takes less time than it did on the day of the Italy game. The police seem better organised, and the roads leading from Manhattan on to the New Jersey turnpike are clearer. From the outside, the Giants Stadium is amazingly beautiful to look at. As we get off the bus, take photographs of each other and briskly inflate anything in a fifty-yard radius that can physically be inflated, Eamon Dunphy arrives in the front seat of a large limousine. (The rest of the limousine, I should stress, arrives also.) Like the Giants Stadium, Mr Dunphy too is amazingly beautiful to look at from the outside, so happy and positive and quite absurdly content do I feel this morning. I close my eyes and try to imagine an inflatable Eamon Dunphy. It seems like a good idea. Perhaps when I go home to Ireland I will put a proposal together for the IDA, so that I too can open a factory and manufacture inflatable Eamon Dunphys. You'd have to be careful about where you placed the nozzle, though.

Inside the stadium, everyone is in great form. I find myself sitting in an area which contains neutral observers, as well as Norwegian and Irish fans. Off to my right, I can see Mr Inflatable Woman in the middle of one of the Irish areas, with his companion sitting – now topless – on his shoulders and jigging up and down, in the manner of drug-ravaged teenage girls in the film of the Woodstock concert. Every once in a while, he makes her wave her hand at the crowd.

They all wave back. He stands up on his seat, wraps her arms around his neck and her thighs around his waist and kisses her full on the lips. Everyone roars. I wonder what this man does for a living back home in Ireland. After some consideration, I decide he is either a senior clerk with the Revenue Commissioners or a recently appointed auxiliary bishop.

The seat beside me is still empty. Beside that, two well-dressed middle-aged men are studying the match programme and delicately eating ice creams. They are Americans, and they have just come along to have a look at the game. They have heard all about how well the Irish fans are behaved, they tell me, and they've never been to a soccer game before, so they just thought they'd take the day off work and drop along. They are both consultant psychiatrists, as it turns out. This makes me astoundingly nervous, for some reason. They keep peering at me as though what I have just said is very interesting. They keep nodding and saying 'really?'

Ten minutes before the game, a prime specimen of the best of Jackie's army comes lurching up the stadium steps, huffing and panting and spewking out of him like a runaway train. He is naked from the waist up. He has thick green concentric circles painted around his nipples, a green nose painted on his torso, and a leering green mouth painted around his navel, which is pierced with a ring so big that even the Pope would find it a bit OTT. As soon as I see him, I just know he is destined for the seat beside me.

I am right. He pushes past the two psychiatrists, dripping sweat all over them, and slides in beside me. 'Howya pal,' he nods, 'howa they hangin'?' I assure him that I have no complaints. He then does the worst thing that anyone in the world can do. He grasps hold of his nose between his pointing finger and his thumb, and he exhales heavily, several times, thus evacuating the contents of his nostrils all over his hand. He wipes his soiled fingers on his hair and then down the side of his trousers. He burps magnificently, pulls a beer from his bag, snaps open the ring and offers it without a word to one of the psychiatrists beside him.

'Er, no thank you very much,' the chivalrous shrink says. The fan offers it to the other one, who also declines.

'What's wrong wit yooze?' he says. 'Are yez fairies or wha'?'

'Just not thirsty,' one replies.

He peers astonished at the non-thirsty psychiatrist, as though he has just been let in on the third secret of Fátima. Then he nods, says 'fair nuff so' and gazes at me. He opens his mouth and, without taking his eyes off me for even a single second, pours the contents of the can down his throat as though trying to extinguish a fire. He burps again – 'Jayzus, the latest release on the Oirland label' – sits back in his seat, scratches his crotch, puts his hands to his mouth and roars, 'COME ON YE BOYS IN GREE-AN.'

Now, it is an odd thing, but being something of a newcomer to the game of two halves I have observed at this World Cup that most fans will not sing on their own. They always wait for somebody else to start the singing, and then they will join in, no bother, and join in at full volume. But they will not start a chant themselves. It is a wonder, in fact, that chants ever get started at all. There must be one guy, I remember thinking at the Mexico game, one guy in this enormous crowd of eighty thousand people, who actually starts off the chant.

Well, I found him. He is sitting beside me now, singing away with gusto. 'YILL NEVER BEAT THE OIRISH. YILL NEVER BEAT THE OIRISH.' This goes on, I swear to you, for about four minutes, the phrase just being repeated again and again, until eventually, almost out of boredom, it is taken up by the Irish fans in the next section of the stadium. One of the American psychiatrists leans over, his eyebrows raised as though he is about to ask me a question. I prepare myself to assure him that I had a very good relationship with my mother, thank you very much, but actually he just wants to know if Ireland have ever been in the World Cup finals before. My reply is interrupted by your man, now bellowing ferociously, 'WE ARE GREEN, WE ARE WHY, WE ARE FOOKY DYNA-MY, NA NA NANA, NA NANA, NA NAHH.' He stands up and begins slapping out a rhythm on his ample breasts. The rest of the fans in our section start singing.

He sits down again, looking contented, and realises with a sudden start that there are Norwegian fans sitting in the row in front of us. His eyes take on the enthusiastic light of a disturbed schoolboy who is about to pull the legs off a frog. He starts loudly imitating the Norwegian fans' voices, in the manner of the Swedish chef character from *The Muppet Show*.

'Hoorgy, goorgy, woorgy, a woooorgy, woooorgy,' he titters, in his singsong intonation, sounding more like a frantic Texan evangelist praying in tongues than an excited Norwegian. 'Boorgy, voory, woorgywoorga-hwoorgy.' They ignore him. After a moment or two he gives one of them a playful smack on the back of the head.

'OOORGY, BOORGY?' he says, 'A HOORGEE?' They still ignore him. He reaches out, takes a light hold of one of their collars and begins to drip ice cold beer down his back, screaming with maniacal laughter while doing so. At last, one of the Norwegian fans turns around.

'You are a really funny guy,' he says. (Devastating irony is obviously very big in Norway.)

'Ooorgy, coorgy, woorgy,' replies the pride of Jackie's army.

'You are hilarious guy, really.'

'Ah don't be such a dry shite,' he says, 'OOORGY, OORGY, come on, will yez do it!'

The band troop on to the pitch below. All the way through the Irish national anthem the guy beside me picks his nose, examining what he has found up there as though it might be a precious diamond or a Category 1 ticket for the next round. And all the way through the Norwegian national anthem he stands to attention, one arm by his side, one hand clasped to his naked bosom, eyes closed in a gesture of sincere respect, singing loudly 'OOORGY BOORGY WOORGY'.

The match begins. Two minutes later, Roy Keane is booked. Mr Oorgy Boorgy gets up and screeches something so abusive that you couldn't put it in a family publication, unless the family happened to be the Borgias. From then on, every single time the referee awards a foul against Ireland, this guy has something to say about it. It starts off mildly enough. A murmured 'Jayzus Ref, yeh're a shagginwell dope,' or a poignantly sighed 'Ah, give the ref a pair of sunglasses and a white bleedin stick.' The two Americans smile, with the gentle benevolence of those who make a very comfortable living indeed out of dealing with dangerous lunatics.

But after some time, he starts to get more excited. 'You filthy little Columbian BOLLIX,' he roars, 'that was never offside you manky little disgusting dickhead.' He has veins in his neck the size of ropes. I wonder if he is going to have a heart attack, and I fervently hope he is. But after a while, I find that, actually, he is quite an interesting commentator on the game. Any time he roars at the referee, it means that Ireland have done something wrong or illegal and have been deservingly punished, and any time he says 'yess, ladss, yesss, yesss, put 'em under PRESSURE', it means that we are playing really badly, and that the likelihood of an Irish goal is receding almost as fast as Jackie Charlton's hairline.

'REFF, YOU'RE DEAD.' He starts stabbing the air with his finger and jumping up and down, sweat pouring off him in meandering rivulets. 'You're dead, Ref, yew are dead, I'm warnin yeh now, I'll see yew outside, pal, and I'll be dug ourra yeh, you poxy little hooer's melt yeh.'

Ray Houghton is deftly tackled by a couple of Norwegian defenders. 'It takes bleedin' two of them all the same,' the Pride of Erin cries. 'IT TAKES TWO OF YEZ, DOESN'T IT, YEZ FOOKIN' VIKING EEJITS.' This goes on all the way through the first half, the interval, and the second half. When the rest of the fans are exhausted into relative silence by the heat, your man is still roaring and cursing at full volume. 'YEH LITTLE COLUMBIAN COONT YEH, I KNEW YER AUL WAN WELL AND SHE WAS ONEY A BRASSER.' Fifteen minutes before the end, the two psychiatrists slip silently away, still grinning like apostles in a renaissance painting. I imagine they must have got invaluable material for a research paper on the therapeutic effects of frontal lobotomy out of the Jack's army experience.

The game ends in a nil–all draw. All around me, fans are trying to calculate where Ireland have come in the group, what the goal difference is, where we will play our next match. Now, I scored an E in Inter Cert pass maths – that's a bad grade, by the way, not an ecstasy tablet, for the benefit of younger readers – so this kind of thing is very difficult for me. Let's see, Ireland beat Italy and Italy beat Mexico and Norway beat ... I sit very still, my brain feeling as though smoke is coming out of it. All I hope and pray is that, whatever happens, we don't have to play in Orlando again.

On the bus back to the hotel, I sit beside the chap with the inflatable woman again. Shee-Shee is looking a little less than her best at this stage. Her paint has started to melt in the heat, her breasts are sagging like burst balloons and her head is drooping and flailing as though she is severely the worse for drink. It seems that in the course of the match she has suffered a number of fatal cigarette burns from mischievous fans. Her loyal consort keeps dolefully raising her lithe midriff to his lips and blowing hard, trying to re-inflate her, to no effect. She keeps making a hissing sound and then collapsing again in his lap. 'Women,' he says.

That night I go out with some Irish friends. The Irish bars on Sixth and Fifty-First Street are absolutely crammed full of people. It now seems clear that we will have to play Belgium in bloody Orlando, the only city in the world that would make Las Vegas seem tasteful. I have a lot to drink. When I get back to my hotel it is almost two in the morning. Shee-Shee is sitting alone in the lobby, looking by now like she's just gone ten rounds with Mike Tyson. I feel so depressed that I almost sit down and try to buy her a tequila sunrise.

Wednesday, 29 June, New York: Get up feeling miserable as the full reality of having to return to Orlando dawns. When I go down to the lobby there are Irish fans everywhere. Most of them will be going back to Ireland today, because their travel packages only covered the first round of the tournament. Some of the diehards have decided to stay, and are borrowing money from those who are leaving. The generosity of the fans to each other is amazing. Twenty dollar bills are being handed around left, right and centre. I have a good gander at the fans who are staying. I notice that the man with the inflatable woman is one of them. She is now in fully deflated state – as, indeed, I am myself – and she is wrapped around his neck like a scarf. I cannot tell you how nauseous this makes me feel.

The fans who are staying are waiting for someone from the travel company to show up. All through this trip there have been problems with the Irish travel agency with whom most of the fans in my hotel have been travelling. They are each paying about two grand to be here, and, hey, call them old fashioned, but they feel that two grand is a lot of dough, and they deserve to be treated with just a modicum of respect. Through no fault of the very nice tour guides working over here for XXXXX Travel (sorry, can't mention them, because no doubt they'd try to sue), there have been a lot of screw-ups. Granted, the World Cup has presented what I believe are called in the business community 'major challenges' to the Irish travel agents (the main challenge being, how in the name of God will we spend all the money we're making out of this?), but the fans' trip, which should have been the experience of a lifetime, has too often been an unending nightmare of long queues, missing hotel rooms, amazingly long airline delays, shabby and inadequate or non-existent transport, lost luggage and delays in getting their match tickets. XXXXX Travel appear to have sent over a mere three people to handle the needs of several thousand people. They have had months and months to get all of this stuff right, but in too many cases they appear not to have done so. The other travel agents have done a decent enough job. And I am sure that there must be hundreds of contented XXXXX travellers. But all I can honestly tell you is that in two and a half full weeks of travelling with the Irish fans, I have yet to meet a single one. Quite the contrary. 'I'd never go with XXXXX again,' one of the supporters said to me last night. 'They couldn't organise a shag in a knocking shop.'

I myself have got off relatively lightly. The most serious difficulty I've had to contend with is being stranded alone and friendless in Orlando last week, booked into a hotel which had been demolished a month beforehand. But one XXXXX traveller I spoke to really did know about suffering. His suitcase had been lost twice during the trip, and he had been given a whopping seventy-five dollars – about fifty quid – to buy two weeks worth of clothes. 'I haven't changed me knickers in DAYS,' he sighed. Another man had been presented with a 650-dollar hotel bill, for a stay he had paid for in full before leaving Ireland. Many of these fans have extremely imaginative – not to say unprintable – opinions about what should be done with Mr XXXXXXXXX XXXXXXXXX, the owner of XXXXX Travel. I don't think he will be getting too many Christmas cards from Irish soccer supporters this year.

I manage to find out where the three XXXXX Travel reps are staying and call all three, leaving messages for them to ring me back as a matter of absolute urgency. About eight hours later, one of them does. I am out. She never calls back. By sheer chance, I bump into one of the reps in the hotel lobby. She was supposed to be here hours ago but did not show up until now. She looks tired, is walking with a pronounced limp, and is clearly overworked. She says she will call me back later today about getting me a flight to Orlando tomorrow. Guess what? She never does.

Thursday, 30 June, New York: Just after eight in the morning I manage to speak to the XXXXX Travel rep again. She sounds very tired, and I do my best to sympathise. She says she thinks she can get me on a flight to Orlando, leaving from Newark at 1.00 p.m. She will meet me at my hotel at 10.00 a.m. and give me all the details.

The sports report on the morning news says we will now have to play Holland, not Belgium. I stroll up Eighth Avenue and have breakfast with a couple of fans in a diner. Over scrambled eggs, I read a report on yesterday's game in one of the New York tabloids. 'The Irish cheered as though they were at a wake' it says. I read this again, several times, wondering whether it is a misprint, or yet another example of deep American understanding of other cultures. Picture the scene. The mother, played by Mia Farrow, says, 'Ah son, I've some terrible news altogether for you, your poor father's after dyin'.' The son, played by Tom Cruise replies, 'WAHHAYYYYYYYYYYYY, YIPPEEEEE, OH WHAT A BEAUTIFUL MORNING, OH WHAT A BEAUTIFUL DAY.'

On the way back to meet the rep I notice that the remaining fans have draped their tricolour flags and banners out the windows of the hotel. Passers-by stop and gaze up at the building, wondering what is going on. Taxi drivers honk their horns. I am suddenly struck by the sheer exemplary determination of these fans to enjoy themselves in the face of grim adversity. I decide to stop feeling sorry for myself. I sit down in the lobby and wait for the rep to show.

Needless to say, she does not turn up at ten. Or ten thirty. Or eleven. Instead, she calls me twice from her hotel to say she will be late. In the end, she calls again to say she won't be turning up at all. She gives me my flight details. Kiwi Air, leaving from Newark in an hour and a half, I really would want to be leaving now, she says.

I explain that I would like my hotel bill for the night before to be charged to XXXXX Travel, as we have agreed, and she suggests that she has not had time to sort this out, so I will have to pay the bill myself. When I have finished choking with crazed laughter, I explain that I have no intention whatsoever of paying this bill. 'I have two hundred fans here in front of me to sort out,' the rep says, as though dealing efficiently with large numbers of soccer fans would be a very unusual thing for a sports travel agency to do (which, in the case of XXXXX Travel, it apparently would be).

Out to Newark Airport to collect my ticket for Orlando. The weekend of the Fourth of July is coming up, the busiest travel period of the year in America. The traffic is absolutely woeful. Arvo the Armenian taxi driver seems to be obsessed with the fact that the gay Olympics have just ended in New York. 'They're all fallin' in love with each other down there in Greenwich Village,' he says, grimly shaking his head. 'Can you believe it, a guy fallin' in love with another guy?' Certainly not if the guy was you, Arvo, I muse, silently.

When we eventually get to Newark Airport, Arvo tells me the fare will be a hefty forty-five bucks. He then tries to rip me off by inventing a twenty-dollar 'Newark Airport Surtax'. He wants sixty-five greenbacks in all, he explains. I explain to Arvo in polite terms that I don't know how these things play back in Armenia, but I did not come down the fucking river on the last fucking canoe. He insists on my paying this tax. There is a frank exchange of views. I get out of the car and rouse a nearby policeman from his reveries.

Now, New York policemen are very unusual creatures. For a start, they all look far more like robbers than cops, and, indeed, recent widely publicised reports into their colourful activities would confirm that many of them should, in fact, be wearing tights over their faces rather than badges on their chests. Also, they seem to regard dealing with the public as some sort of unpleasant and preposterous imposition. (They should all take up new careers with a certain Irish travel agency, come to think of it.)

Anyway, Officer Monroe sighs deeply and yawns through his nose as I explain my plight. He shakes his massive head, brushes the dandruff off his manly shoulders, shambles over to the waiting taxi and raps on Arvo's window with his wedding ring.

'You breakin' this guy's balls here?' he murmurs.

'No, officer,' Arvo replies.

'He sez you breakin' his balls.'

'He whut?'

'Well, to be fair,' I point out, 'I didn't actually say that, Officer.'

Officer Monroe turns to me. 'Thought you sez he was breakin' you balls.'

'I said he was overcharging me.'

Officer Monroe starts examining his fingernails. 'Izzy breakin' you balls or not, pal? Cuz iffen he ain't breakin you balls, hey, I gut woik to do here, y'know what am sayin'?'

A lively debate about the state of my balls, vis-à-vis broken-ness, then ensues. Eventually we agree that Arvo's understanding of the American tax system may be in some need of brushing up. I will pay the forty-five dollars, and Arvo will go down on his knees and thank God and his Holy Mother and the Blessed Trinity that in the circumstances I am prepared to even do this much.

'Ya betta nut be breakin any more uv ya passengers' balls, Mac,' Officer Monroe advises.

'I'm not, Officer,' Arvo says. 'See, he didden unnerstand me. He's a foreigner. He don't speak English so good.'

'Cuz any more ballbreakin' gets done around here,' Officer Monroe explains, and he pauses for what seems an eternity, before plunging into the uncertain and murky depths of a conclusion, 'and I mo be doin it.'

Officer Monroe strolls back to the wall against which he was so energetically leaning when I rudely woke him. Arvo slides out of the cab, looking somewhat crestfallen. He opens the trunk and steps back, generously allowing me to remove my own suitcases, which I do. I then very reluctantly open my wallet and pay him what I owe him. He stares at the half-inch thick wad of banknotes as though I've just handed him a fresh dogturd. Then – wait till you hear – the ungrateful little toerag has the nerve to ask me for a gratuity. I can't believe it!

'How about a tip, Mac?' he says to me.

'Why certainly,' I smile, 'Use a deodorant, Arvo. You'd get to meet more girls.'

I trundle my luggage the seeming ten miles through the terminal building, sweating, hyperventilating (this must be what they call Terminal Illness), and get into line with a huge crowd of Irish fans, feeling like I'm about to have a massive coronary or a complete emotional breakdown. After a 20-minute wait I am called to the counter. The guy behind the counter has the worst bad breath I've ever had the misfortune to inhale. I mean, he's very pleasant and everything, but he really does honk like he ate

71

a broiled skunk sandwich for supper last night. I say I want my ticket, and I want it now.

He tickles the keys on his computer for some moments. Needless to say, the ticket has been booked by a XXXXX Travel employee, so Kiwi Air have never heard of my reservation. The guy actually chortles at the very idea that they have a pre-paid ticket for me. He then tries to call XXXXX Travel in Manhattan, but – surprise surprise – none of their representatives is available. I demand to see the guy's superior. He comes over and says there's nothing he can do. So I demand to see his superior. He comes out and says there's nothing he can do either. I'm about to ask to see *his* superior, but the queue of angry Irish soccer supporters behind me is getting long and hostile and I feel if I keep demanding to meet people's superiors, I'll go all the way to the top and end up meeting God or something, an eventuality for which, after two weeks at the World Cup, I am not as well prepared as I might be. Rather than meeting God, I end up paying $177 of my own dough for my ticket. This done, I notice that there is a young disabled Irish supporter in a wheelchair behind me, in obvious distress. He has been waiting with a friend for almost an hour, in severe heat, to collect his ticket. It is actually astonishing that people can be treated like this.

The flight is OK. The only truly scary thing about it is the air hostesses' orange foundation. (And before anybody writes in to complain, I know you're not supposed to call them air hostesses any more. I know that! I know they're In Flight Supervisors or something, but hey, how come I'm still just a bloody passenger? If they want to be In Flight Supervisors, fine, but if I have to shell out 177 bucks for something that's already mine I want to be at least a Temporary Airborne Supervisee or some damn thing.)

Three drunken Dutch fans are sitting behind me, belching in harmony and opening bottles of lager with their teeth. There is absolutely no need for them to do this, as the air hostesses – sorry, the Aviation Hospitality Operative Technicians – have bottle openers a-plenty, but boys will be boys, it seems, even in a sexually liberated society such as Holland. I close my eyes and pray hard that one of them will wrench out a ventricular molar, in which case I will be only too happy to offer to do a bit of emergency root-canal work with a spanner.

We land at Orlando airport, which somehow amazes me. The way things have been going today, it would not have surprised me to land in the middle of the Gaza Strip. The airport bar is full of Irish fans. Having been – I confess it frankly – a little sick of them by last night, this morning I found that somehow I missed them. I don't know why that should be, but it's true. We all have a drink together in the bar, where the TV is showing a repeat of yesterday's utterly epoch-making nil–nil draw between Ireland and Norway. We cheer and roar all over again, as though by doing so we can somehow change the outcome of the game.

I would like to stay in the bar with the lads – *oh my God, what's happening to me? I've started to refer to them as 'the lads'!* – but although I am enjoying myself my nerves are badly at me. I really do feel tense. I have a very negative feeling about today. So I take a spectacularly expensive taxi to my hotel, or, at least, it takes me there, to the Floridian on Republic Drive. It looks all right.

'SETTING THE STYLE FOR GREAT LITTLE HOTELS', the neon sign announces. Maybe this time, just maybe, just once, XXXXX Travel will not have screwed up!

The Floridian Hotel turns out to be owned by a tribe of Florida Indians, or, rather, a tribe of Florida Native Americans, (apologies to all Apache readers) and I am fascinated by this. Just what I need at this moment. A politically correct hotel. When the very pleasant chap behind the counter asks me if I have a reservation I have to restrain myself from saying 'yes, but heck, I'm sure it's not as nice as yours'.

Naturally enough, the people at the Floridian Hotel, like the people at Kiwi Air, are blissfully unaware of my very existence, and, despite my rep's best assurances, have no booking at all in my name. I explain that I am travelling with this Irish agency called XXXXX Travel. The chap smiles understandingly. 'Ah yes, XXXXX Travel,' he says, and he purses his lips and nods with the air of one consoling a good friend on the sudden murder of a close relative. He turns and says something in Spanish to a passing colleague, gently jerking his thumb in my direction. All I can pick out are the words '*XXXXX*' '*Irlanda*' and '*pobre bastardo stupido*.'

His colleague comes over and peers at me in amazement, as though I am Gulliver suddenly arrived in the land of the Lilliputians. I am actually kind of enjoying my new-found status now. I am The Guy Who Travelled With XXXXX Travel And Lived To Tell The Tale. His eyes widen. 'XXXXX Travel,' he sighs, and he makes a whistling sound with his teeth, '*Dios mio*.' I shrug manfully and say aw shucks, it was nothing. He reaches out to firmly clasp my shoulder in a heartfelt gesture of solidarity between oppressed peoples. I reckon I've got a room.

The chaps behind the counter are really very nice indeed. They give me free coffee and a cigarette and they move people around until they do manage to find me a room, but they explain regretfully that I will have to pay for it myself. This is about as surprising as the news that Tuesday follows Monday. I hand over my credit card, which at this stage is beginning to melt into a Salvador Dali-like shape from severe and frequent misuse. The concierge forces a bundle of brochures about Disneyland and Sea World into my quivering hands.

I go up to my very nice room and lie on the soft bed in a crumpled heap, studying the Sea World brochure. Sea World is yet another dismal Orlando theme park, only, unlike Disneyworld, it is full of real animals in tanks rather than fake ones in ridiculous costumes. Still, though. I have a few days to kill before the Holland game, so a trip to Sea World with some of the Irish fans might be interesting. Yup. I might just do that tomorrow. After all, I see in the brochure that Sea World has a special exhibition on just now all about the Bermuda Triangle, which is, of course, just what you would come all the way to Florida to find out about. The Bermuda Triangle! Where weird and inexplicable and terrifying things happen to the unwary and unsuspecting voyager! Wow! Isn't that something?! I just can't wait. Count me in. Though on second thoughts, I feel I don't actually need to pay good money to experience the Bermuda Triangle. Travelling with XXXXX Travel is kind of the same thing.

Sunday, 3 July, Orlando: Get up early and have a very nice Floridian Hotel breakfast beside the very nice Floridian Hotel swimming pool. (God, journalism is tough sometimes.) The local Sunday paper has an article about an Orlando woman who works for the government in Washington. She is in trouble because the FBI claim to have found a little dope in her hotel bedroom. (President Clinton denied it was him, apparently.) Later, after I have swum five slow lengths and worked hard on my tan, I trot along to visit Sea World with some of the Irish fans who are staying at my hotel. As soon as we arrive, my good mood evaporates.

Sea World is basically an overgrown aquarium, and if you like seeing dumb scaly helpless animals entertaining dumb scaly helpless Floridians, then Sea World is the place for you.

We all pay our money and troop in to see the performing dolphins. We are first subjected to a tedious lecture on how incredibly well-trained and intelligent they are. I find all this a bit hard to swallow. If they were that bloody intelligent, in my view, they would be working the West Coast or Caesar's Palace in Vegas, or, at the very least, appearing in The Gaiety pantomime with Maureen Potter, and not floundering around in a bloody wojus kip like Sea World.

We are then told what terrible creatures fishermen are, because the friends and relations of these poor liddle dolphins are getting caught in the evil anglers' tuna nets every single day of the week. We are all to buy something called 'dolphin-friendly tuna', from now on, we are told. A bit bloody selective, isn't it? 'C'mere you nice little tuna, till I spread mayonnaise all over you and put you in a sandwich, but dear oh dear, let's be nice to the sodding dolphins.' I remind myself to ask for a well-done dolphin steak for dinner tonight.

I watch for a while, absolutely captivated, as the dolphins do really intelligent things, such as head-banging a beachball across a swimming pool and catching gobloads of malodorous mackerel. Wow. Give them a bloody PhD why don't you. Then some musclebound beachbum in a G-string smooths his way into the pool and does a really stunning trick which involves repeatedly balancing on a dolphin's nose while it streaks up and out of the water with the speed of a thermonuclear missile. The Americans in the audience seem to find this almost religiously inspiring. They are quite hysterical with applause.

The steroid-stuffed prettyboy then puts his arms around the dolphin's neck and allows himself to be dragged around the pool, his gob gurgling in the surf, like a great big unholy gobshite. If the dolphin had any real intelligence it would haul your man down to the bottom and half-drown him, but no. Dolphin and man do a lap of the pool, and yet more totally innocent mackerel get consumed. Again, the applause would burst your eardrums.

What happens next is upsetting. One of the younger female members of our party seems to take a bit of a shine to him – the beachbum, that is, not the dolphin – and she insists we all go over to talk to him after the show. I am, needless to say, very secure and not at all threatened by this. She introduces herself to Guy and asks how he manages to keep himself so fit. Guy blushes and stops trailing his knuckles in the dust and runs his fingers through his mop of blond hair and says aw gosh and gee whillakers and so on, before revealing that he has 'isolated his major muscle groups'. I am utterly fascinated to hear this. My own muscle groups are so isolated they are practically in solitary confinement. Anyway, Emer from County Cavan seems to be delighted by garrulous Guy and his incredible performing muscle groups, and promptly invites him to join us for lunch. I am horrified by this sudden development, but it seems there is no escape, so I have to comply. It is a very warm day, so I suggest we eat al fresco. Guy says no, he would prefer pizza. When I have finished scowling maniacally, I congratulate Emer from County Cavan on managing to get a dose of the hots for the only living creature in Florida who is less intelligent than a dolphin.

After this unspeakably enjoyable victory, Emer and Guy head off for a bite – out of each other no doubt, as well as out of a 12-inch pizza – and the rest of us all trawl in to have a look at the various sharks and killer whales which have the dreadful misfortune to inhabit this lousy gaff. The great white shark, which ordinarily would take the leg off a donkey and not think twice about it, seems a little intimidated by the Irish fans, and, let's face it, you can't really blame him. I mean, how would you like to be woken up early on a Sunday morning by a large group of perspiring individuals in green shirts, green sombreros and green shorts, all singing 'Oooh-Aaaah, Paul McGrath' and reeking of stale Southern Comfort? Well, maybe you would like that, maybe I am being presumptuous. But I would not, and, as it turns out, neither would your average shark.

The poor toothsome beastie lies motionless on the bottom of its tank like a surly bored teenager watching the heavy metal half hour on MTV. One fan, observing the scene, claims that this is all a swizz, and that the shark's teeth are not real. I say I didn't know they made false teeth for sharks, but he gamely maintains that they do, and it's a well-known fact. He has false teeth himself, as it turns out, and he insists on taking them out to show everybody. 'It was our fortieth anniversary recently,' he says to me, 'and the aul wan, yeh know, the war department, she says to me, "Honey, I'd like yeh to nibble on me ear the way yeh used to". Burr I told her, "No, I won't bleedin' bother, be the time I get me dentures in, sure yeh'll be asleep."'

We all find this very amusing, but for some reason the shark does not even grin. From time to time it peers anxiously up at us, as we rap on the glass and cry 'come up, yeh bowsie' and 'howya Esther Rantzen' and 'wouldja smile, yeh dozy aul hoor, yeh'. But all this has no effect. It refuses to come up and give us a flash of its molars, whether false or not, so with a final hummed chorus of the theme music from *Jaws* – da NAH, da NAH, daNAH daNAH daNAH – we abandon the great white to its bloodthirsty daydreams of an Irish soccer-fan sandwich.

Next stop is the manatee tank. Now, a manatee is not what Peig Sayers called her husband. Rather, a manatee is a large bulky aquarian herbivore, a bit like a swollen walrus, only with cute eyes and inadequate flippers. It moves around pretty slowly and clumsily, and in its more private moments has the depressed and doleful expression of a creature that somehow knows it should really have disappeared from the earth many millennia ago. (You see this pained look on the face of the Reverend Ian Paisley sometimes, particularly when the SDLP do well in elections.)

Yet evolution, which has dealt so ruthlessly with the dodo and the dinosaur, and which is really giving the duck-billed platypus something to ponder when it gets up of a morning, has been inexplicably kind to the manatee. Somehow it has just kept plodding along through the centuries, while all around it much more resilient and handsome creatures have vanished from the football pitch of history as quick as recidivist South American strikers being given red cards and consequent early baths.

One single look at it, and you can see that the manatee was not designed to survive in any environment other than Sea World. It is utterly pitiful. But, unlike the shark, at least it makes an effort when it notices us. It breast-strokes its way awkwardly up to the top of the tank and plummets down again, its dive as graceless and pathetically unconvincing as one of Jurgen Klinsman's. It hauls its bloated carcass back up to have a gander at us – 'what's up witcha gorgeous?' one fan says, 'jaze, yer the image of the mother-in-law' – then it claps its flippers, bloats its cheeks and releases from its bowels an enormous manatee turd, which ascends all the way up to the top of the tank and floats there for some time before disintegrating. We all clap and whistle. That, after three weeks away from home at the World Cup, is how sad we are. We are applauding incontinent aquatic mammals.

We stare at this ungainly creature for some time, waving our Irish scarves at its window. After a while, it seems to respond to the colour green. I don't know whether it is my imagination, but every time an Irish scarf is brandished, its hapless mug seems to break into an encouraging grin. It keeps coming up and head-butting the window, its great mouth gaping and leering. The manatee is described in my guidebook as 'the last beautiful surviving link to our dark prehistoric past'. It is thus, I suppose, to the aquarian world what physiotherapist Mick Byrne is to the Irish soccer team. As such, I feel it is worthy of considerable respect. In fact, I like the manatee so much that I intend to ask at the gift shop whether they sell stuffed ones.

Monday, 4 July, Orlando: The morning of the Holland game I wake up early. The cold which I have been so vigorously fighting off since the start of the World Cup is now upon me, big time, major league, with fries to go. I am sneezing and coughing and spluttering and trembling and there is enough moisture flowing from my scarlet eyes to fill a good size manatee tank. I am banjaxed, I really am. I clamber from the scratcher, feeling miserable, and I stagger to what the great and good Lord Chesterfield called The Noble Room.

My internal workings are, well, not really working. I will spare sensitive readers the full details. Suffice it to say that I have diarrhoea so bad I feel I could excrete through the eye of a needle at fifty yards.

I wonder what to do about this. I mean, I have a very long and stressful day ahead of me. I decide to get dressed, go down to the pharmacy and buy myself milk of magnesia, vitamin C pills, cough bottle and a good nasal spray. Preferably the kind of nasal spray used by Maradonna. They don't have it, sadly, but they know where I can get it. I am to go to a certain back alley in the bad part of Orlando, find the red door, knock three times, sniff loudly and say, yo dude, 'Fat Diego' from Buenos Aires sent me down for half a pound of Colombian nose candy. (I'm not really to do this, if their lawyers are reading. I made that bit up.)

Back at the hotel, I swig down all my medicaments, but I don't feel any better. I feel a little worse, in fact. Ten minutes later, as I don my Opel shirt and my mirrored green sunglasses, I suffer another terrible internal attack and break the hundred-yard record in a dash to the jacks. I don't mind telling you that I am pretty worried by now. Lavatory facilities at the Citrus Bowl are not what they might be, and I do not wish to stand in a queue for fifteen minutes and miss an Irish goal. (Poor innocent fool me, I have forgotten that to miss an Irish goal a person would have to stand in a queue for about twelve years.) I ponder my problem for some time. In the end, I decide to just trust in fate and bring along a good stout pair of bicycle clips.

The coach arrives at the hotel to convey us all to the game. We clamber on board, singing 'Here We Go, Here We Go, Here We Go' and other such patriotic ditties. On the way down International Drive we pass a busload of Dutch fans, and there are frantic choruses of 'Cheerio, Cheerio, Cheerio' and 'California Here We Come'. One man on our bus opens his window and sings, 'When it's Spring again, I'll bring again, Eejits from Amsterdam.' The Dutch fans stick their trumpets and trombones out their windows and blow them at us. 'Eejits from Amsterdam,' your man roars again, 'we'll wipe the bleedin' floor wit yez.' What he suggests should be done with the trombones will not bear repetition in a quality newspaper.

Everyone on the coach seems confident of victory. But it may not be as simple as that. When we get to the Citrus Bowl and file in, clutching our inflatable green crocodiles and enormous plastic shamrocks, we see that there are a lot of Dutch fans already in their seats, clutching inflatable orange windmills and enormous plastic tulips and looking strangely smug. They look like they have been there all night, for some reason. For the first time in this World Cup, we Irish supporters will have to contend with a more or less equal number of foreign fans. It is just not fair!

The man sitting in front of me is so fat that the back of his neck looks like a plastic packet of hot dogs. He is wearing an orange football shirt and a large preposterous hat shaped like an Edam cheese with a slice slivered out of it. My God, is he big. He looks like a barrage balloon on legs. The waistline of his trousers is far too low, so that a good half of each of his enormous pendulous buttocks protrudes. You could park a bicycle in the cheeks of his bum. He turns and beams at me, in a strangely unsettling manner. 'We will beat you today, yes, Irishman?' he says. 'Oh, I don't think so,' I grin.

'Yes, yes, yes,' he nods, 'I think we will beat you today.'

'You'll never beat the Irish,' I counter, brilliantly.

'Ha,' he says, 'If you think we do not beat you, then you are a very stupid facker.'

'HaHaHa,' I simper. He turns around, opens his beer and begins loudly singing something in a strange guttural language which I suppose must be Dutch. Back home in Ireland I am pro-European, pro-Maastricht, the works. Sitting here in the Citrus Bowl behind this circumferentially challenged Netherlander and his globular nether regions I realise with a sudden start that I want to get my hands on the little Dutch boy who put his finger into the dyke in the children's bedtime story and slap the bloody gob off him.

While waiting for the game to start I have a read of the paper. It leads with a story on the murder of Andres Escobar, the Colombian player who scored an own goal and thus knocked his team out of the World Cup. Underneath is a story about an Argentinean man who bet his neighbour that Argentina would win the tournament. This fellow put up his wife – I am not kidding you – as the stake, and when the Argies got knocked out by Romania, he duly handed the missus over to your man next door. Sadly, the good Señora's reaction is not recorded for posterity, but I imagine she must have been pleased enough to hop over the back fence. Let's face it, when your sweetheart has wagered you on a major international sporting event, you have kinda lost that lovin' feeling.

There is another fascinating story about how much the Irish fans have been drinking in Orlando. A local doctor has written that alcohol abuse might well be a serious social problem in Ireland, which, naturally enough, to me is really a major revelation. I ponder writing Doctor Incredibly Perceptive MD a letter pointing out that alcohol abuse is not so much a serious social problem as the national sport in Ireland, and that if they had World Cups for being scuttered, Ireland would win hands down. Apparently, he writes, if you have eight beers a day the size of your brain actually shrinks. That's the bad news. The good news is that it makes watching English situation comedies so much more entertaining.

The players troop out to a great roar of applause and the game begins. Right from the start, the Dutch are all over us like a cheap suit. The Irish fans cheer and sing, but somehow we know today is going to be tricky. But at least both sides are playing to win, and this makes the game quite stirring to watch. Then, however, Terry Phelan attempts a pass so clumsy that even Casanova would have found it a bit outrageous. This woeful mistake lets the Dutch get the ball. They express their gratitude by taking it and briskly burying it in the back of the Irish net. The fat fellow in front of me practically ascends body and soul into heaven, so screechingly enthusiastic does he become. Bloody typical. Very unsporting people, the Dutch, I've always said it.

Well, all this is a bit of a downer, as you can imagine. As you sit there in the hundred-degree heat, you can't help chewing on the grizzly fact that Ireland have never actually scored more than one goal in a World Cup match. Things go from bad to worse. The Dutch start to take over the game, and soon they are running us ragged. And then that terrible moment comes. It is as though time stands still. Poor dear Packie Bonner, who is very much the hero of the Irish fans, fumbles the ball into his own goal.

Now, I don't know if you have ever heard the sound of a large number of Irish men groaning simultaneously – I mean, I went to a Catholic boarding school, so, you know, I got to hear it almost every night for some years – but take it from me, it is not a pretty sound at all. We are all speechless with shock. Down in the goalmouth, poor Packie looks like he wishes the yellowing patchy grass of the Citrus Bowl would simply open up, swallow him down and spit him out in bubbles. He clenches his fists and hangs his head in pure unadulterated despair.

Well, I think I know how he feels. The likelihood of Ireland scoring two goals against a side like Holland was pretty slim, let's face it, but we have an ice-pop's chance in the bloody Kalahari of knocking in three. It is simply not going to happen. The Irish fans go very quiet. One of them opines – jokingly I must point out – that Packie Bonner is bloody lucky he comes from Ireland and not, like poor old Escobar, from Colombia.

Our hearts go out to Packie. Watching him pace up and down the goalmouth, his face the very picture of horror and misery, is distinctly unpleasant. I cannot help but recall that the last person in Irish sporting history to make such a clanger of a mistake was Dick Spring TD, who, while playing full-back for the Irish rugby team some years ago, famously dropped the ball on his own line and allowed Scotland to score, thereby defeating Ireland. (Not only can Dick not pass the buck very effectively, but he can't pass the bloody ball either.) So poor Packie should console himself. We may have been knocked out of the World Cup, but I can see a very bright future indeed for him as Tánaiste.

The game drags dolefully on and ends in bitter despondency and disappointment. Jack and the players are generously applauded at the end, but it's nothing like the unbridled adulation that echoed around the Giants Stadium on the day we beat Italy, or the day we drew with Norway. Even the Mexico game, when we lost, whipped the fans up into a frenzy of appreciation. That's the amazing thing about the Irish fans. They are the only supporters at this World Cup who will tell you – and mean it – that it's not necessarily winning that counts, it's playing the game with a bit of an attitude. But today has knocked the heart out of us. It's not just the fact that we've lost the match that is bugging us, nor even the fact that we're out of the World Cup one whole round earlier than last time. It's the uncomfortable and as yet unspeakable realisation that we were bloody well awful, and we know it.

The bus back to the hotel is very quiet. The fans troop on in silent twos and threes, heads hung low, still wearing their green shirts, their ludicrous hats, still carrying their green inflatable beer bottles and plastic alligators, their faces streaked with green and orange paint. They look as outrageous – even as ridiculous – as ever, but you suddenly see them in a new and revealing light, as they slump into their seats and light cigarettes and sit staring out the windows in total silence. Absolute loyalty crushed is not a pretty picture.

One man gets on with his ten-year old son, who is sobbing bitterly, his hands held up to his eyes. They walk slowly down the back of the bus and sit down together, and the boy sinks his head into his father's chest and puts his arm around him and cries. His father strokes his hair and says nothing. He just gazes straight ahead of himself, gnawing his lip, shaking his head, his own eyes moistening. I catch his eye and he tries to smile. He looks away, out the window, then he looks back at his son. 'Sure, it's only a game, soldier,' he says, softly. 'There'll be another day, don't worry.' He ruffles the boy's hair, but the poor kid can't stop crying. He takes his hand and squeezes it. 'Ah don't, soldier,' he whispers, 'don't be upsetting yourself.' At this very moment, I can tell you, it is very hard to make jokes.

Church Street, Orlando, 9 p.m.: The huge open-air after-match-night party coincides with America's Independence Day.

In the packed streets of downtown Orlando there are so many people wearing orange that you would swear it was the Twelfth of July in East Belfast and not the Fourth in Florida. The defeated Irish fans have cheered up a little and are mingling happily with the victorious Dutch. Up on a stage seemingly made of tied-together beercrates, a hirsute Irish band is playing 'The Road To God Knows Where'.

We're on the one road
It may be a long road
And it's the road to God knows where
We're on the one road
It may be a long road
But we're together now, who cares?
North men, south men, comrades all
Dublin, Belfast, Cork and Donegal
We're on the one road
Singing along
Singing the soldier's song.

Near me, a crowd of Irish fans are wearing giant orange clogs, and enormous hats in the shape of windmills and tulips. They are dancing around in an unwieldy ring and chanting 'You'll Never Beat The Irish', which, in the circumstances, is pretty damn brave.

For a moment, I am moved to suggest that they should actually be chanting 'You'll Never Beat the Irish (You'll Thrash The Living Daylights Out Of Them)', but that would be unforgivably cruel and ungenerous.

Down the street, there is a large fairground machine which takes the shape of a circular metal ring about six-foot wide mounted on an electronic platform. You pay five dollars to get strapped into this thing and spun around at about fifty miles an hour for five minutes. If you don't gawk your ring up after this experience, you are practically given the freedom of Orlando.

A huge crowd of Irish fans are clamouring around this machine, desperate to have a go. I watch one man I've got to know from the hotel clamber up on the platform and get strapped in. As the circle starts to spin, his friends shout out in encouragement 'greasy fried egg', 'mowldy banana' and, unimaginatively enough, but perhaps most effective of all, 'bag of puke, bag of puke, bagga steamy steamy puke'. Others simply make vomiting noises. BHUAAGHHHH, OH JAYZUS, BHUAAAAAARRRGH. They clutch their ample stomachs, roll their eyes and retch. BHUAAWWRGH, UNGH, UNGHARGHHHHG. All the time he rotates, a blur of green and white misery, until finally nature takes its course and he spews so copiously that everyone has to run and duck for cover.

I watch as this fellow is efficiently untied – the keeper of the machine keeping him well and truly at arm's length – and released into the dubious custody of his cheering companions, who sponge him down, clap his back and tell him what a fine fellow he is. 'Jaze now, ye've balls on yeh the size of church bells,' one of them says, which, I think, must be a compliment, although, to me, it sounds distinctly uncomfortable. I wonder what it is about defeat that makes grown adults behave like this.

I fall in with him and his pals and we wander further down the street together, drinking beers and chatting. Everyone is trying hard to have a good time, but you can see in their expressions that actually they're feeling pretty down. 'I'd as soon be at home in bed,' one man confides. 'I'm not in the mood for a party at all.' On the corner by Church Street Station, a large scrum of Irish and Dutch supporters are dancing and singing.

You put your left leg in
Your left leg out
Your left leg in and you shake it all about
You do the hokey-cokey and you turn around
That's what it's all about.

As I watch them, a sudden and terrible thought strikes me. Maybe that is what it's all about. Putting your left leg in and your left leg out. Is that what it's all about? I mean, you know, you work hard, you pay your taxes, you try to be a good moral person and do the right thing, but maybe it is all a waste of time, because maybe, oh my God, maybe *doing the hokey-cokey, putting your left leg in and your left leg out* is *really what it's all about!*

We stroll on, around the corner of Church Street. A PA system is blasting out songs by Irish bands. 'In The Name of Love' by U2 segues into 'Here Comes The Night' by Van Morrison. The street is chock-full of Irish fans, clustered around the bars on the pavements. A few of them are dancing around, but only half-heartedly. Most of them are just drinking. And then suddenly, a strange thing happens.

The sound of Philip Lynott and Thin Lizzy comes blaring down from the loudspeakers. There is a tumultuous roar of recognition from the Irish fans. They wander from the bars into the middle of the street. They all start to jump up and down and sing along and dance, they clap their hands in the air, first one section of the street, then another section, until in a few moments the whole street is singing, as far as your eye can see, right down to the junction, which must be half a mile away. It's an amazing sight. And the sound! I don't know if you've ever heard 'Dancing In the Moonlight' sung by ten thousand Irish soccer fans, but for some reason I cannot really figure out it is unforgettably moving.

It's three o' clock in the morning
And I'm on the streets again
I disobeyed another warning
I shoulda been in by ten
Now I won't get out till Sunday
I'll have to say I stayed with friends
But oh, you know it's a habit worth formin'
If it means to justify the ends

And I'm dancin' in the moonlight
It's got me in its spotlight, it's all right,
I'm dancin' in the moonlight
On a long hot summer night.

It is a wonderful moment. Somehow, it lifts the whole night. The fans are embracing each other, hugging the Dutch fans, hugging the waitresses, the policemen, hugging the police horses for God's sake and the guys and girls selling beers and ice creams. And singing 'Dancing In the Moonlight'. The laughing voice of Phil Lynott, reminding us in some weird intangible way that being Irish always has its consolations. So we lost. Big swinging deal. We lost. It's not the end of the world. Everyone is singing together now. 'Dancing in the moonlight/It's got me in its spotlight/It's all right.' The Irish fan beside me is apoplectic with pleasure. He is singing along with the guitar solos, at the top of his voice. His right hand is strumming his trouser zip and his left is held out parallel to the ground, fingers wriggling spiderlike on invisible frets. His head is shaking from side to side. He takes off his Ireland baseball cap and throws it high into the air. 'It's all right,' he sings, the veins in his neck throbbing, 'dancing in the moonlight, on a long hot summer night!'

I wander along by myself now, and after a moment or two the crowd sweeps me into a guy I know, an Ireland fan from Derry. He is right in front of me, in a green jersey, and he is wrapped around a young black woman in an orange jersey. Kissing is not quite the word for what they are doing. They look like they are each trying to get a taste of what the other had for breakfast. When he finally comes up for air he peers at her adoringly. 'Are you from heaven or what?' he says. 'Close,' she replies, 'Wisconsin.' 'Dancing In the Moonlight' ends to a roar of applause, and 'Linger' by The Cranberries comes on. The three of us go for a drink, and we bump into more people we know in the pavement bar. The night is warm, and the humid air smells sweet.

You think about these wonderful fans, and what a joy it was to be here with them. Overhead, the Fourth of July fireworks suddenly begin to roar into the sky. They spit and fizzle and bang, filling the air with shimmering light and gorgeous colour. The dance music stops and the sound of the American national anthem fills the street. People stand to attention. For a moment, as you sip your drink and munch your hot dog in a rebelliously left-wing manner, you are – you have to admit it – touched by the seductive spirit of American patriotism.

You think about the brave pilgrim fathers, the American constitution, Jefferson and Lincoln, the freedom of the individual, the separation of church and state, the right to free assembly, the desperate immigrants fleeing poverty and persecution to come to the land of the free and the home of the brave and struggle for a better life. You look around, at this great crowd of people, all standing heads bowed, arms by their side, in attitudes of reverent respect. You get a lump in your throat. Then you take another big bite of your hot dog, and you swig your beer, and you think, 'Feck this anyway for a phoney game of cowboys, I wish they'd bloody put on Phillo again.'

From
The Irish Male at
Home and Abroad
1996

Getting to Know the Lord

It is just after three-thirty on a rainy London Monday afternoon and the moment is fast approaching for which God put me on the earth and made me a journalist. After all the years of suffering and loneliness and poverty, all the relentless hackery, all the unappreciated experimental theatre reviews and the failed feature article ideas, I am here. It's the big time. I am in Lord Jeffrey Archer's bathroom! *LOOK AT ME, MA. I'M ON TOPPA DA WOILD!* Not the bathroom of his country residence, the old vicarage, Grantham, once inhabited by the poet Rupert Brooke. No, I am in one of Lord Archer's other bathrooms, the one so elegantly surrounded by his luxury penthouse flat on the banks of the River Thames. It is, it must be said, a very nice bathroom indeed. And my proudest moment is coming soon. But I am not enjoying myself.

I am so nervous at the prospect of meeting my hero. I close my eyes and take deep breaths. I open my eyes again. I pace the floor. I try to whistle. I notice suddenly, for some reason, that there is hardly any bog roll. But that's OK. Nothing to worry about there. I do, after all, have a copy of Lord Archer's latest book, *Twelve Red Herrings*, in my holdall. If the worst comes to the worst. Not that you would actually use *Twelve Red Herrings* for that particular purpose. And I really do mean that sincerely, folks.

I pace the floor again, relentless anxiety flickering through my nerve endings. I am so thirsty. There is no glass. I turn on the cold tap and try to get my mouth underneath it. I accidentally splash water all down my front. It is all a disaster. I try again. I actually have to crane my neck and pucker my lips and put them around the end of the tap and suck. Good God in heaven, I am sucking the cold tap of the most popular novelist in Britain! It just doesn't get very much better than this.

Getting in to see Lord Archer was a bit of a big deal. I turned up five minutes early and explained myself to the laconic concierge, who showed me into the lift and pressed the button. 'When the lift stops,' he intoned, gravely, 'just push the door. And you will be in Lord Archer's apartment.' Hey, the man has his own lift door. That's how rich he is. His own lift door! I don't even have my own ironing board.

'Good afternoon,' one assistant said, as the door opened.

'Welcome,' the other said.

'Can I use the bathroom?' I said.

But I am so nervous now that I cannot actually pee. The knowledge that there is nothing but wall space between an author of Lord Archer's godlike magnitude and my own lowly self is making me so tense that my urethra is practically prehensile. Lord Archer's soap! My God, Lord Archer's towels!

Look, this man is really famous. He is the cultural wing of the Conservative Party. He is to the modern Tories what Jean-Jacques Rousseau was to Abraham Lincoln. And then there's all his famous mates to consider, too. I mean, Lord Archer has some pretty glitzy and influential friends, you know. And he's well known for the posh society parties he throws here in his luxurious gaff. So who knows what noses have been briskly powdered within these walls? Who knows who has slugged down the champers and popped in here to Jeffrey's jacks for a spot of quick relief over the years? Perhaps John Major himself has pointed the Prime Ministerial percy at this particular porcelain? And which of that shower of Tory bastards, to use Mr Major's affectionate term for his colleagues, have had a satisfying tinkle in here? Perhaps Cecil Parkinson has gingerly lifted this very seat? Perhaps Michael 'Tarzan' Heseltine has rearranged his Little

Richard hairstyle in that very mirror? Perhaps, oh my God, perhaps even Mrs (now of course Lady) Thatcher has ... no, no, I'd better stop. The excitement really is getting too much for me. And anyway, I am now ready to meet The Lord.

I complete my ablutions and venture out, down a long corridor hung with framed political cartoons and into Lord Archer's living room. I stop in my tracks. The living room is bigger than my entire flat. If you were to fart now, perchance, no matter how discreetly, there would be a resounding echo. There are white armchairs and big fat sofas, two huge glass coffee tables piled high with art books. There are paintings on the walls, a large English classical scene and a couple of L. S. Lowry oils. Through a half-open door I can see a bedroom containing an enormous canopied four-poster bed of the type I feel sure Madonna must own.

An efficient young woman comes in and asks if there is anything I would like. What a question. An immediate and rather totalitarian communist revolution, I am thinking, but all I say, cringing moral coward that I am, is, 'A glass of water, please.'

'Fizzy?' she enquires.

'Yeah,' I say. 'Fizzy.' (I don't want to appear unsophisticated. I am in with the literary set now, after all.)

From somewhere above me I hear Lord Archer's booming voice. I look up and see that the apartment is designed in what I believe is called in polite society the 'split-level' manner. He is up above me, where he belongs, on the telephone, discussing, no doubt, some contract or another. 'Right,' he keeps saying. 'Yes. Right. Now look, this is too important to get wrong, OK?'

I chew my nails. With a sudden and terrible start I realise that I want to go to the toilet again. I wonder if the bathroom is vacant, or if it's being cleaned by the butler. But it's too late. Lord Archer descends the stairs with the proud grace and swanlike majesty of Scarlett O'Hara in a Savile Row suit. I proudly shake the very hand that wrote *Kane and Abel* and *Not a Penny More, Not a Penny Less*.

Lord Archer is surprisingly small. He is well preserved and lightly tanned and a little chubby around the midriff. He looks a bit tired today. Perhaps he has been counting his money. I wonder, just for a moment, whether this is the correct moment to ask him if his toilet is vacant. Perhaps not. But even if his toilet is not vacant, his oleaginous smile certainly is. Hey, it's a swings and roundabouts thing.

I sit on one of the big sofas and Lord Archer sinks into an armchair, putting his feet up on the coffee table. He puts on his glasses and reads over the letter he has received from the *Sunday Tribune*, requesting this interview. The letter mentions in passing that I know his editor at HarperCollins, the London publishing house that has just signed him up for a multi-million-pound three-book deal.

'How d'you know Stuart?' he says. 'Were you at college with him?'

'No,' I simper. 'I used to be published by him.'

'What do you write then?' he says.

'Novels,' I say.

He looks at me, beaming, his eyebrows raised. 'Do you?' he says. 'Do you really? Well, well, well.' He regards me the way senior members of the British Royal Family regard Rastafarians from the inner city whom they occasionally have to meet at charity functions. 'Do you? Really. How marvellous. Well, well. How marvellous for you.'

Lord Archer is wearing a beautifully cut two-piece suit, an immaculate shirt, a red-cream-and-blue striped tie and glittering gold cufflinks shaped like the House of Commons portcullis. He is nicely turned out, but his black shoes are in need of a good polish. For some odd reason, this does not surprise me at all.

I take a deep breath and kick off by asking his Lordship to tell me about an average day's writing.

'I rise,' he says, 'at about five in the morning.' (You see? Greatness already. You and me, being peasants, get up. But Lord Archer 'rises'. What a marvellous sight it must be, Lord Archer rising at five in the morning.) 'I work from six until eight. Ten until twelve. Two until four. Six until eight. Go to bed about nine-thirty, ten. Get up at five the next morning. I will do that for a first draft, which takes about six weeks, every word hand-written, and then I will do probably, oh, the last book was fifteen drafts, every one handwritten, and took two years. So it's a long, tough process. Anyone who imagines' – suddenly stops and beams at me – 'I am not saying this to *you*, Joe, I am saying it to your readers – anyone who imagines that you can knock a novel off is living in a dream world.'

But people do imagine that, I point out. People often say, 'God, I'm so broke, I think I'll knock off a crap bestseller and make lots of money.' And then they usually say, 'Look at that Jeffrey Archer. He makes millions out of his books and they're a load of atrocious auld blather.'

Lord Archer casts his eyes towards the heavens and smiles tolerantly at the pure idiocy of these poor imbecilic creatures, before shrugging manfully and shooting me an all-boys-together glance of artistic solidarity.

'Ah well,' he says. '*You* know only too well, Joe, eh?'

'Oh yes,' I say. 'Yes, Lord Archer. I do.'

He joins his fingertips and chortles again, at the ludicrous idea that anybody might think he actually spends all year long in his four-poster scratcher and then writes his books in a weekend. 'I think the easier it looks, the more convinced they are they can do it. And if they realised how much work went into making it look easy, they wouldn't say those things. To be fair, Joe, there are several of my friends who have tried. They say – His Lordship affects a devastatingly hilarious 'cockney' accent at this point – "Oi've known Jeffery all me life. Oi'll 'ave a go." And they had the courtesy, in some cases, and the good manners, to say, "It is not as easy as it looks."' (Snorts with laughter.) 'Otherwise everyone would be doing it!'

He has the most amazing laugh. HAHAHAHAHA. If you crossed a burst of machine-gun fire with the sound of a steroid-stuffed woodpecker attacking a tree, you would come up with something not unlike Lord Archer's laugh.

'I don't enjoy writing,' he confides. 'I find it very hard work.' Now, I must say that this surprises me greatly. I have been keenly studying his ample *oeuvre* in preparation for meeting him, and, God, now, I would have sworn that any author who could actually pen the immortal sentence 'Only a blind man could have missed what was likely to happen next, and although I might not have been blind, I certainly turned a blind eye' was utterly in love with the myriad possibilities of the English language.

Other people – knockers, has-beens, philistines and left-wing lesbian-loving begrudgers – seem to think his books are a steaming pile of fetid guano. But not me. I love them. Lord Archer is quite rightly celebrated for all his famous charity work, but nothing to me is quite as charitable as his writing. There is, for instance, no clapped-out and unfortunate old cliché so hackneyed that Lord Archer will not find a good home for it. Consider the story 'Trial and Error', the opening salvo of *Twelve Red Herrings*. 'The hours turned into days, the days into weeks, the weeks into . . .'? You guessed it. 'Months'. What is the hero's friend as good as? 'His word'. What hours did the hero work? 'All the hours God sent'. What are Yorkshiremen well known for? 'For being blunt'. What do crime reporters turn up to court in? 'Their hordes'. (Not their taxis.) What do they follow every word of the trial with? 'With relish', of course. And with mustard and mayonnaise, too, I suppose.

For me, the playfully ironic use of language is what is ultimately most impressive about the maestro's style. 'I devoured them hungrily,' the hero tells us, of his fish and chips. (Like, how else would you devour something?) 'I was put in a cell with a petty criminal called Fingers Jenkins. Can you believe, as we approach the twenty-first century, that anyone could still be called Fingers?' Well, the answer to that is a very firm, 'No, I couldn't, Lord Archer, we stopped giving fictitious criminals names like Fingers very shortly after Charles Dickens departed the corporeal realm.' You see, a thing like that would give a lesser author cause for mild concern, yet it didn't stop Lord Archer. Oh, no. He is truly an artist who blazes, as he would say himself, his own trail. He paddles his own canoe, he has his nose to the grindstone, his back to the wheel, his head on the ground and his feet in the clouds. Not only does he bring his literary horse to water, but he also makes it, in a very real sense, drink. And every word handwritten, too.

'I can't type,' he explains. 'I don't know how to use any machinery.' It is a very long time indeed since I have heard a type-writer described as 'machinery'. Again, again, the revolutionary use of language. 'Also, I have a feeling at the end of a six-week session, it's ... it's ... it's a bit puritanical, but I have the feeling that I have done it. It is my work. It doesn't belong to anyone else.' He pauses and nods and beams at me. 'I like that,' he says. I reflect that if there's one thing Lord Archer shouldn't worry his fluffy little head about, it's the possibility of other authors any-where in the whole wide world claiming that his work belongs to them, and not him.

Lord Archer in conversation has two expressions. There is the smile, of course. He smiles like a man who has had emergency corrective facial surgery in a Third World country. And then there is the serious, concerned look. This means not smiling, basically, and knotting up his eyebrows, and sometimes removing his spectacles and sucking on the bit that goes over the ear. When I ask him to tell me some of his views on the short story form, he flips into serious mode. The eyebrows are so knotted they are practically Gordian. The spectacles are so thoroughly sucked they are nearly hyperventilating.

'Well, I think I am a storyteller first and foremost. I mean, lots of people write short stories. And they're not short stories at all. They're described in the press as, you know, so-and-so-and-so-and-so, the world-famous author, has written twelve short stories. Often they're twelve essays. Or twelve very well-written pieces. But short stories are ...'

I lean forward, waiting for enlightenment.

'Short stories . . . they have to be stories. H. H. Monroe wrote stories. Maupassant wrote stories. Ummmm, Somerset Maugham wrote stories. Graham Greene even. Fitzgerald even.'

Gosh. As I listen to Lord Archer, I am practically overcome with gratitude for his revealing so kindly and incisively to me that Scott Fitzgerald wrote stories. I pick up my copy of *Twelve Red Herrings* and flick through it while he expounds. Actually, I just want to take my eyes off his spectacles, which by now are so moist they are practically orgasmic. I must confess, it is a tad difficult to detect the influence of Scott Fitzgerald and Guy de Maupassant on such delicate examples of the Archerian prose style as the following:

> *Under the terms of the flotation, fifty-one per cent of the shares would be retained by Rosemary and myself. Jeremy explained to me that for tax reasons they should be divided equally between us. My accountants agreed, and at the time I didn't give it a second thought. The remaining 4,900,000 one pound shares were quickly taken up by institutions and the general public, and within days of the company being listed on the stock exchange their value had risen to £2.80.*

This, again, is from 'Trial and Error'. As is the following little gem: 'Funny, it wasn't the fact that Jeremy had been sleeping with my wife that caused me to snap, but that he had the arrogance to think he could take over my company as well.' Cracking stuff, huh? *Tender is the Night*, roll over and die. When I place the book with reverence back down on the coffee table and look at Lord Archer again, the spectacles too are on the table (smoking a cigarette and asking how was it for you?) and their owner is still wittering on about stories. 'Stories. Stories. Yes, other people write ... ummm ... essays. And write very erudite important pieces. And they're not stories. I tell a story, you see. So, they're certainly stories ... You see, a story, to me ...'

(Sheesh, I guess what the guy's saying here is, he writes *stories*, OK?) I ask whether people ever come up to him and tell him anecdotes as raw material for his … er … stories.

'Yes.' He shakes his head and closes his eyes and does his tolerant smile again. 'But I'm afraid ninety-nine out of a hundred are useless. I was just on a tour of Australia and New Zealand. And I foolishly said in one speech, "I'm always searching for a good short story." And three people came up to me afterwards and told me three of the most pathetic stories I've ever heard in my life. And I had to smile and be polite.'

I convey my sympathies. It must be awful, I imagine, having to deal with a whole room full of over-excited Jeffrey Archer fans, particularly in an Antipodean climate. 'But sometimes someone gives you an absolute gem,' he says, 'like "Cheap at Half the Price."' (This shattering masterpiece is about a woman who tricks her husband and her lover into each forking out half a million pounds to buy her a necklace. I felt it was very reminiscent of early Kafka, with faint echoes of late Enid Blyton.)

'I mean,' Lord Archer continues, 'a girl stopped me in the street just straight after lunch.' ('Girls' seem to stop Lord Archer in the street quite often, the lucky old bounder.) 'And she said, "The whole of New York is talking about 'Cheap at Half the Price'. And everybody wants to know who the girl is." And I said, "Well, that's very flattering." She said, "We're all asking each other 'Who is this amazing Consuela Rosenheim?'"'

Funny, that. I had just been lying awake in a lather of sweat every night for six weeks asking myself the same question.

All this stuff is so extraordinary that it is almost impressive. Lord Archer really does expect you to swallow that in the week in which we are having this conversation, the week of the beginning of the O. J. Simpson trial and Gerry Adams' first visit to America, 'the whole of New York' is discussing his book. It is a quite remarkable and utterly convincing pantomime of self-belief. 'But why do you write, Lord Archer?' I say, in a heartfelt manner. 'I mean, *why*? Do you ever ask yourself that?'

He ponders for a moment. He gives the specs another good lick. 'It's certainly not for the money,' he assures me, fervently. 'I don't need any more. I could live out of this country, of course, and not pay my tax. Or I could have yachts and dancing girls … But I don't.'

'Oh, no,' I say. 'As if.'

'So,' he says, 'I don't write for money. I have enough to last me the rest of my life. And more than I need. Far more than I need. I don't want that printed, because then I'll have a thousand begging letters the next day, but as you can see looking here' (he gestures around the digs with a faintly regal flick of the wrist), 'as you can see, I don't need any more. So it's not the money.'

So what is it? He purses his lips and shrugs and attempts a kind of aw-shucks-little-boy-lost grin.

'I do enjoy people stopping me in the street in every country. In every country on earth. That is thrilling, Joe. And anyone who says it isn't is a nut. And in your country in particular, if I walk down O'Connell Street, I mean, I can't get from one end of O'Connell Street, you know, to the other in under two hours. In under two hours! Without them coming up to me and going' (closes eyes and grits his teeth), ' "Wah wah wah wah wah wah wah wah wah." And they all go at you. And I love it.'

This is actually the noise Lord Archer makes. Wah wah wah wah wah wah wah wah wah. He sounds like either a runaway police car or a former member of The Supremes. I am very concerned about this. I mean, I actually live in Dublin and nobody has ever come up to me in O'Connell Street and gone 'wah wah wah wah wah wah', for even five minutes, never mind two whole hours. A terrible thought strikes me. These people coming up to Lord Archer in O'Connell Street and going 'wah wah wah wah wah wah' for several hours at a time, thereby preventing the poor man from going about his proper business – are they really his fans, or are they in point of fact deranged and potentially violent smackheads prematurely released from custody?

But he loves it, he says. There is nothing in life really better than being stopped in the street by his fans and listening to them go 'wah wah wah wah wah wah' at him. It makes all the hard work worthwhile. He seems to have a huge need to be liked, I say. Does he have any idea why this is?

'It's just human, isn't it?'

Well, yes, I concede, it may be just a human need, but Lord Archer does seem to have it big time, with extra mayo and fries to go.

'Yes, well, if you take the trouble to write, you want people to enjoy it. Aren't you the same, Joe?'

'Well, I suppose so.'

'HAHAHA,' he laughs. 'Yes. You see. HAHAHA. HAHAHA.'

When I take my fingers out of my ears, and the dull ringing sound eventually recedes, I suggest that surely there's more to it than this. Perhaps, I suggest, Lord Archer is trying to compensate for something. Did he have a happy childhood?

'Yes. Very. In Weston-Super-Mare.'

And what about this chap who keeps popping up in the papers these days, claiming to be Lord Archer's long-lost brother?

'What about him?'

'Well, is he? Your brother?'

'I don't know. He might be. He might not. I haven't met him.'

'He says he met you at a cricket match a few years ago.'

Lord Archer shrugs. 'I meet a lot of people. People come up to me, Joe, every day, you know, and they say all sorts of things to me.'

'Things like, I'm your long-lost brother?' (Or things, I ponder, like wah wah wah wah wah wah wah?)

He shrugs, and gazes in silence at his fingernails.

'So you don't really know whether or not you're an only child.'

'I am,' he says. 'I think I am.'

I point out to him that the mystery of the disappearing brother is symptomatic of a problem I encountered often while researching this interview. The facts of Lord Archer's early life tend to get shifted more often than an attractive junior researcher at the Tory Party annual conference. Did he, for example, attend Brazenose College, Oxford?

For the first time during our conversation, the smile fades. Lord Archer looks a trifle miffed. The handsome face is attempting to work its muscles back into grin mode, but it's not quite succeeding. It's all coming out instead as a rather disquieting leer. Lord Archer looks like an irritated Muppet. 'Call them,' he says. 'You just ring them up later and ask them.'

'Why can't you just tell me?' I ask.

'No, no, no,' he says, still attempting to grin. 'You just ring them. It will only cost twenty pence. You ring them and see what they say.'

He fiddles with his wedding ring, twisting, twisting. He takes it off and pops it from palm to palm as though it is suddenly very hot to the touch.

'Call them,' he says.

'All right, I will,' I say.

'Good,' he says. 'You do that. You ring them.'

It seems like a good moment to stop. I have taken enough of the great man's time. There are stories to be written, after all, and begging letters to be answered. I hang around for a few minutes, wondering if there is something I could steal and watching the photographer arrange Lord Archer by the window so that we can see the House of Commons and the Thames in the background. His Lordship looks very comfortable indeed in this pose. You even begin to suspect that he might have done it a few times before. What a guy. What an old pro. (Not that Lord Archer would know anything about old pros, of course. Old prose, maybe. But old pros, no.)

And we are just leaving, the photographer and I, when a funny thing happens. There is a big white statue out in the hall, by the lift, and the photographer asks very politely if he can take a picture of Lord Archer beside this statue.

'No, no,' Lord Archer snaps. 'You can't photograph that. That's my wife's. Not mine. You can't photograph it!'

I am halfway down in the lift before it occurs to me. What a genuinely strange thing that was to say. But then, I guess that's The Lord for you, ain't it? They do say he moves in mysterious ways.

Live and Let Diet

Now look here, I'm a new man. I am. Swear to God. I can express my feelings. I am in touch with my feminine side, my inner child, my personal karma. I cry at films. I iron my socks. I hug trees so hard there's been a bit of talk in the neighbourhood. You name it, I do it. And yet, and yet, here I am walking into Brown Thomas to get my first-ever facial massage feeling every bit as calm as a condemned criminal about to ascend the scaffold.

What the hell is wrong with me? I am sweating. I am nervous. I have chewed my fingernails down to the knuckles. If the cheeks of my bum were clamped together any more tightly I'd be able to crack walnuts with them. Why?

Yes, yes, yes, I know Irish men are uneasy about looking after their skin. Of course they are, This, of course, is because of our historical role models. Would Patrick Pearse have had a facial massage? Would Éamon de Valera? Would they heck. Yet the truth is, we've all had a surreptitious little dab in the mott's cold-cream when she hasn't been looking. So it isn't a macho thing with me, oh no. I think I'm uneasy because I'm putting myself into the hands of experts. Like most Irish people, I'm uneasy about experts. This is because I don't know what they're going to find out about me. Plumbers, doctors, washing-machine repair guys, it's always the same. They always make me feel embarrassed. Is the woman who's going to massage my face going to take one look, throw up her hands in horror, shriek piercingly and accuse me of treating my epidermis the way my mechanic says I treat my car? I've assumed, of course, that it's going to be a woman. In fact, my masseur turns out to be a bloke called Dave, who is from Manchester. As I shake hands with Dave, the full import of this descends on me. My God Almighty. In a few minutes' time, a Mancunian is going to be stroking my face. I cannot tell you how calm this makes me feel.

We go into a little white room which has the soft redolence of a dentist's surgery. Good God Almighty, is this guy gonna massage my face or do a bit of emergency root-canal work? I take off my jacket and lie down on the table. Dave puts a towel around my neck and tells me to relax. I whinny with high-pitched laughter. I'm now so relaxed I'm speaking in a soprano voice so striking that Dame Kiri Te Kanawa would be emerald green with envy.

He starts by telling me he's going to wash my face. Fine. I've even been known to do that myself sometimes, I tell him. He produces a bar of soap which costs nine pounds. Nine pounds?! I wouldn't spend nine pounds on a shirt! Dave grins beatifically. It costs nine pounds but it lasts you nine months, he says. He himself has a bar that has lasted a year. I can't help hoping that it ain't the one he's going to use on me.

I close my eyes and wait. I feel the lather being smeared all over my kisser. It's not too bad. Damn it all, it's quite nice actually. Dave's dextrous fingers knead and pummel my puss until it tingles. Then he washes off the soap and smears on this gel-like substance which exfoliates the skin. Exfoliation is a polite word for scraping. If any of you guys have ever snogged somebody without having shaved yourself properly beforehand, 'exfoliated' is the correct scientific term for the way they look afterwards.

The exfoliating jelly is then removed from my boat race, which is now tingling so exquisitely that it feels like it's got pins and needles. A new lather is efficiently prepared and thickly plastered onto me. Dave explains that this is a revolutionary and special kind of shaving foam that moisturises your skin while softening your stubble. It's an absolutely vital product, Dave says. Indeed, you think, how in the name of God above did our grandfathers manage without it? While he is massaging this into me, he enquires whether there's anything I'd like to ask him about my face. I wonder where to start. Why couldn't it have been Alec Baldwin's, for instance. Dave titters dutifully.

Off comes the shaving foam. At this stage my mug feels pink and naked as a baby's bum. But we are not finished yet. Dave purses his lips in a disconcertingly thoughtful manner. He feels that I need a bit of anti-ageing treatment. I have one or two tension wrinkles, he tells me. I didn't when I woke up this morning, I reply. They must have burst splendidly forth the minute I walked into BT's. He produces a bottle of lotion and briskly uncaps it. This is the business, he says. If you use this stuff for three days it makes your skin look 45 per cent younger.

I am thirty-two years old now, so 45 per cent younger, in my case, would make me look about seventeen and a half. I am not so sure I want to look seventeen and a half again. When I actually was seventeen and a half, I had acne so bad that my face looked like the surface of the moon. Still, Dave is not to be discouraged. On goes the anti-ageing cream, like icing onto a Christmas cake. I lie back and feel it seeping into my cells. When it comes off, I don't really look 45 per cent younger, but I have to say, I feel it.

The whole process takes about forty minutes and I'd warmly recommend it. It is every bit as relaxing, calming, soothing and pleasurable as being touched by a Mancunian can be. And as forms of exfoliation go, it's definitely the second best in the world.

But then you can't help wondering: what is the point of having a face as soft as a new dishcloth if the rest of you is not up to scratch? Look at me, for God's sake. I am out of shape, out of kilter, out of energy and almost out of time. When I was young I loved displaying my body to the world. These days I am afraid to lie on a beach in case I get hit on the head with a bottle of champagne and launched by President Robinson. In college I was thin and lithe and svelte. These days I could wear my stomach as a very attractive kilt.

This is the reason why I have been on a strict diet since the start of this year, and I must say it's been going quite well. I did have a weak moment recently when I read an article about liposuction, a revolutionary new technique where you pay to have a small incision made in your body through which your fat is sucked out. I was initially very excited about this, and, indeed, had managed to make contact with Elle MacPherson's agent. But then, on further research, I discovered that you have no control whatsoever over who does the sucking, and, indeed, where they make the incision. So I decided to abandon that thought and continue with more traditional methods of weight loss.

And it's been tough, I have to say. For breakfast I am allowed an egg. That's it. One egg – as in hen, not ostrich – and a cup of tea or coffee. An egg might sound healthy to you, but I feel sure it is not. I feel sure that an egg just lies around in your stomach all day, fervently attracting dangerous corkscrew-shaped microbes and wicked intestinal parasites which would look under a microscope the way Noel Gallagher of Oasis looks in real life.

Anyway, egg consumed, I get down to the day's work. Boy, am I in a good mood! I mean, who needs a big plate of sausages, bacon, beans, mushrooms, and black and white pudding (swoon) when you can have a whole egg?! My energy levels are so gasp-makingly high at this stage that I can work for a full twenty-five minutes before having to go back to bed in a darkened room with the duvet over my head and a bottle of gin.

When I get up again, my 'mid-morning snack' is 'one cup of coffee'. Phew! I am so bloated by now that I have to tickle my tonsils with a peacock feather and make myself throw up.

For lunch I am allowed a crispbread and a tomato. Great, huh? I explained to my ferociously expensive dietician that a tomato might make a very agreeable lunch for a rabbit, but not for a fully grown adult male human. She smiled the smile of a woman around whose waist a small bracelet could be comfortably accommodated, and explained that, of course, I would sometimes be allowed to deviate from this dietary purgatory. If it is my birthday, I am allowed to masturbate briefly over a photograph of a bowl of tiramisu. If it is a Sunday, or a big family occasion, I am permitted to be lightly spanked on the arse with a piece of steak. On big family occasions I am also allowed to smear myself with mayonnaise or sink my fingers into a bowl of custard and wiggle them about for two minutes.

Mid-afternoon comes around then. Now, I don't know about you, but what I feel like around three o'clock is a smoked cod and chips with a side order of onion rings, a large slice of chocolate cake and several pints of Guinness. What I am allowed to have, however, is 'a piece of fruit'. For the first week of my diet I took 'a piece of fruit' to mean an entire melon, or perhaps a pineapple, including the skin and the leaves and a good chunk of the bark. But no, my patient dietary adviser advised. 'A piece of fruit' means a small piece of fruit. 'Like a kiwi fruit or a piece of mango or something simple like that.' Good God. Any woman who considers a piece of mango something simple has a very bizarre notion indeed of simplicity and clearly does not live in a neighbourhood where the local supermarket is a Dunnes Stores. (Mind you, for the money she's charging to put me through this misery the woman could buy her own mango plantation.) An apple or an orange is what something simple means to me. It takes, oh, a whole fifteen seconds to delicately wolf this down and a further two minutes to masticate the fuck out of the pips.

After this, the hours between mid-afternoon and dinner do tend to drag, I must say. However, I have discovered a good way of quelling hunger pangs, which is to smoke lots and lots of cigarettes. Thus, in the name of fitness, I shall probably die of lung cancer or coronary thrombosis. The fact that at least my coffin will not have to be carried by the former East German shot-put team is, of course, some consolation.

Dinner, when it arrives, is a veritable banquet. A bowl of clear soup or Bovril (yeah, Bovril!), followed by six ounces of meat or fish and either a salad or 'a portion of vegetables'. Now, my feeling about Bovril is that there is only one circumstance wherein it makes an attractive meal, and that is if you are halfway up Mount Everest and so fucking cold that you are seriously contemplating sliding into a sleeping bag with Chris Bonnington. And as for six ounces of meat or fish, well, six ounces might sound like a lot to you, but let me just put that in perspective. This book weighs about six ounces. The salad, needless to say, must be as undressed as a newborn infant. The portion of vegetables has to be small enough to fit in a leprechaun's condom. Dessert is a heaped spoonful of natural yoghurt. Yum, yum. I am told by some of my women friends that a heaped spoonful of natural yoghurt makes a very effective treatment for certain vaginal infections, and I am indeed glad to hear this, because it certainly doesn't make a very effective dessert.

My lithe dietician has recommended all sorts of ways of getting used to hunger, such as not thinking about food, drinking lots of water and going to bed early. But I find that rolling around on the floor and crying hysterically for several hours at a time helps, too. For supper – I ask you, supper, how can the skinny cow sleep at night? – I am allowed a crispbread with a slice of cucumber. All this for six months so far, and I have lost half a stone. Off my bloody wallet.

But people are very supportive when you are on a diet. They stop you in the street and offer you diets of their own for consideration. A sweet thought, but I need a new diet right now like a moose needs a hat stand. I am on the Saddam Hussein of all diets. My daily calorific intake is equivalent to that of a fully grown adult gnat, but I think it is working. I have lost seven pounds, and believe me; I have suffered a staggering purgatory for every single measly ounce. And while it is not yet quite true that you would see more meat on a butcher's bike on a Friday afternoon than you would on my detumescent midriff, I am making progress, and for this I must be thankful.

Yet the thing is, a diet will only take you so far. My dietary adviser told me recently that the time had now come for exercise. I had to 'give my metabolism something to really think about', she said. I assured her that my metabolism had plenty to think about, large plates of steak and chips in particular. But she didn't even laugh. This woman has actually studied the molecular composition of cellulite, and I guess that does peculiar things to your sense of humour. But anyway, I took her advice, and thus it was that I found myself recently signing up for the 'Bums'N'Tums' aerobics class in the gymnasium frequented by my sister.

Now, to say that the aerobics instructor was not exactly a rocket scientist would be something of an understatement. He was, in fact, thick as shite in a bucket. For some reason or another the women in the class seemed to have taken to him, but I really couldn't figure this out. The fact that he had the face of Gabriel Byrne, and that his body looked like it had been chiselled by the late Michelangelo Buonarroti out of a large block of granite, made absolutely no difference to my assessment of him. I mean, there's so much more to sexual attractiveness than pretty cheek-bones, rippling thighs, outstandingly defined buttocks, stunningly perfect triceps, enviable pectorals, etc., etc. Personality and a good sense of humour are so much more important in the long run, myself and the only other male member of the class agreed afterwards, as we soaped down our spare tyres in the communal shower. But we weren't too critical of our instructor, because, poor man, the prominent bulge in his Lycra trousers had almost certainly been caused by a distressing sporting injury of some sort.

Let me tell you, I was glad the aerobics session was over. There is something disconcerting about hopping maniacally around a dimly lit hall, hyperventilating to the strains of 2 Live

Crew while trying not to let your tracksuit bottoms fall down. 'Work that body,' the instructor kept bawling, 'come on, girls, let's funky things up here!' Now, you can credibly say things like that if (a) you come from South Central Los Angeles, or (b) you are a member of Spinal Tap. But this chap sounded like he came from South Central Stillorgan. He strutted about the hall like a peacock on steroids barking 'yeah' and 'I loik it' and 'yeah, yeah, dew it to me, baby!' in his Dortland accent, while we bounced around the walls like sweat-soaked little steel ball bearings in a broken-down pinball machine. Then, as I lepped about wishing fervently that I was dead, he sauntered over and glared at me with his hands on his scrawny hips. He let out a hollow sardonic laugh. 'Kick thews legs,' he said. If I had kicked them any higher I could have been taken for one of the Tiller Girls with a bad case of rabies. But he was not happy. I noticed that he shook his head sadly from side to side as he chortled at my efforts. Then he opened his mouth and screamed, 'Come ON! You're not troying! I said go for the burn, Joe!' If only he had said, 'Go for a pint of Guinness and a kebab,' I would have been so happy to concur.

When the class was over I lay on the floor of the changing room and thought about my life. How had any of this happened. One day you are young, trim, hopeful, the next you are being bawled out by a suburban troglodyte who thinks he's one of The Temptations. I staggered to my feet and weighed myself. I had lost two ounces. Two whole ounces! I put my clothes on and went straight to the pub, where I had a pint of lager and a packet of crisps. And that, I feel sure, gave my metabolism something to bloody think about.

But it doesn't work like that. Oh, no. You might be full of resolve to forget about the bits of your body you exercise, but then what happens? Yes. The bits you can't exercise start acting up. Your toenails start ingrowing. Your eyesight begins to fade. Your hair starts greying, or begins to grow in your nostrils at the same rate at which it falls out of your scalp. I was over beyond in New York on business earlier this year, a fine city full of lovely avenues, fantastic nightlife and organised gang warfare involving nasty sharp implements. As regular television viewers will know, the buildings in New York are tall, slim and graceful, in inverse proportion to the citizens, who tend to be short, fat and clumsy. But still, New York is a great town, so rightfully celebrated in story and song. How many of us have heard Francis Albert Sinatra croon those immortal lyrics 'Da Da Deedle-Dum, Da Da Deedle-Dum, Da Da Deedle-Dum' and felt our very souls thrill to the thought of the place where, if you can 'make it', you can 'make it' anywhere? Where else could he be singing about? Yes, alright, possibly Cootehill, County Cavan. (It's up to you! Coote! Hill! Coote! Hill-Da-Da-Deedle-Dum, etc.) Or perhaps Dundalk? (It's up to you! Dun-Dork. Dun-Dork.) But no, New York is the subject of Ole Red Eyes' affectionate paean. And anyway, there I was that Saturday night, cruising down Fifth Avenue in a yellow cab, feeling full of life and strange mischief and tequila sunrise, when something awful happened to me.

The ache began right at the back of the left side of my top gum. I immediately did the responsible thing. I ignored it and lit a cigarette. But by the time the cab had got to my destination and the laconic taxi driver had extracted a half-inch-thick wad of dollar bills from me, the pain felt like Satan himself and all his unholy minions were prodding the left side of my bonce with a red-hot ice-pick.

Well, in a way I was lucky. Because if you are going to get a toothache outside of office hours, New York is the place to get one. It is a twenty-four hour city. Whatever you want, you can get it in New York at any time of the day or night, with perhaps the sole exception of intelligent conversation, for which you have to book several weeks in advance and pay cash. Like sadomasochistic prostitution or sushi, however, after-hours dentistry is no problem if you have the readies, and so I located a dentist's surgery and conveyed myself there without delay.

It was some years since I had been to see a dentist, and so I was feeling more than a little apprehensive. I hate to admit it, but I had neglected my teeth. I don't know why, because one's teeth are among one's best butties. Think of what they go through with you. Think of all you make them chew, all that gets stuck between them, think of the abuse you give them, think of their lonely and unfulfilled lives, yellowing prisoners in that malodorous hot wet cave, your beak, without even a video machine or a pack of cards. Yes, yes, you give them the occasional brush, the odd sporadic lick if it's Christmas. Big deal. But do you floss? No, you do not. The only floss that ever gets near your mouth is the pink kind that comes on sticks by the seaside. That, in a way, is the problem.

Anyway, I sat in the reception room practically hyper-ventilating with pain and weeping openly. The open weeping was not caused by the pain itself, but by the thought of the bill, which the charming assistant had kindly gone through with me, explaining that they would take cash, credit cards, travellers' cheques, or, failing that, my first-born child.

The dentist, when she appeared in the room, was dressed like one of the NASA scientists from the film *Close Encounters of the Third Kind*, in a white zip-up bodysuit, face mask, heavy boots and thick plastic gloves. She lurched over to me and said hello. 'May the force be with you,' I replied, and she asked what seemed to be the problem. The problem, I made clear, was that the pain in my shagging kisser was enough to make the Pope blaspheme. She clamped my mouth open and began to prod my teeth with a long thin metal implement that looked for all the world like something you would use to eat a lobster or perform a circumcision, or, perhaps, both. 'Wow,' she kept saying, 'wow,' in a tone that simultaneously conveyed both bloodcurdling horror and an odd kind of wonderment. 'I'm guessin' here ya havvin bin to a dennist for a whoile, huh?' she asked. 'Unnnghgh,' I agreed. 'How many yeeze?' she enquired. 'Aragahangh,' I told her. 'Hmmmm,' she said, 'S'what I tawt.' Every so often she would helpfully jab her skewer into one of my molars with the delicacy of a mountaineer hammering a crampon into a granite rock.

115

Sometimes this would reduce me to a helplessly screaming wretch, whereas other times it would make me want to spring from the chair and hurl myself through the window and down into the busy streets of Greenwich Village. 'Does dat hoyt?' she would ask, after scraping me down from the ceiling and pouring me back into the seat. 'FunghinESSSSewefunghinooopidwarghonnn,' I would reply. She was either very well trained or just naturally perceptive, I reflected, as she got out her hose-pipe and whacked it into my mouth.

The next five minutes were like something out of the worst moments of the Counter-Reformation. Old Princess Leia produced a syringe and needle and stuck it into my gum, repeatedly, all the time telling my yelping and ululating body that this 'would help deal with the pain'. She then flicked a few switches on her bleeping console, cracked her knuckles and reached for her drill, selecting for my tooth the same drill-bit a navvy would use to bisect a paving slab. The bit sank into my poor misfortunate molar and the unmistakable aroma of rapidly powdering tooth-matter began to fill the air, along with a high-pitched whine (myself). Indeed, I felt like a bottle of wine in the process of being uncorked.

Only God and His Holy Mother really know what she did to me, but for the amount of money it cost I could have flown home to Dublin first class, put up in the Shelbourne bloody Hotel for the weekend and bought Irish passports for myself and the whole family. Even after all this time, I am still not convinced that this would not have been the better option. 'At least you'll have a nice smile now,' The Brother quipped. Yes, indeed. I certainly feel like smiling all right.

The week I got back from the Big Bagel I got the flu. It was Christmas week, too. (Thank you very much indeed, God, for giving me the flu the very week before your only son's birthday. Junior needn't think he'll be getting a present from me in future!) Everyone else in the country seemed to have it, too; but me, I had it big. I've had some very nasty diseases in my time, as regular readers of the *Sunday Tribune* will know (I've now broken it off with that ban garda from Ringaskiddy, however, and the penicillin is beginning to take effect at last), but I do not think I had ever had this strange ailment before.

This germ was so virulent that I felt I could actually see it. The vile little creature doing the hokey-cokey through my bloodstream had, I felt, loud clothes, long pointed teeth and a hairstyle broadly reminiscent of a rugby player's armpit.

Just in case you have never had this flu yourself – and if you haven't, poor reader, you will have it very soon, because it's so contagious that you can get it from reading this book – let me explain some of the main symptoms to you. A number of things happen when you have this flu. Your nose, of course, ebbs and flows like the broad majestic Shannon. Substances come out of your nostrils that you have not seen since that nasty Dilophosaurus spat all over that poor little man in the film *Jurassic Park*. Your mouth is as dry as a downtown Tehran disco-bar. Your throat and eyes ache. You shiver and shake and shudder like the early Elvis Presley. You cough and splutter and wheeze. You wake up every morning with the inexplicable yet certain feeling that Good Rockin' Dopsie and The Cajun Twisters are playing an extended boogie-woogie session in your head, and they ain't unplugged. And the main symptom, of course, is that you desperately, profoundly, wish to die.

Another symptom is that you stagger around your house or flat stark naked all day. This is because it actually hurts you to put on clothes. Your skin actually aches when you have this flu. A sheet or a shirt, it makes no difference, your flesh actually feels like several layers of it have been removed with a red-hot spatula. There are other odd feelings. If you try to comb your hair, your scalp feels like it is being pricked by a million deranged acupuncturists very much the worse for strong drink. Your energy level completely collapses. If you manage to raise your head long enough to hawk feebly into a crumpled hanky, you feel that you have swum the English Channel on your back.

Pills, potions, serums and lotions: none of them work at all. In the course of my perennial dealings with the bug I have swallowed, imbibed, inhaled, sucked and inserted more chemical substances than Keith Richards did while he was working on 'Sympathy for the Devil', and every year it's the same. I end up feeling not so much like Death-Warmed-Up as Death-In-A-Bloody-Cranky-Humour-First-Thing-Of-A-Monday-Morning-When-The-Telephone-Bill-Has-Just-Arrived.

This year when I got the flu I slept like a baby. That is to say, I woke up every three hours screaming, crying and wetting the bed. The bathroom department, do you say? Do not talk to me about the bathroom department. The bathroom, now, I will not go into, while the flu bug is exploring my innards. This is because when I do go into it, after a lonely half-hour trek across the landing floor, punctuated only by extended spells of curling up on the carpet and gibbering, I find it very hard to get back out. I don't think you want the details. I think you know what I am saying here. Some days, as Voltaire (or was it Locke?) once put it so cogently, the bottom falls out of your world. Whereas other days the world falls out of your bottom. Suffice it to say, I have suffered over the years.

Anyway, enough of this disgusting stuff. Let us talk more of health, grooming and beauty. In the search for manly deportment, a good haircut can go a long way. Look at President Clinton. Who can forget that great scandal last year when he delayed the take-off of Air Force One because he was having a haircut? The haircut cost $300 and was done by a man who trades under the name of 'Paulo'. Jesus. The most powerful man in the world, and he's getting his hair cut by a bloke with only one name.

Ah, the memories that came flooding back as I read the story of Slick Willie's appointment with the tricky trichologist. It was on my fifteenth birthday that I truly became a man. My mother let me get my hair cut in Herman's Klipjoint in Dun Laoghaire. This was a watershed, because to my friends and myself – shorn monthly like miserable ewes in what we regarded as the torture chamber of the old barber's shop in Glasthule – Herman's Klipjoint was the paragon of taste. Herman's Klipjoint did not sell haircuts. It sold a lifestyle. You could tell this because of the 'K' in the word 'Klipjoint'. It was modern. It was post-Vatican II. It had pictures of Kevin Keegan on the walls. It had an eight-track cartridge player – remember those? – and a full set of Steely Dan eight-track cartridges. Damn it all, it had blow-driers, for God's sake, and far from blow-driers was I reared.

I belong to a generation that saw washing its hair once a week in the bath as the height of personal hygiene. And yet, as I sat in the swivel chair that day in Herman's Klipjoint and had my hair blow-dried to within an inch of its life, I thought that I had arrived. The barnet was sprayed and lacquered and back-combed and frizzed. It was crimped and ironed and sculpted. Several of the fundamental laws of science were broken by my hair that day, including the law of gravity. I looked, when I emerged from Herman's Klipjoint, like a chrysanthemum in a tank top. And I felt that I was riding a wave. A permanent wave. In school on Monday morning the teacher took one look at me and said he wanted to help me out, which I thought was nice of him. 'Which way did you come in?' he added, however.

In the years that followed, my love of such establishments faded. Even that oh-so-cool post-modern 'K' began to bother me. It was trying too hard, I soon came to feel. I remember noticing as a teenager, on annual holidays in rural Ireland, that nightclubs which had neon signs outside flashing the words 'Nite Klub' were always dreadful places, whereas establishments that used standard English spelling were not.

I thought about all this the other day when I went into town to get my hair cut. These days I usually go to a barber shop, a civilised place where the barber does not talk to you. But it was closed, and so, feeling hirsute and raggedy, I was forced into one of those modern gaffs, the 1990s equivalent of Herman's Klipjoint.

No sooner was I in the place, than I began to suffer a strange and uneasy feeling. I have since checked with colleagues, and I now know that what I was experiencing was the clearly definable psychological phenomenon known as Trendy Hairdresser Anxiety (THA). Take this, for example: I am sitting by the sink waiting for 'Blake' to come and wash my hair. After ten minutes there is no sign. After twenty, still nothing. I begin to feel: They Have Forgotten Me. Now, apparently, this is a major symptom of THA. Lots of people suffer this in fashionable hairdressing establishments. Pretty soon afterwards, I start thinking: They Are Deliberately Ignoring Me. This, too, is a common phobia.

Finally 'Blake' comes and washes my hair. While he does so, we have a chat. For some reason, 'Blake' wants to know two things about me: (a) am I not working today, no? and (b) did I manage to 'get away anywhere' this year? He is quite persistent about this. He really does want to know. I try to change the subject. It seems that 'Blake' is not his real name, but his 'professional name'. Did he name himself after the great Romantic poet, William Blake? I enquire. No, he says, as a youth he was a fan of the TV programme *Blake's 7*. His real name is Morris, he finally confides, and Morris is not a good name for a hairdresser.

After a time, 'Blake' leaves me, sodden hair dripping down my neck. I am anxious. I am chewing my nails. But there is worse to come. I am only just recovering from Hairdresser Conversation Terror when I start mumbling to myself: That Person Over There Came In After Me And Yet He Is Having His Hair Cut First. Another paranoid delusion, I have since been told, much suffered by those who patronise such establishments. (Sigmund Freud wrote about it in his seminal work, *Curl Up and Dye: The Oedipus Complex and the Bad Hair Day*.)

Finally, 'Marco' arrives to give me short back and sides. He stares at me for a while before asking what I 'would like done with it'. I wonder about this. He fingers my hair. 'I mean,' he

sneers, 'would you like them both cut or just the one of them?'
Oh my God, he's saying I'm bald! I look at 'Marco'. He looks at
me. 'Blake' comes over and looks at both of us. 'Are you cutting
today, Marco?' he asks. 'Is he cutting?' I think to myself.

The man is a complete bitch.

Cowboys and Engines

Reader, there are some weeks you will never forget in your life and late last year I had one of those. I am talking about the week I finally did my driving test! Although I had attained the age of thirty-two, I had never attempted the test before, even though I did have some lessons once as a student, in an establishment that I seem to recall was called the Saddam Hussein School of Motoring ('Death Before Yielding').

This time around I went to a better school. My teacher, Eamon from ISM in Ranelagh, was a pleasant man with the patience of Sisyphus, the courage of Hercules and the wisdom of Solomon. Through many hours together we studied the intricacies of the three-point turn, the hill start and the smooth right-lane manoeuvre, all of which, three months ago, I would have thought were line-dancing steps. The man's persistence in the face of utter frustration was nothing short of heroic. Again and again, he would repeat the order 'mirror, signal, manoeuvre', like a maharishi chanting a mantra, until even I got the message. Mirror, signal, manoeuvre. I am starting to say it in my sleep.

Another problem was keeping my distance. I don't know why, but this was a problem for me. Youarenotsupposedto-drivelikethis. You are supposed to drive in a nicely spaced-out manner. That's nicely spaced out in terms of your proximity to the next vehicle, by the way, not nicely spaced out on drugs or cheap drink, for the benefit of younger readers.

Despite Eamon's many valiant efforts, the Friday before the test I was still in serious need of improvement. So The Brother, who has been driving since he was a gossoon, admirably stepped into the breach and gave me a few last-minute lessons. He is feeling much better now the blood pressure has returned to normal and the waking up in the middle of the night screaming in abject terror has subsided a little. His last piece of advice to me, as he stepped gibbering out of the car the day before the test, was the following, 'Would you not get out the clippers and do your nasal hair, no? You don't want Yer Man the tester to punt his lunch all over yeh.'

Thus, fully prepared, I turned up to take my test on Monday afternoon. Part One was an oral exam on the rules of the road.

'How would you know a zebra crossing at night?' the instructor enquired. At first I thought this was a joke. I frantically search my subconscious for the punch line. Is it: because he wanted to get to the other side? No. What is it again? Oh, yes. Flashing amber lights. A few more easy-peasy questions followed to which I knew most of the answers. Himself then produced a list of road signs and invited me to identify them. No problem.

Out to the car park, where we leapt into the motor and off we went. The first thing that happened was a pothole so big I got a large number of air miles for successfully negotiating it. Then onwards. A deft right, a couple of lively lefts, the gear changes as smooth as a politician's lies. So far, so good, as the optimist said plummeting past the fifteenth-storey of a sixteen-storey building.

The most disconcerting thing about the driving test, as many readers will know, is not the actual driving itself, but the fact that the tester does not talk to you, except to tell you what to do. There is no chitchat, no light laughter, no commenting on the Keatsian beauty of passing Churchtown or the desirability of the indigenous peoples of that parish, no re-hashing of the Oasis/Blur debate. Nothing. Zilch. Your tester, actually, is not *allowed* to talk to you. You are thus driving along for over half an hour with a person who is staring intensely at you without ever uttering one single social syllable. It is like being married, I suppose.

Anyway, twenty minutes in and things were going fine. I had reversed around the corner with the grace of ... something very graceful. I had demonstrated the hand signals you use to other motorists – or, at least, the polite ones. Everything was groovy and I was definitely in with a fighting chance of passing this test. And then ... we were just about to turn off the main road and into an estate when, suddenly, I saw this drunken hairy-looking gom come bounding and staggering out into the road, where, having reached the exact centre, he stopped and gawped at me. Just stopped. He started to beckon. Sheer terror wrapped its cold hand around my heart. I ignored him. He stared at me and beckoned harder. After some moments he sashayed to the side of the road where he stood and watched as I completed my right-hand turn. I couldn't help feeling he was an actor employed by the Department of the Environment for this purpose.

Back to the test centre toot sweet, where I was invited to park the car. Then, I was requested to follow the tester into the building, where he would tell me the result of my examination. I felt like Danton about to keep an appointment with Madame La Guillotine. I was so nervous I would cheerfully take a chomp out of a teacup. He sat at a desk. He scribbled a note. He turned. He looked up at me. He didn't smile. Then he said I passed! I couldn't believe it. I sprang out into the crisp winter evening, a new man, a grown-up, a driver, waving my certificate of competency in the air, a banner of self-fulfilment! Mirror, signal, manoeuvre. Mirror, signal, manoeuvre. I will never be the same again.

But passing my test put me into a bit of a quandary. The thing is, up until then I had never owned a car. I do not know why this is, because I have owned lots of other useless rubbish in my time, including the complete works of Rod Stewart, the keys to the *Sunday Tribune* executive washroom (i.e. the alleyway beside the office) and a television that only gets RTÉ 2. But anyway, the week I passed the test I finally became a whole person. I went out and bought myself a car!

The Brother came along with me to do the actual negotiating, and I must say, he is a good auld scout to have about you in a situation like this. The thing is, The Brother objects to paying the asking price for anything, as a simple matter of principle. He is the only person I know who haggles about bus fare. If The Brother was employed by Brinks-Mat, he would persuade villains and robbers by sheer logic to take only a million or two during heists and leave the rest behind and persuade them, too, that this was a considerable bargain. The Brother used to be a salesman himself, and despite – or perhaps because of – this, he tends to regard salespeople the way Eric Cantona tends to regard football supporters. (Eric Cantona: the first case in modern football of the shit hitting the fan?) But anyway, he is quite merciless about it.

'We want a car,' said he to the salesman.

'How does a BMW sound?' said the salesman.

'Vroom fuckin' vroom,' replied The Brother, 'now, be serious.'

We selected a car and made an offer. It was a fascinating spectacle, the salesman elucidating the basic principles of profit and loss upon which the entire free-market system is predicated, The Brother responding with his hollow sardonic laugh and his repeatedly mumbled observation, 'Ah, you're a tight-fisted mowldy auld bollocks. You'd hire your auld wan out be the hour.'

He tried, the unfortunate salesman, but when he was reduced to getting out the deeds of incorporation of the company to demonstrate that it was not, in fact, a registered charity, I felt he had lost the argument. By the time we left the premises we had chopped a quarter off the original price and the poor custodian was slumped over his desk, gibbering about his difficult childhood and his elderly widowed mother who, apparently, needed a complicated and expensive eye operation.

The next step was to get insurance. We went to an insurance company and the nice man explained the details. Now, I had heard that car insurance was expensive, but I was not fully prepared for the discussion which ensued. After I had finished cackling maniacally, the insurance broker talked me in off the ledge and got out the forms. The gist was that the insurance company would need an amount of money large enough to pay off the foreign debt of a good-sized Third World country, along with my credit card, my watch, my television, my typewriter, my late grandmother's gold teeth, my trousers ... You know, the usual. They would also require my first child to be handed over to them upon the occasion of its birth, along with regular *droit de seigneur* rights concerning its mother. I listened, quaking with shock. The broker then took the pair of tights off his face and I signed the forms. He put my cheque into a large sack marked 'swag', adjusted his striped jersey and informed me that I was now 'fully covered'. I reflected silently on my fervent wish for the broker to be fully covered also, preferably with lukewarm panther piss.

'You nearly had the shirt off my back,' I quipped.

He licked his lips and glared at me. 'Oh yes,' he said, 'I forgot about that.'

I emerged from the office, naked from the waist up, and got into the car. The Brother was in a bit of a sulk, because car insurance seems to be one thing you really cannot haggle about. I had to bring him into Moore Street and let him loose with two pounds in order to restore his good humour. He came back an hour later with an enormous sack of bananas, three crates of cigarette lighters and a shopping bag full of white socks. And since then, my existence has been pink and rosy. Having a car has really changed my life, I have to tell you. I think having a car is a very healthy thing, in that it does get you out and about a lot more. Now I can drive across to the shops every day to buy cigarettes and ice cream. Now I can drive down to Abrakebabra for dinner every night. It is terrific! I feel better already. If any of you need a lift anywhere, please do let me know.

But the thing is, the happiness does not last. You purchase a car, thinking that this will improve your life. As soon as you do this, you start to have second thoughts. My own first second thought, if you know what I mean, happened about a fortnight after I had got the car. I had just left the *Sunday Tribune* office where I had presented myself for my weekly heartless caning from the editor, and I was wandering down Baggot Street at a leisurely pace, safe in the knowledge that my parking meter had at least a full half-hour left to tick away. Suddenly I saw her: about a hundred yards down the street, this little middle-aged brown-uniformed woman, standing by my car and writing me a ticket! I'll tell you, the bould Sonia O'Sullivan had nothing on yours truly when it came to cantering that hundred yards.

Breathless, I stood by her side and asked what my offence was. 'Expired meter,' she said, in the voice of a Midlands dalek. I said the meter must have been broken. She smiled the patient smile of a woman who has heard it all before. She said there was nothing she could do. Even if she wanted to. My fate was sealed. Once she had started to write a ticket, she said, she couldn't stop. She 'wasn't allowed' to stop; she had to continue to the bitter end. She would 'get into trouble' if she did not write me a ticket now. Once that biro had made contact with that paper, pleas for mercy were quite useless and I was wasting my sweetness on the desert air. I took a deep breath and began to explain a few of the more basic concepts of existentialism: for example, the notion that in the absence of any divine ordering force we as rational human beings can and, indeed, must take responsibility for our own moral and ethical actions. But to no avail. 'You're gettin' a bloody ticket and that's that,' she confirmed. She was obviously a member of the Socratic school.

Next weekend I went down to Galway for a few days, and came back to Dublin on the Sunday night. There I was, cruising merrily eastwards across our green and lovely country in what one of my friends has insisted on christening The Babe Magnet (it is actually a Subaru Signet, which looks a little like a biscuit tin on wheels), happy as Larry and listening to the radio. There was a song playing by The Artiste Formerly Known as Prince (that is, The Artiste Presently Known as Pretentious Wanker – by myself at any rate), and I was happy to hear that he would soon be playing in Dublin because I was looking for an excuse to stay in one of these nights and wash my hair. Anyway. There I am, ridin' along in my automobile, when suddenly, quite out of the blue, the damn car begins to gibber and shake like a person with an unpleasant medieval disease. It is very difficult to render in print the noise that my car is now making, but it is something like 'hungh achock achock achocka thunka'. Before very long, it simply stopped. I got out and made a great show of opening the bonnet and looking underneath, but as I am actually the kind of person who cannot understand how a can-opener works, this display was purely theatrical.

Thus it was that I found myself alone and lost and on the outskirts of Mullingar! (If that sentence was the opening of a horror novel, you'd know you were in for a bloody scary read.) Mullingar is not a town I know at all well, and like most towns in Ireland, it is not a great place to try to find a mechanic at seven o'clock on a Sunday night. I suppose, to be frank, Mullingar is the kind of town about which people from Dublin sometimes laugh quietly and tell cruel jokes. But I will not hear a word against it. No, no!

A fine young Mullingarian fellow called Paul came to my rescue. He located the problem – a dicky fuel pump – patched it up and sent me on my way, advising that this was strictly a temporary repair. Next morning, back in the smoke, I took the car to the garage where I had bought it. I parked it outside, ambled in and explained my problem to a mechanic who was energetically leaning against a wall and scratching his armpits. 'Leave her out there and ring me Chewsdeh,' the mechanic yawned, when I had finished my tale of woe. I handed him the keys and strolled out to the car. There, on the windscreen, was another parking ticket! I ranted, I raged, I cursed. If things go on at this rate I intend to push it over a cliff and spend the money I save on parking tickets employing a full-time chauffeur. Having a car seems to be a full-time job. There is really a lot to be said for walking.

Ireland in Exile

When one realises that his life is worthless he either commits suicide or travels.
Edward Dahlberg, *Reasons of the Heart*

One day when I was in my final year at University College Dublin a man arrived out from town on the bus and began to wander about the campus assailing bemused undergraduates. It turned out that he was a photographer who had been commissioned by the Irish Industrial Development Authority to take pictures for a newspaper advertisement that would persuade wealthy foreign capitalists to come and open factories all over the Irish countryside. He wanted images of handsome and clever-looking students who would be willing to dress up in tweed jackets and Laura Ashley frocks and peer into the lens of his Leica and grin like clams and appear to forget about the fact that they would never be able to find jobs in their own country despite the fact that the PAYE workers of that country had shelled out considerable bucket-loads of folding stuff in order to subsidise their chances of so doing. He wanted young people who would embody the bright new Ireland about which journalists were wittering on at the time. None of the people I knew got selected.

Some months afterwards, a friend arrived at my flat with a copy of this IDA poster, which he had cut out of a newspaper. The slogan beneath the image announced proudly: THE

REPUBLIC OF IRELAND: WE'RE THE YOUNG EUROPEANS. As it turned out, my friend knew one of these young Europeans, a very talented engineer from a small town in rural Ireland, who had just upped and offed to Saudi Arabia, having failed after much effort to find work at home. My friend went through all the faces in the photograph, indicating to me that this person was in America, that one in Australia, several were in Spain or France or Germany and, of course, many more were in England. Most of the young people in the poster had fled the country precisely because of the almost laughably suicidal economic policies that same poster was attempting to advertise. Those who were still living in Ireland were unemployed, and, believe me, in the summer of 1985, they had an ice pop's chance in the Kalahari of finding a job. My friend and I talked for a time about this IDA poster. It seemed strange that all these good-looking young people who were supposed to embody Ireland had actually been forced out of the country simply in order to survive. We had both studied English literature, my friend and I. We had been trained to recognise an irony when we saw one.

We had also studied Irish history. We knew all about our country's unique history of emigration. Famine, depopulation, the coffin ships, the ghettos of Kilburn and Boston, the statistics, the lists, the death of the Irish language, the way emigration became a tradition in Ireland, not just a phenomenon, but actually a way of life. It had been a way of life for our parents' generation and now it was a way of life for us, too. The day we graduated, we practically got handed a plane ticket to London along with our degree. We knew about Irish emigration from reading all about it. As my pal and I sat talking about it that afternoon we didn't know – or perhaps we did know, deep down – that soon we would both know a little more about Irish emigration from personal experience. Soon we, too, would be leaving, like just about everyone else we knew.

It is ten years since I first saw that poster in my friend's newspaper, and I spent eight of those years living in London. Whenever I would come to Ireland during those years I would find myself thinking about that poster. Up until quite recently, a version of it was still running. Last time I saw it, it had the same old picture but a new slogan: THE REPUBLIC OF IRELAND: THE QUALITY BUSINESS BASE IN EUROPE. You would see this ad in the Irish newspapers, or in in-flight magazines. And you would often see it in Dublin Airport.

You might be coming home for a family celebration or a funeral. Or to see a friend. You might just be coming back to Ireland because you were so lonely and freaked-out where you were that you couldn't stick it any more, and you would have rented your own grandmother out by the hour to be back home in the pub by nine on a Friday night having fun and telling stories. Or you might be coming home for Christmas, like the hundreds of thousands of Irish emigrants who come back to this island every year at this time to celebrate, to share, to remind themselves why they ever left in the first place.

And there it always was, this IDA poster, illuminated at the end of the corridor that leads from the air-bridge gates to the terminal building; the ghostly faces of those beautiful Young Europeans. It always seemed so poignant to me, this pantheon of departed heroes, so hopeful and innocent, so frozen in their brief moment of optimism.

You would meet your friends the night you got home, the people who stayed behind in Ireland to tough it out. You'd talk to them about what was happening, you'd get all the news. Some of them would have got married to people you never would have met, because you didn't live in Ireland any more. Some would have broken up with boyfriends or girlfriends. Most would still be trying to find decent work. You didn't really know what these scandals and bits of gossip were, about which people were laughing so knowledgeably as they sipped their pints, but you laughed, too, because you didn't want to feel left out. You pretended you knew what your friends were talking about, because you still wanted to belong. And sometimes there were rows as the night wore on, because you didn't keep in touch as much as you should have, and your friends resented you a little for going, and if the truth be told you resented them a little for staying, although you could never really put your finger on why. But the conversation flowed, as much as it could, with only a couple of awkward moments. When you used the word 'home', for instance, or 'at home', your friends sometimes didn't know where exactly you meant. Sometimes you didn't know yourself.

Before you were aware of time passing, it would be the middle of another Christmas Eve, or the eternal Friday night. Hysterical – almost desperate – joy all around you. The pub full of smoke. The smell of beer. The jukebox on loud, playing The Pogues, U2, The Cranberries, Van Morrison, The Chieftains, Mary Black. Traditional singers. What would the songs be about? People like you. People who left. The Wild Colonial Boy. The Green Fields of Amerikay. The Wild Geese. Thousands Are Sailing. The joint would be jumping. You'd have all your best friends around you, all the people you know and love and it's Christmas Eve and everything is fine now. You're home. You know the score. More drink. Another drunken chorus of Paddy's Green Shamrock Shore. My Love is in Amerikay. Everyone is glad to see you. It's familiar. You're home. And then an extremely odd sensation begins.

Suddenly, about half an hour before closing time, you find yourself looking around the pub and becoming frantically uptight. It's weird. You're feeling completely out of place, you don't know why. You don't get it. Somehow, despite the craic, something is wrong. You're home in Ireland, but you're not home really. Your heart is in London or New York or Paris. But the rest of you is in Ireland. How did this happen to you? It's not that you're unhappy exactly. It's Christmas, after all. You wanted to be here, didn't you? But it's just not right. Take a swig of your drink. The music seems louder, oppressive, raucous. You close your eyes and try to fight back the almost overwhelming urge to be somewhere – anywhere – else. And you realise in that moment that you really are an emigrant now. That being an emigrant isn't just an address, it's also a way of thinking about Ireland.

Some mornings later you'd be back at the airport to fly home – ah, that difficult word again. You'd be hungover so bad you'd look like downtown Sarajevo on legs. Your head would be pounding with tension and confusion as you'd say your goodbyes, embrace your loved ones. In the old days, emigrants went for ever when they went, or came back once in forty years. So different now. Air travel is cheap now, you could come back really soon, and you'd say you would, although you knew you probably wouldn't. And you'd see that bloody poster of the Young Europeans once more, as you trudged your way back out of the country, on the wall of the corridor that runs parallel to the duty-free shop. How they would stare down at you, those pure virginal faces, as you shuffled through the plastic racks of Irish whiskey, clingfilm-wrapped smoked salmon, Tayto crisps and Major cigarettes, wondering what to buy with your mountain of leftover change. You always have a lot of change whenever you've been in Ireland. It's because you drink too much when you're in Ireland, and drinking, if it means anything at all, means the accumulation of change. So you'd be weighed down like a racehorse. And sometimes, just sometimes, as you rattled your coins and felt light-headed with emotion, you'd find yourself wondering what on earth they must be thinking, those speculative faces. But you'd know what you'd be thinking yourself, because it was so very simple in the end. You'd be thinking: run. You'd be thinking: Christmas is over now. You'd be thinking: Go. Run. Don't stop. Get out. Just get on that plane and vanish. Before you change your mind.

We are now, as we have always been, a land of exiles and wanderers. 'The history of transport,' muses a Paul Durcan poem, 'is there any other history?' Well, it's a very Irish question. Ever since James Joyce claimed that the shortest way to Tara was via Holyhead – he clearly didn't do honours Leaving Cert geography – hundreds of thousands of us have followed the unwashed and bright-eyed Dedalus junior on that heartbreaking, exciting and frequently stomach-churning journey across the snot-green scrotum-tightening sea.

Emigration has changed, admittedly, over the years. The sons and daughters of the middle classes emigrate now, in search of higher wages and better career prospects, and, also, if the truth be told, to get away from their parents. Ireland must be the last country in the world where people have to leave the country in order to get their own flat. They fly back home at the weekends to parties in Killiney and Montenotte, these young and successful people of the Ryanair generation. Their parents think it's good for them to be out of Ireland for a while, they figure it broadens their minds. They're right. It probably does.

But we also continue to export our poor, our uneducated, our weak. We throw out our suffering, our homeless, those who are as utterly dispossessed in their own country as any refusenik. We expel those who are inconvenient to our fabulous dream of ourselves. That dream used to be of a post-revolutionary Celtic Erin, where we would all without exception be rural, Catholic, heterosexual, conservative, in a family as nuclear as the Waltons. It would be an Ireland where we would all know our places, respect our elders and betters, wear bawneen jumpers and Aran knickers, smoke pipes and write turgid poetry in Irish about fishermen. Yeats said independent Ireland was no country for old men. How breathtakingly, unusually wrong he was. For the last seventy-five years that's exactly what it's been. A country where being old and male really did clock you up serious points.

More recently, the dream has been of a post-Maastricht, utterly dehistorified tax haven for rich tourists and pop stars, with sixteen channels of satellite TV, full employment at low pay in prefabricated factories and smooth new roads paid for by the Germans. Things are changing now; we can all see it. Ireland is introducing civilised laws, recognising that it needs to be humane in its social arrangements. Some of the emigrants I know will come back. But for others, it's too late. They feel that dreams change, but in Ireland waking up is always the same. Always was. Always will be. For ever and ever, Amen. Which is why they like waking up somewhere else.

Emigration is as Irish as the dear little shamrock or Cathleen Ní Houlihan's harp, yet it is only since the 1960s and the generation of Edna O'Brien that Irish writers have written about the subject at first hand. It has been taken as read that emigration and exile are important themes in Irish writing, like the Big House or the Catholic Church. But if they are, they are intermittent and inconsistent preoccupations. Where are the first-person texts of Irish emigrant life in the latter part of the nineteenth century and the earlier part of the twentieth? With one or two notable exceptions – Robert Tressel's *Ragged Trousered Philanthropists*, say, and the bleak, spare poems and novels of Patrick Magill – they're not there. At the heart of the Irish emigrant experience is caution, a refusal to speak, a fear of the word.

Our emigrant culture has traditionally been described in songs rather than novels, plays or poems. But a friend said to me recently that he was sure all those sententious and mawkish ballads about grey-haired macushlas and shagging shillelaghs were written by people who had never been out of Portlaoise, never mind Ireland, in their lives. I suspect he could well be right. No one who ever really lived in Californ-aye-ay wrote 'Spancil Hill', I'm sorry. Silence, exile and cunning, Joyce maintained, were the true weapons of the writer. But the exiles have been silent too long. Perhaps we will give them voting rights. Perhaps not. In either case, the politicians whose manifest failures have perpetuated Irish emigration would do well to ponder the words of Coriolanus. 'Long my exile, sweet my revenge.'

What the English Sunday newspapers call the 'New Irish Literary Renaissance' has begun to fill the exile's silence with a torrent of words. Now there are green fields all over the planet, and at last they are beginning to appear in Irish fiction. The poet Louis MacNeice wrote about celebrating 'the drunkenness of things being various'. This younger generation of writers is claiming the right to celebrate an Ireland that is various also, in terms that are primarily aesthetic, but also, by implication, profoundly political. The silence of the Irish exile is over now. That is important.

'We are the blacks of Europe,' observes a character in Roddy Doyle's novel *The Commitments*. But that isn't really true any more. Being Irish is something worth talking about, if you're on someone else's turf and lucky enough to be making enough readies to socialise occasionally with the natives. These days an Irish passport seems to give you what people in the advertising industry call a reachier punch, I don't know why. I suspect it's more to do with Gabriel Byrne and *Riverdance* and Van Morrison than Synge, Beckett or William Trevor. People envy you these days in New York or London or mainland Europe if you're Irish. That's been my experience anyway. It's extraordinary. The whole world longs to be oppressed and authentic and post-colonial and tragically hip and petulantly Paddy, whereas many of us Irish just want to be anything else. Still, being Irish abroad – half-invader and half-native – is a fine thing for a writer to be. It means you probably won't get shot in the event of an aeroplane hijack, and it certainly helps you understand just how very Irish you are. Indeed, it sometimes seems to me that you almost have to get out of Ireland to be Irish at all, in some important sense that those who stay sometimes turn out to be the real exiles, whereas those who go are the natives. But for a writer that's material. So no complaints.

We have gone about the world like wind, Yeats said. Wish you were here. Wish I was there. Well, sometimes anyway.

The Lizards of Oz

Australia: The Koala Triangle: a mysterious zone in the Southern Hemisphere where persons of talent disappear without trace.
Barry Humphries, *A Nice Night's Entertainment*

Wednesday, 18 October 1995, 4.30 a.m.: Somewhere over Australia. The in-flight video is showing a very interesting television programme about the natural world. It features wonderful scenes of maggots making endless love in slow motion to Mozart. (Well, not actually *to* Mozart, but … you know what I mean.) I switch off the video. I have had enough insect porn for now, thank you very much. If I was a maggot myself, no doubt I would find this very entertaining, but no, I am not. I try to think straight. This is hard. I left Dublin the day before yesterday, got delayed, flew to London, got delayed, flew to Singapore, got delayed, now I am flying to Australia. Yes, Australia! The other side of the world. I mean, I admit it's true that writers will do almost anything to avoid writing. But a book promotion tour? Of bloody Australia? Isn't that taking things a little too far? I turn the video back on. Two nasty-looking spiders are engaging in serious heavy petting. Thirty seconds later, just as I'm getting interested, one eats the other. I guess they just lost that lovin' feeling.

5.30 a.m.: Melbourne airport. I arrive and am met by the very friendly and professional young woman in charge of publicity at my publishing company. She explains to me that Melbourne is 'the cultural capital of Australia'. This is very fascinating indeed, but I'm finding it just a tad hard to concentrate. After twenty-three hours on the plane I have jet lag the way Abba had flares. My head is pounding. My feet have swelled up to the size of watermelons. My tongue feels like a slab of sandpaper. My skin is not so much dry as desiccated. I look like a stressed prune. I feel like Limerick on legs. The car radio says it is five-thirty in the morning, but my body clock knows different. My body clock knows that it is either half past four next Saturday afternoon or some time in the late 1820s. As we cruise gently into the city, *Good Morning Melbourne* comes on the radio. It is presented by two young Australian chaps who make Beavis and Butthead seem like Umberto Eco.

'G'day, Mite,' one says. 'Hawaii yah this morning?'

'I'm blardy good, Mite. And you?'

'I'm good, too, Mite. I'm the best, or so the woif tells me anywaze. HA HA HA HA. And tell me. Did yah perform your abbo-lutions this morning, Mite?'

'Moi what, Mite? My ... ?'

'Your abbo-lutions, Mite. Your ABBO-LUTIONS! It's a poloyt word for taking a poo, Mite.'

It is very nice, I must say, to be here in the cultural capital of Australia.

The hotel is the kind of hotel in which writers only ever stay when they are on book promotion tours and somebody else is paying. This is the kind of hotel where the staff ask how you are feeling today, how your flight was, what kind of newspaper would you like delivered to your room every morning. That kind of thing. Most of the hotels I have ever stayed in are not like this. In my usual type of hotel, the walls are so thin you can hear your next-door neighbours' inner doubts. In my usual type of hotel, if I get an 'Ah, shut yer trap, poxbottle, I told yeh we're out of bleedin' drink' from a waiter, I feel I'm doing quite well. I settle into my room, which is bigger than my entire flat at home. I try on the fluffy white dressing gown and attempt to iron my overcoat in the automatic trouser press. I run a bath, get into it, fall asleep in it and wake up an hour later thinking that I have died in it.

Thursday, 19 October: Wake up feeling absolutely dreadful and stagger out for a stroll. 'In Sydney,' wrote the great Australian playwright David Williamson, 'people spend their whole lives trying to find a house with a nice view. But in Melbourne, they know there is no point, because there are no nice views. So the pace of life is easier.' Looking around the city I can see what he was on about. Melbournites are friendly and hospitable people, but the place they inhabit is not so much a city as one big airport terminal. It has the transient and prefabricated air of a place that could be taken down tomorrow and shifted fifty miles north. People who live here are obsessed by the weather. If you comment that it's not a very nice day today, they will tell you the exact temperature, the relative position of nearby slow-moving cold fronts and the precise wind-chill factor correct to fourteen decimal points. The other thing they seem to like talking about in Melbourne is their personal problems. Perhaps this is because living in Melbourne means you have a lot of personal problems, I don't know. But certainly, Melbournites outdo even New Yorkers when it comes to spilling the lurid details of their personal lives. For example, the chap behind the bar in the cafe tells me he is upset because his wife keeps threatening to leave him. And she hasn't yet.

'The only difference between my missus and a Rottweiler, Mite,' he explains, 'is that when a Rotty starts to savage you, it locks its bloody jaws *shut*.'

This afternoon, as part of the Melbourne International Literature Festival, there is a public forum on 'Irish Writing and God', at which I have been invited to speak, along with the Irish novelists Brian Moore and Frank Ronan. On the plane to Australia I spent time reading a long article about 'the new multiculturalism' in the country and how 'great efforts are now being made to combat racial stereotyping'. I am utterly fascinated to see how Australia's new anti-stereotypical approach applies itself to the Irish. Three Irish writers, oooh, what'll we get 'em to talk about? Leprechauns? Harps? Foster and Allen? Oh, *I* know: God! Very imaginative. I look forward to the next reading by an Australian writer in Dublin so that I can ask him about the enormous influence of the boomerang on his work.

The audience today seems to be full of nuns. I have not seen so many nuns since I last watched *The Sound of Music*. I stand up and begin my speech by gamely telling my favourite religious joke. How do you know Jesus was an Irishman? Because he hung around with the lads all the time, he thought he was God and he lived with his mother till he was thirty. This goes down very well indeed, as you can imagine. I manage to get out of the building without being stoned to death or crucified.

As I am led to the police car with the blanket over my head, I am very glad that I didn't tell my second favourite religious joke. How do you know John the Baptist was made of elastic? Because he tied his ass to a tree and walked forty miles into the desert.

Friday, 20 October: Wake up feeling appalling. This evening I am doing a reading in the Melbourne Town Hall. One of the other speakers is 'New Zealand's greatest living poet'. As I listen attentively to her performance I am in two minds about her poetry. I cannot decide whether I dislike it, or, on the other hand, whether I hate it. This person writes the kind of poetry we all wrote when we were fifteen and then had the good sense to stop. Each line seems to be made up of the same list of words simply rearranged more or less at random. (These words are: I, feeling, moon, me, emotion, pain, self, emptiness, grief, spots, listless, my, heartbeat, nipple, parents and bastard. Just try reading them out repeatedly in any order you like and you'll probably get a large grant from the New Zealand Arts Council.) One of her poems is about how love is like a kangaroo. I swear to you, I'm not making this up. Me, I have never noticed before how much like a kangaroo love is, but now, having listened to her, I can see how wrong I was. Love and a kangaroo are, of course, practically identical. One is a big, bouncy, unpleasant and unreliable brute that initially seems cute but can actually kill you. The other is a kangaroo. Thanks be to God (him again!), New Zealand also have the All Blacks.

This evening after the reading I discover that the most common Australian slang word for having sex is 'rooting', or 'having a root'. (Yes, yes, yes, you can calm down now. I discover this because somebody tells me over a glass of wine.) This makes one or two things about Australia fall suddenly into place. I had been wondering, for example, why the audiences on this trip have cackled and hooted with ribald laugher whenever I refer to my 'Irish roots'.

Here is an Australian joke, which I now understand. Why is an Australian man just like a koala bear? Because he eats roots and leaves.

Saturday, 21 October: Wake up feeling banjaxed. A local freelance photographer arrives to take my picture. He is an affable cove. As he snaps and clicks at my still jet-lagged self, he tells me an interesting story. When the Queen was last in Australia this photographer fellow was commissioned to cover the royal visit by an Australian newspaper. 'Her Madge', as he insists on calling HRH, turned out to be 'a friendly enough old buzzard'. He tells me all about how he actually met her. One afternoon during a royal walkabout he was snapping away at Her Madge, when suddenly she came strolling over to him and began to casually chat. I ask what she wanted to chat about. The weather mainly. And photography. Her Madge was very interested in photography.

'Do you know,' said Her Madge to my new friend, 'I've got a brother-in-law who's a photographer?'

'And what did you say to her then?' I ask him.

'I said that was a bladdy funny coincidence, Mite,' he grins, 'because I've got a brother-in-law who's a queen.'

Sunday, 22 October: Wake up still feeling bad. This afternoon I fly to Sydney for the second stage of my book tour. The man sitting beside me on the plane has the worst facial tic of anyone I have ever seen. It is quite astounding. Every time his face tics, the plane practically goes into a nose dive. Later, we share a taxi into the city. I don't know whether the excitement of being here in Sydney has affected the tic in some way, but the poor guy is now bouncing uncontrollably around the back of the taxi like a steel ball in a pinball machine, his head banging off the windows. Later still, at a bar near the hotel, I meet the first Sydney journalist who wants to interview me. The interview does not get off to the best of starts:

'So. You're Sinéad O'Connor's brother, aren't you?'

'Yes,' I answer, 'as you so perceptively point out, by far the most important thing about my work is that I am Sinéad O'Connor's brother.'

'But she's so beautiful,' the interviewer says, and she peers at me, with a mystified look in her eyes. I have the uneasy feeling that devastating irony may not be that big in Australia.

Monday, 23 October: Wake up feeling poorly. This morning Viceroy John Hayden has given an interview to the *Sydney Morning Herald*, explaining how he doesn't feel Australia should have an elected president. He seems to seriously want this country, which is 12,000 miles away from England, to continue being part of the British Commonwealth and having Her Madge as first citizen. He finds the Queen a very friendly and supportive person, he says, the most friendly and supportive person he knows. He can talk to the Queen more openly than he can talk to anybody else in the whole world, he says. Wow. I find myself wondering how Mrs Viceroy feels about this. Australians feel a strong emotional link with the British Royal Family, the viceroy explains. Hmmmm. I think about this and wonder if it's true. Most of the Australians I've met don't seem to feel a strong emotional link to anything much except perhaps beer and, of course, the weather. I wonder exactly how you would persuade your average Italian- or Croatian- or Malaysian-Australian of the mystical emotional link she or he is supposed to feel with Prince Charles and his mum. This is not a job I would like to have.

The point about modern Australia is that it has completely transcended its Anglo-Celtic origins and is now comprised of people from all over the planet. Melbourne, for example, contains the largest Greek population of any city in the world except Athens. These days Australia, like I told you, is obsessed with multiculturalism. As a result, Australians do tend to go on a bit about the level of multicultural social change they have achieved. I am suspicious of this. The last place I visited where people talked long and loud about the level of multicultural social change they had achieved was Alabama. A bit of local investigation revealed that what this amounted to in practice was giving black citizens a twenty-minute head start into the woods before letting loose the bloodhounds.

Yet, in the case of Australia this multiculturalism does indeed seem to be a reality. It is not Utopia, by any means, and in the past absolutely horrific crimes were conducted against the Aboriginals. Yet these days it is certainly a less truculent and fitful society than America or Britain when it comes to issues of race. I ask an Australian friend how his country has managed to achieve all this. How is it, for example, that there have never been race riots in Australia? He considers for a moment. 'Apathy,' he says.

Tuesday, 24 October: Wake up feeling a little better. This morning's interview begins with the question 'Do young Irish writers see themselves as the voice of the new Ireland?' When I have finished laughing, I think about this. Maybe it would be nice to be the voice of the new Ireland. Perhaps we could take it in turns. Anne Enright could be the voice of the new Ireland one week, then Colm Tóibín, then Dermot Bolger, then Pat

McCabe, and so on. And during the weeks when we were not being the voice of the new Ireland we could be some other body part. The foot of the new Ireland, or the armpit of the new Ireland, maybe. I myself would like to be the bum of the new Ireland, but that is another story.

Wednesday, 25 October: Wake up feeling almost normal. A week into the tour and the humiliation begins in earnest. Having spent seven days dealing with print journalists, a species I understand and mostly like, I am now doing local radio. Local radio interviewers are the same all over the world. They come in two varieties: (a) the type so emotionally disturbed and mentally subnormal that they went into local radio because they didn't have the personality to work at assembling car number-plates; (b) the type who was very clever in school and has a nice velvety voice and really feels they should be presenting an internationally syndicated show, and is only condescending to put in time in this crummy joint while waiting for someone who does present an internationally syndicated show to drop down dead or fall into a coma.

This morning, the interviewer, 'Happenin'' Henry Horovitz, confesses that he has never heard of me or my book, and that he doesn't actually like reading because it gives him a headache, and that they're only having me on the show because the guest they had originally booked, a part-time postman who can fart 'Waltzing Matilda' while accompanying himself on the Wurlitzer electric organ, has mysteriously cancelled at the last moment. But he's sure 'we'll be able to wing it'. The interview begins. We chat for a while about my book. It is called *The Secret World of the Irish Male*, I explain, and it is funny. 'Oh right,' he says, 'say something funny for the listeners then.' I try my best. Happenin' Henry peers at me intensely, looking every bit as amused as a person who is watching *Schindler's List*. Then he says he's going to take a few calls. Things go downhill from here.

Happenin' Henry: 'OK, yeah, Boris in Woolloomoolloo,

you're through to Joe O'Connor, Mite. He's the voice of the new Ireland, Mite, HA HA HA.'

Caller: 'Hello?'

Happenin' Henry: 'Go ahead, Caller?'

Caller: 'Hello?'

Joe: (attempting the local lingo) 'Hawaii yah, Mite?'

Caller: 'Hello? Are you there?'

Happenin' Henry: 'Yes, Mite. You're through to our studio guest this morning, Ireland's Joe O'Connor, author of *The Male Secret of the Irish World.*'

Caller: 'Hello? Am I through?'

Happenin' Henry: 'Go ahead, Caller.'

Caller: 'Yes. Can you hear me?'

Happenin' Henry: 'Hello? Hello?'

Joe: (getting desperate) 'HAWAII-YAH?'

Caller: 'Hello, yes? Am I on the air now? HELLO?'

Etcetera, etcetera. After a few more minutes of this, Happenin' Henry begins to lose it a bit. He begins rocking back and forth and snorting with maniacal laughter. And I do mean snorting. Happenin' Henry is very possibly the individual for whom the adjective 'stertorous' was originally coined. As the full contents of Happenin' Henry's nostrils come rocketing across the studio table as though they have just been discharged from a double-barrelled cannon, I can't help but feel, phew, the sheer bloody glamour of the writer's life.

Thursday, 26 October: Wake up feeling just about OK. I do a reading with the wonderful American writer John Berendt, who has the following true story to tell: while stopped at traffic lights in his hired car in downtown Sydney he is approached by a large and attractive black woman who asks him for a lift. He opens the door and she sits demurely in the passenger seat. They begin to chat. She has a flirtatious and rather physical manner. She keeps running her finger down his thigh and calling him 'Baby' or 'Sugar'. Her name is Chablis, she tells him, (pronouncing it

Sh'blee, with the emphasis on the second syllable). 'That's a nice name,' he tells her. 'Ooooh, yes, Baby,' she drawls, 'a cool sophisticated name for a cool sophisticated lady.' They drive on, her hand lightly stroking the back of his neck, her lips intermittently blowing gusts of perfumed air against his face. He feels a little uneasy. His playful passenger begins to explain that Chablis is actually not her real name, it is a name that she chose for herself. 'And what was your real name?' John asks her. 'I mean, before you changed it to Chablis.' She peers at him for a moment. She grins. 'Frank,' she says.

Saturday, 28 October: In Australia, just like in every other country in the world, local TV is even more badly organised than local radio. An hour after I have turned up at the studio, the producer for my interview, a very pleasant but harassed-looking young man in a black polo-neck jersey, comes in and explains that they are still building the set. I ask if he would like me to give them a hand.

Another hour later I am summoned to said set, which is designed like a suburban dining room. I make an impressive entrance by tripping on the carpet, somersaulting over the velour sofa and almost demolishing the attractive coffee table. Once we fix the set and get going, the interview proceeds quite nicely. I'm sure both viewers enjoyed it very much indeed.

Sunday, 29 October: Wake up feeling marvellous. Yippee! A great night's sleep. At last I am over my jet lag. I spring out of bed with the easy grace of a young gazelle. At last I can start enjoying myself. Yessss! Now what do I have to do today? An awful realisation dawns. Of course. I have to get the plane back to London today. Twenty-three more hours of nonstop fun and airline food and bugs bonking to bloody Mozart. I promise, I'll never try to find an excuse not to write again.

Amateur Traumatics

It is two minutes to eight on a Tuesday night. I am sitting in the Tricycle Theatre, Kilburn, London. I am terrified. My brother is sitting beside me. I am gripping his arm so tightly that his eyes are bulging like gobstoppers. My stomach feels like I swallowed a pogo stick. My brother is telling me to calm down. He is telling me to take deep breaths. He is telling me that everything will be all right. Thank God I have been on a diet for six months now, otherwise passers-by hearing the conversation would take one look at me and assume that my waters had just broken. The reason for all this anxiety? In two minutes' time the curtain will go up on my very first play, *Red Roses and Petrol*.

I use the word 'curtain', although one thing the Tricycle Theatre, Kilburn, and myself have in common is a bit of an ambivalence where curtains are concerned. So, in two minutes' time the stage lights will be illuminated and actors will come on and start saying things and in the course of the following two hours and twenty minutes the product of months and months of hard work by a quite large group of people, myself included, will be watched by an audience of real people, and then judged by the critics. They will poke it, prod it, tweak its chubby cheeks, hold it upside down by the ankles, spank it lightly on the backside and pronounce it either a handsome little creature with a bright future or a bit of a fucking turkey.

How did any of this happen to me? I never wanted to write a play. And yet, almost a year ago now, I agreed to do so. I should

147

have followed my instinct and said no when I was asked. But I didn't. So here we are. I think back to the long nights of composition. For most of the play's period of gestation I was suffering from a bad writer's block. Let me tell you, there were times when the influence of Samuel Beckett on this play of mine was going to be considerable. It was going to be a very meaningful work indeed, instead of the utterly hilarious, yet oddly affecting, little family drama it ended up as. Here, for the sake of posterity, is the entire first draft:

Curtain up on an empty stage. Enter Actor A, naked, except for a luminous condom. He sits on the floor for half an hour in silence, eyes bulging. From time to time he scratches his crotch. Enter Actor B, dressed as a tramp. He drops his trousers and stands on his hands for half an hour in silence, except for the occasional bloodcurdling scream. Curtain down. Fifteen-minute interval for sipping of gin in the foyer, commenting on how fashionable everybody looks and publicly congratulating the anxious author before privately whispering that he really should have stuck to what he is best at, that is to say, the penning of puerile gags of a dubiously sexual nature in *Esquire* once a month. Back into the theatre. Curtain up. Enter Actor A and Actor B, dressed in black tartan kilts, white stilettos and Republic of Ireland soccer shirts. Actor A: 'I can't go on. I must go on.' Ten-minute silence. Actor B: 'I feel that I will die soon.' Actor A: 'Me, too.' Member of audience: 'You're shagginwell dyin' already, boys.' Fifteen-minute silence. Curtain down. Wild cheers.

But that was fantasy. This is the real thing. The lights come up. The actress Anne Kent, who plays the mother of the family in the play, strolls on and just looks amazingly calm. I cannot understand this. The reality of finally seeing her on a real stage is making me want to be hospitalised. Then her daughter, played by Kathy Downes, comes on and says her first line. I'm sorry to use professional jargon here, but Kathy's first line is what we in the theatrical world sometimes call 'a joke'. She delivers it perfectly. Spot on. And nobody laughs. It's nothing to do with the way she said it. It's not that they didn't hear it or anything. They heard it and they just didn't laugh. Hmmmm. Kathy says her second line, another gag. Again, no laugh. I find myself silently assessing the relative merits of shooting oneself in the head as opposed to employing the noose, the gas oven or a Linford Christie-style high-speed canter down the nearest pier.

I am in the front row. The critics are all sitting behind me. There are a lot of them. They have notebooks! I glance over my shoulder. Rampant paranoia begins to descend. In the fragrant air of the Tricycle Theatre the scratching of biros begins to sound like the sharpening of machetes. Not that it matters what the critics say, of course. As Emerson put it, 'It is the job of those who cannot construct to take apart.' (That's Ralph Waldo Emerson, by the way, not Emerson Fittipaldi.) So I don't care whether we get good reviews or not. Oh, no. I am a serious artist, a miner hacking at the coal face of language, a blacksmith forging the uncreated conscience of his race, a second-hand car salesman extolling the merits of the national Fiat Uno, a professional cyclist getting in his spoke for ... (Could we get the hell on with it here? – Ed.)

Suddenly there is another joke. And the audience laugh. It's not a big howl or anything, more of a speculative titter. I breathe in deeply. Quite soon there's another gag. A guffaw from the audience. I breathe out. I look at my brother. He is practically in tears. I am touched by his fraternal loyalty. I thank him profoundly. 'It's not that,' he hisses, 'but please, if you don't let go of my hand soon I'll have to scream with the bloody agony.'

I release my brother's hand, which he clamps into his armpit. The audience settle into it. (The play, that is, not my brother's armpit.) More laughs. At half-time I have a drink with my father. He is very encouraging. I know I should not really refer to this fifteen-minute break as 'half-time'. It's not as if the Territorial Army Brass Band are going to march on in formation and play 'Abide with Me' or anything. 'Interval' is the proper word. This theatrical business is going to be difficult to get used to.

Back in for round two. It goes well. The audience, possibly fortified by copious amounts of free drink, continues to laugh in almost all the right places. Then – another piece of sophisticated technical jargon here – we get to what Arthur Miller in his seminal work *The Meaning of Modern Theatre* (University of Massachusetts Press, 1957) once called 'the sad bit at the end'. Anne Kent is so moving that all around me hardened critics are gulping with either emotion or asthma. When the play is over I go to the pub with the actors. I have been off the drink since New Year's Eve and this does strange things to a person's metabolism. After two pints of lager I am pissed. After four I am kissing the actors. After five I am out in the street and kissing lamp posts. Things get a bit hazy then.

Next morning the phone rings at dawn. I wake up and recognise the lamp post beside me. I must say, it is not nearly so attractive first thing in the morning, but I make up my mind to respect it anyway. My father is on the phone. He has read a review in one of the morning papers. The massive financial inducements, offers of sexual favours, etc., seem to have worked. The review is pretty good. Relief is not the word for what I feel. I make a light breakfast for the lamp post and myself. And I sleep, for the first time in days. Never ever again in my whole life will I complain about the difficulty of writing an article for a newspaper or magazine. After what I've just been through, I'd be happy to write the whole magazine, every month, for nothing. It's the one truly great thing about being a journalist. You don't have to sit there and sweat while people are reading you. Although, now that I think of it, I do feel a little bit light-headed at the thought of you finishing this page. So read it again. Go on. It's better the second time around. Honest.

The Emperor's New Clothes

Oh my God. Here I am. At London Fashion Week. I am in a tent waiting for a fashion show to start. Last time I was in a tent I was singing 'Ging Gang Goolie' and wearing a woggle. How the hell did this happen to me? The woman standing beside me must surely be a model. She is astoundingly beautiful. I have seen more interesting-looking women in my life. I have seen more sexy women. Hell, I've even seen more *attractive* women. But if it's pure old-fashioned beauty we're talking about, she's got it, big time. She is the High Priestess of Babelonia. I look at her. I stare at her. You could hang a hat on her cheekbones. I practically start hyperventilating. She goes away.

Look, I don't have a lot of experience with the fashion industry. You're talking to a guy who thinks a supermodel is something really nice you make with an Airfix kit. And designer diffusion is something on which you pour hot water to produce a refreshing drink. Although I did meet Claudia Schiffer once. Well, I say meet. I was in LA to do a job. Sounds real glamorous, I know. When I tell you the job was to interview Billy Idol you may not be so impressed. Anyway, I'm staying in this nobby hotel in LA. I am not used to this. But anyway, I'm in this posh hotel and I figure I'll go for an early morning swim. So there I am, floundering around the pool, overweight, jet lagged, spluttering, eyes streaming with chlorine, and I'm doing my best to swim along underwater, but suddenly I swallow about a gallon of the rank chemical liquid with which the pool is filled and I start to choke. Up I come, spitting and flailing, swallowing back nausea, nose running, hair in my eyes, swimming togs wedged tightly between my pendulous buttocks. And there she is. Claudia Schiffer. Sitting on the edge of the pool. Dangling those legs in the water. Claudia Schiffer. Wearing not so much a bikini as several pieces of deftly arranged dental floss. I gape at her. She looks like some kind of goddess crossed with some kind of angel. I feel my mouth opening and closing like a goldfish. I am a fully trained novelist. At this point I should be able to think of something really charming, smart and amusing to say. What I actually say is, 'Um, um, y-y-you're ... um, I m-m-mean, aren't you, um, er.' Claudia Schiffer looks at me. What Claudia Schiffer says is, 'Do you think you could swim a little more gently, please. You're making me wet.'

I have told all my male friends the story of how I met Claudia Schiffer in LA and how she told me I was making her wet. OK, OK, I may have been a little creative with them about the actual facts of the story. But still. I met Claudia Schiffer, made her wet, and that's that.

Anyway, here I am, at the Pearce Fionda show. Don't ask me who the hell Pearce Fionda is. Perhaps it is two people, Pearce *and* Fionda. Perhaps 'Fionda' is a misprint of Fiona? I really don't know. There are people milling around with mobile telephones and walkie-talkies. Everybody seems to be wearing black. Many people are wearing sunglasses. At the end of the catwalk is a pen, the kind of thing in which a zookeeper might keep wild slavering rabid animals of some kind. In this pen there are at least sixty or seventy cameras with long protruding lenses. Behind them are sixty or seventy cameramen. (They *are* almost all men.) The lights go out. There is silence. Then suddenly the music starts. David Bowie's 'John, I'm Only Dancing'. The lights flash back on. A model appears at the end of the catwalk. She is wearing a cream trouser-suit. She begins to walk down the catwalk, although I don't know if walk really is the most accurate verb to describe what she is doing. Her hips are swaying like a bell. An audible murmur of appreciation surges through the crowd. The cameras are all clicking and flashing now. The sound of seventy cameras clicking is weird. It sounds like some kind of terrible insect. The flashlights flicker. 'It's very lonely,' sings the sound track, 'when you're a thousand light years from home.' Another model appears and sashays down the ramp in a brown knee-length dress. She has spiky hair. She looks sensational. The audience's heads turn to the right, following her to the end of the catwalk, then to the left, as she returns. It's like watching a tennis audience in slow motion. More girls appear, wearing lime-green jumpers, print patterns, Regency-style jackets, black and white patterned fabrics that look like Bridget Reilly paintings. On the soundtrack David Bowie is now singing 'When You're a Boy'. The creature that has just shimmied past me in the see-through chiffon shirt is no boy, I can tell you. Or if he is, he has a very severe oestrogen surfeit. I look at this model, wondering how it is possible for any human being to be so beautiful. How can it be the case, for example, that Jim Davidson and that astoundingly lovely creature now swishing past me are actually part of the same species? If that is a boy, believe me, I've just turned gay.

A few hours later, and I am trying to get in to the Red or Dead show when I see the High Priestess of Babelonia arriving in a taxi. She sweeps through the crowd, up to the door, gets in. I feel cold and lonely. The invitation to the Red or Dead show is an A3-size piece of red paper. A3, in case you don't know, is the size you would get if you opened up a magazine and held it upright. So it's a big enough piece of red paper, is what I'm saying. And it's completely blank, except for a tiny circle, about the size of an old 10p coin, in the bottom left-hand corner, in which is contained the date, the venue and, most importantly, the information that the show will start at 3.45 p.m. prompt. This is very interesting to me, because it is now ten minutes past four and there's no sign of any action. You do tend to wonder how these designers can design clothes a full year in advance but can't start a fashion show on time. But anyway.

The venue is the Royal Horticultural Hall, a vast splendid room with an arching glass roof. It is very impressively laid out.

There is a line of androgynous dummies lined up on one side, leaning, sitting, crouching, as though watching the show. This makes me laugh out loud. There are also little clusters of dummies wearing Chinese army-style costumes. And there are three enormous banners with Cyrillic Russian script. Backward Ns and Rs. The room looks like one of Ronald Reagan's worst nightmares.

It sounds like one, too. As I shuffle through the crowd of black-clad people to find my seat, the PA is playing a song called 'Detachable Penis'. (I promise that I am not making this up.) 'Even though it's sometimes a pain in the ass,' the singer clarifies, 'I like having a detachable penis. Though I really don't like being without my penis for too long.' There's a sentiment many of us can agree with.

At 4.15, a full half-hour late, a slightly disconcerting noise comes screaming from the PA speakers. It sounds a bit like an airplane crashing. This is accompanied by various assorted buzzings, rattles, drillings and sirens. A male model has appeared in the aisle. He is wearing a white vest-style shirt, grey trousers and a thin black leather tie. A girl follows wearing a similar outfit, followed by another girl in an amazing red and black dress. The Red or Dead models are pretty intriguing to look at. In fact, they are pretty *and* intriguing. They're all stunningly attractive, of course, and they have futuristic *Blade Runner*-style haircuts. But they have an earthy quality, too. They seem like real people you might actually see in the street where you live. If the street where you live happens to be Elm Street. Or Sesame Street.

There's a chap in a yellow and orange T-shirt and black trousers, another in a really nice tight grey suit, a girl with cropped hair in a red woollen dress. There's a black and red skirt, a few very sexy evening frocks. A svelte bloke in a long grey coat with epaulettes, another in a black string vest. There's an industrial theme – cogwheels and images of Chinese workers – but there also seem to be elements of glam in the purple tie-dye style trousers and the low-cut black leather dresses. There's a cool sophistication, too, in the classy navy and gold minidresses.

There are fishnets, feathers, false manes of hair reaching down to the ground, and stilettos. The whole thing is done with humour, style, street-smartness and drama. 'Bella Lugosi's dead', roars the singer on the soundtrack. Maybe so. But if he wasn't, he'd certainly like this show a lot. He'd probably want to be in it. The High Priestess of Babelonia liked it anyway. I heard her say that to this really good-looking geezer linking her arm as they swept from the room together. 'It was very fun,' she is saying, 'wasn't it?' He is agreeing with her. 'Yes,' he says. 'It was very fun.' I stare at him. He looks like Brad Pitt. But I bet he has not got a good personality and sense of humour like me.

Later that night I attend Philip Treacy's show, which is being held back at the tent. Indeed, I am standing beside a television crew just inside this massive tent that has been erected inside the grounds of the Natural History Museum when something exciting happens. The cameraman's mobile phone rings. He answers it.

'Drop everything,' he barks to his crew. 'Kylie's here.'

'Kylie. Fuck. Where?'

'She's outside. Now. She's willing to talk to us. Quick. Come on, for fuck's sake.'

They begin to take apart the camera and pack up their equipment. A man in a red suit appears and begins to shout. 'What are you doing?' shouts the man in the red suit.

'I thought you said we'd got Kylie,' shouts the cameraman.

'Not Kylie, you fool,' sighs the man in the suit. 'It's Katie. Katie Puckrick. From *The Word*.'

The cameraman sighs. He turns to his crew. He shrugs. He begins reassembling his camera.

I look around. A short man has arrived in a leprechaun hat. A woman comes in with a large black feather appearing to protrude from her head. It really doesn't suit her. She looks like a stressed chicken. Boy George and Jasper Conran and Simon Le Bon are here. Simon Le Bon walks right past me. He's *that* close. I could have reached out and single-handedly strangled the man who wrote 'Wild Boys', but I didn't. History will not give me this chance again. Bryan Ferry arrives. He is immediately swamped by photographers, reporters, cameramen. The television lights cut swathes through the darkness around Bryan Ferry. He is sitting in the front row. Minutes later a person whom I think is Noel Gallagher of Oasis arrives wearing a white jacket and looking a bit like a waiter. He is mobbed by the media. Bryan Ferry has now been left on his own. It is a slightly poignant sight, for some reason, Bryan Ferry glaring gloomily down the row of seats at a person whom I think is Noel Gallagher of Oasis being swamped with attention.

The show begins. More wonderful weird exotic hats. There are hats like giant shells and crowns and platters and yashmaks and masks and veils. Incredible. Suddenly I see the High Priestess of Babelonia again. She is standing just across the aisle from me. I smile at her. She seems to be smiling at me. My God. She is actually smiling at me. *This is it.* I grin back like a lobotomised zombie. I find myself thinking back to the Claudia Schiffer incident. I'm not going to make the same mistake again. I breathe in deeply, suck in my stomach and take a step forward.

Unfortunately for me, the step forward also turns out to be a very steep step downwards. I topple, arms flailing at the air, and fall flat on my arse. My glasses go flying through the air and smash. As I try to stand up, I twist my ankle and fall over backwards, right through a flap in the tent. What I'm saying is that *I am actually outside the tent now*, in the darkness and the rain, my hands deep in Kensington mud. I grope my way back in and start feeling around the floor for my glasses. When I find them I realise that I have lost one of the lenses.

The High Priestess of Babelonia looks down at me as though I am something malodorous she has just found stuck to the sole of her shoe. I grin optimistically. 'Oh, dear,' she says, and she turns away. Oh, dear. I guess my behaviour is not 'very fun'. I know it is not, in fact.

Next day I turn up early for the Clements Ribeiro show. The same camera crew are here from last night. I position myself beside them. They are talking in peculiar hissing sounds. 'Anyone good 'ere?' Pause. 'Nao. 'Aven't spotted anyone, 'ave you?' Pause. 'Tracey McLeod is over there.' Pause. 'Oo the fark is Tracey McLeod?' Pause. 'You know. That blondie bird off *The Late Show*.' Pause. 'What the fark is *The Late Show*?' Pause. 'Oh, forget it.'

The Clements Ribeiro clothes are all very nice, I must say. There are a lot of black-and-brown-and-check patterned things. The music is Latin-cum-Arab with a bit of Indian thrown in. She Who Must Be Adored is here with a bloke. Probably her brother, I tell myself. At one point she turns, puts her long, slender arm around his waist and kisses him. Hmmmm. Obviously a very close family.

Later that night I head for East London to the Alexander McQueen show, which is taking place in a church. Everyone is talking about this event. It will be 'controversial' apparently. There are intimations of nudity. Perhaps this is why there are so many people here. If you could imagine an episode of *Absolutely Fabulous* directed by a Nazi, you would get some idea of the scene outside Christchurch, Spitalfields, as I join the brawling throng trying to gain entrance. There are perhaps five hundred people out here all dolefully waving their invitation cards in the air and looking miserable. There is one door, which was obviously designed for a very pious and thin Protestant to get through. I am not pious, thin or Protestant. After a while I decide to go for a walk around the block and come back. Spitalfields is a very interesting part of East London, I must say. On one corner stand three of the local girls, all dressed in mini-skirts, thigh boots and low-cut blouses. They must be quite cold, I figure, given that a gale-force wind is blowing down the street. I wonder why they are wearing such charmingly revealing cozzies. They do seem very friendly, I must say. So friendly that they keep approaching the cars that pull up in front of them. They bend over and talk to the men driving these cars. What can they be doing? Giving directions, I suppose. They are so friendly, indeed, that occasionally they even get into these cars to give, I suppose, even more detailed directions. What a charming and jolly place the East End is.

Back to Christchurch, feeling very Pearly Queen. The scene has calmed down a bit now. I manage to squeeze into the church, which is full and decorated with a lot of candles. The *Elle* photographer has been ordered to take my photograph. This is very embarrassing. I have to plonk my anorak-which-is-missing-two-buttons-wearing self beside this very glamorous-looking woman while the *Elle* photographer snaps her flash at me repeatedly. After a while the glamorous-looking woman turns and asks me why I am having my photograph taken. I say I am writing a piece for *Elle* magazine. She looks at my anorak, which is missing two buttons. 'Really?' she says. If she grins any harder her eyebrows will disappear into her hairline. The show begins. The McQueen clothes are pretty wonderful. From simple enough grey hipster trews to big black woolly coats with flared sleeves, from grey flannel jump suits to dresses that change fabric mid-sleeve.

The show ends and everyone agrees that it was wonderful. The taxi driver is from Belfast and talks in a very attractive Reverend Ian Paisley accent. He asks me what I write about. 'Fashion,' I say. 'Aye, really,' he says, 'I like fashion myself.' I am astounded. This man is the only living entity I have seen in the last forty-eight hours who is actually less fashionable than myself. He is wearing a shell suit and filthy trainers and a tea-cosy hat. 'Oh, aye,' he says, 'I love fashion, I take a very keen interest in it.' I gape at him once again. I am utterly gobsmacked. 'Really?' I say. 'And tell me, what kind of fashion do you like best?' He pauses, grins, lights a cigarette. 'Salmon,' he says. 'Salmon fashion.'

The rain begins to fall more heavily now, as night comes down over the East End.

The French Letters

Friday, 29 March 1996: South of France. '*Parlez-vous Français?*' asks the woman behind the counter in Nice airport.

'*Mais oui,*' I reply. '*Je avais le certificat du départ.*'

She wrinkles up her nose in confusion. '*Quoi?*' she asks. I am astonished by her ignorance. Surely to God, everyone knows that '*le certificat du départ*' is perfect French for 'the Leaving Cert'.

I do my best to explain but she doesn't seem to follow me. This is upsetting. I am here in France because of this thing called *L'Imaginaire Irlandais*, I say. It is a big festival of modern Irish culture. It has taken two years to organise. She gazes at me blankly. I take out my dictionary and look up the word 'novelist'. It is quite a nice word. *Romancier.* I point to myself. '*Romancier,*' I say. She apparently is unmoved. I am in trouble now.

A few minutes ago I discovered something important. There I was, congratulating myself on my sartorial elegance. This is not something I do very often. Yet there I was, in the arrivals terminal of Nice airport, having just arrived from Paris, and was doing just that. Kneeling on the floor of the terminal opening up my suitcase and looking for my sunglasses. Where did these rather attractive multicoloured knicks come from? The awful truth dawned. I had somebody else's bag. I had picked up someone else's bag during the changeover in Paris! (Mr Gerry Brown of Dublin, the things I know about you. Ten grand in a brown paper bag and the negatives are yours.)

Thus, alone, weary, friendless and broke, I book into the airport hotel. The only channel in English is the 24-hour *Flintstones* channel. I am so miserable and lonely that after two hours watching, I begin to think that Wilma's actually got quite a cute smile. I am dying for a shave, but my razor, like everything else, is in a bag in Paris. I ring reception and ask if they stock shaving materials.

'Hello,' I say to the receptionist, 'can yeux send me up a hghazohgh, please?' ('Hghazohgh' is, of course, the correct pronunciation of the French word 'razor'.)

After I shave I go out for a walk. The only thing I have to say about Nice is that it isn't really. Nice.

Saturday, 30 March: Nice. After a fitful night, my case arrives from Paris and this makes me as happy *comme un chien avec les deux mickis*. Shortly after this, The Better Half arrives on a flight from London. This makes me happier still. While I've been waiting for her I noticed a town on the map of southern France called La Grande Motte. I am in a childishly gleeful humour this morning, possibly because after two days I have been able to change my clothes, and so I find the name of this town very amusing indeed. La Grande Motte. It sounds like the French translation of a Roddy Doyle novel. I decide to amuse the girlfriend by referring to her as 'La Grande Motte' from now on. She does not seem to find this even nearly as amusing as I do. This may be because she is English and everyone knows they have no sense of humour. Her real name is Anne-Marie Casey, she points out, and that's what she would like to be called. I study Ms Casey's expression. It is the expression of a Londoner who has been on an airline for too long, thank you very much indeed. I am suddenly and acutely aware that while we have been going out together quite happily for a time now, this could all go down the pan in the space of a millisecond if I ever *ever* call her 'La Grande Motte' to her face again. Good God, aren't women unreasonable sometimes?

We leave Nice for Saint-Tropez, where we are staying in a cheap hotel that claims to be a converted fisherman's cottage. (What the fisherman converted from is not made clear, but I suppose it was Roman Catholicism.) Brigitte Bardot made this town famous when she appeared in the film *Et Dieu Créa La Femme*, which is French for 'Brigitte Bardot capering around with no clothes on'. I like this town, I must say. And if I ever have a son, I'm certainly going to call him after a saint. Tropez O'Connor. Got a certain *je ne sais quoi*, huh?

Sunday, 31 March: San-Rémy-de-Provence. I notice that my French is getting better all the time. For instance, I am in a café having my mid-morning snack when I say to the waiter, '*Garçon, qui portay les choccies à la table? We. Vouz. Portay une grande piece de cet cakefaction à moi, sil voo play, et look vitement about it.*' It is funny how a language comes back to you with a bit of practice. Of course the other solution to the communications problem is the one being employed by the middle-aged English couple at the next table. Not speaking *un worde de français comme moi* they are reduced to the next best strategy: speaking English very slowly and loudly.

'YES,' they say, 'WEEE WOOOOD LYYYKE a CUPPP of COFFFEEEE, PLEEEEEASE.'

'Yes,' the waiter replies. 'I am not deaf actually.'

Monday, 1 April: Montpellier. The first day of my own participation in L'Imaginaire Irlandais. This is a pleasant small city, famous for having 300 days of sunshine per year. Unfortunately, today isn't one of them. Myself, John McGahern, Evelyn Conlon and Jennifer Johnston are reading tonight. This goes pretty well. I get a bit of a lump in my throat actually, watching these fine writers read, and then hearing their words read out in French. It's the proudest I've felt about Ireland for quite some time. Afterwards, the only drink available is Irish whiskey or French dessert wine, but I actually like waking up in the mornings without having spent half the night before vomming like a one-arm bandit, so I decide to have water. During the reception, some bald French geezer in a suit wanders over and starts going on about what a rare sight it is, an Irish writer drinking water, what happened to ze spirit of Brendan Behan, Patrick Kavanagh, Flann O'Brien, etcetera. The spirit hasn't really been the same since they drank themselves to death, I reply. Top Of Ze Morning, he says. May Ze Rhoad Rhize To Meet Yeux. Pogue mahone, I reply.

In the far corner a three-piece band are playing the kind of Irish traditional music that you only ever hear outside of Ireland. A woman in a black dress suddenly starts doing Irish dancing. I had thought hurling was a traditional Irish sport until this moment. I am standing in a breeze-block office building on the outskirts of a provincial French town watching someone *aon-dó-trí* to Wolfe Tones covers. How did this happen to me?

Later that night our hosts, led by the splendid Mr Thierry Guichard, take us all out to a restaurant called *L'Assiette de Boeuf*. The rest of Europe is terrified to eat anything that has ever passed through a country where a cow has even appeared on the television, but here in good old no-nonsense Montpellier they give us a plate of beef carpaccio which practically has a swishing tail. It is delicious. The food is just sensational. This is great. *L'Imaginaire Irlandais, c'est magnifique*. We are all in a very literary state by the end of the evening.

Tuesday, 2 April: The Espace République, Montpellier. Tonight's reading features last night's line-up with the new added talents of Eoin McNamee and Hugo Hamilton. The reading is very well organised and attended. After the reading there is the launch of the *L'Imaginaire Irlandais* catalogue. Doireann Ní Bhraoin, the Irish commissionaire of *L'Imaginaire Irlandais* is here, and she makes a good short speech. Following her good short speech, a right-wing French politician makes a long bad speech. Ireland so cultural, blah blah, the New Europe, blah blah, unity in diversity, blah blah, unaccustomed as I am, blah blah, *votez pour moi*, blah blah.

My book *True Believers* is about to be published in French and I meet the two translators, Gérard and Pirique. They are wonderful chaps. We spend a pleasant half-hour discussing the difficulty of rendering certain Irish slang expressions into French. 'The old sod' was particularly challenging, apparently. '*Le vieux sodde?*' I suggest to the boys. French for me is *un morceau de gâteau*.

Another dinner laid on by our extremely hospitable hosts here in Montpellier. The local gastronomic speciality is a mashed potato dish called *alioli*, which has the consistency of molten rubber. *Alioli* would have come in very handy back in the bad old days when we couldn't buy condoms in Ireland. It would have made a much more natural and much more Irish substitute for clingfilm.

Wednesday, 3 April: Surprise, surprise, out to dinner again. French waiters are legendary for their stunning rudeness. The waiter tonight actually laughs when I ask if I could have a tomato salad. Like a tomato would be a very unusual thing to find in a restaurant. I notice that the French couple at the next table are almost as rude to the waiter as the waiter has just been to me. As a result they seem to get served very quickly and in a friendly and efficient manner. I guess the best way to get a French waiter's attention seems to be to act in an even more rude and aggressive manner than he does. Thus, logically, the *absolutely* best way to get the attention of a French waiter is to enter the restaurant, march straight up to him and staple his balls to a table before attempting to ask for the menu. I may try this approach later in the trip.

Thursday, 4 April: Arrive in Paris and check into the hotel we have booked. The room has a really lovely view of a brick wall and a barbed-wire fence. It also has one of those old-fashioned revolving fans that makes a noise like a helicopter. The room should be called 'The Apocalypse Now Suite'. I took one look at the bathroom. I had never known what 'a gorge' really is, but, take it from me, five seconds in that bathroom and I know mine is rapidly rising. Check out and move into the Hôtel Des Beaux Arts. This is the hotel where Oscar Wilde died. Given the prices they charge, I am not one bit surprised. He probably just took one look at his bill and keeled over in a gibbering heap. I am all for European integration but, really, fifteen quid for a continental breakfast would bring out the Eurosceptic in anyone.

I am reading George Orwell's *Down and Out in Paris and London* at the moment. When it was published in French it was called *La Vache Enragée*, which, funnily enough, is French for 'The Mad Cow'. Anyway, Orwell says that a person who doesn't want to get food poisoning should never stay in an expensive Parisian hotel. This is because chefs in expensive hotels consider food to be an art form. Thus, they stroke it, pluck it, knead it, arrange it on the plate, make sure all the prawns are facing due north, with the very same fingers they've been using previously to pick their noses, smear Brylcreem in their hair, etcetera, etcetera, and in France, believe me, etcetera really suggests myriad possibilities. In a cheap restaurant, Orwell tells us, they just chuck the food onto the grill, incinerate it, pick off the pubes and then scrape it onto a plate for you. I pass this on for what it's worth.

This morning I find myself chatting with a French journalist who is telling me all about his views on Ireland, which is very interesting for me and is exactly what I came to France for. He loves Ireland more than any Irish person I have ever met. Everything about Ireland is great. 'Even ze omeless people in Dooblin seem so much more appy zan ze omeless people in Paris,' he says. I am actually speechless by now, but he doesn't seem to care. He feels that in addition to having the happiest poor people in the world, 'the Irish invented the comic tradition in literature'. Oh, yeah, right. Et les monkeys might fly out of my cul. I have a sudden vision of an ancient Celt sitting in a cave trying to invent the comic tradition in literature. There he is, scratching his boils and going, 'So these three druids go into a pub for a pint of mead, right, and one says to the barman, take my wife … no, these three members of Na Fianna go … no, how many Finn McCools does it take to change a light bulb … no … hey, a really funny thing happened to me on the way to Newgrange … No. Hang on …'

A large lunch with my beautiful friend, Ms Maggie Doyle. The menu features all sorts of mad concoctions. There is pork broiled in aspic, rabbit charred and minced into balls, veal seared and shredded. It is hard to decide what to go for. In the end, I decide to have lobster slowly bored to death by the maître d'.

The waiter is a nice fellow who is unusually polite for a person in the French catering trade. 'And would you like a little more wine?' he asks.

'Est-ce-que le Pope un Catholique?' I reply, wittily.

On the way home, the woman taxi driver is delighted to hear that I am Irish.

'Ze Quwanbayrheaze?' she says.

'?!' I say.

'Ze Quwanbayrheaze?'

After about ten minutes of this I manage to figure out that she is asking me if I like The Cranberries.

'No,' I say. But it is too late. She has started to sing.

'Yeuz gut me rhapped arhound yer finger, ah hah hah, deux yeux av to, do yeaux av to, do yeux av to, let eet leenger.'

'HOHOHO,' I say. 'You can drop me here actually.'

Tonight I am doing a really prestigious reading at the world-famous Georges Pompidou Centre. I have been looking forward to this for months. When I arrive I find that the venue for the reading is a room on the sixth floor of the Pompidou Centre that has been converted into something called 'Le Dublin Pub', complete with Bord Fáilte-type posters, etcetera. It doesn't look like any Dublin pub I've ever been in, and I don't just mean that the toilets are clean and flushed. As I look around I am a bit flushed myself. I am not sure about the idea of doing a reading in a pub. I mean, yes, I understand that lots of effort and trouble has been taken, but still, it's a pub. It is so important to support these events that help to overturn anachronistic stereotypes and truly reflect the changing new modem Ireland, I feel, as I nimbly dodge the team of formation-dancing midgets in leprechaun suits. (OK, I made that bit up.) But it's still a pub. I am looking forward to the next visit of a prominent French writer to Dublin so that I can turn up to the event wearing my striped jersey, black beret and humorous string of onions.

After the reading, the friendly and extremely helpful people from the Pompidou Centre ask me if I enjoyed myself. I have, in a way. They are the absolutely nicest audience over whose drunken babbling conversation I've ever had the great pleasure to read, I aver. 'La Grande Motte', who is a very polite person, kicks me with unnecessary force in the right calf.

A traditional Irish band led by a man called Mickey Dunne begins to play now. I watch for a while, standing beside a woman from one of the local newspapers.

'Mickey is a common name in Ireland?' she asks.

'Yes,' I say.

'Yes,' she says, 'my husband say there are many Mickeys in Ireland. Particularly in traditional music.'

I feel there is really no answer to this.

Friday, 5 April: 'La Grande Motte' and I get the Métro out to Créteil, a distant suburb of southeast Paris, where the great Québecois actor Robert Lepage is doing his piece *Elsinor*, a multimedia reinterpretation of *Hamlet*. On the way, a fully fledged French lunatic gets onto the train and starts screeching at the top of his voice, '*Chirac, c'est un merde, Chirac, c'est un putain de merde*,' which is French for 'I have certain mixed feelings about President Chirac.'

The reaction of the Parisian commuters is astonishing. They all look into their newspapers as intensely as medieval astrologers scrutinising the skies, every last one of them, while My Nabs continues roaring and bawling on the subject of Jacques Chirac's apparently considerable deficiencies. These people make London commuters seem communicative. '*MERDE!*' he screams. '*CHIRAC EST UN MERDE!*' Then, when the train pulls into a station, one of the passengers lunges for the emergency cord and pulls it violently. The doors open. Six transport police materialise out of the walls and begin to discuss the more complex of Monsieur Chirac's policies with the insane man using a large number of helpful visual aids, namely, batons, handcuffs and slavering Alsatians. As the train pulls out of the station and you witness the ensuing debate, you sense that the loonie may change his mind about Monsieur Chirac's policies as soon as he relocates his kneecaps and gets them sewn back on. The man who pulled the emergency cord is reading his newspaper again. He is smiling to himself, I notice. Touching how the spirit of *liberté, égalité et fraternité* is still as relevant as ever.

Elsinor starts half an hour late. All of the parts are played by two male actors, who, in between acting, manipulate the set, operate on-stage video cameras and do fencing. (I don't mean barbed wire – I mean, with swords.) The show is absolutely sensational, but quite long. Afterwards I am dying to go to the loo, where I have occasion to ponder the truth of Billy Wilder's famous observation that France is a country where the money falls to pieces in your hands but you can't tear the toilet paper.

After this, back into central Paris where LGM and I go to a café, on the Quai de Contes. The café is full of young compatriots of LGM, spotty Englishmen who are in a very Parisian state indeed, to judge by the conversation. They keep talking loudly to the waiters and waitresses about subjects of major contemporary importance to Anglo-French relations, such as Trafalgar and Waterloo. I find myself fervently wishing that the waitress would bring up the Battle of Hastings, but sadly she does not.

One young Englishman is humorously wearing a pair of plastic comedy breasts. 'Ere,' he says, to a passing waitress, 'Quai de Contes, right? Does that mean Quay of the Cunts?' There is uproarious laughter and affectionate applause from his friends at this point, but he is not listening. He is now leaning head forward, mouth open, throwing up copiously all over his comedy breasts and moaning, 'Oooh Ahh Cunt-Oh-Nah.' It is good to see the English sense of subtle ironic humour is alive and well in the new Europe, I remark to LGM. 'HA HA HA,' she says.

Saturday, 6 April: *Les Bains-Douches*. This is French for 'The Public Baths'. It is also French for 'the trendiest nightclub in Paris frequented by clotheshorses and eejits where the only way to get in if you don't want to be totally humiliated by the skinny bouncers is to book for dinner in advance and pay out a king's ransom for a dodgy hamburger'.

Perceptive readers may be able to guess which strategy I adopted. I had no doubts about Herself's trendiness, you understand, but my own was distinctly dubious and I felt it would be bad for the relationship for her to be let in and me to be kicked out.

After the dinner we go to the bar, which is downstairs in the club. The drinks cost 100 francs each. That's thirteen quid. Each. Like, for one. I have actually gotten blind mad drunk on thirteen quid before, but tonight I don't think that's going to happen.

By about 1.00 a.m. the place begins to fill up. I attempt to put what I believe young people refer to as 'my funk into your face', but LGM points out before long that God did not put me on the earth to be a dancer. I'm inclined to agree. Indeed, I don't think I have danced since I was about sixteen, when dancing consisted of standing in a frantic rhomboid of young fellows in the hall of Presentation Boys School, Glasthule, and pretending to play an invisible guitar while simultaneously trying to dodge the snowstorm of flying dandruff. My teenage years also saw the outbreak of the punk-rock pogo, a dance that was much favoured in Prez, because it was very close to actual physical violence. But we are a long way from Prez now. Trendy uptight Parisians dance like they have corncobs up their bottoms to 'dance' music, which may admittedly be catchy, in the very same way that certain virulent forms of the flu are catchy. I try to dance to this too, but my left hip does not seem to know what my right one is doing. I retire to the bar to get some drinks. The barman peers at me as though I am disturbing his evening. He is sipping a drink that looks like something out of the Amazon rainforest.

'*Bonsoir*,' I say, '*Je suis un romancier Irlandais.*'

He nods and takes another sip of his luminous drink.

'*Vouz allez ici often?*' I ask, rather coolly.

He looks me in the eye for what seems like a long time, although, in fact, it is not. '*Pees awf*,' he says.

I turn and gaze upon the sea of gyrating, designer-clad bodies. *L'Imaginaire Irlandais? Je ne regrette rien.*

Border Lines

It was about five in the morning and I was somewhere around the border when it happened. I had been in Donegal doing a reading, and I had to leave very early the next morning to get back to Dublin. I crossed the border into the North to look for a garage that was open, and then I headed south. I was driving quite fast along the motorway. If I tell you the truth, I was breaking the speed limit. But I wasn't too worried, because at five in the morning there's no traffic at all. It was quiet and still, and in the distance I could see the sun beginning to come up over the fields on my left, and on the right the vast slumbering hulk of Ben Bulben. Van Morrison was on the radio. I was smoking a cigarette. I was enjoying myself. I didn't know what was going to happen.

I turned a bend in the road. The scene was like something out of a beautiful dream. There were cherry-blossom trees at the edge of the fields all along the motorway, and the breeze was shaking the boughs and showering the road with white petals. It was an extraordinary sight, the white petals raining down on the motorway like so much confetti. And then it happened.

When I recall the whole thing now, I think I first saw the bird when I was about a hundred yards away from it. There were other birds around, whirling around above the motorway, but I think I did actually see this one just sitting still in the middle of the road. I kept going. I got closer and closer to this bird and then suddenly I was a few feet away from it.

It rose up from the ground and spread its wings wide. But then I think either a gust of wind caught it, or it got trapped in the air stream around the moving car, and for one awful moment it hung in the air as though suspended by some invisible filament before it hit the windscreen with a dull and sickening thud that I don't think I will ever forget.

The whole windscreen went red. It was as though someone had poured blood all over the glass. I jammed my foot down on the brake and the car swerved across the motorway and into the oncoming lane. I felt the adrenalin surging through my limbs and body like a drug. I got out of the car. I could feel my breath coming hard and I could feel my hands and legs shaking. The poor bird was lying on the bonnet of the car, croaking in agony. There was a trail of blood and black feathers all over the metal. The bird flapped its wing and thrashed its head and slipped off the front of the car and fell onto the ground. It was in terrible distress. I found myself talking to it. I actually found myself apologising to the bird for hitting it. It suddenly dawned on me that I would have to kill it.

I am a townie. In my whole life, I have never killed anything larger than a spider. It's not that I'm a big animal lover: it's just never happened. How do you kill a bird? What was the most humane way of doing it? I looked at the bird, trembling on the road, and I decided I just couldn't do it. I decided to leave it there. I went to get back into the car, but just as I did so it let out another terrified croak. I knew then that I would have to end its agony.

I stared at it. Should I try to break its neck or something? Should I just put my hands on its bloodied throat and twist the life out of it? I squatted beside it and went to touch it, but I just couldn't bring myself to do that. I felt ashamed of my own cowardice. I got back up and walked up the road for a while, trying to find a heavy flat stone that I could drop onto the bird. Maybe that would kill it. Finally I found one. I staggered back down towards the car with the rock in my hands. But by the time

I got back to the car I was glad to find that the bird was dead. I lifted its broken body and threw it by the side of the road.

I wondered what to do about the blood on the windscreen and the front of the car. I looked in the boot, but I could find nothing to clean the car with. In the glove compartment I found a half-empty bottle of mineral water, which I poured down the glass. Then, with my bare hands, I started to try and wipe the blood away.

I got back into the car and drove on. It sounds pathetic, I know, but I was deeply upset by the whole experience. I don't know whether it was because I was tired and shocked, but I felt very close to tears, and I don't cry very easily. My nerves were jangling. I felt as though I had jumped through a plate-glass window. Shortly afterwards, things began to get even more surreal. I realised with a start that I was approaching the border checkpoint. I stopped the car. I didn't want to approach the checkpoint at some unearthly hour of the morning with my windscreen covered in blood.

I stopped the car again and got out. It was cold. The morning was very quiet and still. There was nobody around. I wondered what to do. I still had nothing to clean off the blood with. On the back seat of the car there was a copy of the book I had been reading from in Donegal. I started tearing pages out and wiping the blood away, and then throwing the bloodstained pages on the ground beside the car. When I had done the best job I could, I got back in and drove on. In time I came to the checkpoint, which looked eerie. In fact, there were no soldiers or police on duty, or, if there were, they were hidden from view.

I crossed the border and drove home to Dublin. On the way, all sorts of crazy thoughts went through my mind. What I am most ashamed of is that I started to think what had happened would make a really good short story. I felt that the whole incident meant something. I ran it again in my mind. Falling petals, bloodstained pages of a novel, the sound of the dying bird, the silent checkpoint on an unfamiliar road. I felt it was all symbolic of something, but I couldn't think what. It's the most debilitating psychic disease which writers suffer from, the desire to turn unusual experience into the stuff of fiction. It's terrible. It's morally very dubious. But I think I did learn something important that morning. I learnt that some things are symbolic of nothing at all. They stand out starkly in their sheer haunting meaninglessness. I realised that the whole event had meant nothing. It was just a sad stupid thing that happened, that's all. It scared me, but in the end it meant nothing.

Should Xmas Be Axed?

I remember childhood Christmases with a strange mixture of pleasure and fear. There's something oddly disturbing about the day for a lot of children. I remember ghost stories, the sweet smell of pine needles from the tree, mountains of shredded coloured paper lying piled up on the floor. I remember going to the Gaiety pantomime, my first time in a theatre, listening to the magical sound of the orchestra tuning up, being utterly petrified by the villainous Vernon Hayden. I remember Maureen Potter as Aladdin saying the reason Ireland's emblem was a harp was that the country was run by pulling strings. A joke she could still use.

We used to go to my grandparents' house on Christmas Eve. My grandad let us hold our notes for Santa Claus in the fireplace and the rush of air would pull them out of our fingers. He said this was the hand of St Nicholas. It was terrifying, but captivating, too. And I remember my sister Eimear swearing that she saw Santa Claus climbing up our stairs with a sack on his back. I was sure she wasn't lying. I still am. Children always see things that adults can't. And all of us sitting in Glasthule Church solemnly intoning the words of the Bay City Rollers' song 'Bye Bye Baby' to the tune of 'Silent Night'.

Another year I got an infuriating toy football game: a small plastic box containing two pinball flippers and a ball bearing. I remember long nights re-enacting the World Cup with my father on this infernal machine. I was usually Brazil. I think he was Poland. It says something that, back then, neither of us would have wanted to be Ireland.

That was Christmas then. Once you attain maturity, however, Christmas changes. It becomes an excuse for socialising. When you are a teenager, socialising is a euphemism for drinking, fornicating, regurgitating, exchanging bodily fluids and indulging in malicious and destructive gossip, preferably simultaneously. Socialising is a broad, generous term to the young. It includes not only gluttony, sloth and lust, but all the other deadly sins as well. When you are older, however, socialising becomes a terrible chore. A night in the pub becomes dull. Whereas one used to admire the bar staff and silently imagine all the chat-up lines one would attempt if one were not so nervous – 'You've lovely dark hair all down your back. None on your head, of course, HAHAHA, but your back is like a bleedin' shag pile!' – one now finds oneself pining for a chicken madras and *NYPD Blue*. A spell in the nightclub becomes similarly wearing. What is this polluting sound that the young call, with devastating irony, music? What is this epileptic lurching that is called, I believe, dancing? What on earth is, or are, 'M People'? Does the 'M' stand for manky? Maladjusted? When one enters the third decade, a new set of socialising opportunities comes along, each one being even less fun than the last. Let us consider, for instance, that foul and toothsome tsetse fly from the malodorous armpit of Beelzebub's granny, The Dinner Party.

There is a lot of this sort of thing at this time of the year. Your friends, whom you have not seen since last Crimbo, when you grossly insulted them over dessert and puked into their aspidistra on the way home, have decided that it is your turn to have them over for 'supper', whatever that is. Begrudgingly, you assent. You then realise that your flat is not really suitable for entertaining. Is it too late, you wonder, to get a bit of flock wallpaper up? Could you possibly borrow a grand piano, or better still, a concert harp? Is that picture you have on the wall of a Spanish boy crying really going to give the best impression?

And what about the menu? Normally, you might have a cheese sambo for dinner, or, if it is a really special occasion, a toasted cheese sambo. You cannot offer such plebeian fare to your guests. You get out the recipe book some malevolent bastard – probably the one you're inviting – gave you for Christmas last year. You ponder the options. Hmmmm. Quail's eggs hand-rolled in badger dandruff? Zebra spleen splattered with desiccated polenta? Eye of stoat, toe of newt, fresh salmon lung in pee of disaffected Eurocrat? No, let's face it, you'll do lasagne again.

And who to invite? Well, I've read up on this in the gossip columns and it seems that no Christmas dinner party is complete now without a few celebrities. And the best way to attract celebrities to your party is to mention a disease of some kind on the invitation. Society people, particularly in Ireland, are very fond of disease because it gives them the chance to dress up and sashay about looking like Noel Coward characters without feeling guilty for being so rich. Some diseases, of course, are more popular than others on the charity circuit and have really been over-used. But a number of other diseases – scabies, shingles and gonorrhoea, for instance – are still available for inclusion as part of the attraction of your special evening.

Party games are obviously very important, too: charades, musical chairs, pass the parcel (or pass the buck, as it is known at the Oireachtas Christmas party). There's also, of course, Parlour Mastermind, a variation of the well-known TV quiz show where you pick a subject: say, for example, the British Royal Family, 1500 to 1939. Bertie Ahern, who I've always invited to my Christmas gathering, has a really good specialist subject: the Dunnes Stores' Anorak, £15.50 to £16.99.

Every year it's the same. The Christmas party season seems to start in October now. You have not got over Hallowe'en yet, and already the time is here for getting scuttered and dancing around some subterranean fleshpot to a selection of abysmal 1970s Christmas songs that you thought you had forgotten for ever. I am thinking, for example, of 'Wombling Merry Christmas' by, yes, The Wombles. There is only one good use for a womble, in my book, which is that it should be hollowed out and turned into a slipper. And I am thinking of 'So Here It Iz Merry Christmas, Everybodeez Having Fun' by Slade, a work that never fails to bring me out in a rash, although I suppose you do have to respect the only dyslexic band in the history of rock and roll.

There is the wonderful myth that Christmas parties are good places to meet people. Well, I've been to a lot of Christmas parties in my time, and I don't think I've ever met anybody at one. You turn up full of hope. You talk all night to the people you came with, about the people who were supposed to come with you, but didn't. You go home alone and stare at the television test-card for an hour before falling asleep with a cigarette in your hand and setting fire to the sofa. There's nothing you can do about this. It's like age, gravity and the phone company; ain't no point in trying to fight it. Ordinary parties are bad enough. But the Christmas office party is a vile scraping from between the gnarled toes of Satan. You turn up in the pub at 6.00 p.m., full of resolve not to go too over the top. You have to work tomorrow, after all. By 7.30 you are already tipsy. By 8.05 you are laughing for no apparent reason. By 8.15 you are reciting Monty Python sketches. (Nudge nudge, wink wink, say no more.) By 9.10 you are having a vicious argument with your best friend about Bosnia, the North or Aston Villa. By 9.15 the manager is telling you that he doesn't care whether you're a regular or not, any more language like that out of you and you're fucking barred.

You go to the jacks to splash water on your face. You peer at yourself in the mirror. You look like an overgrown intestinal parasite. One of your colleagues is locked into a stall busily getting off with another one. It's not that you're jealous exactly. It's just that every time they take a break from snogging the living daylights out of each other, you can hear them blithely conversing about how strange you are. You notice, suddenly, that there is a cigarette vending machine on the toilet wall. You think this is a marvellous innovation. You have spent fifteen quid before you realise that you have accidentally blundered into the ladies and you are actually feeding all your change into the tampon machine. In the restaurant, you end up sitting beside the one person in the office you truly detest, but you are so drunk that you suddenly find them strangely attractive. You suggest just skipping dinner and going back to your place. You then spend several hours nursing your sore face and pondering the delights of fizzy potato salad and greasy ham. You go to a nightclub. You jig around like a recently released lunatic. Fighting your way up to the bar, you bump into somebody you used to go out with. They are now happily married, with a beautiful child. They have given up the cigarettes and gone into therapy and lost two stone. Hearing all this just makes your night. They ask you if your life is still as disastrous as it used to be, and you laugh out loud and say you always liked their sense of humour. But you notice that, funnily enough, they are not laughing.

When the nightclub closes you go back to the office to have a few more scoops. Before you know it, normally sober people whose professionalism you admire are removing their trousers and photocopying their bottoms. You turn on the radio. John Lennon is singing 'So This Is Christmas And What Have You Done?' You hurl the radio through the office window. You reflect that you should have actually opened the window before you did this. You stagger outside and indulge in that ancient Dublin Christmas tradition known as waiting two hours for a taxi. When one finally comes, you get in. You ask the driver if he's busy. 'Ah Jaze,' he sighs, 'it's fierce fookin' quiet this year, boss. But sure, it's for the kids really, isn't it?' You take a deep breath. You open your mouth. You scream.

And then it comes. And it goes in a day. And then there is the aftermath of the festive season to be undergone. 'How did you get over the Christmas?' is the bizarre question which Dubliners ask each other at this odd time of the year. The quirky enquiry assumes that Christmas is an obstacle of definable height, and that the struggle to get over it is akin to vaulting a barbed-wire fence, trampolining over a moat or lepping a brick wall with those bits of broken bottles on the top of it. It also assumes, by implication, that Christmas is something you could tunnel under, slip surreptitiously around or blow into smithereens using dynamite. Very sadly, none of this is true, however. Like torture, puberty or unrequited love, Christmas is something which must simply be endured. How did you get over the Christmas, indeed. I got over the Christmas the way the Christians got over the fucking lions.

There is only one answer to this question, by the way. The response to 'How did you get over the Christmas?' is now, was always, and will always be, 'Ah, it was quiet enough.' No matter what the actual volume of your Christmas was – if you spent the festive season in a padded cell, or if you spent it with your head wedged between two stereo speakers listening to the finer moments of the *Jimi Hendrix Experience* turned all the way up, Spinal Tap-wise, to eleven, until your ears bled – it was still 'quiet enough'. And no matter what happened to you over Christmas, no matter if the ceiling fell in and nearly set the poor Ma's heart astray, if you had both legs amputated following a bizarre gardening accident, if you accidentally blundered into Lillie's Bordello after the office party and managed to get off with Claudia Schiffer during the slow set, your Christmas was 'quiet enough', and no variation on this dialogue is permitted. Try it out yourself, gentle reader. Ask any Dublin taxi driver – assuming every last one of them hasn't fecked off to the Caribbean with the spondulix they made over Christmas! – ask any one of that proud body of peripatetic philosophers, 'Excuse me, driver, but may I be so bold as to enquire, how did you get over the Christmas?' and just see what he says. Anything other than a piteous snuffle, a resounding fart, and a murmured 'Ah, quiet enough' gets a night on the tiles, all expenses paid by New Island Books.

January makes you happy. You are well and truly 'over the Christmas' by now. At this stage your presents will have been enthusiastically opened, hyperbolically appreciated and then briskly fecked into the dustbin. Unless, of course, a pair of lurid socks, a bottle of aftershave that smells like a sick terrier's sputum and a remaindered copy of that very attractive coffee-table book, *The Complete Combine Harvesters of Bulgaria*, are genuinely what you always wanted for Christmas. It's all over now, Baby Blue! Ain't that grand? By now you will have placated your last unpleasant relation, scoffed your last cold turkey sarnie, endured your last dismal rerun of the Morecambe and Wise 1973 Christmas show. Christmas is no more! The time is here for the making of New Year resolutions.

This, I must say, is the time of year when I am most full of resolve, and I don't just mean the fizzy stuff that tastes unpleasant and gets rid of a hangover. I love resolutions. My favourite resolution is, of course, to give up smoking. My second favourite is to lose some weight. My third favourite resolution is United Nations Security Council Resolution 705, full autonomy and independence for the Palestinian people.

But next year I think I will make a new resolution. I think I will go away to Cuba or China or some heathen place where Christmas is not celebrated and New Year resolutions are not made. It seems pathetic, does it not, being thirty-two years old and sitting under a dead pine tree wearing a paper crown and getting slowly scuttered? It is pitiful. And as for that Santa Claus fellow, I really and truly feel that he is often just not what he seems.

Sanity Clause

Stark staring screaming mad. That is what I must be. Here I am, in Arnotts, on a busy weekend afternoon close to Christmas, dressing up as a fat old dipso with a white beard who consorts with reindeers and dresses like a Lower East Side pimp and lives in rural Lapland and drops down chimneys once a year. I mean, Jeez, what kind of a role model is that for kids? Still, I am trying to get into the part. I am trying to identify with the character. But it is not so much a question of Santa Claus as sanity clause. I must be bloody well bats.

I am utterly terrified. I am sweating profusely. The black boots are a size too big for me. The red floppy trousers are several sizes too small and they look, in any case, like something a member of ABBA would have refused to don on the grounds of good taste. The false beard smells like a putrefying rodent that died of something profoundly unpleasant. I have not had anything quite so nasty near my mouth since I once dated a member of Young Fine Gael. To make matters worse, I have been told that I must remove my glasses. Santa Claus does not wear glasses, apparently. He is blessed with 20/20 vision, which is a very good thing, I guess, if you have to drive a sleigh, particularly at Christmas, when there are so many drunken bowsies on the roads. But without my glasses I am as myopic as a bat with a bag over its head. I am about to make a spectacle of myself, and I don't even get to wear my spectacles. The world is a blur. I am definitely getting onto the union.

The real Santa Claus is giving me some advice about the kids. You talk to them a bit, he says. You ask them what age they are, where they live, where they go to school, what they want to find in their stockings on Christmas morning, apart, of course, from their feet. You tell them they have to promise to be good. You don't promise to bring them exactly what they ask for, because even Santa feels the pinch in these difficult times, but you say you'll do your best. If they want to sit on your knee while they're getting their photo taken, you let them, but you don't suggest it, because parents have got a bit sensitive about that kind of thing in the last two years. I want to stop rearranging my beard and ponder the true sadness of a world where a remark like that could be uttered but I don't have the time because a long queue is already forming outside the grotto. There are several hundred shrieking children eating lollipops and ice creams, and hyperventilating and tripping out on sugar overdoses and yelling and singing and fighting and loudly demanding expensive presents and driving their parents nuts and indulging in that important stage of the early learning process known as grabbing your sister by the pigtails and yanking on them until she fells you gibbering to the floor with a brisk kidney punch. It is my job to pacify these monsters.

My heart is pounding as I grope my way towards my seat. My first punter appears, a lovely little fellow of three or four in dungarees and a Superman shirt. He totters towards me, grinning broadly, hands outstretched. 'Ho, ho, ho, little boy,' I say, 'and what do you want for Christmas?' He promptly bursts into tears of shrieking horror, steps backwards and performs a Fosbury Flop into the arms of his mother. I am not doing very well.

The next customers arrive: two sisters aged four and five. I ask them where they live. 'What do you mean?' one says. I begin to panic. I hadn't realised it was a trick question. 'Emmm,' I say, 'you know, where in Ireland do you live?' The younger one gazes at me. 'In a house, of course,' she says. 'But where's the house?' She begins to giggle. 'In a road,' she says. 'And the road is where?' I say. 'At the end of a lane, silly.' That 'silly' has me worried. I suspect I may be losing a little of the fundamental respect on which the Santa–child relationship is predicated. 'And the lane is near a field and the field is in the sky,' the other one says and roars with laughter. 'Right,' I say. 'Well, girls, emmm, Merry Christmas.' More maniacal laughter. 'HAHAHAHA and the sky is in the sea and the sea is in the world HAHAHAHA and the world is in Ireland and Ireland is in a lake and …' Their father arrives to cart them away and inject them with sedatives. He shoots me a very accusing look. More punters arrive.

The sheer innocent credulity of the younger kids tugs at your heartstrings. The thing is, you've approached all this as a bit of a gas, but you realise that they really do think you are Santa Claus. You can see it in their faces.

They are so excited. Some of them are actually quivering with joy as they come up to you. Their eyes are wide as saucers. 'I love you, Santee! I love you!' Some of them have trouble being able to speak, they are so awestruck. After twenty minutes of all this I am feeling seriously clucky. By the end of the first hour I have practically grown a womb.

They're not all cute, of course. One fellow comes in sporting a skinhead haircut and a Republic of Ireland shirt. He reminds me of someone, but I can't think whom. He spends most of our conversation with his finger inserted into his nostril up to the knuckle. When I ask if he will promise to be good, he stares at me. 'Do yeh have to be good all the time,' he asks, 'or do yeh have to just troy to be good?' It is a question I have asked myself often, usually while drinking heavily, but just at this moment it is a little early in the day for philosophical speculation. You don't have to be good all the time, I conclude, but you do have to try. 'But Santee, are you good all the time?' he asks me.

I don't want to give the kid a complex but I don't want to lie to him either. 'No,' I say, 'I'm bold sometimes, but then I'm sorry afterwards.'

He throws back his head and begins to chortle like either

Beavis or Butthead, I'm not sure which. 'I'm bold sometimes too,' he cackles, 'but I'm never ever sorry. HUH HUH HUH I'm glad when I'm bold! HUH HUH HUH.'

It is slightly disconcerting to realise that actually he reminds me of Damien, the child from *The Omen*. Even without my glasses, I am convinced that I can see the numbers 666 tattooed on the side of his head.

Then there are the kids who kind of know the score. They tend to be eight or nine.

'Are you the real Santee?' one says.

'What do you think?' I say.

'I don't really think you are,' he answers.

'Why not?'

He grins at me. 'Well, if you're the real Santee, then how come you're in Switzers as well?'

I think about this for a moment. It is a very good question. I decide to kick for touch. 'Magic,' I say.

He scowls. 'There's no such thing as magic. There's only one Santee Claus and you're not him, because there's only three weeks until Christmas, and if you were him, you'd be too busy gettin' all the toys ready to be in here talkin' to everybody.' I can see a bright future for this kid. I wonder whether he would like to be Attorney General one day.

A little boy wants 'a new book' for his baby sister. 'Because she's after eatin' the one she had already.' One little girl would like a toy truck, because she wants to drive trucks when she grows up, like her Da. But generally traditional sex roles seem to be as strong as ever. At least half of the boys want guns or toy cars. About two-thirds of the girls want Barbie dolls.

The children are full of questions. 'What do you have for your dinner?' one wants to know. 'Do you have a wife?' 'Do you like Zig and Zag?' 'Do you have any children?' 'Do you have any brothers and sisters?' 'Were you ever small?' 'What time do you get up in the mornings?' 'Are there angels really?' 'Can you sing?' 'Does the sun ever shine in the North Pole?' 'Why is there snow?'

'Do you like Manchester United?' 'What different languages do you speak?' 'What do you do when it isn't Christmas?' 'What age are you?' 'Are you ever going to die the way my granny did?' 'Where do you go on your holidays?' 'Do you know Jesus?' 'Are you the same thing as Jesus?' One particular question – 'But when you were a little boy, who brought presents to you every Christmas?' – is genuinely quite perplexing. All the kids have something to say to Santa Claus. Some tell jokes. 'Santee, did you hear about the Kerryman doin' the Riverdance? He drowned.' And then some of the things they say aren't so funny. I ask one little girl with haunted eyes what she wants for Christmas. She says nothing. I tell her she can whisper it to me if she likes. 'I want Daddy to come back home,' she says, quietly. 'And I want Mammy not to be crying anymore.'

Then there are the older kids, who no more believe in Santa than the Pope believes in Motorhead. They come in to see you because they're accompanying younger siblings, or because they've been forced to by their parents. One kid of about ten strides over, looking sulky, chewing gum, hands thrust into his pockets. I ask what he wants for Christmas. His lip curls into an expression so mocking that he looks like a pre-pubescent Jeremy Paxman. 'Tell Santee what you want,' I coax. He folds his arms and scrutinises the ceiling. His mother lets out a roar, 'Tell him what you want, willya, I'm after payin two fifty for the photograph of yez.' He turns and regards her as though she is something malodorous he has just coughed up and then he turns back to me. 'You can whisper it to me if you like,' I say. He nods. He leans in close to my ear. 'Dja know wha?' he says. 'You're only a fat bollocks.' I am a little taken aback, I must confess. 'Ho ho ho,' I say, clapping him on the back. 'Your arse is bleedin' hew-edge,' he says. I suggest that this is no way at all to address Santa Claus and that he may get an unpleasant surprise on Christmas morning. 'So will you,' he says, 'if you come down our chimney, coz you'll set your fat fookin' arse on fire.' I consider my next move as I chortle seasonally through

185

gritted teeth. But then the sight of Santee grabbing a ten-year-old by the throat, hoiking him clear off the ground and squeezing him until he starts to squawk may not be very healthy for the mental development of those impressionable toddlers around me.

By the end of my stint I have been visited by perhaps a hundred children. I have entertained fervent pleas for mega-drives and Barbie dolls, pistols and prams, teddy bears and board games, mountain bikes and surprises. My head is pounding and I am utterly exhausted as I take my leave of the wailing, caterwauling mass and retreat to the changing room. The real Santa Claus is there waiting for me, feet up on a barrel, watching the telly. 'Howdja get on?' he wants to know. I tell him I'd rather face Iron Mike Tyson than do that again, and he tuts at me. But fifteen minutes later, back in my civvies, I pass by the grotto and see the big guy in action. He is surrounded by kids, pawing his tunic, pulling his beard, screaming and yelling. The sound of wild unrestrained laughter resounds through the top floor of Arnotts. He's joking with them, he's patient and calm and happy. And I have to hand it to him. He's the real Santa Claus, after all. I guess there's some gigs only one guy can do.

Christmas Pavlova

Now I'm not a snobbish woman, and I bloody well resent you thinking I am. I'm in Amnesty International, and Jim's family are practically from Darndale, for God's sake. I write to a black man in Kansas who is going to be put into the electric chair next St Patrick's Day. I have a poor girl from down the country who comes into the house once a week for a bit of cleaning. I know all about suffering. But there are certain things that just aren't right, and I would like to tell you about one of them.

The Christmas is a very stressful time really. I have never enjoyed the Christmas very much. It is something to do with over-excitement. Christmas, to me, is crowds of bowsies in Grafton Street and stupid films full of men acting like goms on the television.

Our Victoria got out of the College of Art a few years ago and really things went downhill a little. She has her French and everything now, but she couldn't seem to focus herself at all. She tried being what they call a conceptual artist for a while. She had an erection or an installation or whatever they call them at a little gallery in town. Jim and I turned up. There were lots of people in black polo-necks and quite frankly I'm sure Jim and myself were the only heterosexuals in the room.

We all stood around drinking Blue Nun and eating lumps of Calvita and pineapple on cocktail sticks. There was a speech by some woman who was on about abortion. Then all the lights went out.

Victoria comes in wearing this boiler suit and carrying a

bucket of green paint. She takes off the boiler suit. Nothing at all on except the radio. I don't know where to look. Starts putting the paint all over herself, shouting out words that an itinerant wouldn't use and I wouldn't repeat. It was about Northern Ireland apparently, the situation and so on. I didn't get it. Jim said she was making a statement. I said you didn't have to put emulsion all over your breasts to make a statement, and since when was he an art critic anyway? Jim would think Louis Le Broquy was a character in *The Godfather, Part Three*.

Victoria went off to the UK last summer to paint a big mural of Nelson Mandela on the wall of a block of flats somewhere and, well, something bad happened to her, and I don't want to go into it. She came back here for a few weeks, then insisted on going off to New York. Nothing would do her except that, so we let her have her way. Well, we didn't hear much then for a time, but really Victoria has always been a little bit of a loner, so eyebrows weren't raised, not for a while anyway.

Last week I got a letter from her. 'Mum, Dad,' letter said. 'I've been back in Ireland for two months. I'm living in Ringsend. I met a fellow in New York and we got married. I'd like you to meet him.' There was a little smiling face drawn in the dot over the 'i' in her name. When I saw that I knew that things were bad.

Now I have to say I was upset, but we invited them around to the house last night, for an early Christmas dinner. I got in a sort of precooked turkey breast thing from Quinnsworth and a couple of bottles of Chardonnay. I warned Jim not to start about anything.

So last night finally comes. Everything, I must say, is looking beautiful in the house. Jim has got the tree out of the attic. He says it looks like a toilet brush, but I tell him he doesn't have to deal with pine needles. At half-seven Victoria arrives. She has lost a little weight, but she looks well on it. She's wearing a lovely black dress. It shows off her figure.

And this gorgeous creature strides up the path behind her. 'Well, well, well,' I think. 'Not bad.'

Richard is about six foot one. His skin is very lightly tanned and his nails are beautiful, I notice, when he shakes hands. He is wearing a kind of a crumpled white shirt, and very tight jeans. He is all there anyway, that is for sure, you can practically read his Visa card number, if you know what I mean, and his shoes are beautifully polished.

'Richard, Dad, Dad, Richard, Richard, Mum, Mum, Richard,' Victoria says. We all shake hands. He has gorgeous eyes.

'I hope it isn't too awful for you, Richard,' I say, 'meeting your mother-in-law.' Well, you have to make an effort.

He takes my hand again, and his fingers are as soft as a girl's. He kisses my knuckles. 'If I'd've known she was so beautiful,' he says, 'I'd've made Vicky introduce us earlier.'

He turns around to Victoria. 'Bubble,' he says. 'why didn't you ever tell me your mother was like Audrey Hepburn?'

'Oh, now Richard,' I say, 'would you get up the yard with yourself?' But my face is very hot, and I feel myself blushing. I show them into the lounge. 'Help yourself to nibbles,' I tell them. He winks at me.

In the kitchen I pour myself a vodka and I put the sprouts on. I don't feel the best. I feel a bit tense. It is a very long time since I have been compared to anything at all, never mind Audrey Hepburn. Actually, I tell a lie, Jim does compare me to the Creature from the Black Lagoon sometimes, but that is just his manner, and I know that basically he is ignorant. I take another sip of vodka and I bring in the smoked salmon.

Richard is very bright. He is the kind of person who actually understands the Beef Tribunal. He is a member of the Dublin South East branch of the Progressive Democrats. He campaigned for Michael McDowell during the last election, he tells us. He seems to know all about transfers and quotas, that kind of thing. His voice is just beautiful. We all agree that it is great about Dr Bhamjee getting in. Jim is already quite drunk. He cracks a pretty second-hand joke about cowboys and Indians, and Richard has the decency to summon up a dutiful giggle.

'And where are you from yourself, Richard?' I say.

'Actually, Geraldine,' he says, 'I'm from space.'

Well, Jim practically vomits he laughs so much. Jim just thinks that is some kind of panic.

'No,' Richard smiles. 'I really am from space, Geraldine.'

I know I'm going to say something now, and I hope it comes out the way I mean it. 'Well now, we're all from space,' I say. 'Women more than men, actually. I often think women are very lunar.'

'Yes,' Jim says. 'You are anyway.'

Richard peers at me. 'I'm from a very small planet called Veeblax One,' Richard says. 'It's quite far away actually. It's a bit of a hike, but it's very beautiful.'

'Get away, Richard,' I laughed. 'You're a terrible chancer.'

'Will I show them, Lambchop?' Richard says to Victoria.

'Yes, Loveboat,' she says. 'Show them.'

So he opens up his shirt and this enormous tentacle, I suppose you would call it, plops out, a big long black thing like a hoover extension, jerking all over the table, sort of throbbing. It has suckers all over it, too. That's what got me. The suckers.

Jim, as you can imagine, is in hysterics now. There are tears rolling down his face.

Richard seems to be encouraged by that. He stands up and unscrews his head. I'm not joking you now. I just don't know where to look. His hair and his face seem to sort of lift right off. Underneath he is a big greyish-white bloated blob, like a jellyfish. He has no eyes at all to speak of. Of which to speak, I mean, sorry. He unzips his jeans and takes them down. He unscrews his false legs. Apart from his tentacle, which looks obscene, he is one big blob of jelly. He looks just like a dessert.

The one good thing is, it certainly wipes the smile off Jim's face.

'Jim, dear,' I say, 'I need help with the sprouts.'

Jim follows me into the kitchen. He has his hand down the front of his trousers and he is scratching his private parts, the way he always does when he is confused.

'Well, it's a turn up for the books,' Jim says.

'Jim,' I say, 'this is Glenageary. Be serious.'

'I know it's Glenageary,' he says. 'Could I ever forget?'

'And what are they going to live on?' I say.

'Veeblax One, I suppose,' he says.

I stand there with my arms folded, looking him up and down. I tell him he is terribly funny altogether, and I ask him if he has ever considered leaving the bank to go on the television. He just turns away.

'It's as long as they're happy surely,' he says.

'Happy,' I say. 'Don't make me laugh. Don't you happy me. No son-in-law of mine is going to have a tentacle, I'm sorry.'

Victoria comes in then. She starts on about how it is difficult to understand, but love is love and all the rest of it. I tell her not to be going on with nonsense. When young people start going on about love is when you have to let them know what's what. You know nothing about love until you have lived with a man for at least ten years, in my book. When you have watched a man take off his shirt and smell his armpits every night for ten years, then you can talk to me about love.

'I'd rather you married someone from Darndale,' I say. 'That's how let down I feel about it.'

She starts to cry then, and I tell her I don't mean it, even though actually I do.

'What about, you know?' I say. 'You know, the physical side, what about that? I mean how would you make love to something like that?'

'Delicately, Mother,' she said, 'very delicately.'

I pour myself another large vodka. We are out of lemons.

'Can you not make an effort?' Victoria says. 'For me?'

Well, I go back in and I try my best, but I have to say the evening goes downhill for me. He is kind of puffing and swelling now, like something you'd see in that programme about the things that live under the sea. Victoria is unscrewing his arms. His mouth is a sort of flap of jelly and Victoria keeps chewing his food up for him before putting it in there. He has no arms or legs at all. No head even, just a little lump. A nodule, apparently, is the correct term, so Victoria tells me. He keeps slithering off the chair and onto the floor, bouncing like a bloody basketball. He moves about with his tentacle, sort of dragging himself along. Every time he rolls a bit he leaves a trail of black slime behind him, all up and down the carpet. It is definitely not very hygienic.

I have bought Jim a new wheelbarrow for a Christmas present and we have to put Richard into it, to stop him from flopping around. We do that, and then we chat a bit more about the weather and the price of eggs. Richard is a great admirer of Monica Barnes, he says. He thinks it is an awful pity that she didn't get in this time, and we all agree. Everything is grand, until the younger ones get back in from the disco. They get a terrible shock when they see him. Victoria suggests a breath of air.

'Oh, he does breathe, does he?' I say. 'Well, that's something.'

Victoria pushes him up and down the patio for a while, in Jim's wheelbarrow. And he is terribly upset, the poor fellow, because he thinks he has embarrassed everyone. Little blue tears are coming out the top of his nodule. Well, I feel awful then. We all have feelings under the skin, I say, even people who don't actually have skin so much as membrane. He stretches out his tentacle towards me and I give it a bit of a rub. 'Please don't tell the Progressive Democrats,' he keeps saying. 'Please don't tell Mary.'

When I go back inside the younger ones are crying, and Jim is trying to reason with them. I tell them they will understand everything when they are older, but they won't stop. I stand up then, and I'm afraid I shout at them.

'You will be happy,' I roar, 'or you know what you will bloody well get. CHEER UP, FOR GOD'S SAKE. IT'S BLOODY CHRISTMAS, ISN'T IT?'

Victoria pushes Richard back into the living room. He seems to have gone a bit purple. 'Richard wants to sing a song,' she says, 'don't you, Sweety Drawers?' I close my eyes and say a prayer to Saint Jude.

Victoria goes up to get her old guitar from the bedroom, the one she had when she was in the folk group in Sallynoggin

Church with all those nice nuns who wear cardigans. 'Make it a good rebel song,' Jim says, and Richard laughs.

I am a fifty-year-old woman, I think. Both of my parents are dead now. I have four children. My husband works in the Allied Irish Bank at Number One Upper Baggot Street, Dublin 2. I live in Arnold Grove, Glenageary. It is the week before Christmas. There is an alien in my living room who is about to sing 'Wrap the Green Flag Around Me, Boys'. Where did my life go so terribly wrong?

Victoria puts her arms around Richard and lifts him up onto the dinner table. He is leaking all over the place. It is disgusting, I think, but she doesn't seem to mind. Richard starts to sing now, and Victoria strums her guitar, and he thumps his tentacle from side to side as he sings:

O the Holly she bore a berry
As green as the grass
And Mary she bore Jesus
Who died on the cross
And Mary she bore Jesus
Our Saviour for to be
And the first tree that's in the greenwood
It was the Holly.
Holly, Holly, Holly, Holly
o the first tree that's in the greenwood
It was the Holly.

And he sings very beautifully, I suppose, but the Christmas is already bloody well ruined for me. I say this to Jim in the kitchen when the two of us are loading the dishwasher.

'What's to become of them?' I say.

He looks out the window, scratching his private parts again. 'Sure, if there's love there, anything is possible,' he says.

That starts me off. 'A lot you know about love,' I tell him. 'The way you talk to me in front of people. You seem to take pleasure in it.'

He turns around to me. His face is like a big white stupid moon. He comes over and he takes my chin in his hand. 'Oh, Geraldine, I'm sorry,' he says. 'You're the most beautiful creature I ever saw in my life.'

'Talk is cheap,' I tell him. 'Cheap, cheap, cheap.'

'You sound like a budgie now,' he says.

And I suppose I do actually laugh, even though he is so horrible to me. He wipes my tears away with his thumbs. He puts his strong arms around me and gives me a big hug and he measures my neck with kisses.

'I don't know why I ever married you,' I say. 'I could have married Brian Devereaux and gone to live in Dalkey.'

'Neither do I,' he laughs, 'but I suppose you're only human.'

'It's just as well someone is,' I say. 'In this family.'

And he takes me by the hand then. He begins to kiss me once again, and he holds me against his body, and I listen to the dishwasher chugging away in the corner. He keeps kissing me very softly on my mouth. He keeps telling me how fond of me he is, and that everything will work out to be all right, and that it's great that we're all here together, and that it will be the best Christmas we've had in years. He pushes my hair away from my eyes.

'You're so precious to me,' he says. 'You're so precious to me, Geraldine.'

That is the word, if you don't mind. Precious. I hold his body very close to me. I put my arms around his neck. We say nothing at all for a few minutes, but that is all right. I hold his fingers in mine. I know that we will make love later on tonight.

And I think about getting the Christmas pavlova out of the freezer, and letting it soften up a little before I put it into the oven.

Banana Republic:
Recollections of a Suburban Irish Childhood

In the summer of 1977 I was thirteen years old and pretty miserable with my life. My parents' marriage – unhappy for a long time – had finally disintegrated in the most acrimonious circumstances. My father had moved out of the house, applied to the courts for custody of myself, my two sisters and my brother, and won his case. On the day he had come back to collect us and take us to our new home, I had asked him to let me stay living with my mother. I felt sorry for her, I suppose, and I did not want her to be left on her own. My father agreed that I could do this. He was very good about it.

We lived in a five-bedroomed house in Glenageary, a middle-class suburb of southside Dublin. There was a large stain on the gable wall, which, if you glanced at it in a certain light, looked like the map of Ireland. I always thought that meant something important, but I could never figure out what exactly. My parents, both of whom came from working-class Dublin backgrounds, had slogged and scraped hard to buy this house, at a time when things must have seemed full of possibility for them. They must have had great plans for what they would do in that house. But in the summer of 1977, with only myself and my mother living there now, the house seemed unutterably empty, haunted by lost expectations.

We fought a lot, my mother and I. She had wonderful

qualities. She also had a passionate and mercurial nature, which the circumstances of her life had somehow forced down a wrong turn, so that it had taken the shape of anger. She possessed a capacity for doing great harm to people she loved, and that must have made her very unhappy. When I think about her now, I try to do so with compassion and love, because, like all unhappy people, she deserved that. But in those days, we hurt each other a lot, my mother and I. We didn't see eye to eye on *anything*. Sometimes she would throw me out of the house; other times I would simply walk out to get away from her. So what I'm saying is that I spent a good deal of the very hot summer of 1977 just wandering around the streets of Dublin by myself.

And an odd thing was happening in Dublin in the summer of 1977. All of a sudden, a strange thing called punk rock had arrived in town. People were suddenly talking about it everywhere you went. Up and down Grafton Street, in the arcades of the Dandelion Market on St Stephen's Green, in Freebird Records – a sleazily glamorous shop down on the quays of the River Liffey – the young people of my own age were all talking about punk rock.

At first in Dublin, punk rock was nothing much more than a feeling. I mean, nobody *knew* very much about it. It was said that it had been started over in London the year before, by a group called the Sex Pistols, who swore at people during interviews and were generally controversial. But nobody I knew had much more knowledge than that. Punk had been initially perceived as just another English invention, I suppose, another weird Limey oddity, in the same culturally wacko league as eel pie, pantomime dames and The Good Old Days.

But that summer, posters for homegrown punk-rock groups – or, more accurately, groups that masqueraded as punk groups – suddenly started to appear around Dublin. I remember starting to notice them, in places like the Coffee Inn on Anne Street, where I used to go and sit for hours over a single Coca-Cola. Posters for The Atrix, The Blades, The Boyscoutz, Big Self, Berlin, The New Versions, Rocky de Valera and the Gravediggers, The Vultures,

The Bogey Boys, The Virgin Prunes, The Radiators From Space. I may be wrong about some of these bands – I mean that I may have got their dates of birth wrong by a few months – but in my mind and memory, they all appeared in Dublin in the hot summer of 1977. I remember seeing the names of these new bands on these lurid posters, how exotic and mysterious the words seemed, how funny sometimes. There was a band called Free Booze, who had called themselves this because it was a good way to catch people's attention. And there was an odd little outfit of northside born-again Christians who played Peter Frampton songs, and who, it was said, would never amount to anything. In the summer of 1977, they were just about to change their name from The Hype to U2.

All these bands had sprung up more or less overnight in Dublin, it seemed to me. And at around the same time, a disc jockey called Dave Fanning, who worked on a pirate radio station called ARD, had started to play punk rock on his show. Also, a strange new music magazine called *Hot Press* had just started up, carrying regular articles about punk rock, reviews of records, news of punk-rock gigs. It was odd. But slowly, punk rock was starting to seep into Dublin. And in the summer after my brother and sisters went away to live with my dad, I spent many nights in my room listening to Dave Fanning, reading Bill Graham or Niall Stokes in *Hot Press*, avoiding my mother and wondering what to make of my life, and of punk rock.

It is important to say that this was a time when Dublin did not really exist on the world rock and roll map. We had Thin Lizzy and Rory Gallagher and a Celtic heavy metal band called Horslips, but that was about it. Foreign acts simply did not play in Ireland. It would have been almost unheard of for a big American or British band to gig in Dublin. The city had no pop culture of any size or significance. But in the summer of 1977, when I was thirteen, into this vacuum stepped a monstrous and slavering spirit.

Punk had a notion of secrecy about it in Ireland, a vague redolence of semi-illegality. Someone once told me that when

Freebird Records first got in copies of the Sex Pistols record *Never Mind the Bollocks*, for instance, the customs officers had obliterated the word 'Bollocks' with strips of red sellotape. And RTÉ, the national radio station, refused to play punk at all. 'Punk rock is junk rock,' announced Larry Gogan, then Ireland's foremost disc jockey. Punk felt kind of taboo. So to people of my age, it felt attractive.

I got a job that July, working as a teaboy on a building site in Dalkey, which was near where I lived with my mother. It was great to get out of the house, wonderful to have somewhere to go during the day. One of the labourers on the site was a tall scrawny fellow called Hubert. Hubert was about nineteen, I suppose, from the working-class suburb of Sallynoggin. His language was atrocious. He peppered his sentences with the word 'fuck', sometimes he would even insert it between the syllables of another word. One day, for instance, I heard him refer to his home town as SallyfuckinNoggin.

Hubert had worked as a bus conductor for a time, before being dismissed in mysterious circumstances and coming to lift blocks on the sites. There were two things that made his life complete. The first was pornography. He had a vast and comprehensive collection of *Playboy*s and *Penthouse*s, which had been sent over every month for some years by his brother in England. (Such publications were not then legally available in Ireland.) Hubert would cut pictures out of these magazines and sell them individually to the other men on the site, thus garnering enormous profits. It was fifty pence for a picture that featured a pair of breasts, I remember, and seventy-five pence for what Hubert called 'a gee' – a word I had never heard before, coarse Dublin slang for a vagina. 'Seventy-fuckin'-five pence a gee-shot,' he would sigh, shaking his head and absolutely refusing to haggle.

The second thing that made Hubert's life complete was punk rock. He loved it. He absolutely adored it, and he would talk to me about it for hours at a time, while we were supposed to be working. He told me about an establishment in town called

Moran's Hotel, in the basement of which there were punk-rock concerts almost every night. Hubert seemed to know a lot about punk rock. It was all about being 'against society', he said, it was about 'smashing the system'. He himself was 'against society', he assured me fervently. There were legions of people in the basement of Moran's Hotel every night of the week who were also 'against society', and they had stuck safety pins through their ears, cheeks and noses to prove it.

The bands who played in Moran's Hotel were against society too, all of them. But the worst of the lot, Hubert confided, the mankiest shower of louse-ridden, no-good, low-down bowsies ever to plug in a Marshall, ram up the volume and hammer out a three-chord trick, was a band called the Boomtown Rats. They were 'fuckin' scum', Hubert would say, and he would smile in a fondly contented way when he said this, as though attaining the state of fuckin' scumhood was a development in which a person could take considerable pride. 'They don't even fuckin' wash themselves,' he would beam, although how he was in a position to know such a thing was always kept secret.

I would have loved to go to Moran's Hotel, of course, but being underage, I couldn't. Yet I was frantically curious about this crowd of licentious and festering reprobates, the Boomtown Rats. I wondered what they would be like. The only live act I had ever seen before was Gary Glitter, performing in a television studio at RTÉ. I wondered if these Boomtown Rats could possibly be as entertaining as Gary. One day Hubert told me that I would soon have a chance to find out. The Boomtown Rats had been booked to play a big outdoor show in Dalymount Park soccer ground. And there must have been a bit of a run on gee-shots that week, because Hubert had bought me a ticket as a present.

That August afternoon, having lied to my mother about my destination – I think I said I was going to a boy scouts' day out – I went to the concert with Hubert and his girlfriend Mona. Mona was a healthy-looking girl, with the arms of a docker and a bewildering vocabulary of swear words. It was a very hot day and the stadium was packed full of people. Thin Lizzy and

Fairport Convention were headlining the concert, but I did not care about that, mainly because Hubert had said these bands were not sufficiently 'against society'. So, like him and Mona, I only cared about the Boomtown Rats. When their arrival was announced over the PA, I thought Hubert was going to ascend body and soul into heaven, Virgin Mary-wise, so screechingly enthusiastic did he become.

I had never experienced anything quite like the phenomenal excitement as the band sloped onto the stage, picked up their instruments and began to play. I felt as though a lightning storm was flickering through my nerve endings. It's something you never really forget, the first time you hear the scream of an electric guitar, the thud of a bass or the clash of a real high-hat cymbal. The lead singer, Bob Geldof, looked like an emaciated and drooling Beelzebub, as he leapt and tottered around the boards, spitting out lyrics into his microphone. The keyboard player, Johnny 'Fingers' Moylett, wore pyjamas on stage, an act of the most unspeakable and unprecedented sartorial anarchy. The bassist, Pete Briquette, lurched up and down leering dementedly, as though suffering from a particularly unpleasant strain of bovine spongiform encephalopathy. And if guitarists Gerry Cott and Gary Roberts, and drummer Simon Crowe, looked relatively normal, you still would have had not inconsiderable reservations about the prospect of any one of them babysitting your sister.

They played their music frantic and fast, incredibly LOUD, with a curious mixture of passion, commitment and utter disdain for the audience. I loved them. I had never heard a noise like this in my life. I was nailed to the ground by it. When they thrashed into their first single, 'Looking After Number One', I swear to you, every single hair on my body stood up and promptly did the Mashed Potato.

Don't give me love thy neighbour
Don't give me charity
Don't give me peace and love from your good lord above

You're always gettin' in my way with your stupid ideas
I don't want to be like you
I don't want to be like you
I don't want to be like you
I'm gonna be like ME!

Now, this was what I called music. I went home that night with my head pounding and my heart reeling. My mother was waiting, of course, and she spent several hours yelling at me, which made my headache even worse. But I felt empowered by the music, I really did. It sounds so naive now, I know, but that's the way it was. I felt that I had witnessed a kind of revelation. I felt that life was actually very simple. All you had to do, if someone was getting on your case, was tell them to fuck away off, that you didn't want to be like them, that you wanted to be like YOU! I told my mother this and she didn't exactly see things my way, to put it mildly. But it was the summer of 1977, you see. It all seemed very simple.

Back in school, in September, I told my friends all about the Boomtown Rats. I had five friends: Andrew McK, Andrew D, Nicky, Conor and John. I think we were friends because nobody else liked us. Also, John's parents were separated, like my own, and Conor's mother had died, as had Andrew D's father. So we felt we had something in common, in some odd way. I think we felt we had experienced more interesting pain than other people, although, of course, being teenage boys, we didn't talk much about such things. It turned out that Conor, a shy and very good-looking fellow, had heard about the Boomtown Rats himself. He had read an article about them – he was the one of our group who used to read articles – and it transpired that several members of the band, Bob Geldof and Johnny Fingers included, had actually *been to our school.*

If I had been interested in the Rats before, my enthusiasm rocketed through the roof now. These leprous anti-establishment scumbags had actually been to *my school.* Blackrock College, the alma mater of Irish President Éamon de Valera – this priest-run joint that had always been famous for taking in the carbuncular and prepubescent sons of the Dublin middle class and churning out obedient wage-slaves – had somehow produced the Boomtown Rats! How had this possibly happened? There was hope for us all, it seemed.

Now, Irish readers must forgive me for a moment while I explain something to others. There is a television programme in Ireland called *The Late Late Show*. Its former host, Gay Byrne, is a genial man of polite manners and generally mild views. It is often jokingly said in Ireland that Gaybo is the most powerful man in the country, and, like many jokes in Ireland – as opposed to Irish jokes – it contains the seed of a profound truth. One evening that autumn, Bob Geldof and the Rats were booked to appear on *The Late Late Show*. Once again, I lied to my mother, so that I could get out of the house and go up to my friend's house to watch this.

The atmosphere in my friend's living room was electric as we uncapped the shandy bottles, passed around the solitary spit-soaked cigarette and waited for the Messiah to descend. Bob shambled onto the screen like an evil bedraggled wino and sneered his way through the interview in a furtive southside drawl. He detested many things about Ireland, he said. He loathed the Catholic Church, he hated the priests who had taught him in Blackrock College, he disliked his father. He had only gotten into rock and roll in order to get drunk and get laid. Almost everything he said was greeted with horrified gasps and massed tongue-clickings from the audience, and wild cheers from myself and my friends. When the interview was over, the rest of the band came on and performed 'Mary of the Fourth Form', a feverish song about the seduction of a schoolteacher by a female student. As the number climaxed in a clamour of drums and wailing feedback, the studio audience was absolutely stunned.

'Well done, Bob,' smiled Gay Byrne, ever the professional. Geldof turned around, scowling, wiping the saliva from his lips with the back of his hand. 'Yeah, well, if you liked it so much,' he snapped, 'just go and buy the record.' Fuck! The guy was giving cheek to Gay Byrne now! Well, this was something new and dangerous. This was practically revolution.

In Ireland, in the late 1970s, this was absolutely astounding talk. This was the decade when one million people – a third of the entire population of the state – had attended a Mass said by the Pope in Dublin's Phoenix Park. This was many years before Mary Robinson, or the introduction of divorce, or the legalisation for gay rights in Ireland. You could not legally buy a condom in Ireland in the late 1970s, never mind go on the television and talk so blithely about getting drunk and getting laid and hating priests and disliking your father. And although I liked my own father a great deal, Geldof's pungent cocktail of motor-mouth arrogance, somewhat unwise trousers and utter disrespect for authority really did appeal to me. In time, I couldn't get enough of it.

Soon after *The Late Late Show*, my friend Conor got a copy of the Boomtown Rats' first record and he taped it for me. It wasn't really punk. It wasn't punk at all, in fact, it was just souped-up rhythm and blues played with a lot of aggression. But there were some fantastic songs on it. 'Never Bite the Hand That Feeds' and 'Neon Heart', for instance. The music was raw, brimming with verve and a crisp visceral energy. But there were other things I admired about it. The songs were full of characters. I liked that. It made the songs seem like they were about real people. And there was a surprising facility for language, a gutsy pared-down approach to storytelling:

Sooner or later, the dawn came breaking
The joint was jumping and the walls were shaking
When Joey sneaked in the back door way
Pretending he was with the band, he never used to pay
He used to know all the people and know all the tricks
Used to lie up against the wall like he was holding up the bricks.

But on the Boomtown Rats' first record there was also a slow piano-based ballad called 'I Can Make It If You Can'. It was a tender song of vulnerability and longing. I kept the tape beside my bed, and I would put on 'I Can Make It If You Can' every morning as soon as I woke up. I felt that this was the voice of a survivor, a guy who knew about pain. I felt he was singing to me, and to people like me, and that there was an integrity to what he was singing about. I played the tape until it wore out and couldn't be played any more. And there were many mornings around that time, I don't mind saying it, when that song really helped me to get out of bed. I can make it if you can.

The thing is, I used to get very down in those days. It began as pretty typical adolescent stuff but it got steadily worse, until it got more serious, until it became real depression. I missed my brother and my two sisters. I missed my father more than I can say, and I wasn't getting on at all well with my mother. I was supposed to go and see my father every weekend, but my mother had gotten to the stage where she would simply not let me do this. She had begun to drink too much. She was also taking drugs, sleeping pills and tranquillisers of various kinds. She must have been enduring some dreadful pain, the poor woman, but at the time, I must say, I only cared about the suffering she was inflicting on me. Her temper, when she lost it, became ferocious and unpredictable. Sometimes she would even try to turn me against my father, and against my brother and sisters. She would insist that I was not to go and see my dad, and I would not, most of the time, because I wanted a quiet life. And often when we did meet – he won't mind me saying it – my father and I had to meet in secret. A father and son, having to meet in secret, in an Ireland that never tired of spouting platitudes about family values. It's a shame things had to be like that.

I was so full of fear in those days that I would often feel fear clenched up inside me, like a fist, literally, like a physical thing. My life sometimes felt meaningless. In time, it actually got so I could see very little future at all for myself. It is a terrible thing to feel so hopeless when you're so young, but I did for a while, and I have to tell you that honestly.

If my memory is inaccurate on this point, then I ask for forgiveness in advance. But thinking back now, I truly do not think that any teacher, priest or neighbour ever lifted a finger to help my family. There were three things, and three things only, which kept me going throughout my early years. Chief among these was the nurturing love and support of my father, which was constantly and unselfishly given to me and to my siblings, again and again throughout those years and since. He never abandoned me, despite what he was going through himself. The second was the support of my brother, my sisters, my stepmother and my friends. And the third was Bob Geldof.

I would listen to his song 'I Can Make It If You Can', and I would believe it. I simply felt that I could make it if Bob Geldof could. I was naive enough to think that, but I'm grateful now for the naivety of youth. I associated myself with Bob Geldof. He became a paradigm of survival, toughness and courage. He would never ever get ground down by anything, I felt, and thus, if I remembered that, neither would I. As time went on, I began to think more about Bob Geldof. It was the only thing I could do. I derived an active personal pleasure from everything the Boomtown Rats got up to. I bought everything they released – 'She's So Modern', 'Like Clockwork', then the album, *A Tonic for the Troops*. I really did think their success had something to do with me. I felt I was involved in it, inextricably linked to it, bound up with it in ways that nobody but I could understand. I felt they were singing to me. I thought of them as my friends, even though I had never met them. Isn't that funny?

In November 1978, anyway, the Boomtown Rats became the first-ever Irish group to get to the top of the British charts. On *Top of the Pops* that week, as he jabbered the words of 'Rat Trap' into his mike, Geldof shredded up a poster of Olivia Newton John and John Travolta, whose twee single 'Summer Nights' the Rats had just ousted from the number one slot. In school, my friends and myself were speechless with joy. Conor cut a photograph of Geldof out of *Hot Press* and we stuck it up in the

Hall of Fame, where the framed images of all the famous past pupils of the school had been hung. We stuck Bob up there, among the bishops and diplomats and politicians who had founded the state in which we lived. His gawky snot-nosed face fitted exactly over a photograph of President de Valera, and this fact had the kind of exotically cheap symbolism that appeals very greatly to fourteen-year-olds. It felt like a victory of sorts at the time, and if I am honest, it still does.

Soon after that, things in the life of my family began to worsen again. My mother took my father to court and somehow won back custody of my two sisters and my brother. It was a decision that would lead to great unhappiness for my family – some would say it was an amazingly stupid decision by the courts. But in holy Catholic Ireland, bizarre legal opinion too often takes precedent over the rights of terrified children, or it did then, at any rate. Things went from bad to worse in the house. There were constant rows, terrible arguments. My father was routinely and absolutely denied access to us, and nobody official ever did a thing to help him. And there was fear. We experienced terror, the four of us children. We never knew from one moment to the next how my mother would behave towards us. There were many times when she treated us well, with the affection and love that I know she had for us. But there were other times when she seemed to see us as enemies, and at those times, the atmosphere in the house was close to unbearable. I don't know how we got through it. I sure as hell couldn't do it now.

I listened to the Boomtown Rats all the time. I would listen to them for hours on end, and let them send me into a kind of comforting trance. 'I Don't Like Mondays', 'Diamond Smiles', I knew the words of their songs off by heart. I would recite them, over and over again in my head, over and over. There were many nights when I went to sleep with the words of 'I Don't Like Mondays' rattling around in my head, many mornings when I woke up still silently reciting them, like a prayer.

In December 1979, the Boomtown Rats came back to Ireland. They were supposed to play a big concert in a marquee in Leixlip, but they had been denied permission by the authorities at the last minute. The Boomtown Rats were seen as dangerous and anti-Establishment in Ireland, such was the murderous innocence of the times. The band took the authorities to court, and lost. That Christmas, my parents were back in court, too. I went along with my mother, but the judge told me to leave. When I came out of the court and into the huge circular hall of the Four Courts building in Dublin, I was upset and crying. An odd thing happened, then. Fachtna O'Ceallaigh, the Boomtown Rats' manager, was standing on the other side of the hall with his lawyers. I recognised him from the newspapers. His case was on at the same time as my parents' case. He was just standing there with his hands in his pockets, looking cool as fuck. He might have been wearing sunglasses, although I'm not sure. But I was very glad to see him standing there. I felt it was a good omen. It made me think of Bob.

Christmas was dreadful that year. Terrible. The atmosphere in the house was one of pure fear. Early in the new year the Rats released – unleashed would be a better word – the single 'Banana Republic', which deftly summed up their feelings about Ireland, by now feelings that coincided greatly with my own.

Banana Republic, septic isle
Suffer in the screaming sea
Sounds like die, die, die
Everywhere I go now
And everywhere I see
The black and blue uniforms
Police and priests.

It was a devastating attack on a society whose achievements in posturing cant and hypocrisy had so far outstripped its achievements in morality, and it was delivered with force and power, at a time when it needed to be so delivered. Nobody but Geldof would have had the guts to do it. I don't know how anyone else felt about it at the time, and to be absolutely frank,

I don't care. I admired Geldof for calling it the way he saw it, and I still do admire him for that.

But it was to be the last big single for the Boomtown Rats. Not long after 'Banana Republic', things started to wane. There were rumours of drug-taking in and around the band, I don't really know if they were true or not. One way or the other, I think the Rats simply began to lose their way as the tastes of the record-buying public started to change. But I still chart where I was in those days, and what I was doing, by remembering their singles. 'Elephant's Graveyard' was January 1981, the month after my parents' last court case. 'Go Man Go' was August 1981, just before my eighteenth birthday, the month my mother had to go into hospital for a fortnight.

We never told my father about my mother's absence. Instead, we stayed in the house by ourselves and we went pretty wild, my brother, my two sisters and I. We stayed up late, we did exactly what we liked, we painted the words BOOMTOWN RATS across the front doors of our garage. We were drunk with freedom. We practically trashed the house. We moved four mattresses into one room, and we slept there, with the door locked. That's the kind of dread we had. We left the Boomtown Rats on loud, almost all the time. That's what I remember now, the blankness in the eyes of my siblings, the intoxicating light-headedness of fear and freedom, the thud of the bass coming up through the floorboards, the nasal roar of Geldof's voice. When you are in trouble, it is odd where you find consolation.

When my mother came home from hospital, it was clear that things could never be the same again in the house. We had tasted something like liberation, and would not easily go back to being suppressed. One Sunday afternoon, three weeks after she came home, my two sisters ran away and returned to live with my father, where they were treated with the love, affection and respect they deserved. They never came back to Glenageary.

'Never in a Million Years' was released in November 1981, just after I started college. That month, things got too much for me at home and I moved out too. My father helped me to get a flat near college. I made some good friends in university but I wasn't happy. I had the habit of telling people barefaced lies in those days, for pretty much no reason at all. I think it was something to do with our former existence at home. It had been an environment where lies had become the norm for survival, and where the truth was often to be feared. So I hurt some of the new friends I had made by carrying this bizarre approach to the notion of truth out into the real world. I also felt ripped apart with guilt and self-loathing for leaving my brother. I sometimes went to meet him in the afternoons – he attended a school just down the road from the campus – but, as had been the case with my father, we had to keep our meetings secret. One day when I went to see him he had brought along the copy of *A Tonic for the Troops* which I had left in my mother's house on the day I had finally run away. That tore me to pieces, I don't know why.

'House on Fire' was released in February 1982, when I was going out with a girl called Grace Porter. 'Charmed Lives' was June the same year, just after we broke up. 'Nothing Happened Today' was August 1982, just after I finished my first-year exams. Almost everything that happened to me in those days, I am able to mark with a song by the Boomtown Rats. They may not be the greatest records ever made, but they're memorable to me, because they were involved with my life, and with the things I was doing, and with the people I knew and cared about.

The single 'Drag Me Down' came out in May 1984. I remember this, because I bought it one cold afternoon in Dun Laoghaire Shopping Centre, before getting the bus up to Glenageary to visit my mother. She was surprised to see me, she seemed pleased at first. We talked for a while, although I don't recall much about what was said.

I remember she asked me if I had a girlfriend now, and I said no, I didn't, for some reason, although in truth I did. I smoked a cigarette in front of her, and she was shocked that I was smoking. We had an argument, then, and we parted on bad terms. It was the last time I ever saw her. My mother died nine months later in a car crash. It was a Sunday morning. She was driving to Mass.

I went to Nicaragua that summer. I was utterly bewildered and confused about my mother's death. I couldn't really figure out what to feel about it, besides a grief of such depth that I couldn't understand it. I think I was probably a bit crazy, and longing to find some kind of frame into which I could fit the events of the last few years more clearly. So I ran away to Nicaragua to be by myself. I took a tape of the Boomtown Rats' last album, *In the Long Grass*, and also a tape of their last ever single, 'A Hold of Me'. In some ways I wanted to forget about home, and in other ways I wanted to remember every last thing.

But it's odd, the stuff that happens. One of the first people I met in Managua was Lynn Geldof, one of Ireland's leading journalists, and also, inter alia, Bob's sister. She's a terrific woman, very smart and bright and funny, and I was lucky enough to get to know her a little bit while I was there. Now, Bob had said some pretty critical things about his family life, but he hadn't ever spoken about Lynn much. I thought she was really lovely, and that Bob was very lucky to have a sister like that.

That was the summer of Live Aid. Many people with left-wing views were uncomfortable with the idea of the project, and I was one of them, I have to admit. I felt that charity wasn't the best way to deal with the problems of the developing world. Maybe I was right, maybe I was wrong, I don't know any more. Like Woody Allen said, don't ask me why there were Nazis, I can't even get the can-opener to work. What I do know is that Geldof was clearly motivated by nothing but humanity, and that if those critics on the Left who took cheap shots at him had displayed something like the same humanity, both in their criticisms and in their politics, the world would be a better place.

I came back to Ireland and returned to college. Slowly, gradually, things began to calm down a bit in my life. But I often thought about the old days, and sometimes when I did, the Boomtown Rats would come into my mind. Their career seemed to have petered out by that stage. Geldof was probably the most famous person in the world, but the band hadn't made a record in a long time, and they seemed to have no plans to do so.

And then, in May 1986, amid rumours that the band was about to call it a day for good, they came back to Dublin to play at a charity event, featuring Van Morrison, U2, The Pogues, Scullion, all the great and the good of the Irish rock world. The Rats played a stormer. They blew everyone away and received a tumultuous reception from the audience. After the main set, Geldof strolled up to the microphone for an encore. He seemed taken aback by the warmth of the crowd's affection. At first – unusually – he didn't seem to know what to say. He appeared a little lost as his eyes ranged over the crowd. 'Well, it's been a great ten years,' he muttered. 'So, rest in peace.'

The thundering drum roll began. The opening riff pounded out. The familiar chords: D, A, G, E. The last song the Boomtown Rats ever played in public was their first song, Geldof's hymn to snot-nosed anarchy and adolescent attitude, 'Looking After Number One'.

Don't give me love thy neighbour
Don't give me charity
Don't give me peace and love from your good lord above
I'M GONNA BE LIKE ME!!

It was at once a powerful homecoming, a stylishly ironic act of self-deprecation and a poignant farewell. And in some odd and quite profound sense, it seemed like a farewell to me, too, a final goodbye to a time in my life that was over now. As I watched the show on television that day, I knew that I would leave Ireland again soon, that I would not come back for a long time, that I would try to forget about most of my past.

I came to England four months after that. I went to Oxford to do a doctorate, didn't like it much, dropped out. I came to London then, decided to stay there because I liked its anonymity, its vast size. All the things that other people hated about London, I loved. It was a great place in which to get lost, and that's what I did for a while, just kept to myself and got lost.

Gradually I lost touch with my old school-friends. I had ups and downs in my personal life, times of great joy, too. I moved flat three or four times, and somewhere along the way I left behind all my old Boomtown Rats records. But I remember their force and power still, the healing power of their righteous indignation. And I suppose that sometimes the words don't seem quite as electrifying now as they did in Dalymount Park on a summer day when I was thirteen years old and breathless with discovery. But that doesn't bother me much. Because great pop music sometimes heals us in ways that we don't understand, or in ways that seem unbelievably trite or trivial when we look back. Great pop music is about the people who listen to it, and the circumstances in which they do so, and not really in the end about the people who make it. Maybe that's what's so great about it. I don't know.

A few years ago I wrote a novel called *Cowboys and Indians*, about the love of rock music, among other things. In the winter of 1991, after a reading I did in Dublin, a girl I used to know in the old days came up to me and said that my friend Conor, who had given me my first Boomtown Rats tape, was dead. Things hadn't worked out for him in Dublin, she said. He had left Ireland, like so many of the young people I knew. He had drifted around for a while, ended up in Paris, and been happy enough there. But then something bad had happened to him – she didn't know what exactly – and he had died.

I was so shocked. I could not believe what had happened. I had a lot to drink and I lay awake for hours, just thinking about the past, unrolling images from my childhood as though looking at a film. I cried that night. When finally I fell asleep I dreamed about poor Conor. Sometimes – very occasionally – I dream about him still, and when I do, it's always the same happy dream. I see his laughing shy face on the day we stuck the photograph of Bob Geldof up in the Hall of Fame in Blackrock College. I hear him whispering, 'Let's do it, Joe, come on, don't be afraid.' It's not the worst way to remember him. And I'm sure the Boomtown Rats are up on the wall in Blackrock College officially now. But we beat the authorities to it, me and my friend Conor. We beat them by a whole decade.

Two years ago, I was on a television programme in Ireland to talk about my novel, and Bob Geldof was one of the guests. I was extremely apprehensive about meeting him, because he had been such a hero of mine, and because he was connected to so many painful memories, I suppose, and, also, because I've met enough pop stars to know that they usually have the intelligence quotient of a piece of toast. But he was absolutely great. He had the air of a survivor. He seemed like a man who had come through.

In the green room after the show, he introduced me to his sister Cleo, and to his father. (He described his father as 'the real Bob Geldof'.) He was very polite to everybody, he made real efforts to include people in the conversation. We chatted for a while about nothing at all, his eyes flitting around the room as he talked, his hands running through his straggly hair. When the time came to go I asked him if he wanted to come out for a jar, but he said no. He was going out for a meal with his family. So we shook hands and he got his stuff together and sloped from the room with his father and his sister, a guitar case under his arm. It was like watching a part of your past walk out the door.

I never got the chance to tell him what was on my mind that night. There were too many people around, and, anyway, I suppose I hadn't really found the words I was looking for. But when I think about it now, what I wanted to say was actually very simple. It was this: I didn't have the worst childhood in Ireland by any means. I had some things that other kids could only have dreamed about. I had them because people who loved me worked hard and made sacrifices to ensure that I would, and for those blessings I am grateful and always will be. But there were bad things, too. There were dark days. I don't say it to blame or to hate, just to acknowledge that there were very dark days. Just to tell that truth. We in Ireland need to tell the truths of our past if we are to build up the decent and compassionate and merciful home that all our children deserve to live in. This country could be an absolutely wonderful place. For me, it wasn't always. And Bob Geldof helped me through. When I was a scared kid, who felt that there was little point to life, his music and his example were second only to the love of my father and my stepmother and my brother and sisters in keeping me going through all the terror and misery. It helped me survive. It helped me sit out the dark days, and wait for the better times to come. They did come. They often do. And I don't care whether nobody likes the music now. Tastes change, and times change, and so they should. Besides, a hell of a lot of people didn't like it then. But I did. Big time. His music embodied a world-view with which I felt I had some connection. It opened my eyes to things that had never occurred to me before. Like the greatest pop music, it was fun, unpredictable, alive, iconoclastic, intelligent, witty, danceable, tender when it wanted to be, tough as nails when it had to be. It just made me feel better. It healed. And it made me think I could make it, if *he* could. A foolish and adolescent belief, if ever there was one. But in a world where I had to grow up too fast, at least Bob Geldof and his band allowed me to be foolish and adolescent just once in a while.

I'm grateful indeed, for that little, or that much. I'm very grateful for that.

From
**The Last
of the Irish Males**
2002

Are YOU an Irish Male?

What a piece of work is a man! How noble in reason! How infinite in faculty! In form, in moving, how express and admirable. In action how like an angel! In apprehension how like a God! The beauty of the world! The paragon of animals!

William Shakespeare, *Hamlet*

Sometimes in the streets I am stopped by total strangers who recognise my finely chiselled features from the literary supplements, not to mention the Wanted posters, and who need to know if they too are Irish Males. You can usually tell the answer merely by looking at the questioner. If, for example, he is wearing the jacket from one suit and the trousers from another, and if both garments look like they've been recently washed in a washing machine, then the chances are probably fair to middling.

But tell me this. Are you an Irish Male? Do you believe a woman's place is in the home? That real men don't eat quiche? That boys don't cry? Do you pine for the dear old dirty days before metrosexuality made a mess of your mind? Here then is a simple questionnaire which will help you calculate your IQ (Irishmale Quotient). Simply select and tick the relevant answer; then, at the end, add up your points. (If you can't actually add, ask your mammy to do it for you. God knows, she does everything else for you.)

1) **Your idea of a good night out is:**
   a) fifteen pints of snakebite and a doner kebab with the lads.
   b) a romantic dinner for two with your girlfriend.
   c) a romantic dinner for two with someone else's girlfriend.

2) **Competitive sport is:**
   a) a barely veiled form of fascism.
   b) a pleasant-enough diversion but not to be taken too seriously.
   c) *Come on, United! MURDER the lousy bastards!*

3) **Given the choice of ten seconds of fellatio from Debbie Harry (circa 1979) or forty happy years of monogamy and fatherhood, you would choose:**
   a) the latter.
   b) the former, but absolutely hate yourself for it later.
   c) … er … is this a trick question?

4) **You wash your hair:**
   a) once a year when you bathe.
   b) every day when you shower.
   c) never, but you truly believe that if you don't wash it at all, it washes itself after a couple of weeks.

5) **Aerosol Deodorant is:**
   a) for girls.
   b) not really acceptable to those who are concerned about the environment.
   c) a midfield player with Dynamo Kiev.

6) **A friend is getting married and has asked you to organise his stag-night. Your ideal image of such an evening is:**
   a) a few beers, a curry and a bit of a chat.
   b) the world première of the new Brian Friel play.
   a) going to an abattoir to shoot cows.

7) **You like to discuss your feelings in an open, direct manner:**
   a) very frequently.
   b) very rarely.
   c) … huh?

8) **The last time you actually cried was when:**
   a) one of your parents died.
   b) Ireland so narrowly failed to qualify for the World Cup.
   c) you caught your pubic hair in your zipper.

9) **Physical contact with another male is acceptable:**
   a) at any time.
   b) in a boxing ring/rugby scrum/car-park fight.
   c) when he is giving you the Last Rites – and even then there should be witnesses present.

10) **The dishwasher is:**
    a) a useful domestic machine.
    b) a strange box-shaped object in the corner of the kitchen, the function of which you have never been able to work out.
    c) your pet name for the wife.

11) **The tumble-drier is:**
    a) a machine for drying laundered clothes.
    b) a 1920s dance craze.
    c) a sexual position.

12) **Sometimes you break down:**
    a) in tears of happiness.
    b) in tears of sadness.
    c) in your Hiace van on the Naas Dual Carriageway.

13) **Irony is:**
   a) the humourous or mildly sarcastic use of words to imply the opposite of what they actually mean.
   b) a powerful dramatic convention developed by the ancient Greeks.
   c) the art of ironing well (as practised by the Mammy).

14) **Sex without commitment is:**
   a) a meaningless experience.
   b) morally wrong.
   c) the perfect end to the perfect night.

15) **You want to get most women you meet into:**
   a) intelligent conversation.
   b) bed.
   c) a phonebooth.

16) **Your idea of helping out with domestic chores is:**
   a) dividing them up fairly and happily doing your share.
   b) opening your own bottles of beer.
   c) not flicking cigarette ash on the carpet.

17) **How often do you clean the toilet in your house?**
   a) very often.
   b) not quite as often as you know you should.
   c) never, but then again you pee in the sink, so why should you?

18) **Scruples is:**
   a) a subject that is worth thinking long and hard about.
   b) a question of knowing right from wrong.
   c) the name of a night-club in Mullingar.

19) **You would cheerfully enter your family's poodle:**
   a) in a beauty pageant for canines.
   b) in a Talented Pets contest.
   c) if nobody else was available at the time.

20) **Marriage is:**
   a) the bedrock of society.
   b) a word.
   c) a whole fucking sentence.

21) **The cornerstone of a successful marriage is:**
   a) good communication and a sense of humour.
   b) not getting caught and denying it if you do.
   c) apathy.

22) **Most of your previous girlfriends were:**
   a) sometimes difficult to understand.
   b) very nice people but it just didn't work out.
   c) inflatable.

23) **Your ideal woman is:**
   a) your Mammy.
   b) Saint Bernadette.
   c) Jackie Healy-Rae in a dress.

24) **The Clitoral Orgasm is:**
   a) a complete myth.
   b) often the subject of articles in *Cosmopolitan*.
   c) an important river in Central Bulgaria.

25) **Since you were fired for fraud, finances are a little tight. Your seven-month pregnant partner suggests a part-time job might be the answer. Do you:**
   a) agree and immediately start applying for interviews.
   b) resist and say you're not feeling well.
   c) say 'Ah, Jayzus, love, I couldn't ask you to do that'.

26) Cunnilingus is:
a) an intimate and exciting form of foreplay.
b) a mortal sin that makes the Virgin Mary cry.
c) a sub-division of Ireland's national airline.

27) Your favourite sexual position is:
a) y'know … the usual one.
b) the other one.
c) either of the above, but with your socks still on.

28) What do you do immediately after sex?
a) hold your partner tenderly and whisper soft words of love.
b) roll over and go to sleep.
c) ask for the loan of your bus-fare home.

29) Children are:
a) a blessing in a marriage.
b) sometimes demanding, but ultimately a source of wonderful joy.
c) the reason you can't lie in bed scratching your arse until lunchtime any more.

30) Lesbianism is:
a) a perfectly valid lifestyle choice.
b) morally repugnant and deeply sinful.
c) well-worth paying to see performed live.

Now add up your points and consult the following table:

Q1 (a)2 (b)0 (c)1		Q16 (a)0 (b)1 (c)2
Q2 (a)0 (b)1 (c)2		Q17 (a)1 (b)0 (c)2
Q3 (a)0 (b)1 (c)2		Q18 (a)0 (b)1 (c)2
Q4 (a)1 (b)0 (c)2		Q19 (a)1 (b)0 (c)2
Q5 (a)1 (b)0 (c) 2		Q20 (a)0 (b)1 (c)2
Q6 (a)1 (b)0 (c)2		Q21 (a)0 (b)1 (c)2
Q7 (a)0 (b)1 (c)2		Q22 (a)2 (b)2 (c)2
Q8 (a)0 (b)2 (c)1		Q23 (a)1 (b)0 (c)2
Q9 (a)0 (b)2 (c)1		Q24 (a)0 (b)1 (c)2
Q10 (a)0 (b)2 (c)1		Q25 (a)0 (b)2 (c)1
Q11 (a)0 (b)0 (c)0		Q26 (a)1 (b)1 (c)1
Q12 (a)1 (b)0 (c)2		Q27 (a)0 (b)1 (c)2
Q13 (a)0 (b)1 (c)2		Q28 (a)1 (b)0 (c)2
Q14 (a)1 (b)0 (c)2		Q29 (a)0 (b)1 (c)2
Q15 (a)0 (b)2 (c)1		Q30 (a)0 (b)0 (c)5

More than 40 points: You are so Irish Male that you should probably seek immediate counselling or apply for a sex-change operation. The chances of you ever forming a stable relationship – and by that I don't mean 'with a horse' – are really very slim indeed unless you mend your ways immediately. You suffer from low self-esteem, and correctly so. You have all the attractiveness of a tape-worm in Doc Martens and your intelligence is on a par with that of mayonnaise. Have you ever considered living in a cave? You probably should. If the bats and dung-beetles would let you in.

Between 20 and 39 points: You seem to be a reasonably well-adjusted fellow. Yes, you have your moments of drunkenness, sloth and goatish lechery, but in general you are calm, charming, in touch with your feelings, polite, restrained and frequently, if not comprehensively, washed. With a little effort you could have a career in politics.

Between 10 and 19 points: A New Man such as yourself is so rare that you should be in a glass-case in the National Museum. Several of my sisters would like to meet you.

Less than 10 points: You *are* actually a man, are you?

Flatley Will Get You Nowhere

Lady readers will find this difficult to believe, but it used to be thought that the Irish Male was not good at dancing. Yes, I know, it is almost impossible to credit, and yet, believe me, that was the case. The muscular coordination and sheer physical grace he employed to such devastating effect upon the hurling pitch or handball alley seemed to desert him inside the night-club. Nor was the happy agility he displayed when scuttling up a mountainside after a lost sheep ever observable on premises licensed for the jitterbug, jive or boogaloo. God moved in mysterious ways, and so did His finest creation – the Irish Male.

Perhaps the strobe-lights put him off. (I mean the Irish Male, not God.) Perhaps he was exhausted from his hard day struggling with the silage. Perhaps it was what happened when he found the sheep that wore him out and sapped his vitality. (For in certain parts of rural Ireland the truth of the Good Book is often quoted: *The one sheep that was lost hath now been found. PARTY TIME!*)

Many theories were formerly advanced to explain the Irishman's strange ungraciousness. Whatever the cause, the effect was not good. An Irishman dancing was like a rhinoceros doing yoga. Ungainly, unnatural – yet horribly compelling to look at.

Understandably the Irish Male was written-off as a non-dancer. Lacking the swerve of the Italian or the strut of the Frenchman, out of step with the civilised world, Pat was doomed to a life of cruel mockery, dismissed by hoofers everywhere as choreographically illiterate. But then, a few years ago, anthropologists began to re-examine the evidence, in particular the intricate patterns of Irish Male night-club behaviour. Dusty textbooks were scrutinised, experts consulted. Field trips were undertaken to the Irish Midlands, that region known in academia as 'Darwin's Waiting Room'. And so it came to pass that the scholars discovered an absolutely astounding fact about the nocturnal activities of *homo erectus Hibernicus*.

He was dancing all along – *but in his own unique way!*

Yes, he was dancing to a different drum. Not for him the Twist, the Watusi or the Mashed Potato. He scoffed at the Pogo, the Tango and Mambo, he barred the Beguine, the Bolero and Body-Pop. These were ugly shufflings, hideous foreign gyrations, un-Christian lurchings designed to corrupt. The Irish Male had devised his own wholesome dances, and today we are happy to share those with you.

The Bar-Prop

This strangely beautiful form of Irish Male dance is usually performed by a herd of younger specimens, but is sometimes attempted individually. The male enters the night-club and hauntingly staggers for the bar. There, in a movement as swift as it is subtle, he leans quickly forward, rests his elbows on the woodwork, and pertly sticks his bottom out, often to rapturous and prolonged applause. Poignantly he raises his eyes to the television screen. There they remain for the rest of the night. This is a tremendously difficult position to maintain (particularly while drinking heavily), but a really well-trained ballerino can keep it up for days at a time, even while making regular overtures to the bar-person.

The Lep With The Lads

A large rowdy circle of young native Irish Males performs this ancient tribal dance, which is part mating-display, part initiation ceremony and part fully fledged football riot. Details of costume are vitally important here. Each brave will know the ritual's intricacies, having learnt them as a nipper on his grandfather's knee. Neckties are removed and affixed about the head. The jumper is whipped off, the arms knotted loincloth-style around the waist. (In extreme cases, the trousers may go too.) The shirt is opened right down to the navel, revealing the obligatory grey string vest given by the Mammy last Christmas. Then it's on with the Quo and away we go!

> *DOWN DOWN, DEEPER AND DOWN*
> *DOWN DOWN, DEEPER AND DOWN*
> *GET DOWN, DEEPER AND DOWN*
> *DOWN DOWN, DEEPER AND DOWN*

Ah, the Yeatsian delicacy of the lyrics.

The main feature of the dance is that the feet do not actually leave the ground, but remain firmly planted while the body jigs rhythmically up and down, enabling the blubber to slap the ribcage in time with the music. Grunts, barks and ululations are optional. The head rocks vigorously back and forth, filling the air with a blizzard of dandruff. As for the more detailed upper-body movements – the arms are used either to clutch the most adjacent Irish Male or thrash one's invisible Stratocaster.

Brief respectful invocations of each other's tribal ancestors are often chanted, for example 'Hey, Leppo, yer granny's a fookin' ride.'

The Lunge of Love

This is an exquisite and enchanting form of Irish courtship *pas-de-deux*, performed by an Irish Male and Female who have only just met. The two partners modestly slow-dance for a time, all the while making polite chat about such light-hearted matters as the affairs of the nation, their musical tastes and whether frequent attendance at these premises has become customary –

'So tellus, love, jeh cum here often?' The initial stage being properly completed, the male delicately approaches; the female retreats with maidenly modesty. The man shimmies forward again, the movement courtly and elegant. His hands respectfully move southwards and clench her buttocks. Firmly she removes them. The moment has come. He LUNGES forward and deftly inserts his slab-like tongue in her mouth, wiggling, waggling, probing, poking. The movement is completed with the traditional knee in the balls and that ancient ceremony known as the Calling of the Guards.

The One-Handed Celtic Urinal Shimmy

This is the Irish Male equivalent of 'The Dying Swan', a poignant and desperately moving hymn to existential suffering. Though it may just as easily be attempted in the privacy of the home – indeed it often is in mine – the usual venue for this deeply affecting dance is the male public lavatory of the average Irish night-club. Enter quietly any weekend evening around midnight and you will see it in all its pitiful glory.

There he is, the Irish Male, swaying at the urinal, much the worse for strong drink. One hand is firmly clamped to the wall in front of him, fingers splayed in an attempt to gain purchase; the forehead may also rest against the tiles and the tongue may hang out a bit and drool. The body is slowly rocked from side to side; the knees sag, the shoulders slump. Soft groans of distress add to the profound sense of tragedy. The performance even has a religious dimension – 'Jayzus Mary and Jozeph,' he moans devoutly, 'I'll never fookin' dhrink aghain, I swear.' He begins to swallow hard, his abject face turning forty shades of green, until – '*Bwaaaaaaawwwghgh-ghgghhghgh*!' With that piteous mantra, full catharsis is achieved (all down his shirt and tie).

The Space-Cadet

This is another piece for the soloist, possibly related to the 'Sundance' ritual of many Native-American tribes, though it is mentioned in the annals of ancient Ireland and was often performed by Cuchullain himself.

All these centuries later the mystical dance is still performed. The young Irish Commanche, having smoked perhaps too deeply from the pipe of peace, totters to the very centre of the dancefloor and begins rotating in ever decreasing circles, waving his arms like a windmill gone mad and crying gaily at the top of his voice 'Fatboy Slim! Fatboy Slim!' until the security staff are called to put him out.

The Father of the Bride

This dance, an essential part of the Irish nuptial ceremony, is exclusively reserved for weddings. In it, the bride's father performs a holy rite of abject self-humiliation as a sign of his continuing love for his daughter. The dance traditionally commences with a courteous cry from the singer/drum-machine-operator of the wedding band: 'Hey, baldy, get up there now and give us a twirl.'

At this point the poor man struggles to his feet, as the wedding band – 'Boogie Knights' or 'Hi-Way Star' – strikes up the opening recitative of that beloved Irish traditional tune 'Amhrán na Éan' ('The Birdie Song'). The important thing is for the dancer to possess absolutely no sense of rhythm whatsoever, rather to display all the grace of an octopus on dry land as he disco-dances with one of the hefty bridesmaids. From time to time he clicks his fingers in the air, gestures which bear no relation at all to the beat of the music. Sometimes he shakes his bottom from side to side, inducing loud mirthful roars from the assembled guests. Elements of flamenco are often in evidence, particularly in the playing of invisible castanets. Occasionally the bride's father also attempts to incorporate 'the twist', which was all the rage back when he was young in the late 1400s. The dance concludes with violent jeering, gratuitous flash photography and bottle-throwing.

The Walls of Limerick

This fine old dance brings together the corps-de-ballet of Irish Males for a rousing finale to any evening. In deceptively simple formation they totter to a wall and in unison graciously urinate up and down the side of it, while singing a lusty chorus of 'The Fields of Athenry'.

Now you know how to dance like an Irish Male. So git on up! (I know I do.)

The Irish Male:
A User's Manual

It was the great Leo Nikolayevich Tolstoy who wrote: 'All Irish Males can be a pain in the ass; but each Irish Male can be a pain in the ass *in his own way.*'

Women readers will sadly concur. They will know that living with an Irish Male is on very rare occasions not the blissful paradise it customarily is. He is by nature a solitary beast – really he lives inside his own shell. If the Italian is a stallion, the Irishman is a tortoise. (Witness his remarkable fondness for hibernation, especially on mornings when the bins must be taken out.) Not that there is anything wrong with that either, for as devotees of the fabulous Aesop can attest, even the tortoise may gain in the end. Mainly by cheating and lying, but that's another story.

But yes, the Irish Male finds it hard to converse in an open fashion. Compared to him, a brick is eloquent. Thus he finds sharing his thoughts and emotions almost impossible. This reticence came home to me forcefully a short time ago when a close friend I have known since my difficult childhood confessed that he had fallen passionately in love with me. 'But you can't be gay,' I said in amazement. 'We used to go out to night-clubs together looking for girls.'

'Jesus,' he said. 'I thought we were dating.'

You see what I mean? The Irish Male does not notice silent signals. His social antennae are not finely tuned. Misunderstanding is the sea through which he haplessly paddles, with only his bafflement and incomprehension for armbands.

If confusion and lack of empathy were his only real crimes, the Irish Male might reasonably ask for the benefit of the emotional probation act. But alas, there are several more additions to the charge sheet. When it comes to the business of courtship, for example, the Irish Male has a lot to learn. It isn't that he is unromantic, as such. It is just that your average Irishman, when pursuing a woman, is a bit like a dog chasing after a car. He wouldn't really know what to do if she stopped. Yes, as they age, they gain a bit of experience. It is a well-known fact that older Irishmen can keep matters going for longer in bed. But then again, when you really think about it, who wants to shag an old man for a long time?

So, ladies, if you must live with an Irish Male – and please do ask yourself whether there are not real alternatives, such as emigration, lesbian separatism or entering a convent – there are a few points which are well worth remembering.

Being an Irish Male myself, I forget them all. But here are some I made up earlier.

The Irish Male Is Always Right

It is a surprising but well-established biological fact that the part of an Irish Male's brain which admits to making mistakes (the *cortex maximus apologeticus*) actually shrinks during early adolescence, finally disappearing around the age of fifteen. How this happens we don't quite know – and obviously if we did we wouldn't tell YOU – but by his mid-teens the cortex has been entirely replaced by the frontal rationalisation lobe and the cranial utter-denial node (*cerebellia non mea culpa, honestus*). Parents can tell this has begun to happen to their teenage sons when they start saying things like 'It wasn't my fault I burned down the school' or 'I know I tattooed the baby, but she was asking for it'.

As the Irish Male achieves what is euphemistically called

maturity, a new sponge-like tissue called the evasionary gland develops (*glandus irresponsibilius et molto stupidissima*) until it fills almost half the cranial cavity by the late-twenties. (Its growth seems to become much more pronounced immediately after mating.) Again, there are a number of tell-tale verbal signs, e.g., 'Look, I don't see what we're doing as going out together, as such. We're just having a large number of consecutive one-night stands.' Or, 'All right, so I slept with your mother and showed the photographs to my friends, but I only did it twice and it didn't mean anything.'

As the years roll on, the evasionary gland swells even further. By the time the Irish Male is thirty, it will have expanded to fill his whole head, resulting in his widely noted inability to listen. It's not that he doesn't *want* to listen, it's just that his ears are under severe pressure. By now he is biologically programmed for utter pomposity and self-righteousness and may even have embarked on a career in the church or literary criticism. Once this happens there is really no cure, although a stake through the heart at a crossroads at midnight may be worth an attempt.

So now you women can see why we Irishmen have a problem admitting we're wrong. That's right. It's not our fault. In fact it's probably yours. So really, you should show a bit more understanding. We Irish Males are victims of our own biology. And it isn't as though we're not making an effort. Take myself, for example. I often point out to my wife that whenever I *am* wrong I immediately admit it. It is just that I am never wrong. But even if I were, I would be right to be wrong. And she would be wrong for questioning that. And I would be right to point that out. And she would be wrong if she didn't agree. And we find this approach works quite well for us. At least we did, until she divorced me.

The Irish Male Is Fond Of Cursing

OK, OK, you have a point here. If they took the four-letter words out of the English language, most Irishmen would be fucking speechless. But this love of effing and beeing shouldn't be taken too seriously. It is only a form of affectionate punctuation.

I remember once being in a pub in Dublin – all the other times I don't remember at all – where I witnessed an extraordinary scene. A man was sitting alone at the bar, deep in mystical contemplation of his pint, when the door opened and another fellow, bedecked from head to toe in black, entered the premises unobserved by the former. The new arrival crept up to My Nabs at the bar and quickly tapped him thrice on the shoulder. The philosopher turned, a smile of surprise and delight playing about his lips.

'Would yeh FOOK OFF, yeh fat fooker-yeh,' he happily cried. 'I haven't seen yeh in BLAYDIN' AGES!'

Only in Ireland do men greet each other thus. Although even making allowances for local cultural idiosyncracies, I thought it was a bit much to talk to an Archbishop like that.

You Will Never *Ever* Compete With His Mammy

Look at her, the fossilised old reptile. You hate her, don't you? With a pure, clean, WHITE-HOT kind of hatred. Look at her thoughtfully stroking her beard. Making little comments about the dinner you've cooked. Sitting there in her Christmas party hat. Frightening the children. Frightening the dog.

Hallelujah.

Behold – His Mother.

God in heaven, look at the state of it. Face like a bag of rusting spanners. You wouldn't say she was ugly exactly, but last time you saw her she had potato-sacks over two of her heads.

And it's *ALL HER FAULT*, what you have to put up with. It was she who raised your so-called husband to be the incapable dweeb he is. She's as bonkers as he is anyway. Bloody madwoman. Treacherous COW! When she finally dies, there'll be one minute's violence. Smile at her. Offer her some gravy. That's right, have some more, you vile ugly hippo. Oh? You think it's a bit lumpy, do you? Dear, oh dear. How very sad.

You hope it bloody CHOKES her, the vicious troglodyte.

Remember the second time you went out with him? What did he say when you asked him back for coffee? That's right.

'Oh ... urm ... The Mammy wouldn't like it.'

'I wasn't asking your Mammy,' you pointed out.

That was your first-ever row, wasn't it?

Look at her, the evil conniving baggage. Pretending she 'doesn't really drink' when she'd get down on all fours and suck the amontillado out of the shag-pile if you spilled a drop. Remember how she ruined your wedding day? Had to be the centre of attention, didn't she? Had to have everything her own way, despite the fact that you paid! Because he – her useless, brainless GOM of a son – spent all his wedding savings on *gravelling her driveway*.

You know she gives out about you behind your back, don't you? When he's driving her home, when he's taking her shopping, when he's painting her house, when he's mowing her lawn. She doesn't like how you bring up the kids. Doesn't like the shirts you buy him. Doesn't like the fact that you work. Doesn't like ANYTHING, EVER.

And you know what's coming next, right? Oh yes you do, come on, don't pretend. *He wants her to come and live with you!* Yes, he's been building up to it, bit by bit. You know that sneaky way he goes on, the low coward. Can't bear to say it out like a man, just tries the occasional pluck on your heartstrings. How she 'isn't that bad when you get to know her'. How you'd 'have to laugh at the way she goes on'. How lonely she feels now his father is gone, kicking around by herself in that house full of memories. (Not that his father's *dead* or anything. He's just bloody GONE. And who could blame him?)

Well she can get a bloody tenant in, because she's not coming here. No WAY. Over your dead body. You'll even help her put the ad in the paper. You've thought up the wording already. ROOM MATE WANTED – MUST BE HEAVY SLEEPER WITH POOR SENSE OF SMELL.

Oh? Surprise, surprise. She doesn't like the way you've done the parsnips. Go on. Pick up the turkey and brain her with it. The judge will understand. You'll get time off for good behaviour. Go on. Right in the kisser. You know you want to. Yes. Do it now. *DRUMSTICK THE WITCH!*

The Irish Male Believes He Is Good At DIY

You know the story. You have seen it unfold.

Normally your adult Irish Male cannot be roused to vacate the sofa, except if the house is actually on fire. If he gets off his backside to dander down the end of the garden, he nearly sends you a postcard saying WISH YOU WERE HERE.

But once in a while, a strange thing happens to him – do not argue, it is the call of the wild. There is nothing you can do, this is something quite primal. (It is often brought on by the vernal equinox.) He will start expressing a frightening desire to repair or refurbish things around the house. If that occurs, and it almost certainly will, you should move children or pets off the property immediately.

Yes, you are confused, and you are right to be. He knows nothing at all about manual labour and precious little about labour of any kind. The phrase 'Good With His Hands' was not coined for this man. (Not in *any* sense, if you know what I mean.) But all of a sudden he is rummaging around in the garage for a hammer, borrowing a bricklayer's hod from a chap across the road, speaking with the authoritativeness of Isambard Kingdom Brunel about joists and flanges and lengths of four-by-two.

You point out that you only need that dodgy bookshelf in the living room straightened. Really you can do it yourself. But look at him, the monster, as he reaches for his spirit level. Observe the patronisingly understanding smile. 'If a job is worth doing, dear, it's worth doing properly. So off you toddle and make me a sandwich. And don't be worrying your pretty little head. This' – he brandishes his tool – 'is MEN'S WORK.'

Away to the kitchen you retreat with the children. You try to

distract them but the poor wains are crying. The terrible thud-
ding, the whine of the drill, the shrieks, imprecations and dark
Satanic oaths – it keeps them awake for several nights; you would
swear he was building the ark in there. Finally, a week later, he
flings open the door. Bruised, bleeding, bog-eyed with exhaustion,
his arm in a tourniquet improvised from a cushion-cover, he looks
as if he has undergone ten rounds with Mike Tyson.

'Woe-man,' he grunts. 'Must come. See my work. Ungh.'

You enter what used to be your living room. There is a large
star-shaped hole in the gable wall. The ceiling has collapsed and
the carpet is in shreds. A drumlin of rubble has obliterated the
sofa. The floorboards have been ripped up to serve as
scaffolding. Water is gushing down the chimney. You have
bribed the children not to cry, but when they see the devastation
they just can't hold back. By now he is standing beside the
bookshelf, fingering his spanners and screwdrivers and pliers. He
raises the drill and coolly blows on the bit-end – the gunslinger
who drove Wild Bill from the town.

'That's a nice piece of work if I say so myself,' he avers. 'And
when you think of all the money we've saved.' He runs his
fingertips lightly along the shelf. It immediately collapses,
sending the Waterford Glass bowl you inherited from your
grandmother into a spin across the room, where it shatters into
a thousand shards, one of which takes an eye out of the cat.

'Of course,' he continues, 'the drill was defective. And
anyway, Tiddles had it fucking coming.'

The Irish Male Knows All About Packing

This is the source of many a domestic altercation, but in fairness
the Irish Male can't be blamed for it all. His female companion
is equally guilty, if not more so. (*See Section 1 – He Is Never
Wrong.*)

When presented with the prospect of vacational travel, she
feels she must pack every single item of clothing she possesses. It
does not matter that you two are going to Majorca in the middle

of July. She *needs* those woollen long-johns and tea-cosy hats. And even if she doesn't, *you never know.*

Her suitcase is stuffed to bulging point. For even a one-night stay at a wedding down the country the following items will be *sine-qua-non* for the Irish Female: sandals, dresses, eiderdowns, hats, lotions, potions, mixed emotions, fifteen pairs of shoes, hot-water bottle, make-up, lipstick, tights, socks, intimate garments, sun cream, moisturiser, mosquito repellant, mosquito attractant, diarrhoea pills, cough bottle, whalebone corset, photographs of children, hair of the dog, rub of the relic, complete and unabridged works of my good friend Marian Keyes.

The Irish Male, on the other hand, tends towards the opposite extreme. He is by nature a light traveller. On a four-year expedition up the Amazon he would take along a change of socks and a copy of *The Racing Post*. And he mightn't even bother with the change of socks.

Here, as in all things, compromise is the solution. Simply agree never to go on holiday. It is far too stressful and not worth the money.

The Irish Male Will Not Communicate Openly

In his ground-breaking study 'Towards A Psychology of Being' (1962) the great psychologist Abraham Maslow expounded his theory of 'the hierarchy of prepotency' as a means of explaining human motivations. Observing that 'man is a wanting animal' he argued that 'one desire is no sooner satisfied than another takes its place'. To give his theory graphic force, he famously represented human needs as a pyramid. At the broad bottom of the triangle he placed absolutely essential physical requirements such as shelter, food, water and warmth. Higher up the narrowing pyramid he represented the higher yearnings, such as love of beauty, appreciation of the arts, spiritual awareness and so forth, leading finally to the apex – complete self-actualisation. But Maslow ran into trouble when attempting to apply his theories to the Irish Male. Indeed, as he wrote to a renowned colleague, Dr Rollo May, on 9 June, 1948: ... 'even my "Human Pyramid" itself becomes totally inadequate to explain the basic components which the Irish Male requires for a fulfilled existence. I believe, old friend, that I shall have to construct another diagram, especially for him.'

Sadly Maslow died before he could publish his research on Irishmen. But here, for the first time, is his previously unknown representation of Irish Male interests, which the great scholar labelled 'The Irishman's Christmas Tree':

Me.

Beer.

The lads. The Mammy.

Sandwiches. Sky Sports. Occasional ride.

Pub football team. Clean pair of drawers of a Monday.

Old reruns of *Starsky and Hutch*. Acute and frequent

hypochondria.

Porn stash under the floorboards.

The budgie

The dog

The kids

Navel fluff

Oh yeah ... the wife

The Irish Male Can Be Sarcastic

OK, I admit it.

But I like people who are sarcastic. I don't know why. Yes, sarcasm is the lowest form of wit, but if you think about it, the individuals who tell you this so confidently usually don't possess *any* form of wit. The people who tell you this usually think that politicians who are rabidly opposed to asylum seekers 'have a point really, when you think about it' and worse, that 'at least they're stimulating debate'. Stimulating bloody debate! As though *that* excuses anything. Good God. If Hitler had only thought to say he invaded Poland 'to stimulate debate' his face would be on the Euro now.

But anyway. As the Third Epistle of Saint Michael to the Jaggeraguans tells us, 'You can't always get what you want. But if you try sometimes, you can get what you need.' So it is with humour. Some kinds are better than others. Yes, a brilliantly Wildean epigram incorporating a series of multilingual puns and several allusions to Greek mythology is what we must aim for at all times. But no power in the world has quite the devastating force of a simple 'Oh yeah, really' delivered at just the right moment and with just the right degree of sceptical detachment.

Think about it. For example, when His Holiness, Pope John Paul II, told us young people of Ireland that he loved us, if we had all chanted back in one great big saracastic roar 'OH YEAH, *SURE* YOU DO' instead of bursting into a spontaneous chorus of 'He's Got The Whole World In His Hands', the course of modern Irish history would have been radically changed. (Those were more innocent days, of course, when the whole world was *all* we suspected leading churchmen had in their hands.)

I remember, when I was much younger, going out with a girl who was never sarcastic. It was great. Well, no it wasn't, I'm being sarcastic. We would enter some dubious pub where the glasses had not been cleaned in several centuries, where the clientele was so cheesy it could have been melted down and spread on toast, where the malodorous barman looked like he shaved regularly with a piece of sandpaper – in fact there was more toilet paper hanging from his chin than there was in the men's jacks. I would say, 'Wow, this is a bit of a palace, isn't it?' And she would say, 'God, really? You reckon? I think it's pretty disgusting actually.'

For a while I think I must have found this charming. Sometimes when we fall in love, what we are attracted to is the seemingly artless public display of qualities we could never dream of acquiring ourselves. Perhaps I was still in that phase of retarded adolescence where the dream of being, y'know, a complete person, still held some kind of spurious validity. I was attracted to this woman because she 'believed' in things I didn't. Like 'nature'. We would be strolling down the street and she would start going on about flowers, leaves, little birdies, dogshit, the planet, etcetera. I would start going on, sarcastically I must admit, about how little birdies should be hollowed out and turned into carpet slippers. And she would laugh. And I would be more sarcastic. And that was how we related to each other.

After a time, though, her innocent sincerity, her total lack of sarcasm, started to drive me screaming mad. We would be sitting there skulling into a take-away vindaloo and watching *George and Mildred* on the telly (yes, I know how to show a gal a good time). Then said dismal sitcom would end and I'd say, 'Bleedin' *hilarious*, huh?' to which she would smile sweetly and respond, 'I didn't think it was funny at all really'. And at that point I would start chewing the nearest light-bulb.

The poor girl. We would sit up late at night discussing 'God', a fictional character whose many exploits she was fond of relating. At this stage I had honed my sarcasm to the point where I could dismiss millennia-old belief systems with a scarcely discernible raising of one eyebrow. I told myself I looked like Jeremy Paxman, but, actually, I must have looked like a fat Alvin Stardust.

In the end I decided to deal with my sarcasm by being more open about my emotions. I confronted her, saying, 'Listen, I know I'm sarcastic sometimes, but really you mean an awful lot to me.' She smiled and said she was breaking it off with me anyway, to take up with some Aran-wearing ornithologist geek she'd met at a born-again Christian prayer meeting. A charismatic, she said. Reader, let me tell you candidly, I had thought hurling was a Gaelic sport until that moment. I mean, you should have MET this guy. How anyone could use the adjective 'charismatic' about him is still, after all these years, a mystery which for me is right up there with the Blessed Trinity. But anyway. There I go being sarcastic again. One of these days I better try to give it up.

Yeah. Right. Sure I will.

BELIEVE IN YOURSELF! Our highly sophisticated computer system can DEFINITELY have you out dating TONIGHT — or at least in the quite near future, possibly. And that is ABSOLUTELY GUARANTEED!

Mr B Ahern of Dublin wrote, 'Dear Idiot, How can I ever thank you for helping me find love at last.' Garda Sergeant Boris Ossory (retired) of Co Laois joked, 'Tears of happiness are trickling down my cheeks — and my new wife's!' Dr JP Magillycuddy of The Reeks, Listowel, said, 'On my knees I BEG you to accept my life-savings in appreciation for all you have done in brightening the boreen of my existence with the headlamps of love.' These are extracts from GENUINE LETTERS not made up by our receptionist Bridie during her lunch-hour. (Names have been changed for reasons of honesty.) And we have THOUSANDS MORE too humourless to mention.

As soon as we receive your remittance we will waste no time in IMMEDIATELY ~~spending it on drink~~ rushing you a carefully selected list of fascinating single women, any one of whom would be a privilege to know. If you are not LITERALLY ONE HUNDRED AND TEN PER CENT HAPPY with our service, we will refund your money WITHOUT DELAY, IN TOTAL, NO QUESTIONS ASKED.***

AT IDIOT© WE CARE. SO YOU DON'T HAVE TO!

So go on. Take a few moments to change your life. Because hey, Mister — you know you deserve it.

(Send cash only. Cheques and butter vouchers will NOT be accepted.)

*** some terms and conditions may apply

Your Details

Mr _____

Address _____

Age (mental and physical) _____

Prisoner Number _____

I am SERIOUSLY interested in changing my life and finding true and everlasting love with an Idiot©.

☐ Yes

☐ No (tick appropriate box)

I understand that in the interests of finding REAL LOVE, I am hereby waiving all the legal rights to which I am entitled under the Protection of Consumers Act, 1971.

☐ Yes

☐ No thank you, I wish to remain unloved and lonely

(Tick appropriate box)

Marital Status

☐ Single

☐ Widowed

☐ Divorced

☐ Christian Brother

Education

☐ Primary

☐ Secondary

☐ University

☐ None – but vague feeling of superiority anyway

Build

☐ Scrawny

☐ Boringly average

☐ Fat

☐ Gargantuan

Eyes

Please indicate number ——

 Green

☐ Blue

☐ Red

☐ Glass

Your Degree of Attractiveness

☐ Preternaturally hideous

☐ Plain

☐ Barely presentable

☐ A fecking lash

Your Logical Reasoning Skills

a) The opposite of 'happiness' is:

☐ Woe

☐ Misery

☐ Despair

☐ United losing

b) The opposite of 'woe' is:

☐ Happiness

☐ Joy

☐ Delight

☐ Giddy-up

Your Personality

If you *have* a personality, tick which traits closely describe you. If you don't have one, you needn't worry; our Director-General has multiple personalities and we'll loan you one he isn't using.

 Conventional

☐ Eerie

☐ Intense

☐ Groping

☐ Catatonic

☐ Rampant
☐ Self-destructive
☐ Dishonest

Your Interests

Please tick for a liking, cross for a dislike, or leave blank for no preference:

☐ Wining and Dining
☐ Whining and Pining
☐ Strangling small woodland creatures
☐ Cinema
☐ Nose picking
☐ Politics/History
☐ Pets
☐ Farmyard animals (please state if you have a conviction)
☐ Mixing with friends (if any)
☐ Current affairs
☐ Extramarital affairs
☐ Biting your toenails
☐ Gardening
☐ Music
☐ Pleasant conversation
☐ Unpleasant conversation
☐ Other

Your Attitudes

Tick for yes, cross for no or leave blank if you don't feel strongly:

☐ I am looking for an old-fashioned girl
☐ I am looking for a sophisticated modern woman
☐ Anything in a skirt would do me just fine (except a Scotsman)
☐ Even a Scotsman might be all right
☐ I just haven't met the right girl yet
☐ I met the right girl but she happened to be a nun
☐ I am ready for a serious, committed relationship

☐ All my friends are married so I may as well be too
☐ No way am I desperate, absolutely NOT
☐ OK, OK, I'll take the bloody Scotsman

Your Ideal Partner

☐ Nymphomaniac recently released from solitary confinement
☐ High priestess of Babelonia
☐ Lollipop lady
☐ Student nurse, masseuse and part-time Wonderbra girl
☐ Lash-wielding Mistress of Utter Submission (Limerick only)
☐ Daily communicant
☐ Andrea Corr
☐ All of the Corrs simultaneously (Jim optional)
☐ Six-pack of Heineken and twenty fags

Please send your completed survey and cash to: IDIOT, New Bribeland Books (Offshore Account) Ltd, c/o Ansbacher Holdings, 71 Rue Traynor, Jersey 417 NQA (No questions asked. And none answered either.)

Faking Friends with the Irish

Picture the scene.

You are in a pub where the barman is called Seamus. You are enjoying a plate of corned beef and cabbage, washed down with Bushmills, Murphy's or Guinness. The antique jukebox is playing 'Danny Boy'. On the wall behind the bar is a framed photograph of John F Kennedy, another of Michael Collins, a third of Samuel Beckett. Where on earth are you?

That's right. North London.

You have entered 'an Irish pub' for a good night out. You are tired of The Duke and The Cock and Feathers. The Prince of Wales has no appeal. Fecky Flanagans is what you want now. Down the street from Murder Mulligans. Across the way from The Emerald Oil.

You know the kind of place I mean. Sepia-tinted photographs of thatched cottages beside lakes. Posters of Georgian doors in Dublin. Tables made out of redundant agricultural machinery. Begorrah! *Bejayzus*! How very Irish it all is. Why, even the condoms in the vending machines are green. And as for the tampon-dispensing unit in the ladies loo? Oh no, those *aren't* tampons. Those are banshees' fags.

These stupefyingly vile places bespeckle the whole world now. The Irish bar in all its quasi-Hibernian horror. From Hamburg to Paris, from Bangkok to Rome – wherever you go stands one little corner of a foreign field that will always be Irish, no matter how ridiculous that might be. Hansi or Luigi or Lee

Ho Hung will be ripping it up to the sound of the fiddle. But England has more 'traditional' Irish hostelries than anywhere else on the face of the planet – certainly many more than we have in Ireland, or ever did have, if it comes to that. And as for London, to judge from its pubs, the city has turned into Oirland-on-Thames.

This dreadful proliferation of the Irish pub, this excruciating epidemic of ersatz Éire. Is there any way we can all band together and stop it? What can it mean? How do we explain it?

Bored with trying to understand the Irish – and who could possibly blame them for that? – the English have lately decided to imitate us. They want to be Irish too, bless their hearts. And why shouldn't they? Often I think they are remarkably good at it. To be honest I think they are much better at being Irish than we are. Whenever I see English people enjoying themselves in a London-Irish pub I realise that history means nothing at all. 'Feck!' they shout. 'Are you having the craic? ... er ... Top o' the mornin. *Diddly-deee!*'

Irish readers will know all too well that up until recently a *truly* authentic Irish pub was usually a filth-encrusted, draughty, malodorous hovel with a leaky roof, corrugated iron walls and a hole in the ground down an alley as a toilet. That is not what you find in Camden and Islington but in Ireland not too long ago that would have been common enough. When I think of the Dublin bars I frequented in my student days my heart begins to pump and sputter. There was no fine menu featuring Yeatsburgers or Baked Behans, no autographed portrait of Shane McGowan, no selection of potent cocktails named after characters in James Joyce's novels. A packet of nuts was all the food you could ask for and the regular punters would laugh if you did.

The glass-collectors were not smiling russet-headed colleens, but grim-faced viragos with blackened teeth, or sullen pimply teenagers saving up for emigration. The walls were adorned with jolly Irish notices saying, 'DON'T ASK FOR CREDIT AS A

TRUNCHEON IN THE KISSER MIGHT OFFEND'. The furnishings weren't distressed but the customers were. The barman was not an Aidan Quinn lookalike with a lovely little song perpetually on his lips about his wee grey-haired mammy in the County Donegal. More often than not he was an outright bollocks who would gnaw his own leg off for a tenpenny piece.

Oh, how we pined for the bars of London, those of us who knew we would soon take the emigrant boat. Buxom barmaids! Dartboards and pork scratchings! Skittles! Warm bitter! Watney's Red Barrel! Dot Cotton in the corner sharing a sherry with Doctor Legg. Bunting out the front on Coronation Day and a bunk-up out the back on Christmas Night, followed by a punch-up with Big Grant Mitchell and a roll in the cellar with Wellard the pub dog. How could any self-respecting Irishman want more?

But no. Alas. It wasn't to be. The fashion for 'Irish pubs' took off just as soon as we stepped from the mailboat. London bars began to fall in love with faked Irishry. It was as though our horrible past was stalking us.

Back home in Ireland people soon came to realise that business opportunities were presenting themselves across the Irish sea. The mighty English, we soon realized, were the only people in the whole world who really *would* give you money for old rope – provided the old rope had once been in a Dublin alehouse. Attics were ransacked, old buildings stripped. We emptied our skips, threw open the museums and sent the dusty contents across the water to be nailed and hammered to the walls of faux-Irish speakeasies.

This exporting of crap was good for Ireland. It really helped to clean out the country. Other European nations have wine lakes or butter mountains. In Ireland we had a Tat Pyrenees. But soon we were recycling whole mountains of old junk, selling them to the ancient enemy to put in his pub. Lord in Heaven, what sweet revenge.

But the Irish pubs of England wanted more and more. Soon

the demand reached crisis proportions. Slowly, inexorably, Ireland was sucked dry of drek as every last little piece of it was exported to England's inns. For a brief period in the mid-1990s there was actually a serious Irish junk-drought, an epidemic of craplessness.

Grot was rationed by the Irish government, tat and garbage strictly limited. Mothers with young children were allowed small weekly supplies of Val Doonican album covers; a granny with good connections could sometimes get her hands on a battered old harp or a plastic leprechaun. But still the Irish pubs of Britain demanded more. *Give us postcards of donkeys! Faded icons of Saint Patrick! Busts of Bob Geldof carved out of turf!* In no time they became completely insatiable. But we had no more bits of old junk to sell. We soon realised there was nothing else for it. We started *manufacturing* bits of old junk.

Thus it is that deep in the peaceful Irish countryside there are now many large and successful factories churning out broken spinning wheels, battered ancient books with their jackets ripped off, rolls of atmospheric spider-web to be sold by the yard to the Irish pub market. Once a poor and backward country, these days Ireland has the healthiest economy in Europe. Now you know why. It's all down to you.

So remember tonight, as you sink your pint, in Buggery Boylans or the Shamrock Shebeen – authenticity is absolutely everything. If you can fake that, bejayzus, you've got it made. Big time. In spades. With shillelaghs to go. Cheers now. Pass the credit card. *O Danny Boy …*

The Land of the Free –
Or at Least the Very Cheap

Friday, 13 September
Look, I'm tired, OK? I am hot and exhausted and hungry and stressed. I only got off the plane from Dublin to New York two hours ago. I have jetlag the way Noddy Holder had spangles. I am in a bad mood and it's getting worse.

'Why did you write *Sweet Liberty*?' the television reporter is asking me, for only the fifteen-hundredth time. 'I mean, this book about all the towns named Dublin in the United States? What exactly is it that you feel you are saying about the Irish in America?'

'One, two, three, four,' I reply.

She nods in a solemnly encouraging fasion.

'Five, six, seven, eight,' I continue.

'Really?' She flashes a smile that must have cost thousands to achieve. 'How *very* fascinating. Will you share more of that story with us?'

'Oh yes indeed,' I affirm. 'One, two, three, four. HA HA HA. And four, three, two, one, as a matter of fact. But then again, when you really think about it, ten, nine, eight, seven, six, five, four, as James Joyce would have put it.'

'Marvellous,' she grins. 'And you tell it so beautifully. You Irish folks have *such* a wonderful way with words.'

I should explain that we are doing cutaway shots. 'Cutaway shots' is televisual jargon for annoying the very LIFE out of people being interviewed. How this works is as follows: having answered all of the interviewer's enquiries, they then take the camera off you and point it at the interviewer and do portions of the interview all over again, now filming the person asking the questions. Only this time round, as the sound engineer has explained to me, it would be much easier for editing purposes if I didn't actually answer the questions in an intelligible manner, and if I just said 'one two three four' in response. Do I think I can do that? I confirm that having spent five whole years studying English in UCD I think I can just about manage it, yes. In fact I say 'one, two, three, four' better than anyone else in the literature business. I am known all over the world for that. Not even Seamus Heaney says 'one, two, three, four' the way I do.

'Looking forward to your book tour in America?' the interviewer asks.

'Well, Donna,' I smile, 'I'm really glad you asked me that question. Because one, two, three, four, five, six, seven …'

I feel as low as tits on a giraffe. My tongue is a yellowish-grey sock. My head is pounding like the Manic Street Preachers are rehearsing therein. My feet have swollen in my brand-new book-tour shoes.

'One two three four, one two three four.'

Sometimes being a writer seems very glamorous indeed.

Saturday, 14 September

Up early and get a taxi downtown to my interview at Radio Free Éireann.

I know you will be surprised to hear that Radio Free Éireann takes a broadly Republican line when it comes to the Irish national question, but it is all done with refreshing irreverence and a good deal of self-mockery. The presenters are two extremely friendly and funny fellows who fall around laughing when any of the phone-in contributors says anything at all. One of them takes me to task for criticising a New York Irish priest who said in a sermon that Portlaoise Prison should be immediately destroyed by

God. I point out that I am all in favour of God destroying Portlaoise Prison, once he destroys the rest of Portlaoise as well.

Later in the day I turn up to do a reading at a bookshop in Woodlawn, which is in the Bronx. Tens of thousands of Irish people live in Woodlawn. Unfortunately only five of them come to my reading.

The silence in the shop is astounding, as we all stand around and look at our shoes and fervently hope that nobody breaks wind, because the resulting echo would be utterly deafening. The manager explains that today many of the local populace are engaged in 'A Day On The Bog'. This is an important annual cultural event, involving the shipping into Woodlawn of several tons of Irish turf, the spreading of same on a local race-course, and its subsequent and celebratory digging up. Why anyone in even half of their right mind would want to go all the way to New York to dig turf is beyond me, but there it is. 'Give me your tired, your poor, your needy,' said Lady Liberty, 'and I will let them dig turf in the Bronx.'

Woodlawn is also famous for having a large cemetery, which contains what is left of Irving Berlin, Oscar Hammerstein, Herman Melville and the great Duke Ellington. Peripatetic Irish authors, please note – if you ever do a reading in Woodlawn, do it in the boneyard. You just might get a livelier crowd.

Sunday, 15 September

Day off. Go for a stroll in the attractive and thriving neighborhood of Times Square. Very friendly locals. Extremely outgoing. So friendly and outgoing that many of them walk right up to you in the street and shout, 'GIMME SOME FUCKIN' MONEY RIGHT NOW' in your face.

As well as the touching hospitality of its habitués, Times Square is noted for the breathtaking variety of its exciting cultural institutions, such as Petie's Porno Palace, The Lap Dance Lounge, Murray's Thai Massage and Big Benny's Bazoom Room ('Fifty Pretty Girls and One Ugly One').

I notice that one of the nearby artistic cinemas is currently showing a sensitive and delicately crafted work set in the Deep South, about the affecting relationship between an elderly white lady and her poor black chauffeur.

It is called *Driving Miss Daisy Crazy*.

What a nice town New York is.

Monday, 16 September

Get up early and fly to Washington where my book-signing session at lunchtime goes OK. I meet two folks from Roberts Rinehart, the American publishers of *Sweet Liberty*. These are Edwin Van Zant and Shelley Daigh. Shelley will be accompanying me on the rest of the tour. It is her job to drum up publicity for the book and to make sure that the rest of the tour goes smoothly, but most of all it is her job to make me get receipts for any expenses I may incur. She seems absolutely adamant about this. There will be no expenses pay-out for anything that doesn't have a receipt. She says this quite a number of times and does not look like a person to be trifled with at all. Her nickname back in the office is 'The Bulldog', she tells me proudly. Subsequent to this revelation, Edwin fondly informs me that she is 'the Eva Braun of Roberts Rinehart'.

The Bulldog keeps using the phrase 'the wrath of Shelley' to describe what happens when she gets upset. (For example, when an expenses claim is submitted WITHOUT A RECEIPT.) Pretty soon I decide pretty firmly that the wrath of Shelley isn't something I ever want to see. I actually like having kneecaps, after all, and don't want to have to carry them home from America in a plastic bag.

Washington is abuzz with talk of the forthcoming election, also with memories of the recently deceased criminal fraudster and Nixon henchman, Spiro Agnew. Tonight there is a launch party for *Sweet Liberty* at the Irish Embassy. Big enthusiastic crowd. Bits of cheese on cocktail sticks. Someone tells me that America has really changed a lot since the bad old days of Vice-

President Agnew. Yes, I joke, in these days a lying State Governor with severe legal problems can make it as far as the actual *Presidency*.

This goes down very well indeed, as you can imagine.

Tuesday, 17 September

Fly back to New York. The American newspapers all carry the epoch-making story that Senator Bob Dole fell over on his backside the other night while campaigning for the Republicans in Chico, California, the only town in the United States to be named after a Marx Brother (apart from Zeppo, Texas). Some journalists have put this forward as evidence that Mr Dole is too old to be still active in politics. They may have a point. Shortly after his tumble he reportedly made a reference to his deep admiration for 'the Brooklyn Dodgers', who actually departed Brooklyn in 1957. Next week he's going to Paris to discuss NATO with Napoleon Bonaparte. Still, Dole seems like a nice old codger. And at least when he met the Japanese ambassador recently, he didn't vomit on him like former President Bush once did. (I am not making this up.)

Back at the hotel in New York a reporter from a tremendously major newspaper such as the *The Staten Island Picayune* or *The Boise Idaho Leprechaun* fails to turn up to interview me. Shelley's eyes take on the expression of Linda Blair in the more memorable moments of *The Exorcist*. He, it seems, 'shall feel the wrath of Shelley'.

I decide to leave the room before her head starts revolving.

Wednesday, 18 September

This morning I wake up to the somewhat startling news that the mayor of Dublin California has issued a statement about *Sweet Liberty*, condemning it as 'a work of fiction'. Hmm. It is an odd country indeed where the worst thing you can say about a book is that its contents are fictional. Someone faxes me the front page of Dublin California's local newspaper, which boasts the screaming banner-headline IRISH AUTHOR DUMPS ON DUBLIN CALIFORNIA beside a photograph of myself looking sulky.

The article goes on to describe how my book 'goes through Dublin California block by block, like a literary wrecking ball'. My publishers seem very excited about this, on the basis that there is no such thing as bad publicity. I often wonder whether this cliché is true, but Shelley feels it is, and I'm not going to argue. She points out that Hugh Grant's career in the United States actually *improved* after he was caught soliciting a hooker. She then goes on to ponder aloud whether I would be prepared to get myself into a Hugh Grant-Divine Brown-type situation in order to publicise *Sweet Liberty* a little further. I tell her yes but I don't think prostitutes give receipts.

Extremely well-attended reading at the Glucksman Ireland House in NYU. I am introduced to the audience by one of my heroes, the Irish-American journalist Pete Hamill. During his remarks he says I am 'disgustingly young' but I point out that in fact I am merely disgusting.

Afterwards I go for a drink with the wonderful staff and a mate from Dublin, Peter McDermott. We are all in a highly literary state by the end of the evening. Indeed, literature is discussed so very thoroughly that I keep waking up with an awful pain in my head.

Thursday, 19 September

Fly to Boston, where I meet my father Sean and brother Eoin. With massive kindness way beyond the call of duty, they have flown over from Ireland to keep me company for a few days on the tour. Poor chaps, this will be very expensive indeed for them.

American hotels seem moderately priced when you look at their rate cards. But when the bill eventually arrives the unwary traveller can get quite a shock. By the time they add on the Standard Sales Tax, State Tax, Local Tax, City Tax, 'Room

Occupancy Tax' – like, what ELSE are you going to do with a hotel room if not *occupy* it? *Take it for a walk around the block?* – Service Charge, Concierge Commission, Maid Tax, Air-Breathing Tax and Looking-At-The-Waiter-In-A-Funny-Way Tax, the bill for a hundred-and-fifty-buck room can quite easily be $50,003.01

Sean, Eoin and I have an agreeable time looking around Boston. It is a graceful civilized town, if a wee bit snobbish. That night in the bookshop I ask the manager if he thinks many people will show up for my reading. A strangely stressed smile invades his face. 'I'm not gonna lie to you here, Joe,' he says. 'Tonight is gonna be an intimate occasion.'

As I stand at the podium and gaze down at the crowd of nine, two members of which I share actual DNA with, I am struck once again by the great American capacity for euphemism.

Friday, 20 September
Today is my birthday.

Well whoop-de-bloody-doo.

They say you're only as old as the age you feel. In which case, I probably died six years ago.

Eoin, Sean and I go to lunch at *Maison Robert* ('It means Robert's House in French, guys,' the Concierge helpfully explains). In the jacks of that fine establishment, I meet a waspish English bloke who proudly informs me that his mother was 'a titled lady'. I tell him mine was too. Leinster Middleweight Champion.

Saturday, 21 September
Get up and bid my beloved relatives safe return to Ireland. They decline my bribes to stuff me into one of their suitcases, smuggle me on board and convey me homewards. So me and the Bulldog fly to Chicago where the signing session at The Joy Of Ireland Gift Store is a disaster of almost Biblical proportions. We rack up sales of a massive seven books, four of those to a clearly

insane old lady who seems to be under the impression that I am Roddy Doyle.

Mr Richard Kosmacher, who runs the store, is clearly upset that so few people have turned up. I try to console him as best I can, though really I feel it should be the other way around. Yet I do have a genuine sense of pity for Richard, for he too shall soon be undergoing 'the wrath of Shelley'. As he watches her eyes begin to narrow, I hope to God he has made a will.

In the peaceful two-hour gaps between waiting for punters to show up and buy my book I scan the morning newspaper. There is an interview with the great diva of soul Dionne 'Walk On By' Warwick, who is apparently involved with a television channel called 'The Psychic Friends Line'. I confess that I find this somewhat surprising, because only last week in New York I read *another* article about Dionne Warwick, pointing out that she had recently been injured by someone throwing a brick at her.

With all those psychic friends she has, you'd think she'd have known to duck, wouldn't you?

Sunday, 22 September

Day off. I call Richard Kosmacher to see if he wants to meet for lunch, but today is Yom Kippur, the Jewish 'Day of Atonement', and Richard, being of that faith, is consequently busy with Things of the Spirit. I bid him fond farewell and promise to keep in touch. I can't help feeling that God will forgive him a lot sooner than Shelley will. And that Shelley may require more painful atoning.

Monday, 23 September

Me and the Cuddlesome Canine get the train to Milwaukee, which isn't a very exciting town. The streets, in fact, are almost deserted, except for the occasional small group of citizens huddled together in a doorway to watch paint dry.

Very tired as we drive to the hotel. The most positive thing I can say about the room is that it contains a fly-swatter, which comes in handy.

When you buy a book the author receives about one tenth of the cover price. The cover price of *Sweet Liberty* is fourteen dollars.

Tonight at my reading in downtown Milwaukee, I boost my annual income by one dollar forty.

Tuesday, 24 September

Fly from Milwaukee to Denver, Colorado.

Here we meet the Bulldog's husband who drives us to Boulder, the commodious city which contains, among other things, the international headquarters of Roberts Rinehart. I am a tad disconcerted to notice that the first thing Shelley does when we get to the office is whip out a badge of a snarling bulldog and proudly clamp it to her lapel. She really is an unusual person.

I am led around and introduced to all the fine, intelligent and strikingly good-looking people who toil away in Roberts Rinehart for the greater good of literature. I am quivering with anticipation at the thought of being reimbursed for my neatly filed and remarkably comprehensive sheaf of *per diem* receipts. But sadly the company accountant is not in today. She is out stealing the pennies off deadmens' eyes.

A pleasant and strikingly beautiful young woman with the unusual name of Isis has just started working at the office. I ask if by any chance she is named after the Bob Dylan song of that title and am overjoyed to discover that she is. Her second name is Layla – after the Eric Clapton classic. I tell her she got off remarkably lightly. She could have been christened 'I Shot The Sheriff'.

Back to Denver with minutes to spare, then the Bulldog and I take the shuttle to Seattle, where the hotel room is so small you couldn't raise veal in it.

Again I am worried about tonight's reading, but to my

considerable surprise it goes quite well, except for the presence of one dribbling loon in the audience. When it comes to time for questions he thrusts his hand roofwards, glares at me, and asks if people in Ireland have ever heard of Seattle?

I kick for touch by simpering madly and swallowing a few big slugs of water. I ask myself if this is a trick question. Does he mean the Native American chieftain after whom this beautiful city is named?

No, he means Seattle.

I say yes, we are a very civilized country, we have flush toilets and we've heard of Seattle.

'You guys get *Frasier* over there in Ireland?'

I say that not only do we get *Frasier* in Ireland, I've actually had a couple of one-night-stands with Ros.

He then asks me who I think should play Brendan Behan in the forthcoming film of that writer's life. I say Sylvester Stallone. Everyone laughs, except this guy.

He's glaring at me like he wants to strangle me with his bare hands, rip out my liver and feed it to his psychiatrist. I am quite glad I have the Bulldog here to protect me.

Back at the hotel I can't get to sleep. It sounds like the room next door is occupied by two Sumo wrestlers with Tourette's Syndrome working their way slowly through the *Readers' Digest Guide To Sado-Masochism and Bondage*. Finally drift into the arms of Morpheus (my teddy bear) and get a really good night's rest which lasts for, oh, an hour and a half.

Wednesday, 25 September

Get up early and watch the TV news. Things are getting freaky in this country. Everywhere you look people are trying to ban things. The people of Oregon are currently voting on something called Ballot Measure Nine – amusingly misprinted 'Ballet Measure Nine' in today's *New York Times* – which will give status of law to the hoary old prejudice that homosexuality is 'abnormal, wrong, unnatural and perverse'.

Personally I've had enough of all these people telling us who it's OK to sleep with. You're gay? Good for you. You're straight? Congratulations. You want to bonk a llama? Hey, if it's cool with the llama, it's cool with me. You're getting it on with your living-room bookcase? Well, bring her down to the pub on Friday night and let's all get a look at her! Bro, Sis – if *YOU'RE* happy, *I'M* happy.

But here in America that is not how things work. The most multicultural democracy on the face of the earth and pretty soon you're going to need a permit to read *Doonesbury*.

Shelley and I fly to San Francisco. I go shopping for presents. Shelley goes shopping for receipts. Amazingly long queues in all the stores. People are shoplifting to save time, not money.

Mixed memories of San Francisco. Last time I was here I stood on a nail – it's a long and crashingly tedious story – and ended up hobbling to Casualty in a local hospital. There were maybe twenty people in the emergency room, and nineteen of those were holding urine samples. It was like a scene from Octoberfest.

Ah, sweet recollection. I won't say the queue was long but the guy in front of me had a musket wound. The first question the doctor asked me after a four-hour wait was, 'How will you be paying for your treatment tonight, sir?' Wincing and groaning and trying not to bleed all over the floor I replied, 'with my life, sweetheart, if you don't pick up the fucking pace.' Tony Bennett may have left his heart in San Francisco, but I left my entire life savings.

This time around things are better. I manage not to skewer any part of my person and tonight's reading goes very well indeed.

Thursday, 26 September
At San Francisco airport I bid goodbye to the Bulldog, who gives me a kiss on the cheek and one last bark of affection. She feels the tour has gone well, all things considered. I am in two minds

about that myself, but I'm certainly not going to argue the toss. Some people might feel that an eight-thousand mile journey to sell forty-two books might not be a total success, but I am not one of them, and neither is Shelley.

'Main thing is, we got the receipts,' she points out.

And I really have to agree with her there. Particularly because she's biting my leg.

Fondling Foreigners
in Frankfurt

(for Lar Cassidy, in fond memory)

The flight from London to Frankfurt is full of publishers. You can tell they are publishers because they are weighed down like pack-mules, with briefcases and hold-alls and supermarket bags full of thick typescripts. Modern technology, which has put a man on the moon, cannot produce a novel typescript that does not look and feel and weigh like a telephone directory. Often, of course, they read like a telephone directory also, but that will not stop these airborne publishers from selling them to other publishers, who will in turn sell them to *more* publishers, who will print them up and sell them to wholesalers, who will sell them to bookshops, who will finally sell them to unwitting members of the public, who will hurl them into the bin after reading one page. And a key part of this wonderful process is that annual form of madness known as the Frankfurt Book Fair.

I arrive, get off the plane and gaze upon the attractive foyer of Frankfurt airport, which is roughly the colour of a cancerous lung. I am looking for the person who is supposed to meet me. He, she or it has failed to turned up.

Hmm.

I look around and consider my position. Most of the German I know is of the comic-book variety. But I imagine that phrases such as *Donner und Blitzen*, *Achtung Achtung* and *HANDE*

HOCHE, BRITISCHER SCHWEINHUND! may not be all that useful in booking a hotel room.

I start to walk around the terminal, attempting to look like a published Irish novelist. This is more difficult than it might initially sound. Spiritual angst crossed with traces of faint residual hope is the mix you have to try your best to project. But quite often it comes off as violent constipation.

After a while I bump into another lost and bewildered Irish writer, Belfast's own Mr Glenn Patterson. I don't know what it is Glenn is trying to look like, but if it's a pitiful Dickensian orphan he certainly is succeeding. He tells me his own driver has also failed to show. So Glenn and myself get a taxi to our hotel, which he happens to know is in a town called Raunheim.

Raunheim is a small town to say the least. It is, quite frankly, a bit of a kip (*eine kleine krappendümpf* in German.) Many places in this area were bombed by the Allies during World War Two. Raunheim escaped the bombing because the Allies looked down from their Spitfires and assumed they must have bombed the shit out of it already.

We pull up outside the Best Western Wings Motel. The building has all the beauty and charm of something stuck to your shoe. 'Thank God,' Glenn comments, 'it isn't the Second Best.'

I should explain that Glenn and myself are here as part of the 'Ireland And Its Diaspora' festival which is being held at the Frankfurt Book Fair this year. Every Irish person who has ever written a poem, published a novel, or sat half-drunk in a pub and merely *wished* they had written a poem or a novel, has been airlifted to Frankfurt at the expense of the German and Irish governments to discuss what they feel about Ireland and its diaspora. They are all staying at the Best Western Wings Motel, an hour's drive from the centre of the city.

This is an impressively cunning exercise in crowd-control by the main organisers, the Irish Arts Council. Knowing a thing or two about young Irish writers, they realise full-well that putting forty-seven of them in a hotel in downtown Frankfurt on an expense account would be a recipe for an irretrievable break-down in diplomatic relations between Germany and Ireland. But *this* hotel is so far out of downtown Frankfurt that I seriously wonder whether it is not actually in Belgium.

I know the person in the room next to my own must also be a young Irish writer because I can hear him pacing the floor in iambic pentameter. Meanwhile my television is switched on, and the screen is flashing out the message WELCOME TO RAUNHEIM HERR O'CONNOR. I lie on the bed and look at this for a while, thinking intensely literary thoughts, such as 'I wonder if there is a minibar?'

After a while the flashing message starts to annoy me. I get up and try to switch it off but I can't. There is a small sticker on the table warning people NOT TO SWITCH OFF THE TELEVISION FOR NO REASON AT ALL PLEASE. I contemplate simply chucking it out the window, plug and all, in true rock 'n' roll style, but decide this would not be good for the image of Ireland, not to mention its diaspora. So I pick up the remote control and make another attempt to make the offending screen go dark.

I now notice that it is possible to receive in-room porno-graphic movies, all of which have arrestingly alliterative titles. So I am now terrified to change channels in case I accidentally order up 'Lipstick Lesbians Get Lusty In Leipzig,' 'Horny Heidi Humps Helga in Heidleburg' or even 'Fondling Frisky Foreigners in Frankfurt'. I mean, yes, to be absolutely candid, I don't have anything against fondling foreigners in Frankfurt, per se, you understand, in fact if the opportunity were to present itself I might even ... never mind. It's just that I don't want to watch a film about it, particularly one that might show up on my bill.

The person in the room above me, however, clearly doesn't feel the same way. To judge from the wild gasps, lascivious whoops and low guttural groans coming through my ceiling, either he is energetically availing of the in-room entertainment or he is a more enthusiastic literature fan than you often find.

'Oh my God,' a voice cries. 'It's so big. Oh, Jesus! I've never seen one so huge before. *Oh, God, yesss! It's FUCKING ENORMOUS.*'

Of course, he might not be watching pornography at all. He could be talking about John Banville's latest advance.

I leave the room and amble down to the lobby, where Glenn is having a cup of coffee. He has just read in today's newspaper that Gerry Adams is among the Irish writers who will attend the Book Fair this year. I ask Glenn if Mr Adams will also be staying at the Best Western Wings. 'No no,' Glenn jokes. 'The Provisional Wings.'

Myself and Glenn take a taxi into Frankfurt. I discover that I left my money in my bedroom, so being an all-round decent segocia, Glenn munificently stumps up the fare. But the Best Western Wings Motel is so far from the city of Frankfurt that the sum comes to almost fifty pounds. Glenn then realises that he has lost his complimentary entrance ticket to the Book Fair and will have to buy another to gain admission. He has only been in Germany for two-and-a-half hours and already he is seventy smackers down on the deal. It is lining up to be one hell of a weekend for him.

People tell you that the Frankfurt Book Fair is big. Indeed they struggle to find adjectives that can possibly convey just how staggeringly, awesomely, implausibly large it is. You could take all those superlatives and multiply them by infinity and you still wouldn't even be halfway close. It is vast. It is massive. It is momentously humungous. There are many whole towns in rural Ireland where people get born, grow up, meet partners, fall in love, have children, retire and die, that are a good deal smaller than the Frankfurt Book Fair. It is actually quite macabre, from a young author's point of view, to wander the halls and gaze upon the hundreds and thousands of books that get published in any one year. I confess I had expected, as a young Irish author, to be greeted by mobs of screaming literature fans, all falling to their knees before me, sprinkling my path with fresh rose petals, thanking me for the continuing regular production of critically acclaimed, yet commercially successful, literature. But no. An author at the Frankfurt Book Fair is basically an inconvenience. Which is funny. Because none of these people would be here if it wasn't for us, as I explain to Glenn, as he stares into his rapidly emptying wallet with a look of considerable emotion on his face.

'*Gott in Himmel*,' he says. But in a very literary way.

Several hours later and several kilograms lighter, Glenn and I manage to find the Irish Pavilion. I reflect how it is so heart-warming to take part in these events which challenge outmoded and unhelpful stereotypes of Ireland, as I stare at the posters of thatched cottages, round towers and red-haired colleens dancing jigs beside tractors. The posters have been supplied by the Germans, apparently. They must have thought the Irish Pavilion, staffed and organised and designed by Irish people, and full of Irish writers, and made of Irish materials, and paid for by Irish taxpayers just wasn't quite Irish enough. And hey – who can blame them?

A thirty-foot-high blow-up doll of Lemuel Gulliver is standing proudly erect outside the pavilion, like a gigantic bouncer in period costume. Mr Gulliver, as you will know, is the central character in the classic novel *Gulliver's Travels* by Jonathan Swift ('Verily I could not putte it downe' – *Ye Iryshe Tymes Booke Supplemente*, December 1726). I can't help wondering, however, whether Swift would have liked his famous creation being used in this way. After all, his own views about Ireland were somewhat mixed. He left money in his will for the building of the first mental hospital in Dublin, adding, in a pithy codicil, that had he been richer he would have bequeathed enough dough for a twenty-foot wall to be constructed around the entire country.

After a time I bump into Gunter and Klaudia, whom I met at a literature festival in Berlin three years ago. We all go along to a Thai restaurant for dinner. The stunningly attractive waitress is clearly not a literature fan and thus fails to recognise either myself or Glenn. 'Be careful, it's hot,' she keeps saying, whenever she places a dish on the table. After a while Glenn seems to feel that the only adequate response is 'Me too, baby'.

After dinner we all go to the literaturhaus (German for 'pub') where the brilliant Frank McCourt is giving a reading from *Angela's Ashes*, the German title of which is 'Limerick, *Nein Danke*'. (It isn't really.) 'A happy childhood isn't worth a fuck,' he says, in answer to a question from the audience. I laugh so loud that it gets a bit embarrassing. I intend to tell my children this at least once a day.

The night is just beginning to hot up nicely when the man with the Raunheim bus turns up and sternly explains that we have to get onto it. Grumbling and moaning, we all do.

Back at the Best Western Wings Motel we are overjoyed to discover that there is a night-club in the basement. The poor barman looks very worried. I would estimate that on average the night-club in the Best Western Wings Motel gets about four people on a Friday night; three Austrian businessman and one hopeful local hooker. Tonight it is crammed to the doors with Irish writers, drinking, dancing and discussing poetry. Indeed, we are all in a highly poetic state by the end of the evening.

Up early the following morning. My head feels like something died in it. My tongue looks like it needs to be scrubbed clean with a toothbrush. Glenn and I get the bus into the *literaturhaus* where we are doing a reading together. The reading goes well and afterwards there are questions. One girl wants to know why so many wonderful writers come from Ireland. I feel it is probably the weather. It is always so cold and rainy in Ireland that there is very little to do all day except stay at home and produce literature.

When the event has finished, I have some meetings. I have meetings with my Swedish publishers, my Italian publishers, with the foreign rights department of my British publishers, with my Japanese publishers, with my French publishers and, accidentally, with Maeve Binchy's Norwegian translator. The day begins to feel like a strange and terrible nightmare. Before too long I have no idea who I am talking to any more, nor what language I should be apologising for not being able to speak. I bump into Glenn again. By now all his money is gone and he is considering selling his body so he can afford a cup of tea. I am considering selling mine too. But where Glenn is considering selling his by the hour, I am considering selling mine by the kilo.

We go for a walk and discuss the hell out of literature. Outside the Irish Pavilion, we notice a group of three Germans staging some kind of demonstration. The word 'OUT' is printed on their T-shirts. I wonder if they are from a Gay Rights group. But no, on closer examination we see that the word 'BRITS' also appears on the T-shirts, conveniently positioned just before the word 'OUT'.

Yes, it appears that these three Germans are the Frankfurt chapter of the Free Ireland Campaign. Glenn goes over to explain that while he actually lives and works in Belfast he is absolutely sure that Fritz, Heidi and Heindrich, who have once been to West Cork on a bicycling holiday and who actually own several Planxty CDs, not to mention some Aran jumpers, have a much more profound and sophisticated understanding of the many complexities of the Northern Ireland situation than he does himself. But they do not seem to recognise irony when it presents itself. Every time they use the phrase 'ze six counteez' I am showered with saliva.

People have begun to gather at the pavilion for the next event. Suddenly a strange and disquieting thing happens. A long, loud hissing sound can be heard. Naturally I assume it is the Free Ireland Campaign being rude. But no, it is actually the giant inflatable Gulliver. Some appalling disaster, possibly involving cigarette burns, has befallen him. He sags, begins deflating and tilts over face-forward, like a drunk leaning his forehead against a urinal wall. I can't help but feel that this is an omen. The endlessly genial Lar Cassidy, who has organised this event, starts looking around for a bicycle pump. I try to avoid making eye contact with him. I love Ireland as much as the next man, but I do know where to draw the line. If Lar cannot find the bicycle pump it certainly won't be myself who ends up giving Gulliver a patriotic blow-job.

Inside the pavilion a large crowd has turned up to sit there in awed silence while Glenn, myself, Anne Enright and Evelyn Conlon discuss Ireland and its diaspora, live and unplugged. We do this for some time. Glenn says the word 'diaspora' sounds like some disease you might get from a toilet seat. But that is facetious. It actually sounds like the name of one of those small emerging statelets produced by the break-up of the former Yugoslavia.

When the diaspora has been vigorously discussed to the shattering fulfilment of the German public, the event ends and I visit the stand of my British publishers. There I meet three people from my American publishers. They are busily trying to buy the rights to my next novel. I am somewhat bemused by this, since I have not as yet got around to the tedious business of actually thinking it up and writing it down. But this does not matter at the Frankfurt Book Fair. This is a place where people actually have huge auctions, involving telephone-number sums of money, for two or three pages of a new novel. For one page, sometimes. For a single paragraph. A blurb. A title. A word! Sometimes they will have an auction for *the idea for a novel*. I swear to God I am not making this up. Frankfurt is an event where highly paid professionals buy and sell what does not exist. I myself made a quick fifty thousand Deutschmarks by telling a Japanese publisher about an idea I don't intend to actually *get* until 2013. I also sold the translation rights to an afterthought, movie rights to an attitude, and serialisation rights for several irrational prejudices and a vague hunch.

That night I go out with my German editor, Hans-Jurgen Balmes, and two of his *freunde*. We drink beer, shoot pool, tell rude jokes, discuss whether the linguistic strategies of the contemporary novel can play any truly radical role in the new millennium, y'know, guy stuff. Hans-Jurgen explains that all the prostitutes leave Frankfurt during the Book Fair, because publishers are too mean to pay for sex.

After dinner we go to the bar of the Frankfurterhoff Hotel. I am now in a state where saying the word 'Frankfurterhoff' is proving quite a challenge. This is the hotel where very rich publishers and mega-successful authors stay when the fair is on. The hotel is booked up many years in advance. It is said that someone in publishing has to actually die before you can get a room at the Frankfurterhoff during the Book Fair. Indeed, just to get a seat at the bar requires a senior editor to have a mild heart attack.

My English agent, Carole Blake, is here, chatting with my French agent, Maggie Doyle. They buy me many drinks and indulge my insane, exhausted ranting about the sheer size of the Book Fair. Although they have been working at an inhuman rate – Carole's diary looks like a train timetable – they look like they've just had ten hours sleep. I, unfortunately, look like downtown Limerick on legs. I am so tired that I could cheerfully lie down in the gents' toilets and go to sleep.

Except I can't even get into the gents' toilets. Not until Frank McCourt dies.

Amore in Amalfi

The driver we have arranged to meet us at Naples airport is an hour-and-a-half late 'because there is much traffic today'.

I glare at him. By way of response he gives one of those large, nonchalant Italian shrugs. The kind that says: 'I am a relaxed Mediterranean type but if I have to kill you for business reasons, I will.'

Me, I would have thought there would be much traffic most days in a city such as Naples. That if you were a person who made his bloody *living* from driving you would bear this little fact *in mind*, you know, that you might even *leave your house a bit early*, or perhaps even ... My first wife and current travelling companion tells me not to go inflicting my own cultural standards on people whose nonchalant philosophy of life is not the same as my own, so I apologise to the work-slacking Latino lounge-lizard and he thoughtfully allows us to carry our own luggage to the car. (I wouldn't mind, only the wife is six months' pregnant so she finds it hard to manage my golf-bag.)

In we clamber and off we go, and an hour later, after a knuckle-clenching drive up the cliff-top roads and dirt-tracks to Ravello, we arrive at our hotel, the Palazzo Sasso. (Named after a local medieval nobleman, Prince Palazzo Sasso, who invented period costume.)

I don't actually know too much about the geezer, but with pillars and fountains and courtyards and terrazas, his former digs are certainly something to see. The whole place has been recently and thoroughly 'upgraded'. Think Graceland crossed with Government Buildings and you will be close to the interior-design concept.

Obviously the upgrading has not quite reached its completion. Our room – featuring allegedly 'free' champage and fruit – offers a stunning view of the Gulf of Salerno, not to mention the building site (*sito de contructione* in Italian) which is conveniently located beneath the balcony (*balconia*). But Antonio, the baby-faced and very pleasant desk-clerk, assures us that this is nothing to worry about. The work is almost completed; the workers are very quiet. 'You will not even know they are there,' he smiles. I don't know why we believe him but poor fools we do.

We unpack our clothes and the large library of childcare books which Once Twice Three Times A Lady feels we should read on our weekend away. We do indeed read, for at least four seconds, and then at my insistence we go out for a stroll around the neighbourhood.

Ravello is the kind of unspeakably pretty little Italian town that looks like it came in a flatpack box from a stage-set warehouse. It has small dark cafés, ice-cream parlours ('the best ice-cream in the world' – Jacqueline Kennedy), a couple of spooky churches, a small piazza where toddlers play football with nice old duffers. Couples stroll. Fiats buzz. Old ladies in black sit gossiping on the benches. It is so Italian it's just not true. You expect to see the youthful Robert De Niro skulking about in the shadows, planning to pitchfork various people who once offended Mama.

One admirable thing about people of the Italian persuasion is that they do seem to love a pregnant lady. My first wife and myself remark on this fact as we stroll the neat and dusky streets. Women passing give her empathetic smiles. Men rush to open doors and offer chairs. 'When will you be three?' one waiter graciously asks. This is all quite nice when you come from Ireland, a country where pregnancy is still occasionally regarded as a vaguely embarrassing minor ailment. (The day before the holiday a photographer at a wedding – not our own I stress – had suggested that Herself might like to move out of the front row and conceal herself at the back since 'Yeh know like … I mean … y'know … the aul bump like.' I asked if he'd had a mother himself, before venturing the opinion that it was a pity she hadn't crossed her legs in mid-delivery and choked him.)

As we saunter along, arm-in-arm, we talk about the many responsibilties of parenthood. It is hard to describe the cocktail of feelings exactly but it is a subtle mix of joy, angst and impending poverty.

That night we eat in the hotel restaurant (*restaurante de hotelia*). This is the kind of place where you get sorbets between the courses but you don't enjoy the food because you are worrying about the bill, not to mention the bewildering selection of tableware – which features lobster-crackers, crab-disembowellers and something that looks like its principal use might well be the debollocking of horses. When I see the menu I understand the veritable arsenal of cutlery. You don't come to the Palazzo Sasso for coddle and chips, nor even that jewel of Dublin cuisine, the batherboorga. If it ever crawled, scuttled, slithered and wriggled along the seabed, or adhered itself to a rock/hull/drowning sailor's leg, you can eat it in Ravello, usually half-raw.

But the wine is really exceptionally nice. The Face I Can't Forget, of course, has been eating for two in recent weeks. And I, for my part, have been drinking for two. (It is nice to be supportive at a time like this.)

By the time we retire I am in a thoroughly Italianate state, as happy a dog *con due mickiz*. I totter onto the balcony and look out at the moon, the stars, the tiny fishing boats in the waters below. 'Isn't it beautiful, Dear?' I call to My Sexual Plaything.

'Zzzzzzzzzzzz,' she replies.

Hmmm. I suppose I had better get used to this. I have been told by associates who have already reproduced that connubial bliss tends to happen a good deal less frequently when there is a new baby residing in the house. I drift off to sleep and have a strange dream. There she is in the bed, my Main Squeeze, and I have only whipped off my night-shirt when the whimpering, then the screaming starts. 'You better pipe down,' I tell her. 'Or you'll wake that baby.'

At 8 a.m. we are awoken by a phenomenal noise (*uno racketo stupendo*). The stereotype of Italian workmen is that they are lazy and inefficient, but oh no, not here in Ravello, oh no, that would be *asking too much*! By 8.03 it sounds as though the Colosseum itself is being strenuously erected outside in the garden. I stagger to the shutters and haul them open.

Below I see a veritable army of labourers doing extra-ordinarily noisy things with large bits of industrial machinery. Diggers and trucks and cement mixers are pounding, while a jackhammer is busily mincing my brain. For no reason at all obvious to me, a very fat man is repeatedly hitting a tree with an iron bar. The hem of his shorts had slipped half-way down his ample buttocks, resulting in a remarkable example of that unforgettable phenomenon known on London building sites as 'The Dagenham Smile'.

The Other Half Of My Soul is already on the phone, calling around all the other hotels in the area to see if they will take us in. We pack up our clothes and our child-rearing books and go down to the lobby to say goodbye to Antonio.

He couldn't possibly be more charming or understanding about the fact that we are leaving early. He tells myself and Mi Chica Bonita 'when you have your baby, you must all come back'.

We taxi down the hill to the local town, Amalfi, which in medieval times was the regional capital of a major city-state and is now the regional capital of tour-buses, souvenir shops and al fresco heckling of girls. The bones of Saint Andrew are lodged in the cathedral and a great big statue adorns the square, of local boy Mr Flavio Gioa, who invented the compass, thereby guaranteeing that whole generations of aspiring orienteers would have something to argue about at weekends.

We stagger into the Hotel Santa Caterina and throw ourselves at the desk-clerk's feet, begging for hospitality at any price. Foolish move, as it turns out. He turns his beady eyes upon us in the manner of a Roman Emperor in a Hollywood epic who is about to lazily intone: 'You there, Centurion – the fat one amuses me. Have him stripped, washed and brought to my tent.'

'Do you have a reservation?' he wants to know. I am tempted to reply, 'Several, actually, but we're prepared to put them aside if you give us a room.' He scrutinizes his book, softly shaking his head. I feel like a sinner at the gates of paradise. (*Los gatos de paradiso.*) They do have one room left, he finally says.

Great!

Well, strictly speaking, it is more of a suite than a room.

Oh?

It costs one million lire per night. Which translates into approximately £402.

Now I don't know about you, but I have had entire holidays that did not cost approximately £402, many of them not too bad either when you got used to the scabies. We consider our position, the wife and myself. We do have a little money put by in case our beloved child-to-be ever needs something like an expensive cot. She looks at me. I look at her.

'Sod him,' I say. 'He can sleep in the bath.'

Yes, I think, fumbling for the Visa card, one important thing about international travel is that you make adequate financial preparation for the rainy day. This may well be one of those rainy days. In fact, as the wife points out, it is!

Outside the rain has begun bucketing down. Lighting is cracking the sky in two. A bitter wind is whipping up the waves. A giant black cloud shaped just like a pound-sign is drifting in from over Capri.

Wooooo! it seems to say. I am coming to get yoooo.

The suite to which the desk-clerk leads us is the size of a small house and has been decorated with no thought for expense, not to mention taste. It does, however, have its drawbacks. Situated at the very end of the building it is only twenty yards from the main road to Naples, which is not necessarily where you want to be on a relaxing, restful holiday. 'It is a very quiet room,' the clerk announces confidently, over the drone of cars.

'Pardon?' we say.

'IT IS A VERY QUIET ROOM, HONESTLY. IT IS VERY PEACEFUL.'

But it isn't quiet. In fact it is noisy. It sounds as though several juggernauts are actually driving through the bathroom. I ask the clerk how he thinks we will get any sleep. The trick, he explains, is to close all the shutters and put the air-conditioning on at full-blast. I can't believe he is telling us this. He truly has a neck like *los bollocks de la jockey* (Frankie Dettori). For £402 a night I would expect the manager to personally make his aged mother go and lie down in the road to stop the traffic, but She Who Must Be Obeyed feels we have no choice and as always she is annoyingly correct.

For the second time in two days we unpack all our clothes and our pregnancy books.

We lie on the bed together and watch a little Italian television. A very little Italian television that doesn't work very well.

We switch to what is advertised as 'the Culture Channel'. Before us on the flickering star-spangled screen, two scantily clad women on roller-skates shimmy and glide, dancing around to a song called 'Captain of Her Heart'.

'That must have been difficult to learn,' the wife says. No doubt it was. But was it worth it, you wonder.

There follow an episode of *Only Fools And Horses* dubbed into Italian, which is without even one single doubt the weirdest, most disturbing thing I have ever seen in my life, comparable, I would imagine, to a really bad acid flashback lasting twenty-eight minutes. And yet it does have its educational moments. (For the benefit of linguistically curious readers, 'strozzo' seems to be the Italian for 'plonker'.)

By now culturally satisfied, not to say exhausted, we flick to an American cable channel. Over a soundtrack of Richard Clayderman music, two silver-haired old people are strolling arm-in-arm along a sunset beach. 'Are you aged between sixty-five and eighty and thinking about life insurance?'

'*Huh?*' I ask myself. Isn't eighty cutting it a tad fine?

I am reminded of the story of the American couple who at ninety and ninety-one were the oldest people ever to seek a divorce. Asked by the reporters on the steps of the courthouse why they had waited so long, they are said to have replied, 'We were waiting for the children to die.'

After two hours or so the rain stops. The sun peeps out from behind the black clouds. 'Come out,' it seems to say. 'You poor gullible suckers.'

We gather up the pregnancy books and the few little knick-knacks which women seem to need for sunbathing – towel, sarong, flip-flops, hairbrush, straw hat, sun-screen, moisturiser, P.D. James novel, camera, tripod, Swiss Army Knife, postcards, pens, nail polish, laptop, mobile phone, fold-up desk – and lumber down to 'The Beach Club'.

The Beach Club does not feature a beach, as such; nor to be honest is it actually 'a club'. It is a flat expanse of tarmacadam beside the sea, administered by two handsome local youths in tight shorts. The wife seems to think there is something attractive about them but, as I point out, they probably don't have a sense of humour or a fine mind like what I do.

'Mmmmmmmm,' she agrees.

I open my copy of *Babies And What To Do With Them*. But I don't have very much time to read because now it is time for lunch.

In the adjacent dining area I notice that the menu offers such thought-provoking savouries as 'Baby Octopus Drowned in Tomato Sauce'. Perhaps impending fatherhood is making me a wuss but I decide I'm not really in the mood for cruelly murdered squidling and order instead a tuna and tomato sandwich. Said item, along with two glasses of fruit juice and one small chicken salad which, without any doubt, once had a piece of chicken waved over it, brings the bill for lunch to £36. At this stage our son's Harvard education is beginning to look dubious. (We will have to pretend he is thick as a plank but quite rich so we can get him into Oxford.)

Now depressed and downhearted, I repair back up to the room. Outside there is 100-degree Fahrenheit heat and blazing sunshine. But I am in bed, in a haze of despondency, under the covers to protect myself from the rattle of the air-conditioner, trying hard to read *Loving Discipline* which is not a sex manual for Tory MPs but a handbook for aspiring parents who don't want to beat their children. The noise of the traffic gets louder and louder. The walls are so thin I can hear our next-door neighbour's inner doubts. Tension rises. Tempers are frayed. The Wind Beneath My Wings and I have an argument. I don't speak to her for a couple of hours.

That night we get a taxi back up to Ravello where we intend to have dinner in a local restaurant (*restaurante de locale*). This five-kilometer journey sets us back £20. But that's not the bit that really gets us. Two hours later, faces stuffed and wallets depleted, the taxi driver breaks the startling news that to go *back* to Amalfi costs £28! I will not say that Ravello's taxi drivers are robbers, as such. Just that they should be wearing tights over their faces.

Still at least we are back in our lovely suite. And at least things seem to be looking up. And at least we have abandoned our plans for judicial separation. And it is, of course, at that precise moment that the disco begins in the restaurant above our bedroom.

Now I am as fond of disco music as the next person. But I do have to admit that by one in the morning I am starting to get just a little irritated. Again and again my ears are assailed with cheerful exhortations to boogie awn down, shake my thang and put mah funk into various people's faces. Given the choice of putting anything into anyone's face right now, I think I would choose a loaded Magnum.

Louder it gets, the bass throbbing. 'It's fun to stay at the YMCA,' I am repeatedly assured through the ceiling. By now I am wishing that is where we're staying. At least we might be able to get a bit of kip and it wouldn't be costing us £402 a night.

But it is when the karaoke kicks off that I really do get angry. I feel my throat-muscles begin to tighten as the raucous chorus commences above me – 'When the moon in the sky is a big pizza pie, that's amore.' But that ISN'T amore. That's fucking DRUGS!

I pull on my dressing-gown and go complaining to the reception desk, or, as it is known in Italian, *el desco de receptione*.

I try to explain to *el portero de la notte* that I can't sleep. He smiles and says there is nothing he can do for the moment.

'But there must be something?'

'No no. Nothing.'

Sad, isn't it? Italians once built the Roman Forum, subjugated the mightiest armies in Europe, ruled a vast and awesome empire encompassing almost all of the known world. Now they can't even stop a singalong of pissheads.

Next day we rise in a bad mood, but cheer ourselves up by setting out to arrange that greatest of all holiday pleasures, hiring a car which you know you are not going to use, but that's not the point – it's there if you need it. The car is delivered, a nifty little Fiat. We drive smugly up and down past the Amalfi taxi rank for a while, making hand gestures of a vaguely Italian nature out the window.

Since we would like to be in a position to feed the child at least sometimes, we decide not to have lunch in the hotel today, but to bring our custom to one of the trattorias in the town. We pull into the local car park.

'*Buongiorno*,' I say. 'How much?'

'Italian?' asks the attendant.

'No.'

'From where?'

'Ireland.'

He thinks for a while. 'Five thousand lire.'

I hand over a bundle of notes.

'Would you like to buy me a cup of coffee, my friend?' he smiles.

I wonder if the parking attendant is propositioning me sexually. But no, it soon becomes quite clear that the invitation is a euphemism, a colourful romantic Italian way of saying 'Give me a gratuity or I will vandalise your car'.

Off we go for lunch, following which the wife discovers that a large bottle of mineral water which costs four pounds back at the hotel is available in the town for just under one pound. I suggest that we buy a few extra bottles and see if we could claw back some of the weekend's unforeseen expenses by selling them on to the other guests. Then it's into the car and off for the daytrip!

See Naples and die, they say. Having now driven in that city, I understand what they meant. One is always nervous of lazily repeating stereotypes and perhaps we were there on a bad day, but I would rather have my eyeballs prised out by the teaspoon of Beelzebub than ever drive a car in Naples again.

Trucks actually speed *at* us, as though in attack. Motorbikers seemingly intent on hara-kiri crisscross in great roars of diesel. Little old ladies on scooters zoom into our path, cackling and scowling like demented Valkyrie. Motorway exits loom up and disappear. In the distance Vesuvius keeps flashing by. Before long I am feeling pretty Vesuvian myself.

We pass a sign that says 'BIENVENTO A NAPOLI' on a mural depicting an armour-clad legionaire. The banner in his hand reads SPQR, an acronym of the ancient motto of Naples ('Some Parts Quite Revolting.')

Somehow we end up in a grimy backstreet. Two staggeringly

large ne'er-do-wells look up from their antipasto and begin lurching across the alleyway in our general direction, dragging their knuckles in the dust as they walk.

'Lost, *si*?' one monster grins.

'Yes. I was wondering if you could give us directions. Back to Amalfi.'

He thrusts out his hand. For one awful moment I wonder if he wants me to hold it.

'Money,' he says.

'Don't you dare ask me for money, you unshaven, dog-breathed cutpurse,' I reply immediately. In my mind.

'How much?' is what I actually say.

'Twenty.'

'Twenty lire? Gosh that seems very reasonable, doesn't it, Dear? If you hold on a moment, I ...'

'TWENTY THOUSAND!' he barks.

I reach into my emaciated wallet and give him thirty. He pockets the notes and glares at me for a while.

'The traffic in Naples, she is bad today, *si*?' he says.

'Oh yes,' I simper. 'Yes, very bad. But it's really a terribly nice place, after all. We're really finding it thoroughly enjoyable, myself and my six-month pregnant wife who would be all alone in the world if anything were to happen to me, murder for example.'

He looks at me and sniggers. '*Strozzo*,' he says.

Then he turns around and walks away.

Jingle Bills:
The Post-Millennium Irish Family Christmas

Whenever I tell foreigners, and particularly English people, that I am the eldest of eight children, they smile understandingly and sometimes quite enviously. 'Ah,' they say, with a wistful sigh, 'the typical Irish Catholic family.'

I think they have a mental image of the eight of us sitting around a turf fire with our gentle, grey-haired Mammy and gruff but oddly poetic Da, all of us strumming banjos, crooning 'Boolavogue' to each other and writing long poems in Irish about fishermen. The Von Trapp family meets Ógra Fianna Fáil.

In fact there were four children in my parents' marriage, which ended when I was thirteen years old. My father is happily remarried to a wonderful woman who had three daughters in her own first marriage. She and my beloved father have a son of their own and I very much think of him as a brother. That makes eight kids. At least I think it does. Sometimes I have to stop and add them all up. Yup. Eight. At the last count.

We don't all keep in constant touch. We often forget each other's birthdays. Only rarely have we all been in one room simultaneously – and that's probably the reason we manage to get along.

Yes, we have our ups-and-downs. Some of us argue, others fall out for a while. But there is one thing which always gives me true hope for the future:

WE HAVE MANAGED TO SPEND ALL OF
CHRISTMAS DAY TOGETHER WITHOUT ANY SINGLE
ONE OF US BEING ACTUALLY STABBED.

And it's coming again. You know it. Don't fight it. There is
really no point in your pitiful denial. It doesn't matter when you
are reading this book. It might be August. It might even be
January. But it's coming again.

It's *always* coming.

Yes, Christmas actually comes but once a year. Thanks be to
God and Her Holy Mother. The season of jolly jangling music
in the streets, and styrofoam snow piled up in shop windows.
Crackers that don't crack and fairy lights that don't light and
Christmas trees all shaggy with smug aplomb. Office parties and
television repeats and perpetual hangovers and Grandad in the
corner sucking the vodka out of his jumper as he wistfully recalls
to the dazed company, all smacked out of their heads on the
angel-dust in the spiced beef, how he got a ball of tinfoil for a
Christmas present every single year until he was forty-seven and
he was happy as a hogget in SHITE with that, not like these
young pups today with their Nintendo machines and
micturating Barbie dolls and mountain bikes and Playstations,
not that it matters anyway because it's his last Christmas on this
earth, and won't he be happy as Larry to go.

Then there is the purgatory of Christmas shopping. Come –
gaze into the crystal ball. There you are, head pounding, in the
subterranean torture chamber that is your local branch of 'Toys
R Bloody Expensive Considering They Break So Soon'. Your
companion is a hysterical nine-year-old relative who is
screeching that her entire life will be ruined and she will grow up
unhappy and never be able to form stable and meaningful
relationships AND IT WILL BE ALL YOUR FAULT unless she
is immediately supplied with a large inflatable hirsute animal
that makes a farting noise when you pull the string attached to
its navel. At this stage, you have actually surrendered. You are
weeping openly. You have your cash in your trembling sweaty

hands. You would willingly throw your money and the deeds of your very soul into a bucket wielded by Satan, if only you could find a sales assistant who would release you from this tinselled gulag. But you can't. Because there isn't one. They're all having the day off. And you know *why*?

TO DO THEIR CHRISTMAS SHOPPING, THAT'S WHY!

Buying for children is bad enough. Buying for children can give you a breakdown, reduce you to a wreck, destroy your mind for ever. But buying for women?

Be afraid.

Men, of course, are useless at this. The Irish Male's idea of a romantic Christmas present is a collapsible monkey-wrench or new carburettor. Even the New Man can get it wrong on this point. A woman I know told me quite recently that she had broken it off with her former boyfriend because of what he bought her last Christmas.

A tennis racket.

Now in truth it seemed to me that a tennis racket was actually quite an original present, a well-thought-out non-sexist gift, a token of egalitarian love in the new century, a subtle tribute to her athleticism and strength. But no, she corrected me, it was a BLOODY TENNIS RACKET! She then levitated towards the ceiling, spitting thumbtacks and bullfrogs.

As well as ending many promising relationships, the holiday season also affords the opportunity for playing all the old favourite traditional Christmas games, such as Musical Chairs, Lick The Bowl, Find The Christmas Pop Song That Doesn't Make You Punt Your Muffins, Avoid The Carollers, Find The Taxi, Snog The Weird Ex, Make The Returning Emigrant Feel Vaguely Uptight In The Pub On Christmas Eve, Fight Off The Mugger and – because it's really for the *children* of course – Leave-the-Slice-of-Cake-Out-For-Santee-Or-He'll-Give-All-Your-Presents-To-Somebody-Else.

And speaking of Santee, how did *he* ever catch on? Wouldn't any healthy society have him locked up immediately? I mean, just hang on one second and let me get this straight. An ancient, overweight Norwegian alcoholic in a red suit and kinky boots, with no visible means of support despite his massive wealth, is going to slither down my chimney in the middle of the night and creep into my bedroom to fill my stocking?

I have a gun. And I'm waiting, Fatboy.

Ah yes. Jolly old Christmas. All those lovely cheerful songs.

On the twelfth day of Christmas my true love sent to me:
Twelve ulcers throbbing,
Eleven puddings burning,
Ten letches letching,
Nine drunkards puking,
Eight grabbers goosing,
Seven Richards Cliffing,
Six toddlers screaming,
Five crOOning BINGS —
Four bawling aunts,
Three French strikes,
Two Ninja Turtles.
And a repeat of The Partridge Famileee.*

'Still,' they will tell you, the Christmas-loving monsters, 'It's a family time, isn't it? All the family together. What on earth could possibly be better than THE FAMILY ALL UNITED AT CHRISTMAS?'

How about having cocktail sticks stuck into your eyeballs?

This Christmas, when you see an image of the Bethlehem manger, have a good long hard look at it. It's an icon of the supposedly perfect family. OK, OK, so it doesn't stand up to even basic scrutiny. *She's* an unmarried mother from a religious minority, *he's* a semi-skilled migrant labourer with poor employ-ment prospects. And Jesus Christ Almighty, that cute little kid

---

* From Charles Dickens, *'Twas the Night Before Christmas and Daddy Was Smashed* (Oliver Twisted Books).

in the swaddling clothes is gonna grow up to wander around the desert in a frock, cause enormous civil disturbance, vandalise a temple and come into serious conflict with the law before being arrested, tortured and nailed to a tree. I mean they're not exactly The Waltons, are they? But no, no – this is a *family* time. Nothing to do with screwing money out of you, honest. We just want you to enjoy YOUR TRADITIONAL FAMILY.

Years ago when there actually *were* traditional families – if, in fact, there ever were – perhaps all this ludicrous mumbo-jumbo was fine. But nowadays things simply ain't so simple.

You waken on Christmas morning feeling like Death-in-a-Duvet. You try to remember who you snogged last night at the office party, after you all got ossified and photocopied your bottoms. There were so many cows, dogs and asses in the room, you thought you had stumbled into the moving crib. You definitely remember getting off with somebody earlier in the evening. You're sure of that. Who could it have been?

Oh no.

Oh Jesus, no.

As the theme music from *Psycho* begins stabbing through your mind, the terrible memory slowly dawns. Your former girlfriend caught you in the pub jacks busily snogging YOURSELF in the mirror.

Your stomach is churning. Your bedroom is spinning. Next time it spins your way you're going to avail of the centrifugal force and jump. Oh *Christ*! Your brain is melting. What did you ever do to deserve such pain? You lurch down the stairs, and there it is. Gathered by the tree. Waiting for you.

The traditional Irish post-millennium family unit.

Yes, gone are the days of the Irish family being the Ma, the Da, the kids and the dog, all of them Catholic, conservative, heterosexual, faithful if married, and virginal if not. There are seventy thousand separated people in Ireland these days, buddy! That means a whole heck of a lot more Christmas complication.

In addition to relations both full-time and temporary, the room is crammed with boyfriends, girlfriends, exes, foundlings, waifs and strays, children and pets. So nice to have those children around at Christmas isn't it? So lovely the way they skip and chant and sing the jolly Yuletide song they wrote especially just for YOU:

Hear the Christmas bells all jingle
Pity that you're fuckin' single.

If the composition of the Irish family has changed, the power structures within said constitutionally protected entity have mutated also. This all started a few years back when the Irish family began to *communicate*. What a disaster. Make no mistake about it; open, honest, uninhibited sharing of feeling has no place whatsoever within the family unit, as fans of *The Godfather* can well attest. As soon as Irish parents started 'to rap', 'chew the fat' or 'shoot the breeze' with their children, the whole institution of the family subjected itself to unwithstandable pressure. And Christmas in Ireland is not a good time for pressure.

Used to be, one word from Dad and everyone nodded their fervent agreement while secretly resolving to do exactly as they liked. But the day after the divorce referendum was passed, Dad packed his bags and promptly legged it. Off to a Buddhist monastery down in West Cork to get in touch with his inner child. Sometimes he sends the occasional letter, signed Bhagwan Shree Majooma Gosht – though your mum always knew him as Mickey-Joe Mooney. Now it's one word from Stepdad and he's given a long lecture on the patriarchy by Auntie Vera, who's come to stay until New Year's Eve, and who's never liked your stepfather anyway, and who has a beard that Castro himself would be proud of since she accidentally took an overdose of Nandrilone bodybuilding steroids instead of her HRT.

Your mother doesn't like your eldest sister's boyfriend. But he had to be invited to dinner this year because last year he wasn't, and it all ended with a tearful punch-up in the cake. This year Mum went along with it, but she's unhappy. Hey, call her old fashioned, and yes, just because he's done four years for burglary, that doesn't *necessarily* mean he's not a nice person. But does he *have* to pour his soup out into a saucer before swigging it? And does he have to keep referring to the dog as 'that bitch'. And if he absolutely must wear his mirrored sunglasses inside the house, couldn't he at least brush the dandruff off the lenses first?

No, Mum is uneasy about your big sister's boyfriend. But she ain't too crazy about your younger sister's girlfriend either. Carly, she's called, and she turned vegetarian the same year she discovered her clitoris, she is happily explaining to Grandad, who's choking on his dentures with the excitement of it all. Live and let live, that's what Mum tries to practise. But did Carly really *have* to turn up to Midnight Mass last night in her QUEER NATION sweatshirt? Back in Mum's day, choice of orientation meant using a compass instead of a map to find your way to Sodality meetings. A dyke was something vague in geography class: something Dutch boys put their fingers into. Now, it seems, Dutch girls also put their ... No. STOP! She doesn't want to go there.

Three-year-old nephew Tarquin is bludgeoning his sister because Santa forgot to bring the batteries for his cute little Machine-Gun/Learning-Aid. Four-year-old niece Madonna is fashioning postmodernist sculptures from bits of dogturd she found under the Christmas tree – her mother warns you not to intervene and accuses you of trying to stunt her creativity. As for the Christmas tree, it isn't the best. Your stepfather totally forgot to buy one this year. He was too busy concentrating on scoring some coke. So it was up to the attic at one this morning to search out the ancient bri-nylon model that looks like a mouldy toilet-brush stuck to a tripod.

Granny's here too. Temporarily released from the Old Folks' Home, allegedly on an experimental care-in-the-community scheme, but actually because she keeps trying to burn the place down. Look at her, paper sombrero clamped over the heated rollers. Absolutely no idea of where in the name of Jesus she is. But what the Hell. At least she's happy. And if you were on the drugs she's on, you'd be too.

Grandad wants to tell you what's wrong with the Michael Collins movie that's on the telly AGAIN tonight. He knew Michael Collins *pairsonally*, you see, him and Mick were *like dat*, he knew him well and he was *a daily communicant* and the very idea that he'd be leppin' in and out of the scratcher wit dat tart Julia Roberts is a heinous blasphemy. Stepdad tells him to put a sock in it. Mum tells him to do the same. Grandad insists that he knows what he's talking about. He was 'out' in 1916. Little sister and Carly stop playing footsie under the table and perk up at this point. Is Grandad saying he too is part of the QUEER NATION? No no, of course he's not, he's saying he was 'out' in the General Post Office in 1916. 'AND DAT FILLUM IS A DAMN DISGRACE.'

Food, too, is now a source of utterly explosive Yuletide ructions. In the good auld days of turkey and ham, menu planning was admirably simple. All anyone had to argue about back then was whether or not to have Brussels sprouts. Nowadays Granny's food has to be minced, and little Tarquin's has to be pulped, and little Goneril's has to be mashed and wok-fried because she's hyperactive and allergic as well as dyslexic, and your brother's vegan girlfriend has to have desiccated lettuce or broiled tofu-burgers guaranteed to be produced in a country where they've never even shown a cow on television. She's studying politics in UCD and she's very left-wing and after oh, a vat of red wine, she wants to know how anyone has the loik audacity to eat this amount of fewd when people in the thord world are loik storving. (She almost caused a fistfight earlier when she told your two-year-old cousin Lucretia that Santa's little elves work in loik Fascist conditions and are TEWTALLY non-unionised.)

Aunty Vera is GAGGING for the want of a drink. She's only

staying with you because she was fecked out of the chronic alcoholism unit in John Of God's, so it's Carly's home-made vegan lemonade for her, until she can sneak up to the jacks where she's hidden a dishcloth saturated with gin in the cistern. Your mother heard full-throated sucking sounds coming from the bathroom earlier, but given the various hair-raising possibilities implied by the range of overnight guests she didn't really feel like investigating too closely. She had other things on her mind anyway. She's not allowing herself to have any Christmas pudding this year because she's on a diet. She says she's on a diet 'for herself', as a 'life-affirming, self-nurturing, holistic experience'. She's actually on a diet because last night, when he reeled in from the next-door neighbour's sherry and pornography evening, your stepfather grabbed her, dragged her under the mistletoe and told her she could wear her stomach as a kilt.

Sisters start fighting. Babies start crying. Brother starts sulking. Mother starts screaming. Aunty Vera starts drinking. Stepdad starts singing:

Away in a manger, no-ho crib for a bed
The little Lord Jesus lay down his sweet head
The stars in the bright sky, light up you and me.
The little Lord Jesus
On PAYE.

Bah, as somebody once put it, and humbug.
And as for New Year's Eve? *Don't get me started.*
Should old acquaintance be forgot and never brought to mind? Take it from me, the short answer is YES!

Patrick Pearse and the Easter Bunny

You know, I recollect my dear old Granny talking to me once when I was a lad. Well, two or three times actually to be strictly accurate. But this particular time was just before Easter one year. I think I would have been five or six.

'Joseph,' she said – her memory was admirable – 'Joseph, if you are very good, and if you do not be giving lip out of you to the poor nuns beyond in the school, and if you eat up all your greens, do you know what will happen to my nicens little man?'

I glanced up from my biography of Proust and replied in the negative.

I recall Granny smiling then, and giving me a big huggly-wuggly-snuggly and confiding that if the above conditions were fully satisfied, and if I tried to be that rarest of things, 'a good boy,' a giant rabbit would hop into my bedroom on Easter Saturday night and give me a large egg made out of chocolate.

She grinned. She nodded wisely. And I can clearly remember thinking, as I stared at her loving face, how absolutely great it will be when I am a grown-up, because then I too will be able to take powerful hallucinogenic drugs, just like Granny.

The Easter Bunny?

The WHAT?!

Something in our culture has gone terribly wrong when we celebrate the miraculous arrival of spring by inventing a character which even John Lennon in the post-Pepper years would have found a tad on the spacey side. Santa Claus? The Easter Bunny? Honest to God, the role models we give children. And we wonder why they grow up robbing cars.

Apart from long nights lying awake feeling terrified of giant lagomorphine invaders, my other childhood memory of Easter is the Easter Parade. Younger readers will not remember this, because a number of years ago a government of what I suppose one might call the revisionist persuasion (though 'uptight Blueshirt scuzzballs' is the technical term) decided that the best way to deal with the Easter Rising and its attendant, if uncomfortable, symbolism for our country was to completely ignore it and instead make RTÉ put on *The Best of the Two Ronnies* so we could all celebrate Easter properly.

The thinking was that if we had a parade to mark the Easter Rising, all the inhabitants of our poor windswept rock would immediately rush off to join the Provisional IRA, just as in modern France, as we all know, people don period costume and behead aristocrats every Bastille Day. But anyway. There used to be an Easter Parade, and my parents used to bring us to it.

Oh, how we looked foward to the Easter Parade! Forget Mayday in Moscow or East Berlin, here was a display of military might. You could see the entire Irish army pass by – all seventeen of them and their bikes. Also marching would be those valiant praetorians, the FCA or 'Free Clothes Association'. If you were really lucky they would have on display many pieces of high-tech equipment, such as penknives, compasses and complicated knots.

Now, seven-year-old boys do not have much of an understanding of Ireland's important tradition of neutrality, nor of the essential and courageous work of our international peace-keepers. When you are seven and possesed of a Y-chromosome, you do not want to see your country's army wielding hurley-sticks. You want to see them carrying THERMONUCLEAR MISSILES. So the Easter Parade, like most things in childhood, was more exciting to anticipate than to actually experience.

Except for one aspect.

Every year it would be the same: out of the middle of the ranks of soldiers he would come capering, some poor unfortunate recently recruited private, dressed up in that most secret of all deadly weapons – the Irish Army's Easter Bunny suit. To see him gamely lepping about O'Connell Street, flapping his arms and chewing his giant plastic carrot, would make the parade seem worth a whole year's waiting.

Yet for all his absurdity the Easter Bunny is quite a revealing beastie, if we think about him for even a moment. The plain fact is that before Christianity appropriated the pagan festival of spring for its own highly specialised ends, Easter was actually a celebration of the one activity at which rabbits truly excel. And I do not mean going 'Nyeargh, what's up, Doc?'

Yes, Easter was the rite of renewal and birth, and, in that beautiful spiritual context, was very much about shagging. If we could enter a time machine and go back a few millennia to see what our ancestors were doing on Good Friday, they would not have been saying the Sorrowful Mystery, I'll tell you that much. Easter is the one festival that truly belongs to us all, not to any single church or sect or party. It is a milestone that says life is worth the living, its secret meaning still sometimes capable of being read, even through the layers of crapology with which we've smothered it.

I mean, come on – *chocolate EGGS*?

What do you want? A telegram or something?

The Secret World
of the Irish Mammy

A few years ago St Patrick's Day and Mother's Day happened to fall on the same Sunday. Well a thing like that can make you think. Particularly if you can't be bothered to get out of bed.

What do we really feel about mothers here in Mother Ireland, the world capital of po-faced devotion to mammydom? Oh yes, we sing about the mammy when we're rat-faced drunk and we bung her a bunch of daffodils every Mother's Day morning, which we stole from the forecourt of a garage down the road. And musha, why wouldn't we? She's our mammy, after all.

Many traditional Irish ballads celebrate the special role of mothers, including the following beautiful and poignant example from the 1920s in South Kerry. It is sung to the tune of 'Spancil Hill', with a tremendously deep feeling of beer:

Oh Mammy, you're a livin' saint,
An angel in a dress.
You always have a lovely smile
When you're sweepin' up the mess.
When I'm loadin' up me weapon, boys,
For to aim it at a Brit,
I think about me mammy's smile.
And I shoot the little shit. *

---

* Quoted in *Five Hundred Songs of Mother Ireland* by Dr Oedipus O'Beard (Maam Cross Publications).

Such stirring examples of native song expressed our patriotic feelings about the Mammyland. And our mammies had a unique place in our affections. For example, as Gemma Hussey's book *Ireland: Anatomy Of A Changing State* points out, if you look up the word 'mother' in the index to the 1937 Constitution, the document on which every single Irish law is predicated, you will notice the words, '*Woman – see family and sex*'.

Nice, huh?

Must have been really convenient for Irish mammies to be shown with such clarity just what they were for.

Oh begob, we were historically, hysterically, mad about the mammy. On Mother's Day we cooked the lunch. Well OK, she actually cooked it the day before but at least we managed to heat it up without setting fire to the kitchen. Because we *loved* our mammy. We LOVED HER TO DEATH. And just to really prove our love, a Dáil motion of 1925 stopped her getting divorced; a law of 1927 excluded her from jury service. Well, we didn't want our mammies sitting in the courts or anything. Sure it's men who decide what crimes are, not ladies! And when it came to setting up the Censorship Board, our mammies were once again excluded. We wouldn't want our mammies reading dirty literature, vile sweaty guff about lezzers and malcontents. It might take their minds off washing our pants.

Strangely enough, a great number of books which the male censors thought were acceptable promoted an image of our mammies as victims or virgins. But that didn't worry us. 'Sit back there, Mammy, it's Mother's Day,' we cried. 'Here's a box of chocolates and a few balls of wool. Would you ever knit me another jumper?' Our mammies were helpfully banned from the civil service in 1925, to allow them more time to clean up our bedrooms. Ten years later they were told they couldn't have any of those nasty English contraceptives. We liked them being our mammies so much, we decided they should be mammies over and over again!

Yes, we sent her a card every year. It expressed our gratitude and profound appreciation in heartwarmingly sentimental little verses such as the following:

Mammy, how I thank you;
You really are my friend;
All the love you give me –
Love without end.
And when you get to Paradise,
Our Lord Himself will say:
'Welcome, dearest Mammy –
NOW WHERE'S ME SHAGGIN' TAY?!'

OK, so we didn't always feel as well-disposed as that. Occasionally we thought our mammies were getting strange modern ideas. We didn't like some of the clothes they wore. When a mammy is a mammy she should *dress* like a mammy. So we got the bishops to write a few pastoral letters about 'immodest fashions in female dress'. And the priests would put on their nice lacey frocks and flowing silken gowns and read to our mammies from the altar, telling them not to be dressing like tarts.

By 1937 the bishops were busy with other things. Yes, they were happily writing the new Constitution with the occasional bit of interference from the actual government. There were three TDs at the time who were mammies. But these were naughty, *unhelpful* mammies. They wouldn't just shut up and make the sandwiches, the way a proper mammy should. No, they kept on making speeches, yapping out of them – you know the way the ladies do. They went so far as to claim that mammies had rights! Well we had to talk a bit of sense into them. So we got the newspapers to do that for us.

Here is an absolutely genuine quote from an *Irish Independent* editorial of the time:

'Many men (including, it is whispered, the President) think
that a woman cuts a more fitting and more useful figure when
darning the rents in her husband's socks by the fireside than she
could hope to cut in a Parliamentary assembly …'

---

* William Butler Yeats, 'The Song of the Wandering Mammy'.

Now. That softened their cough for them, didn't it? We didn't send *those* mammies a Mother's Day card. Naughty mammies. Bad mammies.

For thirty years after that, there was barely a peep out of the happy Irish mammy. She was busy at home, where she needed to be. She had fourteen children, after all! And every Mother's Day we brought her breakfast in bed, where she was happily giving birth to the next babby while simultaneously ironing us a shirt in which to emigrate. All this feminist nonsense about our mammies being oppressed. All that liberal hokum about miscarriage and still-birth rates being the highest in Europe. Our mammies *loved* their wonderful lives. And didn't they have their own mammy in heaven – The *Blessed* Mammy – to put in a word for them when things got a bit tiring?

No, the Irish mammy had a wonderful time. On Mother's Day, Daddy would give her a little break. Or sometimes even a compound fracture. But that was a terribly rare occurrence. In fact no Irish mammy ever had to live in a violent marriage, so there was no need at all to give them legal aid, or change the laws to allow them to have abusive husbands removed. So that was handy! They were *never* deserted or abandoned with their children, so the taxpayer never had to give them welfare. Think of all the money we saved! As for the few very bad mammies who did run out on their husbands just for punching them every night for ten years – well you will always get the rotten apple. (As Eve found out!) But even then we didn't turn our backs on them. Oh no. In order to protect that misguided mammy, the Criminal Conversation laws were introduced, entitling her ape-like geek of a husband to prosecute anyone who gave her a cup of tea and a sandwich. I ask you, what could be fairer than that? *Every* day was Mother's Day here in Ireland!

Admittedly our mammies were considered their husbands' property. But that was what our mammies wanted. And what man in his right senses wouldn't look after such a valuable possession? This is what the young women of today completely fail to understand – our mammies didn't mind that until 1965 they could be disinherited by their husbands. Not at all. They thought it was great! And they didn't mind that they weren't entitled to the dole, or that their only legal status was as dependents of males, or that Children's Allowance payments were made to fathers and not mothers. And as for getting equal pay for equal work?

They were mammies, for God's sake! Their work was being walked on!

Late last year, I was listening to Marian Finucane's radio programme, when a young woman called to say she wanted to take up boxing but was having difficulty finding a trainer. Would any of the listeners have any advice? A much older soft-spoken reticent woman rang to say she found the idea utterly horrifying. It was undignified, common; so unladylike.

'I mean, Marian,' she implored, 'can you imagine the Blessed Virgin Mary in a boxing ring?'

I have to confess, I found the picture intriguing. *In the Red Corner, ladies and gentlemen, wearing the black trunks, the undefeated heavyweight champion of the world – Iron Mike TYSON! (Booooo). And in the Blue Corner and wearing the sky-blue veil, tonight's contender – something of a newcomer but she's full of grace, an immaculate little mover with some good combinations. Make no assumptions, she's virgin on a title! Your appreciation please – FOR THE MOTHER OF GOD!'*

Now that would be a fight worth getting Sky for.

Ms Finucane had to point out that young Irish women did *lots* of things these days which it might be hard to imagine the Blessed Virgin Mary doing. As indeed they do. Things like vote. Or watch *Ally McBeal* on a Wednesday night. Or employ other modes of transport than assback. It was a funny moment. But it was poignant too.

The historian Dr Margaret McCurtain has remarked: 'Around Irishwomen, as in a cage, were set the structures of family life.'

You won't be seeing that on a Mother's Day card.

Nor the words of the great Irish socialist, Hannah Sheehy-Skeffington: 'Ireland will never be free until Irish women are free.'

But sure there you go. That's women for you now. Never bleeding happy, are they?

Flicks, Chicks and Getting in a Fix

The very first film I ever saw in a cinema was *War And Peace* starring Henry Fonda and Audrey Hepburn. The cinema stood on the main street in Dun Laoghaire. It isn't there any more, and I can't remember its name, despite much brain-racking and carpet-pacing (The Adelphi, maybe?). Anyway, it was fantastically exciting to be going to the pictures at all, and I was knocked out by the storming sound and fabulous fury of the movie with its epic battle scenes and colourful costumes and generally swashbuckling style. But what was even more gripping than the film itself was the fact that it was so long it had to be shown in two parts. Part One was running for one week and you couldn't see Part Two until *the week after that*! For a nipper reared on the ten-minute culture of children's TV this was an astonishing and quite revolutionary concept. Over this I could not get.

Apart from the fact that the film concerned Russians and people bayoneting each other and glamorous women flouncing around in crinoline, I couldn't really follow the story of Part One much, but I loved it anyway. I spent the whole of the ensuing week salivating with anticipation at the thought of returning to the cinema for Part Two, in which, as I recall it now, Audrey Hepburn looked even more beautiful than she had in Part One. Well, perhaps I had grown a few more hormones in those seven days. Anyway, 'Natasha' was the name of the character she played. I promised myself that if I ever met a Natasha when I grew up I would marry her. And I did, once. But that's another story.

Shortly after this experience my parents and I went to see *Butch Cassidy and The Sundance Kid* in the same cinema. It wasn't as good as *War And Peace* because it was only in one part and it didn't feature Audrey Hepburn, or, indeed, any characters at all called Natasha or dressed in furry hats or bayoneting each other. But it was still pretty good.

The other cinema in Dun Laoghaire was the Pavilion, a vast, pastel-coloured, ornately corniced building which was as quintessentially 1950s as a little red Chevy. (Sadly the Pavilion is now also defunct, transmogrified into a yuppy apartment block.) You could see a film on a Saturday afternoon in the Pavilion for ten pence, and my brother and sisters and I often did. I suspect that many a marriage in the greater south Dublin area was saved, or at least prolonged, by the existence of the Pavilion Cinema.

In school there was a film every Friday night at seven o'clock in the hall. A gentle, compassionate priest called Father Al Flood was in charge of this event. At the start of each year he would select two or three boys for film duty, and one year myself and my pal James Boland were the lucky winners. The job involved Father Flood driving us into town after school on a Friday in order to collect that night's film from the distributor's office, which, as far as I remember, was just off Westland Row, and then driving us back to the school, where we would get the reels out of their big metal circular boxes and set up the projector and generally think we were really something.

The Friday night films were typically such fine, intelligent works as *The Guns Of Navarone*, *The Great Escape* and *Tora! Tora! Tora!*, which is a deeply educational and multiculturally sensitive work about the bombing of Pearl Harbour by evil Japanese loonies. From time to time Father Flood would tire of this kind of thing and for a few Friday nights there would be films with religious themes, such as *The Ten Commandments* and *Brother Sun, Sister Moon*. These were not nearly so entertaining, although it was rumoured that several people had ACTUALLY DIED during the making of *The Ten Commandments*. It was a lot of fun watching out for those bits.

Father Jarlath Dowling was another wonderful man. He taught music in my school for many years. I seem to recall that he actually *lived* in the music room; his small bed, which always looked as if it had been recently savaged by a wild animal, sat looking forlorn in the middle of the floor, surrounded by trumpets and tubas and drums.

Father Dowling was fanatically interested in old movies. He had a pull-down screen and a rattling projector in the music room. Often he would show us a Laurel and Hardy short or a Marx Brothers feature when we should have been listening to Beethoven or Brahms. He was a plump, passionate, fiery man with a head as bald as a billiard ball. Whenever he either lost his temper or laughed for any length of time he would sweat heavily, and his face would go red and heat up, with the result that the sweat on his scalp would turn into steam. When this happened – and it happened not infrequently – it looked like Father Dowling's head was oozing smoke. It was quite an effect. It really was. He could have sold tickets and made a lot of dough.

I remember one time during a music class Father Dowling decided that we really should see *A Night at the Opera*, which had the blissful virtue of combining his two greatest enthusiams. The screen was pulled down, the chairs were pulled up, the curtains were drawn and off we went. Father Dowling was sitting just down the row from me. And about five minutes into the film, he started to laugh.

At first, it was what comic books call 'a titter', and then it grew to a strangled chortle. Shortly after this he began to guffaw and then to snort. He tried to control himself. He sat sculpturally still, his legs tightly crossed, his face scarlet, the occasional apologetic cluck of mirth bursting forth from his massive frame. But it was no good. Before long he was rocking back and forth on his chair, slapping his thighs and actually honking with helpless, unrestrained laughter. And then the poor man just lost it completely.

He couldn't stop. What I can only describe as a blast of laughter exploded out of him. It sounded like one of his beloved trumpets being played by a lunatic with Gargantuan lungs. He howled. He bawled. He groaned. He cackled. The Marx Brothers cantered across the screen and Father Dowling opened his mouth and ROARED and bellowed with laughter. He jumped to his feet and lurched up and down the music room clutching his enormous stomach, barking with sheer abandoned joy, big tears of gaiety rolling down his chubby cheeks. Thirty seconds later the entire class of nine-year-old boys was in utter hysterics. The principal must have heard the noise because he burst in shortly afterwards to find out what was going on. He glared in astonishment at Father Dowling, who was now uncontrollably sobbing with hysterical glee and leaning on a radiator with a hanky stuffed into his mouth – and then he glared at us, and then he glared up at the screen, where the Marx Brothers were now doing a dance. And then the principal started laughing. Which made Father Dowling laugh even more. And then the smoke started coming from Father Dowling's head. Which made us nearly widdle with laughter. And so on. It was astonishing. The Catholic Church introduced me to Marxism. It's the happiest memory I have of school.

Another movie recollection, less pleasurable although more poignant, is the first real date I ever had. It involved the Forum Cinema in Glasthule, a large bag of popcorn, a lot of hope and Denim deodorant and a very nice girl from Monkstown Farm. Her name was Patricia Keegan and she had gorgeous hair. I had met her the previous Saturday night at 'Prez', the Presentation College Disco, Glasthule. She, like me, was sixteen-and-a-bit. (She a bit beautiful. I a bit nervous.)

The movie we went to see was *Midnight Express*, which

turned out to be about an unfortunate American youth called Billy Hayes who gets imprisoned for twenty years in Turkey for smuggling drugs. To say the work portrays negative images of that country would be something of an understatement. The people who run the Turkish Tourist Board must have shat themselves when this was released.

Let me tell you, if you are trying to make a good impression, this is NOT a good movie to see on a first date. Poor Billy Hayes. Torture, gang-rape, nudity, squalor, filth, cockroaches, endless cursing and public masturbation – *Midnight Express* featured all these thought-provoking themes and more. Every five minutes, it seemed to me, Patricia emitted another near-puking noise, or plaintive wail of abject disgust, and scowled in my direction like I was some sort of pervert for bringing her to see this hideous gore-fest. I, for my part, kept my eyes locked on the screen. Because by now pure shock had drained the power from my neck muscles.

The film climaxed with a scene of a prisoner biting a fellow inmate's tongue out and spitting it across the room in glorious Technicolour slow-motion. If I live to be a hundred-and-fifty, I will never forget the sound which issued forth simultaneously from the darkness beside me. It was the sound of Patrica Keegan going 'oh Jeeeeeeeeeeeeeezis'. As I watched that tongue flying through the air I somehow sensed that the chances of my own tongue making any contact whatsoever with Patricia Keegan's later on in the evening were receding fast. And I wasn't wrong.

She broke my heart when she finally dumped me. Every time I see *Midnight Express* I still think of her. And the funny thing is, after all these years, I still reckon Billy Hayes got off lighter than me.

There's One Yawn Every Minute

Gentle reader, you have probably guessed that as a fully trained, youngish, award-winning novelist – albeit that the award was for ten-pin bowling – I frequently receive letters from the unwashed *hoi polloi*, many of whom want to write Irish fiction as a hobby. Other correspondents are far more serious in their aims. They too would like to be young, award-winning novelists (YAWNS for short) and would like me, perhaps the greatest YAWN in the country, to give them 'some advice'. My main advice would be the following: never sleep with anyone who has an annoying laugh.

But it turns out this is not the kind of advice they want. No, what they want to know about is literature and how to do it. So here are my top tips for literary success:

1) Dealing with the Desire to Write

Ask yourself if you really do want to write. It is true that most Irish Males have a book in them, but in most cases that's exactly where it should stay. Few people are suited to the life of the YAWN, involving as it does a good deal of solitude, angst and gratuitous wearing of black polo-neck sweaters. If you do find youself experiencing a deep and burning inner desire to express yourself creatively, try eating something and often the feeling will go away.

2) When to Start

If you really do want to write, start young. It often occurs to me that when Keats was my age he had been dead for eleven years. This clearly gave him an unfair advantage with the critics.

3) Writing Comedy

Always remember the profound words of Groucho Marx: 'An amateur thinks it's funny to dress a man up as an old lady, put him in a wheelchair and push him down a hill towards a stone wall. For a pro, it's got to be a *real* old lady.'

4) Writing Serious Literature

A work of serious literature is a book with a lot of weather in it. In serious literature wind does not blow. It *howls, shrieks, weeps* or *screams*. To the serious YAWN, rain does not merely fall. It *spatters, patters, spits* or *surges*. Snow invariably lies on the grass *like a coverlet, blanket* or *continental quilt*.

5) Sex

It is often difficult for aspiring YAWNS to handle scenes of sexual activity. This is mainly because they know that Granny is going to read the book when it is published and they do not want to hasten her departure from the corporeal realm, at least, not for the moment. But be brave. Grab hold of your courage in both hands. Remember that it is compulsory to use all of the following words in your sex scene, in whatever order suits your purposes, and indeed your morals: *pulsating; trousers; steaming; Wellington boots* (if applicable); *quivering; tongue; again and again; deeper, tumescent; proudly pert; inwardly; downwardly; swirling ectoplasm of anguished desire; baby oil; heaving; heart-stopping series of Vesuvian eruptions; cigarette; taxi home; chips and batterburger (salt and vinegar optional).*

6) Sending Your Finished Typescript to the Publisher

Most aspiring YAWNS take the time and trouble to enclose a large, stamped-addressed envelope with their first novels. I know from bitter experience that this is a terrible mistake. It is far too much temptation for the publisher to resist.

7) Public Readings

The best audience for your work will be intelligent, well-educated and only slightly drunk. But these days some audiences at literary events can be quite aggressive, going so far as to staple their rotten vegetables to lengths of elastic so they can hit you twice. There is an old English music-hall song which goes: 'They made me a present/ of Mornington Crescent/ They threw it one brick at a time.' For some reason, those lines frequently come into my head when I am doing a reading.

8) Handling Hecklers

When you begin your career as a YAWN, you will be doing many readings in places like Thurles, which I know quite well because I spent forty years there one night recently. The indigenous peoples of these primitive settlements are not well known for their love of literature. So it is always a wise strategy to prepare a few witty put-down lines for abusive hecklers. One response which has been good to me over the years is, 'Listen, pal, I'd like to help you out. Which way did you come in?' If all else fails just open your mouth and scream, 'THE DEVIL MADE ME DO IT!' Then simply continue reading as though nothing odd has happened.

9) Book Signings

It is important that you at least try to listen to what the kind person who is buying your book has to say. Failure to do so may cause embarrassment, offence or even assault. I am indebted to the fine novelist Mr Colum McCann for the story of the young Irish author who was sitting proudly behind the table at his first signing in London. There he is, a vision of loveliness, pen in hand, as the queue shuffles up to purchase books and get them signed. A young woman approaches. He beams, flourishes the biro and asks for her name.

'Emma Chisett,' she smiles.

He signs the flyleaf with a graceful swirl – 'To Emma Chisett, with warmest best wishes.'

The woman peers at this heartfelt inscription, distaste now graven on her lovely face.

'Whatcher write that for?' she asks.

'Well ... Is your name not Emma Chisett?'

'Naow,' she snickers, in finest Cockney. 'I was askin' you 'ow much is it? *Emma Chisett?*'

My Own Personal Irish Male

By now you won't be surprised to learn that for most of my life I've been sure I would never be a father. Nor, to be frank, did I want to be. The very idea was painful enough to make me generally avoid discussing it. When friends or even family members talked about their children, something inside me would simply click off and I'd find an excuse to change the subject. I'm sure one of the real reasons was that my own parents' marriage was unhappy and ended in the courts when I was thirteen. Even after their separation, we children continued to be the focus of their arguments, my father having to fight constant and bitter battles with a woman who was good at many things, but not good at being a mother. So I grew up regarding marriage as a trap for the decent people, almost by definition an emotional torture which having children could only prolong.

Most children of unhappy marriages blame themselves for their parents' misfortunes. I used to also, from my earliest childhood. Therapists, self-help books and often your parents themselves will advise you against this, and of course they are right. But I found it hard to kick the habit.

The guilt I acquired in my childhood had odd effects in later life. I spent most of my twenties sternly reprimanding myself for things which on mature reflection were not really my fault – Shamrock Rovers having to move from Milltown, the rise to power of General Pinochet – while accepting no responsibility whatsoever for things which were, such as heavy smoking, would-be promiscuity and the frequent composition of derivative poetry. My personal life was so fiendishly complicated I couldn't keep track of which lies I was supposed to be telling to whom. In politics I developed a deeply irrational need to feel spurious affinities with other creatures who were suffering badly, such as whales, Guatemalans or the Irish Labour Party. I do not mean to imply in any way that everyone on the Left is motivated by low self-regard masquerading as comradely solidarity. Indeed most of my personal Irish heroes are people who work for social change simply because it is right to do so. But that's not the only reason I did so myself. In those days, feeling better was part of the mix.

And in those days marriage was just another thing to oppose, another weapon in the arsenal of the bourgeoisie. This suited me well; it made bachelorhood a *cause*. I was opposed to marriage like I was opposed to apartheid. 'Free Nelson Mandela' may have been written on my T-shirt, but 'Fight For The Right To Party' was written on my heart.

It wasn't until my early thirties that I met someone who gave me inescapable cause to question my certainty. A beautiful, intelligent, kind-hearted woman who would send me John Donne poems by fax, she was, basically, my kind of gal. And even my attitude to the prospect of having children softened a little during our courtship. To fall in love is to make yourself believe that almost any difference of perspective is either illusory or unimportant. I knew my beloved wanted to be a mother some day and I felt she would make a wonderful one. Whenever she asked if I wanted a family myself, I managed to project a kind of nonchalant agnosticism. And by the time we married, several years later, I had succeeded in dressing up my neurotic unease as a laidback desire to trust in fate.

Fourteen months later my wife discovered she was pregnant. My initial reaction was one of amazement – not just that it had happened, but at how happy I felt about it. For several days I walked around in a haze of cheerfulness and positivity. But soon my feelings became more complicated. It wasn't that the exhilaration of the first week exactly disappeared. It was just that beneath it something else was growing; that old gnawing sense of foreboding and angst.

We decided not to tell anyone our news for a while, for the usual reason – 'in case anything goes wrong'. (Impending parents become quickly adept at euphemism, a skill they will need for the next eighteen years.) The pregnancy felt like a shared conspiracy, a covert game being played by two participants who didn't quite know all the rules just yet. A lot of couples say this is fun, and in a way it is, though for me the secrecy had other uses too. It allowed me an amount of crazy denial. If we didn't tell anyone, it wasn't really happening.

After a short time I began to see that what I was doing was ridiculous, and I tried to confront the reality of our situation. But I found that the only way I could think about the baby was with that particular mixture of empathy and objectivity one might feel for the hero of a novel. And then I realised it wasn't the baby I was seeing in this way; rather that most unbelievable of all fictional characters – myself as a competent, loving parent. The Irish Male: From Lad to Dad.

How could someone as interestingly damaged as myself ever begin to cope with this role? Who was I fooling? Myself? My wife? Statisticians tell us that most children of divorce will end up in unhappy marriages themselves. What if that were to happen to us? It didn't feel likely, but how could you tell? And if things between us ever did go wrong, what kind of separated parents would we make? I can see now that the questions look utterly paranoid. But at the time they seemed logical, *completely* necessary – even if, perhaps unsurprisingly, I kept them to myself.

This probably sounds far-fetched, but in a way I think abject terror was good for our relationship. Certainly it forced me really to consider the promises I had made to my wife on our wedding day. I would silently repeat them, thinking about the words, and whenever I did that, the fear receded. Yes our marriage might fail

– but whose might not? In a way, the risk seemed suddenly the whole *point* of marriage – to make an act of faith with the world. As soon as I stopped worrying about my own painful childhood, I sensed my wife and myself become closer. There were no big chats about the future, we simply seemed to accept that suddenly it was here. If we were silent sometimes, the silence became more comfortable than heretofore. My wedding day was the happiest day of my life, but I honestly think the first month of the pregnancy was in almost every sense the beginning of our marriage.

But still I found it hard to express my emotions about impending fatherhood. I think that's because I didn't entirely know what they were. I had managed to stop thinking I was doomed to be a bad parent, but that isn't the same thing as believing you'll be a good one. I did find the first foetal scan affecting, but I didn't cry, as most of my friends had predicted I would, and I felt a bit guilty about that. As my wife and I walked down the street together afterwards, I felt as if there were a sign dangling over my head – The Fucker Who Didn't Cry at the Scan.

I approached the second scan in a state of apprehension. The clinic in London which my wife attended is also a renowned centre for fertility treatment, and I remember feeling painfully conscious as we waited in the foyer that many of the other couples in the room would give all they had to be in our situation. By now some of our child's features were clearly discernible – an arm, a spine, a ghostly white face. But if I am honest, the sight still wasn't enough to make me feel like a father. The little creature on the monitor screen was more like a being from a faraway planet, some amniotic spaceman unimagined by science-fiction. He turned, he rolled, he moved his tiny head. But even as the nurse finished making her notes, and confirmed that he was doing well, it didn't feel like he had much to do with me.

It was what happened next that I found astounding. Almost casually, the nurse reached out and flicked a speaker switch on the monitor unit. There was a short crackling sound, a few watery echoes. The nurse smiled and raised a finger to her lips for us to be silent. A moment passed. A truck went by in the street. And then the sound of our son's heartbeat filled the small room.

My own heart actually seemed to stop. It was like having a spear of longing driven through me. I will remember that sound until the moment I die, that pulsing rhythm of extraordinary rapidity that called for nothing but to be loved in return. It was about nothing except itself; its own beauty, its own aching vulnerability. It was so very ordinary, yet it felt unspeakably sacred. Unable to speak, I stood still and simply listened, trembling with emotion as I held my wife's hand. More than any music I have ever heard, that sound changed my life as I listened to it. I left that room a father at last.

But in truth that sound implied darker things too, some of which I was grievously unprepared for. The night of the scan I had a dream of my own death, the next night the same; before long it had become a regular occurrence. I'd be drowning, sinking, endlessly falling. Sometimes I would hear the baby's heartbeat.

I'm not someone who often has nightmares, so I found the dreams disturbing in the extreme. I wondered was something terribly wrong with me? Had the fear I'd always felt of parenthood been well-founded, after all? Did I, in shameful fact, simply not want this child? But even as I asked myself those questions, I already knew they were the wrong ones.

When I was younger I think I honestly believed that some-how I would never die. Now, on the point of becoming a father, I finally realised that one day I would. It is the darkest secret of impending parenthood – how birth also gives an intimation of mortality. To bring a new life into the world is to face up to many things, among them the certainty of your own ultimate extinction. 'They give birth aside the grave,' wrote Samuel Beckett. I never knew what those words really meant until the pregnancy.

And yet after a few weeks the bad dreams simply stopped. They never returned, I don't know why. Neither do I have any explanation for what happened next. To say I began to experience a deep sense of calm and acceptance would be technically correct, but it doesn't come close. I have no shred of religious feeling, but the language of sacrament keeps suggesting itself. Suffice it to say, if there is a peace that passes understanding, I think I know what it is now. It is the memory of nothing more than a child's heartbeat, the small persistent puttering rhythm which proclaims that life has triumphed over death, that you can stand up and walk out of the tomb of your own past. Even if that peace eventually fades from my life – even if it were to completely disappear – to have glimpsed it just once is miracle enough. And I owe that blessing to my wife and child.

But I didn't see the baby as anything supernatural. As the scans continued, and our son developed, I found myself pondering the awesome fact of his physicality – his bones, his muscles, his skull and internal organs, the two impossibly black shadows that were slowly becoming eyes. He didn't appear to *grow* as such; he unfurled, he sprouted, he seemed to take leaf. Like a loving heart in a John Donne poem.

Sometimes, in quieter moments, I would allow myself to imagine what it would be like to look into those eyes; to see them gazing steadily back into mine with all the tenderness of filial love, to watch as one day, far in the future, they convey the beautiful wordless message which every father finds so deeply moving: 'Give me some money, Baldy, or I'll invite my friends around.'

The last time I saw our son's face on the monitor screen, it sent a bolt of lightning through my chest. I felt as though I were seeing a ghost. But I was, of course – the ghost was my own. I looked at his face, then I looked at my wife's. She gave me a vaguely playful wink. I truly believe it was the first time in my life that I understood what it is to love completely, unconditionally. The child is father to the man, they say. I only hope I can return the favour – because even before our beautiful son came into the world, he had taught me more about how to live in it than anyone else I have ever known.

What a blessing. What a joy.

My own beloved Irish Male.

RTÉ *Drivetime*
Radio Diaries
2008-2009

Barack Obama Steps Up
9 April 2008

It was a remarkable experience to be in America at the moment when Senator Barack Obama almost lost the 2008 presidential race. His difficulty involved his family minister, the Reverend Jeremiah Wright – the kind of pulpit-thumping firebrand they used to produce in the North of Ireland in the days before peace and love. A sermon delivered the Sunday after 9/11 received particular attention from the American media, who behave like a Tour de France peloton in pursuit of a yellow jersey. 'God damn America,' thundered the Reverend. As election slogans go, it wasn't the best.

Yet what almost lost Obama the election was not the pastor disaster but his own reaction when it came. His speech about race was one of the greatest in American history, certainly the greatest since Martin Luther King – except that in some ways it was more complex than anything King said, with higher stakes and hopes.

Obama was honest, daring, forthright, sophisticated, used words of several syllables and concepts requiring thought. He did not play to the crowd – indeed he asked a great deal of them. Pastor Wright loved his country and the people of Chicago, had worked for them, lived among them for thirty years. Obama did not agree with all of his views – indeed some of them he repudiated, as he had done before. He had not personally heard

Wright's attacks on America. Indeed, Obama's guiltiest secret, it seems to me, is that for much of his life he was not a regular churchgoer at all, which in this self-avowed Republic of Separation-of-Church-and-State has paradoxically become a major crime for anyone aspiring to political office, almost as bad as being unmarried.

John McGahern was once asked if he had disowned the Catholic Church. He replied that to do such a thing would be impossible – it would be to amputate part of the self. In recent years, Ireland has had to confront its multiplicities, which have long been there, whether we like them or not, and in the years to come it will have to do so again, in ways that we cannot yet imagine. For that reason, Barack Obama's speech should be part of the Leaving Certificate course, for it says our aspirations and our fears are somehow connected: we have prejudices, hurts, dislikes, mistrusts, and allegiances to emotions and realities that are sometimes in contest with one another, to the extent of being almost mutually exclusive. Last time I checked, it was called being human. And that's where the problem starts.

America is a society of remarkable complexity, and the way it is caricatured by air-head European liberals does violence to truth as well as fairness. But what is true is that its political culture does not like ambivalence. In the soundbite-driven maelstrom of the 24-hour media, black needs to be black and white white – and those like Obama, who are in several senses both, find themselves suspect and demonised.

Then there is the problem of the Democratic Party, so in thrall to what it considers a notion of justice that it has devised a primary electoral system of such extraordinary fairness that neither of its candidates, Clinton or Obama, can win. What, you might argue, could be fairer than that? John McCain would doubtless agree. For as things now stand, it will be President John McCain who will take the oath of office and lead America into its next adventure.

Aspiring to lead her country, yet seemingly unaware that if

you have said or done anything public since about 1980, someone, somewhere, will have a video of it on YouTube, the exceptionally talented Hillary Clinton has been hamstrung by a weakness for exaggeration. Having brought peace to Ireland, braved gunfire in Bosnia, jammed with the Beatles and discovered the South Pole, Mrs Clinton entered the presidential race the way Marie Antoinette entered Versailles and is now discovering the peasants are revolting. Like the British Labour Party all through the 1980s, so riven by internecine war that Mrs Thatcher kept winning, the Democrats make Cain and Abel look like the Teletubbies. And the losers are the poor of America.

There is no city I love as I love New York, but to walk its streets and glorious avenues is to see things that shame it, or should. People sleeping in doorways in a city where you can arrange for your dog to see a psychiatrist. Where a notice in the window of the doctor's surgery below my apartment reads, 'Come in right now and customize your botox' – while nearby a Vietnam veteran begs. If ever a country needed a figure like Barack Obama, it is the United States at this point in its extraordinary history. If nothing else, to counteract the distortions and choking propaganda that affixes itself to American politics like ivy on a graveyard gate. 'All illegal immigrants should be sent home' is one current hilarity – along with 'a wall needs to be built along the Mexican border to keep them out'. When everyone in America knows they couldn't build a wall to keep illegal immigrants out – because they'd need illegal immigrants to build it.

A Collection of
Wedding Photos
16 April 2008

Recently I met up with two old friends who had surprised everyone by getting married. The wedding was a family affair, held in Boston, their home-town, a city I have always felt a little uneasy in. People say it can be a snobbish and uptight town. In other American cities they have drive-by shootings, but in Boston they have drive-by shunnings.

Mary is a writer and a secondary school teacher. Pat is a taxi driver and a part-time bartender. They were full of talk about the wedding, who was there, who wasn't, who was wearing what, who made the longest speech, and they shone with that particular shining glow of new immigrants to the Republic of Matrimony. Like all Irish weddings, no matter where in the world they are held, there were the usual little sensitivities about who should sit where. There was a difficult brother, a divorced second cousin, an aunt who quarrelled with her sister back in the late 1300s and hasn't been speaking to her since. And there was a granny who delighted the company by sitting down to eat what she announced was probably her last meal on this earth.

They showed me the wedding photographs, which were sweet and romantic, if posed a little too stiffly, as most wedding photographs tend to be, but the unofficial pictures caught a sense of the occasion with all its little dramas and triumphs.

Everyone had red eyes and there were disco-dancing dads. Great Uncle Tommy, out of the old folks' home for the day, was happily eying up the bridesmaids.

I should probably mention, at this stage, that Mary and Pat are both women, and are happily married – they hope for life. Theirs is not a civil partnership, of the type that is now proposed for Ireland – it is a marriage, pure and simple, if a marriage is ever that, and legal in the Commonwealth of Massachussetts, with all the rights and duties of matrimony. To describe the newlyweds as lesbians, while technically correct, is a little reductive and perhaps misses the point. They are simply two people who met and fell in love and who wish to be married, for life. Society was not destroyed, the institution of the family still exists, the world did not spin off its axis, nobody was hurt, except possibly Uncle Tommy when it came to the slow-set, when I believe he was declined by a waitress.

Recent surveys have shown that the Irish public, as usual ahead of their political leaders, are amenable to the idea of legal marriage for gay people, as opposed to the institutionalising of their partnerships in some other form. A friend of mine puts it in rather sardonic terms: 'Of course I'm in favour of marriage for gay people. Why should they be any less miserable than the rest of us?' But behind all the ironies beats a kind of nobility. We are coming of age, facing up to our realities, and a majority of us have now come to terms with the unavoidable fact that a happy marriage harms nobody; indeed it makes life beautiful, and can be an example of what is best in us.

Sometimes anxieties about children are expressed. And we are right to be always concerned about children. But is it right to say to children that a loving marriage is wrong? That a lifelong commitment to live in friendship and intimate companionship is somehow a danger to anyone? There are vigorously heterosexual marriages in which children have been terrorised, where there has been violence, fear and abuse. And if those marriages are thankfully a small minority, they are surely a testament of something we all know – that marriage is not for everyone, but it is for some of us – and if available to some, it must be available to all, in fairness, justice, and the simple human decency which most Irish people still believe in. So I would ask our politicians to ponder very carefully and to listen to what people are saying. Might we stop building separations and find the common ground, and let our gay fellow citizens be legally married if they wish, and give them our blessing for the journey? No one's making it compulsory. It's only an option. Besides, to live in a republic is not only to recognise difference, but also to recognise what unites. We have long known in Ireland that Seán O'Casey was right, when he wrote at the end of *Juno and the Paycock*, that sometimes it is better to have two mothers than a mother and father who hate.

News from the Neighbours
30 April 2008

Not long before my father-in-law, John Casey, died, he gave me a dog-eared piece of paper he had been saving for fifty years. It was an Aer Lingus plane ticket, the first he had ever bought – and he bought it the day he emigrated to London. The price was five pounds and eight shillings – and since this was in the days before Ryanair and Aer Lingus.com gave us low-cost air travel, the price actually *was* five pounds and eight shillings, not some enormous multiple of that.

Like John, I would spend many years in London myself, back in the 1980s when the national motto of Ireland became, 'Will the last person to leave, please turn out the lights.' My wife is a Londoner, and our first son was born there, so like many an Irish person I feel pretty much at home there – which makes me regard the London Mayoral elections with a sense of choking horror. Not since the days of Dick Whittington, perhaps, has the question of who will be mayor of the second greatest city in the world resembled quite such an unbelievable pantomime.

First, there is Boris Johnson, the Conservative candidate, a buffoon of patrician background and right-wing views. This aspirant to high office in Britain's most multicultural city once referred, in his newspaper column, to black children as 'picaninnies' and to Africans as having 'watermelon smiles'. Yet Mr Johnson has tried to reinvent himself for this mayoral campaign, with often excruciating results. He has visited Brixton and been photographed with Rastafarians, who perhaps don't know who he is. And he even likes football, or so he now claims, whenever there is a microphone in view. But the suspicion has persisted in certain quarters that Mr Johnson is a bumbling, fumbling fop who wouldn't know his Arsenal from his elbow. Certainly, if one of the inhabitants of Killinaskully had been educated at Eton, the result might have been like Boris Johnson. Stories persist from his Oxford days, when he was member of a raucous association of braying upper-class twits called the Bullingden Club, and some of those stories are colourful indeed. If Boris is mayor at the time of the London Olympics, dwarf-throwing could be one of the competitive events, along with tying your shoelaces together, belching 'Rule Britannia', and pouring sherry down your best chum's cummerbund.

Those who feel London should not be run by an upmarket D'Unbelievable might consider Brian Paddick, the Liberal Democrat candidate. Mr Paddick, who is among other things gay and a former London copper, seems destined to be known by the British press for all eternity as 'The Gay Policeman' – which sounds like the title of a 1930s musical, probably written by Noel Coward, that your granny once saw while on honeymoon in London and enjoyed while not fully understanding. Mr Paddick feels London should be modernised, which always makes me worry. As though layers of thick old wallpaper were to be removed and replaced with muted tiling from Ikea.

And then there is the incumbent, Ken Livingstone. People say we end up with the face we deserve. But Mr Livingstone doesn't deserve that face. Nobody does.

In his youth Mr Livingstone was the hammer of the ruling class, and once, in my own youth, as an idealistic student, I went to interview him for the UCD newspaper while he was on a speaking engagement in Dublin. To say there was a lack of journalistic objectivity would be something of an understatement. Myself and my left-wing colleagues greeted abashed Mr Livingstone as though we were schoolgirls in the presence of Westlife. Since those days, alas, Red Ken's legacy has been further coloured by accusations of cronyism and corruption. Indeed, if you want to get a London taxi driver going, just say, 'Y'know, I really admire that Ken Livingstone.'

I suppose it shouldn't matter, and here in Ireland, as we know, happiness rains down from the electoral sky and all our politicians are angels. But I have such happy childhood memories of how important London was, how exotic, glamorous and foreign. I remember once, when I was aged about seven, my parents arriving home from having spent a weekend there. They brought back with them the most exotic thing I had ever seen – which my mother had bought in a Wimpy Bar, she told me. I remember how we all held our breath while she slowly unwrapped it, like a pilgrim undraping the Holy Grail of Sophistication. It was a plastic tomato-ketchup dispenser, shaped like a tomato. No wonder the English had an empire.

A New National Animal
7 May 2008

Now that the Celtic Tiger has padded away into the foothills of extinction, it has become all too obvious that we need a new national animal that might symbolise the malaise we are in. Possible candidates might include the Housing Bubble Bunny, the Repossession Teddy Bear, the Negative Equity Leprechaun, the Hospital Trolley Hippo, the Mahon Tribunal Monkey, the Rip-Off Ireland Rhino, and the Bank of Ireland Security Lapse Banshee. The party is over. Good-times Bertie has gone. Brian Cowen is eying us up with rectitude in his eyes, like a bored Roman emperor regarding a floored and wounded gladiator, and we're wondering if his thumb is going to point up or down, but it sure don't look like he's smiling. The buffet of communal wealth – so tasty and luscious – has has been replaced by the national breakfast of credit crunch.

We stand in the filling station, staring bleakly at the ascending digits on the pump, as we fill up the cars we thought we needed with the petrol we can no longer afford. Sixty, seventy euros to satisfy the tank. Used to be, you could get a suit for that. In July, thanks to the Greens and their insistence on saving the world, you will be paying more motor tax than you ever thought possible. This is for your children, so the Green Party says. And your children's children. And your children's children's children. You drive to the daycare where the bill for the children you have *now* has quadrupled; then you sit in the gridlock listening to *Morning Ireland*, where the presenters sound so serious and gravely realistic. And why wouldn't they? The news is so bad that some mornings I want to say – 'Don't speak, Áine Lawlor – just hold me.'

The good times are over, so we are told every day, and we know we are supposed to tighten our belts. The belts were made in China, the builder was Lithuanian, the girl who minded the kiddies was from rural Belarus, but you never knew her full name because you paid her in cash and now you've had to let her go. De Valera spoke of maidens dancing at the crossroads. But I don't think he meant lap-dancing, exactly. Like any party, you wonder did you really enjoy the boom, or did you miss the really cool stuff that was going on somewhere else. Either way it's the morning after now. It's wake up and smell the frappuccino. As a society we asked the bank manager, 'Will you still love me tomorrow?' The answer has two words and several effs. And it isn't Fianna Fáil.

My father once told me that as a young man, just married, he dreamed of having a bank balance of fifty pounds. That amount would protect his household from every sling and arrow of fate. A hundred would have been a true fortune. I thought of this the other day, when our gas bill arrived at home. The amount being requested was more than fifty pounds, more than a hundred pounds, more than two hundred pounds, more – indeed – than the cost of my first car, which at least came with a radio as well. Eight hundred euros. For gas! Nothing more. For stopping myself and my children from freezing to death! For that amount of money I'd want the gas on all the time, powering a series of hothouses or the Olympic flame! I'd want to be invited around to the chief executive of the Gas Board's house for dinner, brunch, or just…a bit of gas. Well, I can tell you right now, my kids better get fit, because next winter my plans for heating the house involve jogging on the spot for an hour every evening while burning copies of the Lisbon Treaty.

In the last fifteen years our national priorities changed. We came to worship Mercedes and Alfa Romeo the way our grandmothers once revered the Virgin Mary. The great Irish poet Derek Mahon speaks of being 'the prisoners of infinite choice'. That's what we were. That's what we became. Every time I check my emails I am offered half-price Viagra, cheap vitamin tablets and a damned good time. These days I might need the first two, in order to avail of the third – and so, I think, would the country.

Nuala

14 May 2008

I don't think I was in Nuala O'Faolain's company more than eight or ten times, but like anyone who ever met her or knew her even slightly, I knew she was someone special. The first time I met her was in London in 1989, when she was presenting a programme about books on RTÉ television. My first novel had just been published and we had arranged to do an interview in a little hotel in Kensington. I was nervous as I waited in the lobby of the hotel, for Nuala's journalism meant so much to me, and to everyone I knew, that really I was meeting a hero.

I wondered what she would be like as I waited in the lobby, this woman who had written with such eloquence and passion of the country she believed could be better. She was interviewing the English novelist Sir Kingsley Amis – and I remember seeing him leaving the room where their conversation had taken place. Amis was a man of gruff right-wing views, but he was laughing to himself as he came out of that room. 'Are you next?' he asked me. I said I was. 'She's bloody wonderful,' he told me as he left.

In an email she sent me last year, she recollected that interview with Amis. He had 'an oddly comforting physical presence,' she wrote, 'like a big, fat, very clean baby.' 'Funnily enough,' she went on to say, 'Conor Cruise O'Brien had the same.'

That day in London, almost twenty years ago, I was wearing a leather jacket. She asked me if she could try it on, admired herself in the mirror; she was funny, warm, with a sense of the ridiculous. She talked about her days at Oxford. On camera she was generous and kind about my book. Once the interview was over, she told me everything that was wrong with it, and she was right about everything she said. She had beautiful eyes, I remember thinking, and every time I saw her again, I noticed that again. She was one of those people the camera does not fully capture, but everyone who ever met her will know what I mean when I say she was a beautiful-looking person.

Her readers all over the world came to see in her work the rare combination of qualities that has been spoken about in recent days. She was generous and could be tough. She was kind and could be irascible. I saw her a few times in argument, when she would never give up, and heard uncountable stories of her kindness and solidarity, which I was fortunate enough myself to have received. She wrote brilliantly, felt deeply, never had a lazy thought. A born communicator, she was in love with the world: sometimes impatiently, always ardently. When she wrote of what was wrong with it, she was burningly precise. She never did *plámás* or sentiment. She was intensely, restlessly, questioningly intelligent – anxious, changeable, moody, amusing, extra-ordinarily well-read, a world citizen, an Irishwoman, a true intellectual, a traveller.

She clearly loved New York, and how would she not, for that vital, noisy, endlessly self-renewing city was made for such brave spirits as Nuala. And she loved rural Ireland and the city of Dublin – the way people talked, their modes of interaction, the small, everyday courtesies that were part of Irish life in the long-gone days of the Irish past she described as being 'black and white'.

Less frequently remembered in Ireland are her immense literary achievements. She won France's most important literary award, the Prix Femina Étranger, and had a No. 1 Bestseller in the United States, a country whose readers took her work to their hearts in the most extraordinary ways. 'My little book is in every bookshop window in America,' she once emailed me about her first memoir. It delighted her to have found her readers.

The last time I saw her was a year ago in Listowel, where she was attending the annual literary festival, Writers' Week. The special, particular atmosphere of that wonderful event suited her down to the ground. She loved the company of writers, loved talking about books, loved gossip and brave talk and staying up late, and mooching around, and music. She looked well, happy, entirely at home. I can remember her beautiful eyes, and the way they shone, as she said, 'Isn't it great to be here!'

She wrote to me in December for what would turn out to be the last time. 'A happy Christmas to you and your family,' she wrote. 'How lovely that you became a father. Chin up for the New Year. Who knows what it will bring? I wish you peace.'

That is how I will remember this remarkable woman, whom I wish I had known better, but feel honoured to have known at all. Known as warm, generous, brave and brilliant. *Are You Somebody?* asked her book. She was.

The Eyes Have It
4 June 2008

There may be people in the world who like looking at Irish politicians. And why not? They're a good-looking bunch. And as a card-carrying liberal, I will defend anyone's right to look at Irish politicians to the very last breath in my body. But I would like them to do it in the privacy of their own homes and not to force others to acquire the habit.

Yet at election time, or referendum time, it's always the same. It starts with one or two posters. Who would mind that? It's only a bit of fun. By next morning, half the town has been plastered with the faces of the local politicians of every party and faction. All night long while you were sleeping, moonlit party activists were scuttling up ladders with staplegun and stickytape. Before long it has spread like a virus across the whole country, to every last lamp post, in every city and village, this chickenpox of vacuousness and smiling self-promotion that masquerades as democratic encouragement. Political posters everywhere you look. Wastepaper waiting to happen.

Exactly why are they needed, these countless posters? What do they achieve, except to litter the Irish landscape more than it already is? With their pointless slogans and bland exhortations, they have all the political content of a greeting-card rhyme – but without the consoling image of the bunch of flowers or ponies in a field at twilight.

What has happened is the practices of the advertising industry have somehow leaked into politics. The soundbite is what's aimed at, preferably meaningless but memorable. This in a country whose traditions of political oratory are not without shining stars. Did Bold Robert Emmet stand up in the dock and cry, 'Freedom for Ireland – Cos I'm worth it'? Did James Connolly, as he faced the firing squad, utter the memorable words, 'The-value-of-socialism-can-go-down-as-well-as-up. Terms-and-conditions-apply'? Did Pearse inspire his men with the rallying call, 'The invader has oppressed us for eight long centuries' – before going on to sing: 'Since Eleven. Eight eleven'?

Who are the Mandelas and Martin Luther Kings who came up with the slogan 'Europe – Let's Make it Work. Vote Yes.' Do those who advocate a NO vote wish Europe not to work? And what does Europe working actually mean? And those on the other side, what are they saying? Would Parnell have addressed a monster meeting with the meaningless jingle, 'Europe isn't listening. Vote no'? A whole lot of cardboard goes swinging in the wind and few of us are any the wiser.

No doubt these posters are printed on recycled paper these days. But that doesn't excuse the sheer waste. Not a red cent, we are told, for little fripperies like hospitals, but plenty of dough for this rain-soaked rogue's gallery gazing down at us as we sit in gridlock. The politicians are fined for not taking them down. They should be fined for putting them up. They're not needed. They're meaningless. They're a snowstorm of tat. Yes! No! Yes! No! It's the politics of the kindergarten playground. They swing nobody's vote, add nothing to the debate. All they do is make me feel I'm being watched in the street. I swear their eyes follow you. Dublin readers – look at that Gay Mitchell Lisbon Treaty poster. He knows your guilty secrets.

My seven-year-old said to me recently, 'Who's that man in all those pictures on the side of the road? And who is that lady saying NO?' We turned it into a game as we happily drove along. I said every time I saw a Gay Mitchell I would give him a sweet and every time I saw a Mary Lou McDonald I would give him a lollipop, and by the time we had travelled less than two miles he had put on several pounds. And it's nothing against those two accomplished and hardworking politicians – every party in the country is the same. People who cannot agree on the tiniest matter are united in the desire to plaster our thoroughfares with images of themselves looking electoral. The hair is brushed carefully, the best suit is put on, the correct facial note is struck for the photographer – a little bit solemn, a little bit humane, as though posing for a banknote. If only one of them would pose in a clown's red nose, or in the comedy moustache that will inevitably be added by Ireland's army of roving graffitiers. Or laughing. Or scowling. Or semi-undressed. Who wouldn't want to see a poster of Brian Cowen in the jocks, effing away at the electorate? Vote YES. Vote NO. Vote MAYBE. Vote OFTEN. And the faces wherever you look.

Empty as a Pocket
and Lisbon to Lose

18 June 2008

It's not often, perhaps, that An Taoiseach, Brian Cowen, raises in our minds the image of Christmas – but recently, on hearing of the Lisbon Treaty defeat, that strange thing happened to me.

In the winter of 1992 I was living in New York, a city that is rarely kind to the needy. My difficulty, as Christmas approached, was that I was broke as a politician's promise. For a month I had been abusing my credit card but it was now 'maxed out'. But I wasn't too concerned. Funds were coming.

I was owed a weighty cheque by a London newspaper for which I had written a series of articles. The cheque had not arrived, despite abundant phone calls to the editor. It was coming, he assured me, honestly it was coming – but it turned out to be coming in the same sense as a Bertie Ahern explanation, or Samuel Beckett's Godot: always threatening to arrive, but never quite making it. The editor and I would exchange a bit of banter about the thrilling independence of the freelancer's life, and then he would hang up and his butler would bring him lunch and his chauffeur would ferry him home to the burbs.

On the day before Christmas Eve I rummaged a handful of dimes from down the sofa and rang the editor from a semi-vandalised callbox. The cheque would be in my mitts by morning, he insisted. It was coming by express. 'Relax!'

Early on Christmas Eve I sprang from the scratcher, imagining all the seasonal treats I would purchase. By noon, no cheque. Two o'clock. Then three. By four, I could see parties of revellers in the tinselled streets, which, like my spirits, were darkening. At half-five, I left my igloo and traipsed fifteen blocks through a snowstorm to the post office. There was a sign in its window. CLOSED it said. HAPPY HOLIDAYS TO ALL!

Back home, I opened the fridge. Oh dear. Not good. A bottle of aspirins, a half-empty beer can, and a substance that might have once been a banana. Deep in the freezer compartment sat a mysterious relic encased in a crusting of ice. When thawed, it turned out to be a packet of lard with a sell-by date from the era of *Saturday Night Fever*. It practically disco'd its way to the bin.

Stayin' Alive suddenly seemed more than just a song title. On Christmas morning I awoke early, got up, got dressed, ate an aspirin for breakfast, washed down with instant coffee brewed with water from the hot tap. I then got back into bed and remained there a hundred years.

Stephen's Day came slowly. An anxious ache was racking my chest. I had a breakfast of what remained of my fingernails, then wrapped myself up and went out to trudge the deserted city. It was like the Antarctic with skyscrapers. Through the windows of gracious apartments I saw families by roaring fires, stuffing themselves, laughing, glugging down wine. Onward I hiked, the two miles to Central Park. I remember the ducks on the ice-glazed pond. Even they looked well-fed, prosperous, happy. Many times I breathed a word that rhymes with duck. I considered bludgeoning one of the smug little gits and eating it.

Next morning I was awoken by a thunderous noise, which was not my stomach, but a knocking on the door. Its creator was a courier with my long-awaited cheque. I would have kissed him but my lips would have frozen us together and anyway I had eaten the mistletoe. It was a public holiday in New York and the banks were closed. But tomorrow I could cash in and gorge myself stupid. Only one more day and the trial would be endured! I felt a surge of terrible glee.

Dizzy with joy, I resolved to make a new start, by bringing my clothes to the nearest laundromat. Practically crooning 'Ding Dong Merrily On High', I gathered a ball of garments that were offensive to several of the senses, and began sorting them into organised piles. In excelsis Deo! Never again would I let such wretchedness overcome me. I shook empty the pockets of an old pair of trousers. Out of them fell a crumpled piece of paper.

I picked it up and unfolded it. I looked at it. I blinked. It was a hundred dollar bill.

It had been hidden there, only yards from me, all those three endless days and nights, while I considered prostitution. And you might think I was elated to have found that money. But that was when I wept.

Funny enough, I thought of this story when I heard the astounding news that the Lisbon Treaty had been rejected by the electorate. Because sometimes what we need is actually there all the time, if only we had the sense to look for it. It appears the Irish don't like being ordered what to do; told by their leaders 'there is absolutely no choice'. Next time the politicians might try persuading – not telling. You never know what they might find.

Bye Bye, Happiness
25 June 2008

In November 2004, having conducted extensive research on the matter, the boffins at *The Economist* announced the results of a major survey into which country was the happiest on earth. They had measured and analysed data under dozens of headings. Computers had churned late. Brains had been stormed. In the end, the blushing winner was summoned to accept her crown. Step forward – the Republic of Ireland!

Yes, November 2004. Not even four years ago, we awoke to the exciting news that we were happy. The quality of life in Ireland was officially unbeatable. Norwegians envied us. The Swedes wanted to be us. All those untrendy, outmoded countries that had functioning social-welfare systems, those cold, northern socialistic places spoilt by little luxuries like rat-free schools, had suddenly realised they'd got it all wrong. Their lives were sad. Ours were gas.

The Scandinavians wanted our spirit, the French our *joie de vivre*, the Italians our cappuccino and the English our playwrights. The world and her husband wanted to be hip, rich and Irish, blinging like a rap-star, yet admirably authentic. We were exporting moneyed grooviness the way we used to export our poor and we'd never had it so good. The national life was like the moment we've all known at a wedding, when the deejay puts on ABBA, and everyone hits the floor. U2, Colin Farrell,

Jack Charlton, Graham Norton, Drink, Girls, Arse, Feck, the Tiger, *Riverdance*, Philip Treacy, The Cranberries, Pearse Brosnan proving James Bond had been Irish all along, a native – where else? – of Navan.

Mother – What happened? Where did it all go wrong? We're shaken. We're stirred. The martini's gone flat. As I scan the morning papers, I find I want to cry. But thanks to *The Economist*, I know they must be tears of bliss. Politicians widely mistrusted. The dole queue steadily growing. A health system so dysfunctional that a week on a trolley is now considered a holiday. Which is just as well. Because an actual holiday means using one of our wonderful low-cost airlines. And with the inevitable little surcharges, such as the Seat Rental levy, and the Landing-On-a-Runway-Rather-Than-In-The-Sea tax, the price of a €6.00 flight can kinda mount up. But I feel sorry for the airlines. I really do. People can take advertisements so literally.

It's hard to find a garage in Dublin now; they've all been sold for apartments. But last week I heard a rumour of one and went there straight away, before someone built a supermarket on the forecourt. I filled the car with petrol – which cost only the proceeds from the sale of my first-born child – and drove into the centre of town. Battling through the morning traffic, being saluted by my fellow motorists with a variety of ancient Celtic hand gestures, I consoled myself with the thought that we are all very happy in Ireland. Stopped at lights, I was approached by a beggar who asked could I spare him €12.75 for a sandwich. His quality of life was clearly enviable. Arriving at my rendezvous, I had the usual light-hearted banter with my colleagues, about how none of them can afford a home, unless it's a shack near some swampland, but the ones who do have one have quietly realised it's worth about half what the bank told them they'd need to buy it. My, how we wept with laughter.

I suppose, when I think of the dismal country in which I grew up in the 1980s, where your chances of a stress-free existence were roughly on a par with those of Osama Bin Laden, life did improve for most of us. Remember full employment? Only voluntary emigration? That sense of a culture more outward-looking and vibrant? The grip of dour authority no longer felt? But now, what have we got as the school disco finally ends, and Brother Cowen starts putting the national chairs on the tables, and asks if we've no homes to go to? (No Brian, we don't – your builder friends didn't finish them, and the repoman now competes with Dustin as the national symbol.) Suspicion of the EU. A return to older ways. The past in the air, like a faint smell of rain. The whipcrack of rectitude. Talk of tightening belts. The team not in Europe. Irish children in poverty. A Taoiseach we didn't vote for. A coalition few wanted. A government who behave like something out of *Hall's Pictorial Weekly*. Ballymagash, with café latte.

But as the great Orwell once wrote: they can't actually outlaw the summer. We should enjoy it before they start trying. Because you know they will.

Still, hope is like ABBA – it will never go away for good. No matter how unfashionable it gets.

The Hardest Working
People in Town
23 July 2008

You might find you're having to work a bit harder these days to make ends meet. The odd bit of overtime. The occasional weekend. Hiring out your kids to a chimney sweep. But there's one group of us that will be enjoying a three-month paid holiday away from the workplace. I don't think I need name them. You know who they are. The hardest-working public servants in the whole troubled country. No, no, not the nurses, the firefighters or the gardaí. What would they need three months' holiday for? Sure their lives are a holiday. I'm talking about the ladies and gentlemen who really deserve a bit of downtime – away from the Kildare Street sweatshop.

Yup, July rolls around and school's out again and the debating chamber of the Dáil is as empty as a promise, as the eleven-week vacation begins. What matters the starkest rise ever recorded in the unemployment figures when it's time to throw the prawns on the barbie? More businesses going bankrupt in the first quarter of the year than in the entire twelve months of 2007? You know why? Because those business people worked *too hard*, that's why. It's a health and safety issue. If only they'd taken a leaf out of the politicians' books. Little bit of me-time. Cos I'm special.

Bertrand Russell once wrote, 'One of the symptoms of

approaching nervous breakdown is the belief that one's work is terribly important and that to take a holiday would bring all kinds of disaster.' The mental health of our legislators is obviously deeply sound, since they are the most holidayed parliamentarians in the world.

What do you do when the building industry comes to a juddering halt? Come to a juddering halt yourself, of course! It's kind of a Buddhist approach. Leave it alone and all will be well. Slap on the tanning oil and decant that sangria. Kick back! Slip on the flip-flops. Hang loose, baby. As the Good Book has it, 'There's a time to surf and a time to wax your board.' And in Kildare Street, the two are never confused.

And don't they deserve a holiday? It's hard work, thinking of euphemisms for what the Knife of Brian has planned for us all. There aren't going to be cuts. Oh no. They're *readjustments*. You'll remember the Everly Brothers once sang that 'Love Hurts'? But it doesn't. Love Readjusts.

But it isn't like the summer is entirely without stress for a TD. The packing is an absolute nightmare. Sitting on the suitcase trying to cram everything in is really very tiring indeed.

If you're a minister, you've even more to put up with. Being driven out to the airport can get decidedly uncomfortable when the air conditioning in the state car is on the blink. Sometimes you even have to open a window, or get your advisor to blow on you softly. And the VIP lounge at Dublin Airport can get pretty tough sometimes. There are days when the chardonnay is served unchilled.

But we mustn't be churlish. Everyone needs a little break. I find vacationing from early July to the middle of September sets me up nicely for the ten weeks of work I then manage to do before Christmas. I need nearly a month off to open all my Christmas presents, but I come back in late January ready for even more public service. I then slave like a Trojan until St Valentine's Day, which is so close to Easter that I just give up work for Lent. Yes, in 2005, the last year for which comparable figures are available, Dáil Éireann sat for a whopping 92 days; the House of Commons for 133; the US House of Representatives, 140; and the US Senate and the Chamber of Deputies in Italy, for 159. But are those countries any happier than we are in Ireland at the moment? Maybe we should just close down the Dáil completely?

And there are always consolations when our TDs go away on vacation. Maybe they'll bring us back something nice – like one of those amusing souvenir garments with a slogan reading. 'I paid for my TD to go on holiday for three months and all I got was this lousy T-shirt.'

Yes, the committees still sit, and the TDs are in their constituencies, and any of them who did nothing for three months would pay the price, come election time. But it's a symptom of the stodgy inertia built into how the Dáil does its business that again and again this issue is raised and nothing is done to resolve it. It isn't the three-month holiday alone that's the problem here. It's the fact that they don't know it matters. Indeed, so remarkably out of touch are several of our TDs that you feel some of them might benefit by an even longer holiday away from the Dáil. A permanent one, maybe. Missin' you already. Now, where's that pina colada?

Baby Come Back:
Ode to the Celtic Tiger
6 August 2008

Economic Lady-Luck is after givin' us the flick…
She's broken it off. We're financially heart-sick.
Worst of all she swears to the skies above
She still loves us as a friend – she's just not *in* love.

Misty-watercolour-mem'ries of the way we were.
She said 'Let's always be friends.' It's not us, it's her.
She just needs some space. It's a trial separation
From the sweet, happy times of economic generation.

Was it just a passin' thing; a fabulous fling,
We all went mad an' indulged in the bling
Of a love too intense, as sweet as nectar,
But too heavily based on the property sector.
It's wilted, we're jilted. We didn't pay attention.
Now money's too tight to feckin' mention.
Where have you gone, you beautiful hunk?
A ship passin' in the night… And now you're sunk!

The other night I was sad; I was feelin' wild,
I opened up the vodka, I got drunk and dialled.
I shouldna done it, my self-esteem was slack,

344

I said 'Please Full Employment – I can change – Come back?'
'I'm sorry that we flirted with Thatcherite ways.
I'm sorry that we spent it all on SSIAs.
And we didn't fix the hospitals we needed to mend.
I said 'Please Celtic Tiger... Let me try again.'

You don't miss your water till your well runs dry.
You don't miss your Celtic Tiger till he growls good-bye.
But when the gross-national-deficit is approachin' a ceiling
Well you know – you've lost that lovin' feeling.
That's life, that's love. The bad news lurks.
You're only figurin' out how the deck-chair works
When the sun goes in and the rain starts lashin'
An' the werewolves start howlin' like a Taoiseach on a session.

My friends all say there's more fish in the sea,
Don't lose your self-respect – but then I hear George Lee,
And somethin' inside me wants me to curl up and weep,
And I can't smile without you, can't laugh, can't sleep.
I'm comfort-eatin' ice-cream an' other foods sugary.
I'm takin' to the drink. Me waistline's gone to buggery.
Keep askin' myself where it all went wrong.
I can't seem to forget you. I CAN'T move on.

What a beautiful boom you were entirely.
We didn't deserve you. We're missin' you direly.
Too brief, time's a thief, and the memory taunts us.
An economic miracle. Now nobody wants us!
And now you're gone, we're losin' the plot.
We're broken-hearted, broke, and we miss you a lot.
We were thick, too quick; we were stupid an' soft,
Now we're sobbin in the hanky – cos Cupid's fecked off...

Some insist we're better off at the end of the day.
Me mother says she's never liked you anyway.

You were vulgar an' immoral an' you made us nervous-
   wrecks –
But she didn't see you through love-tinted specs.
We didn't treat you well; we were clumsy as an elephant,
And we didn't invest in infrastructural development.
That David McWilliams – he WARNED us we're blind.
And like Elvis once put it – now you're always on our mind.

You said you'd had enough; you had nothin' left to give,
You packed your bags and said 'Slán libh'.
We thought you'd be back when the row died down
But we heard it on the grapevine – you're after skippin' the
   town!
Our D.I.V.O.R.C.E. is comin' through this week.
The E.C.O.N.O.M.Y. is lookin'….. purdy bleak.
The A.I.B. they want my house, and so does the Bank of I.
The E.U. don't like us. We're U.N.H.A.P.P.Y.

I shouldn't be callin', my friends'd all kill me,
My shrink would be ragin', my therapist'd bill me.
Cos I need to accept that our love is a ghost 'n'
The priest in confession would gimme a roastin'.
But the greatest love in all antiquity –
Now all we have is negative equity.
I'm feelin' sorrow… I'm feelin' shame.
My heart skips a beat when I hear your name.
If anyone says what a great boom we had,
I feel nobody loved you the way I did.

When you came into our lives, we were livin' in ditches,
No dough in our pockets, no arse in our britches,
And we took to the high-life fast as a blink
Like Hollywood Apaches takin' to the drink.
Extensions to houses! Mansions in Mayo!
Hummers and Beamers and Alfa-Romeos

And four-grand handbags! Diamond bracelets!
Apartments in former Soviet statelets!
… I'm sorry, I'm sorry, it ain't right to phone ya …
Designer labels. Au-pairs from Estonia.
Latte and bistros an' tasteful trattorias.
We had it ALL! … NOW, do you see us?

Here I am on your line an' I'm actin like a whiner,
How strange the change from major to minor.
Now we're through, an' you never even ring,
When to us it was more than a purely fiscal thing.
You gave us a purpose, you gave us some style.
Like baby-Moses in his basket, now we're floatin' in denial.

The Progressive Democrats, Fianna Fáil,
They took their slogan from L'Oréal.
They floated your boat but they just couldn't berth it.
'Free market economics! Because I'm worth it.'

Now you're gone, we keep our feelin's hid.
Those others don't love you like we once did.
The house is worth tuppence. The cost of livin's killin'.
The directors of the banks are only gettin' half a million
By way of bonus. They're tightenin' belts.
Is it somethin' we said? Is there somebody else?
No matter where we wander we're still haunted by your
    name.
Oh my lost Celtic Tiger – wonder who is to blame?

Cos we had it all, like Bogie an' Bacall,
Like Adam an' his Eve before the Fall,
Like Brangelina. Like Beauty and the Beast,
Like Michael McDowell and Dublin South East.
Like Mills and McCartney. Now we're just old flames.
We're a love that dare not speak its name!

But you wanted us once, and we wanted you. An' breakin' up
   is hard to do.
Is it yes, is it no, is it definitely-maybe?
Can we start again, Tiger?... Don't you WANT me, baby?

Most of us have done it, tho' we know we shouldn't do it,
In the cold light of day, well we usually rue it –
Ringin' up your ex with self-piteous rants.
So let's ring the Celtic Tiger for one last chance!

Sorry for cloggin' your answerin' machine.
We don't mean to be bitter. We don't mean to be mean.
But call us back, Tiger, if you feel like a fling.
Just come around and use us, it won't mean a thing!

I'm leavin' my message when the beep goes pause.
Celtic Tiger – We miss your claws.
We don't mean to get heavy, we're just missin' you, Honey.
Call us back ... OR WE'LL BOIL YOUR FECKIN'
   BUNNY!

The Delights of an Irish Summer
20 August 2008

The summer Irish climate is causin' upset.
Our dry sense of humour is … effin-well wet.
The skies should be blue but they're gloomy an' dark,
And if it rains any harder – we're buildin' an ark.
Celestial drenchings, it's been a frustration,
Rainstorms quenching the glee of the nation.
It's the heavens are open, it's cats an' bloody dogs,
It's wearin' sou'westers when we should be wearin togs.

It's dramatic, it's erratic; we're not feelin' ecstatic,
Let's face it, this summer we're turnin' aquatic.
There's floodin' in Dublin every day of the week.
Me toes are webbed! I'm growin' a beak!
An' it isn't bloody fair, it's a load of codology,
A vicious little trick of meteorology.
For God's sake, it's August, would you give us a rest?
Should be rubbin' on sunscreen – not Vic on the chest.

The only kind of consolation, to a rained-on, wrung-out,
    damp-feelin' nation
Is the feel-good medicine of imagination –
Yes, there's stuff you can do to ward off precipitation.

In the shower you're Bono singin', 'Where the Streets Have
No Name'
To the clapping of the hailstones on the steamed-up window-
pane.
Be Elvis in wellies, be Bowie with a brolly,
Be Dickie Rock singin' 'Good Golly Miss Molly'.
You're the Rolling Stones live, you're Madonna, you're
Sinéad.
Can't get no satisfaction if it rains on the parade.
See, nothin's that bad if you shelter from the pain.
So don't let the storm get to you. Sing in the rain!

You're TR Dallas, you're Maria Callas.
You're twenty-four years livin' next-door to Alice.
You dunno what it is as the rains soaks all.
You're Daniel O'Donnell from wee Donegal.

Fill your lungs, sing songs, do somethin' drastic,
Tell your other-half you love 'em and they're lookin'
fantastic.
Write a blog, walk the dog, read a bit of Baudelaire,
Go out an' have a ramble in the wet fresh air,
So what if it's lashin' an' you're catchin' a fever?
Sing, 'I saw her face – now I'm a believer.'

Walk the rain-soaked streets, walk the hail-drenched avenues,
Write a letter to the Mammy to thank her for havin' youse.
So there's rain on the windowpane, sleet in your kisser,
Email a buddy to tell her you miss 'er.
Join up with a gym, have a swim, have a sauna,
Go out for a walk 'mid the flora and fauna,
We could have worse problems than the lack of good
sunnin'
It's a rainy night in Georgia and the Russians are comin'.

Rain is only God's teardrops, don't be so cautious,
Take off the summer sandals, put on the galoshes.
Splash in the puddles. Wallow in the mud.
Insure your dreams against landslide or flood.
Sandbag your soul. Stock up on what's essential.
It's an Irish summer, baby! The joy is torrential!

Put on an old raincoat and saunter the town.
Turn your banjaxed umbrella upside-down.
No pennies from heaven, I'm sorry to say,
But sure who needs cash when you're washin' away?
And the rain falls on all, the great an' the small,
Fine Gael, Labour, Sinn Féin, Fianna Fáil,
And we all know the truth although nobody says it –
When the sun comes back – they'll be takin' the credit.

Count up the rain-clouds crossin' the skies.
Read Hugo Hamilton's novel *Disguise*.
No point in lookin sad with your eyes all hollowed.
Drink a little French wine (but don't get bolleauxed.)
Learn to do boxing, professional, amateur.
Learn to write a sonnet in iambic pentameter.
Stay out of the rain. As a last resort
Take up a hobby. An indoor sport.

Brush up on a language you thought you'd forgotten.
Tell someone you fancy you fancy them rotten.
Book yourself a night-class. The summer's nearly through.
Forgive a traffic warden. They know not what they do.

Be glamorous, be amorous, try livin' with style.
Give your face a holiday, force it to smile,
Cos the rain's gonna end, we'll be sunny men and women
And just in case it doesn't – practise your swimmin'.
Take up the piano. Take up darts.

Don't hurt yourself thinkin of hot foreign parts.
No you ain't in Majorca, and you ain't in Lanzarote.
You're in summertime Ireland where the weather's feckin'
    grotty.

The dampness communal, the rain is monsoonal,
With downpours like this you'd want a flood tribunal.
But don't be morose as the miserable weather.
Give it full-force welly, we'll get through it together.
The sun'll be out, we'll be rollin' in clover,
Thanks be to God, *Fáilte Towers* is over.
Put up the auld feet. Have a strong cup of tea.
Email *Drivetime* at RTÉ dot i.e.
Sayin', 'George Lee I love ya, it's makin me dizzy,'
Or 'Des Cahill's gorgeous – spit on me, Dessie!'
Be a little impulsive, sure who's gonna frown?
Don't dampen your ardour, let the love rain down.
There's sweet consolation, no need to be glum.
And Keelin Shanley's voice – is a ray of the sun.

An Irish Olympic Hero

27 August 2008

When Oscar Wilde was once asked if he played outdoor sports, he replied, 'I have sometimes played dominoes outside Parisian cafés.' But as the dust settles on the Olympics, we might not be feeling so cheerful. We will miss the faked Opening Ceremony fireworks, the little children happily miming their songs, the Swedish wrestler who threw his bronze medal away and stalked huffingly from the arena, the Olympic-size pharmacy that is required by certain modern sportspeople, the ignoring of human-rights abuses perpetrated by the Chinese government, and of course the stirring remarks on that subject by President George W. Bush, the man who gave us Guantánamo Bay.

And yet it's easy to be cynical. Somehow sport still has room for innocence, endeavour, determination – the best of us. And in all the honourable history of Irish Olympians, perhaps no achievement is more immense than that of John Mary Pius Boland, the accidental hero who stumbled into greatness.

Boland, a Dubliner and a fluent gaelgoir born in 1870, studied law at the University of Berlin, and then at Oxford, where he also played tennis, was a capable enough cricketer, and also a big hitter in the university's debating society, the Oxford Union, a launch-pad for many political careers. In that role, in 1895, he hosted a visiting Greek student who gave a talk on his country's resurrection of the ancient and semi-mythical Olympic

Games. The youth of the world would gather again to contend in Athens, as they had not done, at that stage, for thousands of years. Boland was smitten by this ludicrously ambitious idea. He decided he'd have to see it bear fruit.

He visited Athens for the 1896 Olympics, arriving in mid-March of that year. He and his friend, Manaos, the Greek student who had spoken at Oxford, did the usual tourist things – visited the ruins, drank the retsina, and knocked a tennis ball about when it wasn't too hot – but soon afterwards the unsuspecting Boland was landed with a shock. Manaos, a leading light of the Olympic committee, had entered his Irish buddy in the tennis competition as a practical joke. But Boland, a good Dub, not to be phased by a challenge, resolved he would indeed take part. With a borrowed racket and playing in his everyday leather brogues, he beat Friedrich Traun of Germany in the opening match, Rallis of Greece in the second round, Paspastis of Greece in the semi-final battle, and the world champion Kasgaldis of Egypt in the final. The Olympic gold medal – the first ever won by an Irishman – became one of his holiday souvenirs.

Having won the singles championship pretty much by accident, Boland decided, for the hell of it, that he would enter the doubles event with Traun, the German he had defeated in the first round of the singles. And you know what happened next. They beat the Greek team in the first round, had a bye in the semi-finals – the presumably terrified opposition failed to turn up – before despatching Petrokokkinos of Greece and the Egyptian Kasdaglis in the final, thereby adding a second Olympic gold medal to Boland's collection. 'I was lucky,' the modest Dubliner would always insist in later years. His autobiography hardly mentions the triumph.

Since Ireland was happily married at the time to a loving neighbour, some reference books still insist on listing Boland as 'British', along with Wilde, Shaw, Jonathan Swift, and other succesful Paddies. Interestingly, James Connolly – despite being born in Britain and serving seven years in the British Army – is rarely so claimed by the Commonwealth. As for Patrick Pearse, whose father was a Birmingham stonemason, the less said the better, perhaps. The fellowship of international Britishness had its black sheep, as we know, like many dysfunctional families.

Back at home, Boland became far from the last one-time racketeer to be elected to electoral office in Ireland. He became Nationalist MP for South Kerry in 1900, and was something of a star at Westminster, admired for his brilliant speeches and his gift for friendship across party lines. A friend of Kier Hardie, Bonar Law and Churchill, he held his seat for almost twenty years, before being appointed a Dublin Commissioner under the Irish Universities Act, in which role he helped establish and name the NUI. He was also one of the leaders of the campaign to have a statue of Parnell placed on O'Connell Street in Dublin. Ireland's first, and surely greatest, Olympic champion died in his eighty-ninth year, on St Patrick's Day, 1958. When the Beijing extravaganza closed down on Sunday, in a hail of pyrotechnic thunder, it was tempting to think of that modest and unassuming Dubliner, looking down from his cloud, never having told the angels of his achievement, and marvelling at the strange world we live in.

Letter to Myself at Age Four
3 September 2008

Dear Four-Year-Old Self,

Hi. This is me. That's to say, this is you plus forty-one years. I'm writing to you from September 2008. Hope you're doing OK back there in 1967? How are the 1960s treating you generally? Are there flowers in your hair? Have you been rioting about Vietnam and the lack of civil rights, or is that disgruntled noise you're making only the result of belated teething? The Beatles released a pretty good record this year, didn't they? It's called *Sergeant Pepper*. Some say it has a future.

So we've a lot to catch up on. What's all my news? Well, I'm married. Seriously. Yes, to a girl. I know you're not too crazy about them, but that might change. My wife sometimes tells me I have the mentality of you, especially when I'm eating with my mouth open or telling her a joke or leaving my clothes all over the bedroom floor. So it's nice that we're similar. You and me, I mean. Little bit chubby, aren't you? Hey that's great, so am I! You're prone to the odd tantrum when you don't get your own way? Well, I got news for you, kiddo... But never mind.

So I have a son of your age, and another who's eight, and both of them seem so much more confident and happy than you do. You're frightened by the whole world, as how would you not be? That's what the world is for, you believe. Most people in the Ireland around you believe pretty much the same thing. It's one nation under the thumb.

What can I tell you about 2008? Well, we have this thing called the internet. It's a system someone invented a few years ago, of joining up every computer in the world for the greater good of the planet and the species, and bringing all of humanity together. Well, mainly it's used for acquiring pornography and gambling. So really we've made a lot of progress.

You don't even have colour television, I know, and if you did, your parents would actually have to get their backsides up off the sofa in order to change the channels, or the stations, as they are called in your 1967 world. No, *Wanderley Wagon* isn't on RTÉ television any more. We have sort of more advanced ideas of what constitutes entertainment now. There's this show called *Fáilte Towers*, right? You'd love it. It's absolutely made for you. It's where people pretend to run a hotel and viewers give them money for charitable causes. Like hospitals for children and help for patients with Alzheimer's and people with autism or cancer or MS. No, no, the government don't do that. Don't be such a baby. For God's sake, what are you, four?

Oh yeah, I forgot. Ireland is a prosperous and self-confident country now. Don't laugh in your Liga. It's true! I swear. We drive SUVs and jeeps. Those are cars meant for farmers or soldiers going into battle. No, we're not all farmers. In fact very few of us are farmers, anymore. And we're not going into battle. I don't know why we need military vehicles to drive to the shops. Don't be asking such childish questions.

Anyway – the reason I'm writing is that this week my son who's your age is starting in school. And for some reason, it got me thinking of you. Isn't that funny? Big day for you, wasn't it? You probably found it a scary experience. Yes, your teacher, Mother Lawrence, seems a bit tough, I know. No she isn't your mother, she's just called Mother by the other nuns. And she probably wasn't always called Lawrence. At least, I don't think so. Yes, those ladies dressed in black robes are nuns – that's right. There are thousands of them in your Ireland, you see them every day. Nuns on the beach. Nuns in Clery's. Nuns in the audience of the *Late Late Show* waving shyly or gleefully at the camera. Great flocks of Carmelites, Sisters of Mercy, flying around your childhood like birds. No, we don't have as many of those here in 2008. And the ones we do have wear cardigans. The people dressed in black robes these days are called tribunal barristers. The Sisters of Mercy are a punk-rock group.

But you should listen to Mother Lawrence. She knows what's what. Okay, I know she's a bit fierce. But she'll be teaching you to read. And that's going to bring a lot of happiness and pleasure to your life. You mightn't think it now, but you're going to be endlessly grateful to that woman, for her patience, and yes – her love. Okay, so she doesn't do self-esteem. What's self-esteem, you ask me? Oh, self-esteem means generally not despising yourself or believing you're the Antichrist. It isn't thought too useful in the Ireland you're growing up in. Mother Lawrence hasn't heard of it. Nobody has, really. It would be illegal if anyone had.

So I'd better sign off. You'll be busy, I know. The first week of school can be frightening and confusing – but this is just to say, it gets better. My son – your son – is a beautiful boy. He looks like you in photographs. Just less frightened; more smiling. There's times I put my arms around him and feel ghosts are in the room. Take care of yourself, kiddo. You're not alone.

Suburban Spancil Hill:
A Sung Diary
10 September 2008

O last night as I lay drea-ee-ming – about this aul recession,
Me mind being bent on ramblin', fell into a bout of
depression.
When I thought about the Tiger years when every thing was
great,
But sure then it all went pear-shaped – in the black year of....
zero eight.

It been on the 23rd of June, the month before July.
Disappointin' forecasts were released by the shower at the
ESRI.
'Twas gloom and doom descendin' soon, the misery reachin'
a summit
When the ISEC Index of Irish Shares commenced a historical
plummet.

Well I used to drive a Beamer, boys, upholstered plush an'
deep.
For to drive the kids to ballet class, the au-pair had a jeep.
The missus had an SUV, a vehicle meant for the shticks,
For to drive to the Mall at Dundrum, me boys, for a latte in
Haarvey Nicks.

Well I'd stocks an' bonds an' a bit put-away in dodgy
 accounts go leor.
A diversified portfolio – I never – had before.
Investment apartment in Kanturk – an' it rented out to a Pole
Who commutes every day to his office in Bray –
Four hundred mile round-trip in all.

But the bean a tí, she fled from me, when I did lose me job.
She's living with a lesbian in the town of Ballydehob.
The cars was ray-possessed, me boys, me house is not worth
 a shite
An' me AIB shares are worth half what they were, an' I'm
 kissin me pension goodnight.

'O step softly love,' cried William Yeats, 'for you're steppin'
 upon me dreams.'
Overextended borrowings have buggered it all up, it seems.
I'm singin' the sean-nós now, me boys – for me iPod – I had
 to pawn,
An' I'm bangin' away on me belly today for I cannot afford a
 bodhrán.

George Lee does be often on *Drivetime*, boys, with Mary the
 flower of Montrose.
The balance-of-payments deficit is leavin' us over-exposed.
The Footsie one-hundred index's fecked, and other most
 troublin' data.
And the middle-class gettin' kicked in the ass along with less
 privileged strata.

O ochón, ochón, the boom is gone, agus briste is mo chroí.
That miserable wagon Peig Say-ay-ers is less lamentatious
 than me.
I'm singin' it through me nose by heart, I'm feelin' emotional
 pain,

That Ireland long a province be in recession once again.

Well I used to listen to Die-ur Straits, Garth Brooks was
indispensable.

Me tastes were fairly anodyne and some would say
reprehensible.

When I had bread, I liked Simply Red, and nothin more
haard-core,

But sure now I'm broke I've turned to the folk, and I wish I
was Christy Moore.

Yes, I wish I was Christopher Moore, me boys, for to my
mind he's the best.

Standin' up there singin 'Nancy Spain', he's integrity clad in
a vest.

The sweat does be drippin' off him, boys – he's no need to go
to the gym.

Ah the young, the old, the brave and the bold, sure we all
have a soft spot for him.

I went to the bank manager for to ask of him a loan.

He said, 'Johnny, you must – be jo-oh-kin – we're repossessin'
your home!

We're cuttin' up your maxed credit cards – for you owe us
quite a stack,

An' we'll sue your ass from Baltinglass to Spancil Hill and
back.'

Well there's seventy-two more verses of – this ballad of racial
pain.

But I've forgotten most of them since I'm socially usin'
cocaine.

Tryna make me go to rehab, I said BUPA will cost me a
bomb.

I'm a post-Tiger mess: Me internet-address would be
'miserable sod dot com'.

Well me singin' it's fairly brutal, boys, 'twould make the purists cross.

I'll tellya no lie but me deedle-dee-die won't be gettin' much bualadh bos.

The cock! He crew in the evening time, cruel as an ESB bill –

And I nodded off with a triple Smirnoff and the half of a Valium pill.

Oh I dreamed we had it all again – the boom 'twas only startin'.

Full employment in the land! Hair – on Mee-eehawl Martin!

The COCK! He crew in the mo-hor-ning. He crew both loud and hoarse –

And I woke in post-boom Ireland – no arse, within, me drawersss.

Ode to Sarah Palin
1 October 2008

John McCain's advisers said: 'Listen heah, John,
Ask your wife what state your runnin'-mate needs to be
    from,
Cos your own ideas are nothin' short of disasta'.
McCain said: 'Okay, okay… AL-ASKA!'

Next thing you knew you were plucked from obscurity.
People had doubts on your style and maturity.
But you ticked all the boxes on national security.
Picked for your ideological purity.

Dear Sarah: I'm from Éire. Here's my ode to what you're
    doing.
You're half Maggie Thatcher, half Sue-Ellen Ewing.
You're young enough to disco and you're spoilin' for a fight,
You're the born-again bomb; you're the right-wing Snow-
    White.

A lass from Alaska, a small little town,
With the photogenic children you're paradin' around.
It's McCain and Palin! It's Beauty and the Bomb!
The Homecoming Queen meets Mr Vietnam.

The bible-belters' pin-up, they love ya to pieces,
They're impressed, you're the best, you're their favourite polar
    species
And you got their hearts thumpin', singin' halleloo yay-
From the Armageddon button you're a prayer away.

You being selected was new and original,
If you get elected we'll all find religion'll
Play a new part in global occasions.
It's just what we needed – God blessing invasions.

Lots of comments on your looks, it's how the hacks work,
Beside you, ole McCainiac looks like a waxwork.
Iran's gettin worried. Could be makin an exit.
Gettin nuked by you if Granddaddy pegs it.

You've heard all the lines, it's a fresher reality,
The Commander-in-Chief'll be Miss Congeniality.
She's feisty, a fighter, she's youthful, she's groovy
The sexy librarian you saw in that movie.

Yes, you've read all the clichés, seen all the headlines
Hastily written to imminent deadlines,
Sexist assumptions, all part of the plans,
And they're playing right into Republican hands.

But don't underestimate, don't ever forget her, for
A pit-bull in lipstick, to use her own metaphor,
Do well to remember if you're gonna be rude –
This is a candidate kills her own food.

Johnny met her only once, she was placed on the ticket,
Now they're pitching for the White House; she's sassy, kinda
    wicked.
What I'm thinkin' every time I see Palin and McCain

Is: 'Father Jack in a pinstripe – and Calamity Jane'.
He's startin to look like he's poached in preservative.
You're a fresher-faced, hard-line ultra-conservative,
Used to be a beauty queen, in a bikini
Now you're shootin' up the moose – you're Moose-alini.

No one ever heard of it before the convention,
An Alaskan baskin' in worldwide attention.
You're a cuter kinda shooter, you're a hunter with huskies,
Where it's polar and it's colder, you can nearly see the
    Russkis.

Ain't never been to Europe, but hey you don't care;
Once touched down in Shannon, didn't know where you were,
Cos your knowledge of geography's the size of a pinprick
Said you'd been to Iraq – but it was closer to Limerick.

Thought the duty-free shop was in outer Falluja.
Finer points of foreign policy, they sometimes elude ya.
Think 'Some parts Sunni, some parts Shi-ite'
Is the weather forecast in Alaska tonight.

And lookin at your policies I feel my heart tighten
Got the same surname as that guy in Monty Python
And McCain's getting madder, of Mr Fawlty he's a copy,
Angry as old Basil beatin' up on his jalopy.

You love the right to life, on certain occasions,
But you're not opposed to killin' in the cause of invasions.
You're the mom with the bomb, drive those cute kids to
    hockey
Yes, all life is sacred – unless it's Eye-rocky.

Your style, your smile, so orthodental
You put the mental in environmental

365

No secular lady, to Jesus you pray –
Wonder what he'd make of Guantánamo Bay?

I'd like to say more but I know I really shouldn't,
Cos Angry John picked ya – you're perfect – who wouldn't?
You're opposed to welfare medicine, don't believe in
evolution,
Wanna put back the Con into Constitution.
You're a down-home, hard-line, gun-totin' mutha,
One George Bush is goin' but here comes anotha,
You're the neo-con Madonna, you're the short, sharp shock.
No Dan Quayle in a ponytail, you're Rumsfeld in a frock.

Got a son called 'Track' cos his mother likes running.
You could call it a pun, though it's just about as stunning
As a hurley-playing father down in Caherciveen
Baptisin' his daughter 'Camán'... Eileen.

You're a damn fine shot, you don't stand for no messin'.
Think every last American should own a Smith-and-Wesson,
Out hunting in all weathers when it's snowy and rainy.
Hope you don't shoot-up your buddies like Vice-President
Cheney.

Think the bears should be shot. Think the oil should be dug.
Think the only good use for a moose is a rug.
And the thought of you and Johnny-Boy runnin' the show
Is enough to make an Eskimo afraid of the snow.

Sarah Palin, McCain was failin',
And the neo-con dreams were rapidly ailin'.
Now you might get elected by the ice-hard Right –
If so, we can kiss our Alaska... goodnight.

Subterranean Homesick
Budget-Time Blues

15 October 2008

Ouch! It hurt. From your head to your toes,
It's a slasher-movie dressed up in budgetary clothes.
It's Psycho for slow-learners, we were feelin' uncertain
As Norman Bates came peepin' round the bathroom curtain
Dressed up as the Minister, the knife our fate!
Kildare-Street-Chainsaw-Massacre, two thousand and eight.

Shares gettin' lower, stocks gettin' slower,
Ain't got no dough or we'd be gettin' on the blower
To a woman sellin' tickets to the hot Caribbean
Where Ireland's tax exiles, you'd be likely to see'em.
It's gettin' so I'm scared to turn on the news.
Got the subterranean homesick bank bail-out budget blues.

Yes, back in the Sixties when the world was young.
And when life got heavy – the young folks sung!
Top billin' was Bob Dylan and his raspy gravel voice;
John Lennon spat venom if you fancied a choice
But now, these days, when times get hard
Where's the national protest-singin' bard?

Johnny's in the basement, thinking it's outrageous
They're askin' Gerry Ryan to take a cut in his wages!

The budget came early, freaked out the whole nation,
It was bad, bad vibes, and a hard auld station
Country feckin'-well wrecked – when we used to be loaded
But the boom went bang and the bubble imploded.

Hard times for the bankers, hard for their friends,
It's been hard for the builders, no money to lend
So the budgetary cudgels are picked up to bludgeon
The nation existin' in shock and high dudgeon
And the bread's all burnt, the economy's toast,
An' where's Bobby Dylan when you need him the most?

Mr Cowen's lookin' down at the ashes an' the embers,
Mr Gormley's lookin' warmly at the Labour Party members,
Miss Joan Burton's hurtin', the economy's a-slumber,
Richard Bruton's nearly shootin' at his opposite number;
Only Jackie Healey-Rae is safe from harm –
He's goin' back to workin' on Maggie's Farm.

Yes, where can they be, all the protest-singin' bards
And they standin' in an alley with the words wrote on cards.
It's been blowin' in the wind, it's been blowin' through the
    Dáil
That a hard, hard rain is – gonna fall;
And we're all sayin' prayers to the holy ghost,
Where's You-Know-Who when you need him the most?

There's a house in New Orleans called the Risin' Sun
And there's Leinster House in Dublin where the country's
    mis-run.
There's debates on the state and the fate of the nation's
Finances and chances of beating inflation's
Bad grip on the country; we've been hittin' the brakes!
Woke up on Budget-Morning with a case of the shakes.
Cos they're taxin' your income, taxin' the booze,

Taxin' Woody Guthrie singin' 'Tombstone Blues',
Taxin' your flight and taxin' your motor,
It's five grand extra from every last voter!
Taxin' your breakfast, taxin' your bed,
Taxin' the thoughts goin' on in your head

And the bones for your dog and the milk for your cat,
And they're taxin' your leopard-skin pillbox hat,
And they're taxin' the facts and they're taxin' the fictions
'Stead of axin' the fellers who caused these afflictions.
Oh, thanks to the banks; fine executives youse!
We've a case of the two-Brians budget-time blues.

Oh Hallowe'en's comin', you can nearly hear the screamin'
George Lee's dressed as Dracula, Dave McWilliams as a
    demon,
It's the knife of Brian. We'll be bawlin' with fear,
There's a whole lotta shakin goin' on around here.
Yes it's one of the government's budgetary feats,
It's a big bag of tricks – and not so many treats.

If this was a ballad it'd have quite a chorus.
Mr Cowen wants your vote an' Mr Bertie wants the Áras,
Mr Kenny hasn't very many new things to say,
Mr Gilmore's looking ill-more with every passin' day,
Mr Caoimhghin Ó Caoláin is speakin' all day long,
And out here the rest of us are all gonna pay.

Banner headlines howlin', we're all feelin' miffed,
When you're biffed by a Biffo, you stay bloody-well biffed.
Man in a suit lookin' only half alive, wants forty billion euro
    bills, you only got five.
No jobs; Eddie Hobbs from dusk till dawn
Every time you switch the bloody radio on!

Oh lay lady lay, on me big brass bed;
It's a shame I had to pawn it for a breakfast-roll instead
Cos I'm drivin' up from Carlow from a flat I can't pay for
To a job that's gettin' shifted out to outer Bombay for
Globalisation has caused a bonanza.
Where's Bobby Dylan when you're needin' a stanza?

Celtic Tiger skipped town, he's deserted the lot of us.
Now the national emblem is called the Biffopotamus,
The belt's bein' tightened, we're all bein' frightened
And the tension I mention seems soon to be heightened
Cos the budget didn't fudge it when it came to the cuts.
Where's Bobby Dylan? Not here – unless he's nuts.

Yeah, the budget came early, Christmas lookin' quiet.
The whole bleedin' country on an unexpected diet
And who's gonna pay, well you're damn sure to know
That it won't be the people who made all the dough.
We're slim, we're thin, it's scary and strange an'
Where's Bobby Dylan... when the times they are a changin'?

So put on your old albums, keep safe, keep warm,
An' batten down the hatches an' we'll shelter from the storm.
An' remember the eighties, that time of fiscal pain,
Hope it won't last forever, we'll come through the hurricane,
And robbin' a bank is a crime too far,
But when the banks robbed *us* – we bought the getaway car.

Ballad of a Forgotten Hero
29 October 2008

In memoriam, Donogh O'Malley, 1921–1968, Fianna Fáil
Minister who introduced free Intermediate education.

All early I walked through the dawn-streets of Dublin,
By Christchurch and Trinity, grey in the mizzle,
And I met a sad ghost in the realm of Kildare Street
By Buswell's Hotel, in the wintry drizzle.

He said: 'Gentle stranger, if you will assist me –
I'm lost and I'm lonely, I don't recognise
This country I worked for and lived all my life in,'
With fear in his face and bewildered, tired eyes.

He said: 'Something's happened me. I'm baffled by everything,
As though I've awakened in Lilliput's lands.
I'm down on my luck and I have a few drinks on me.
There's a dread in my soul and a shake in my hands.'

He said: 'You've had good years, but what did they do with
     them?
Build the schools, pay the teachers, so no child would need,
And equally cherish the children of Ireland?
That's all that I'd hoped for, what my life guaranteed.

What brave men once fought for, refused to be bought for,
When Connolly, Larkin, and Davitt arose.
I know they're unfashionable, branded irrelevant;
These days the heroes win celebrity shows.

And I don't even mind that; for time changes everything,
But is all that they stood for now thrown all away?
In the schools of the country my own party governs
There's thirty-five children in classrooms today.

That boy who needs help, and that girl who needs more of it,
And that daughter of parents who came from afar –
Why must she pay for the crimes of the billionaire?
Is my country a slum-land? Have we travelled so far?

For I once was a Minister, served in a government
That dared a brave vision, even when poor.
Free education, in a poor if proud nation.
Does anyone know who I am any more?

I am Donogh O'Malley, I loved Ireland's children,
I worked all my life for to send them to school.
And to think when my country was able to help them
My own party hurt them, is callous and cruel.

I wasn't a saint, I was doubtless a sinner,
But my life wasn't meaningless, I answered the call.
When my people had nothing, I tried all I could for them.
I could see teaching children was the noblest of all.

For the child is the future. Excuse such a cliché,
But it's one of those clichés that's actually true.
And to teach is to liberate, to shatter all manacles.
The most beautiful thing a free country could do.

Fianna Fáil my great party, and I stood for our notion
That *Republic* was more than a word on a stamp
And a patriot's duties extended to thinking
The weak should not pay for the greed of a bank.

But forgive me for boring you; it's just that I'm friendless
And a little hungover, forgive my demeanour;
I come from a time when the proud hopes were endless.
Foolish, I know. I was only a dreamer.

I am Donogh O'Malley. No one remembers me.
Banished to ghost-hood; just a name from the past.
And the party I loved now disgraces my legacy.
Could you spare me a copper? For I'm lonely and lost.'

By Buswell's Hotel, in the wintry mizzle,
He crossed to the Dáil gates, gazed sadly inside;
The flag of his hopes at half-mast on the rooftop –
Limp in the drizzle – and the lonely gulls cried.

Does that Banner Yet Wave?
5 November 2008

There are eleven towns called Dublin in the United States and it sometimes occurs to me that I may be the only person on the face of the planet sad enough to have visited all of them. I did this about fifteen years ago because I was writing a book about Irish-America, and it seemed to me that to travel to all of them would be a way of entering that strange place and walking around in its history. For most of these towns were named by our ancestors – those economic migrants and asylum-seeking refugees who looked to a country then undergoing a boom for a homeland of safety and success.

Some of these towns are located in the American South, a part of the country I love. Savannah, Charleston, those sultry, stately cities. New Orleans, the greatest city in the world. There is a Dublin, Virginia, a Dublin, Texas, and there is a beautiful Dublin, Georgia. But in some of them, it was pretty clear, even to an outsider, that any connection with Ireland that had ever existed had blown away with the tumbleweed of time. One night I found myself in a restaurant making conversation with the very pleasant waiter. He asked me, 'Where you from?' I said, 'Dublin, Ireland.' He looked at me a moment or two before smiling amiably and saying, 'Gee. Is that named after Dublin, Georgia?'

All in all, I'd say I spent a month in the American South, just roaming around and looking at things and talking to people and being late for everything and making notes and collecting facts for my book. I never once saw anything we might call 'racism' and I often found myself wondering why. For this had been the homeland of slavery and segregation. A place where human beings – plenty of them Irish – had sold one another, and owned one another, and branded one another like livestock, and gambled for one another at card tables, and left one another to their children in their will. A place where rape was considered an employer's perk and where the truths of how life was lived until not all that long ago are so intensely disturbing that you wonder just how it is lived now. And then one night I found myself in a town not far from one of the Dublins, having one of those small, trivial, unimportant conversations you remember for the rest of your life.

I was in a taxi at the time, having only recently arrived in town. It was a beautiful spring evening. There was blues music on the radio. And until you've driven the streets of a southern American town, as the dusk is coming on, and the air smells of crushed lilac, and you're so very far from home, and anything could happen, you mightn't understand how beautiful the ordinary can be. I asked the taxi driver where he would recommend me to go later in the evening for a beer and a few laughs. 'Well now,' he said, happily, indicating the right-hand side of the street, 'We go over here.' Before adding, 'And they go over there.' For a moment or two, I didn't know what he meant. We go over here. And they go over there. And then slowly it dawned on me that he was talking about race. I asked if there was anywhere in town where everyone went. The blues music played. A moment or two passed. 'Not really, sir,' he said, as though surprised by the question. 'We go over here. They stay there.'

It's a conversation I've never forgotten, for it was an education, a revelation. The greatest things we learn, in my own experience anyway, are not in the classroom, the textbook or the church; they are in the everyday moment of the apparently simple, the thrown-away remark to fill in time. And I thought it often in the days, weeks and months leading to Barack Obama's electoral victory. He chose not to make an issue of his race, to appeal to all who wanted change – all who were willing to alter the world by the simple act of crossing the street. Had you told any black person in the South, even as recently as the 1960s, that in the year 2008 a man whose father was African, and whose wife is the direct descendent of an American slave, would be elected to the most powerful office in the world, you would simply not have been believed. How could you be?

Many years after that visit, I was researching another book, this time in the New York Public Library. It was my novel *Redemption Falls*, the story of a group of Irish immigrants drawn into the American Civil War, when some fought for freedom, and some fought for slavery, and most fought because they were ordered to fight by the wealthy, the people who have never done the dying in any of America's wars. As part of my work I read the transcripts, made in the 1930s, of Edison-recorded conversations with a number of American former slaves. These brave, comradely, irrepressible people, who were bought and sold, their culture destroyed, but who had lived – unlike many of their loved ones – into the era of technology, when a voice could be transferred to a crackling wax disc. One of them, an elderly woman, remembered the words of a powerful old spiritual that would be quoted by Martin Luther King to an audience of millions, but which she herself had often sung – quietly, to herself – in the cruel years when their promise seemed impossible. 'Free at last. Free at last. Thank God almighty, I am free at last.' And it seems to me now, at this beautiful moment for the whole world, that it is not only the descendants of that woman who are free. But all of us, in some small, precious way.

A Farewell Letter
12 November 2008

Dear Free-Market Capitalist System,

Hiya. It's me. How you've been getting along? Oh dear. Kind of a tough year for you, wasn't it? You've been having a bit of a hard time, collapsing and ailing and generally being miserable, and gasping and puffing like a broken-down train, so I thought I'd drop you a line just – y'know – to offer sympathy. And – y'know – to say goodbye.

Need a hug? C'mere, ya big lunk. Let me put my arms around you. They've been saying *very* nasty things about you, haven't they? Poor diddums. Come cry on my shoulder. The poor snookums dote. There, there. Oh, the poor wickle capitalist bunnykins.

You're feeling unwanted. It happens to us all from time to time. Some people think the world shouldn't be organised like a slum that happens to have a casino attached. Crazy, I know! Deluded, left-wing fools. There's this childish, ludicrous, *sentimental* idea that we produce more than enough in the world for everyone to be happy, that no child needs to starve, that nobody need be poor, that hunger could be eradicated all over the planet with less food than we throw away. I know, I know – bloody old hippy nonsense. What the hell is this, the Girl Guides? Why don't they all join hands and sing 'Kum-by-a', right? The muesli-eating, incense-sniffing, recorder-playing

377

eejits, with their naïve bloody ideas and their flared bloody trousers and their Bob Dylan albums and their Che Guevara posters. You know what I'd do? I'd *repossess* some sense into them. That'd soften their cough for them now.

You're the system that really works best. Free-Market Capitalism. You're a lovely little system. You're the answer to everything! If only we could see it. I mean, OK, you chew up our pensions, devalue our houses, cause runaway inflation and rocketing fuel prices, keep half the world starving while the other half is obsessed with dieting and the people who work hardest own the very least of everything, while the people who do no work *at all* own the most – but that's 'natural', isn't it? The natural order. Survival of the fittest and all that craic. I mean, yes, when I say 'survival of the fittest', I obviously don't mean it literally. Because when *you* break down – as you do now and again – the governments all rush to fix you. They take our money and use it to bail out the banks and the insurance companies and the oil companies and their friends. '*Nationalise the banks,*' the lefty moaners used to cry. George Bush is doing it now – the bloody commie! Because the banks don't make *enough* profit. Oh no. Not at all. The banks are actually *charitable* institutions. They're the Vincent de Paul with free cash cards. All those times they loaned hundreds of thousands to people who couldn't afford the repayments – the banks only wanted *to give people a chance*. We should be *grateful* to them. But do you think we are? That's right. We're so selfish. Eaten bread is soon forgotten. Oh, Capitalist System. All the *fantastic* things you have given us over the years: wars, poverty, class divisions, inequality, the way poor people die far sooner than their rich and overfed neighbours – what kind of world would it be without you?

Some people say the model of society should be the family. From each according to their abilities. To each according to their needs. But we all know those families are *very* inefficient. It would be far better if mothers *charged* babies for giving them life, and if elderly parents paid their children for feeding them once in a while. That's the kind of world we'd all like to live in. The survival of the fittest! The natural order! Efficient, profitable and free.

Some people think the point of life is – you know – happiness. Stuff like that. Bloody students. Swilling down the lager and chucking midgets around the disco, and they've the *neck* to be giving lectures to the rest of us. But who could disagree with *your* view, dear Capitalist System, that we're a nasty, greedy, self-serving species, venal, corrupt, brutal and violent, and that is what we are *meant* to be. And the *point* of our lives is to grub around like dung-beetles, amassing the biggest pile we can get. Care about each other? Yeah, right. Give the other guy a break? I'll give him a *compound fecking fracture*. *You* are the only system that can really protect us. So I don't mind you repossessing my house, losing me my job, vanishing me my savings, starting the occasional arms race, filthying the planet – you mischievous little rascal! You do have your little ways, don't you? I don't *mind* that a nurse is paid far less than a man who owns a media empire, or that a teacher is paid a fraction of what an arms dealer makes. Free market, right? Way it has to be. It's all a question of motivation.

In the Communist countries, they used to have these phoney 'elections' every now and again, where everyone essentially believed the same thing; it was really just moving around chess pieces. But we're lucky in the democratic world. We don't have that. Every four years, we have this completely *different* thing we call 'an election', where we decide which group of people, most of whom believe the same things, are going to implement you over the next while. It's not really politics – it's more a question of management. Oh, we put up a lot of posters and fight phoney little wars, a bit like two gangs of overactive kids in a play-ground, lashing at each other with paper swords, while the classroom, and the city, and the country, and the world, are being sold to the highest bidder. It seems to work for us very well. We wouldn't want to try nasty 'regulation' or 'planning' or – heaven forfend! – 'working together' or anything. It just doesn't work. Not like *you* do.

Here's the deal you offer: The only game in town. People sell their labour. They get money. They buy food with the money. The food keeps them alive. So they can sell their labour the next day. And, meanwhile, the people in Africa starve, because the governments in wealthier countries break their promises. Like, *what in the name of God* could be fairer than that? And yet some people say there has to be more to life. *Some* people say this is a bit like a burglar breaking into your house and offering to sell you back your stuff at a profit. But some people *would* say that, of course. Studenty bloody losers. Nuke 'em!

But I'd better sign off. You'll have things on your mind. You've a famine to cause somewhere, and that's a great thing, right? Hey you did it here in Ireland once! Worked like a treat. Because someone's always going to make money out of that too, aren't they? All those things we call 'natural disasters' or 'acts of God'. You and I know the truth. It's not God or nature at all. You don't like taking the credit. You're so *modest*, you really are. So take care now, Free-Market Capitalist System. You did a really great job for us, all those years we had you. Missin' you already.

A Francis Street Boy
19 November 2008

There's been a lot of talk recently about hard times, new challenges. I find it's got me thinking about my father. Sean was born in 1938, in the Liberties of Dublin, the city's oldest neighbourhood, a place of great independence and amazing histories, near the stern black cathedral where Swift had thundered the gospel, near Thomas Street Church, where Robert Emmet was executed. In Sean's childhood and teens there was mass emigration, a sense of the celestial irrelevance of the poor to the fantasies of the Republic they lived in. It was a different world, a different time. The Celtic Tiger would have been unimaginable.

An oaten aroma drifted up from the brewery and the barges plied the Liffey, bringing barrels of Guinness to the world beyond a child's imagination. A city boy, he loved animals, especially birds; he roamed about the Liberties exploring. The grid through which he moved had its landmarks and lighthouses – Saint Nicholas of Myra church, Francis Street School, Meath Street, the Coombe, Johnny Rae's ice-cream shop – place-names that will mean much to all who hailed from the Liberties. The map of an Irish childhood.

Francis Street, now, has antique shops and cappuccino-bars. But in the years of Sean's childhood it wasn't like that. He grew up in a safe home where there were strong values of loyalty and family – where music was valued, and reading, and dependability; keeping your word; being there for one another – but in the streets beyond that home he saw barefoot children, parents beyond coping, hard sights. A restless, questioning boy, he had a talent for English at school. It was an ability encouraged by his beautiful sisters, who adored him. My aunts bought paperback novels and shared them among themselves. Indeed, such avidly hungry readers were those gorgeous young Dubliners that when one of them would become impatient for her turn with the paperback, another would sometimes tear out a page and pass it across the kitchen table, so that often you had five or six siblings all reading the same book, each on a different chapter. A magazine, *The Bell*, containing short stories and poetry, was often in the house, and Sean availed of it. He was the sort of boy who enters contests, learns definitions, runs in races, sometimes gets into fights, feels promises deeply, believes the answer to almost anything can be found in a book and is sometimes impatient as a wasp. I see him in many Irish men and women of his own generation. And I see him in my own beautiful sons, in my brothers and sisters. And I am happy when I see him in myself.

He left school at the age of thirteen and worked to help support his family. Later, as a young father, he dived into his books again. He studied at night, did exams, worked by day, in time qualifying as a structural engineer. He opened a little practice in Dublin and in time it grew. He had a kind of mantra of determination you'd often hear him saying, 'Feck them all bar Nelson.' (Only he didn't say 'feck'.) I remember once, as a teenager, asking him, 'Dad, why not feck Nelson too?' He replied, 'Because son, he's fecked already.'

Churches, schools, office blocks, libraries – they formed themselves on the drawing board he kept at the house. Often, when I went to bed, he would be working at that board, in shirtsleeves, his tie flung over his shoulder. And often in the mornings, as I got ready for school, he would be there again – his eyes raw with tiredness – so that it seemed to me, as it may have seemed to him, as though he had stood there working all night. He sang as he shaved; little Dublin songs or bits of Italian arias. And at night he would read to me before I slept. He loved the Victorian writers, the old poets like Lord Tennyson, to whom he had been introduced by Brother Thomas Devane in Francis Street school, in the Liberties. And I can never read any poem without hearing Sean's beautiful Dublin voice. Calming as a hearth on a rainy night, it was a voice that revealed whole worlds. It was how I had learned to read, or certainly why I wanted to; his finger tracing capitals on the yellowed old pages of books that seemed to breathe wonder into life. That I wanted to be a writer one day, I owe to Sean – to his voice, his love of learning, and of course to his stories.

What fantastic stories he had, but there's one in particular I remember still. It was about a Francis Street boy who bought a goldfish. And one day, to see what would happen, he took it out of its bowl, just for the briefest second. And it didn't die! So the next day he took it out for two seconds. And it still didn't die. And every day he would take it out, for a little longer each time, until soon he could take the goldfish out of the water for thirty seconds and it wouldn't die. And he continued like that – one second longer every day – and the goldfish got slowly accustomed to these longer periods out of the water. And soon, he could take that goldfish out of the water for nearly a full minute, and still it was healthy and well. And then one day, he was taking the goldfish in its bowl to school, because he wanted to show the teacher this remarkable thing – a goldfish that can remain out of water for, like, five minutes! But he stumbled while walking alongside the banks of the canal. And didn't the goldfish fall out of its bowl and into the water. Where it drowned. 'And that's a true story,' Sean would smile. And somehow, I still believe it is.

And I also believe, without his solidarity and courage, that his life, and therefore mine, would have been different indeed. All my life I have been given chances he did not have. The same is true of many of us. It's hard not to panic when times change very suddenly, as they have for most of us in what seems only a few months. But to read with a child can never be taxed; nor can the belief that there are deeper solidarities than the merely financial. Things were not better in the old days. Nobody sane could say that. But the example of that generation of Irish people has much to offer. It could be a time to remember where we came from.

Political Grumpiness
26 November 2008

People have been saying Brian Cowen is a bit grumpy of late. I think we should cut the poor man a little slack. Given all he has to put with, his occasional bouts of crankiness are rare as a Ryanair ticket in FÁS. Yes, the incident some time ago in the Dáil when he used an early sixteenth-century word that rhymes with 'muckers' attracted a fleeting controversy. He responded, you'll recall, by threatening to use his influence to have the leader of the opposition howled down. But then, it's nice for Fianna Fáil backbenchers to know what they are for. Yes, it's always deeply moving to go and sit in the public gallery of Dáil Éireann and see the parliamentarians screeching, baying, yelping, barking, performing Nazi salutes, thumbing their noses and giving out about how badly behaved young people are these days.

Mr Cowen is far from the first political supremo to go a bit moody now and again. Indeed the late Mr Haughey, in a famous interview with John Waters, turned the air about as blue as General O'Duffy's famous shirt (which was not of the Charvet variety). John Major once famously referred to his own cabinet as a pack of something beginning with *b*, and he didn't mean bathing beauties. And the great Paul Keating, former Prime Minister of Australia, once remarked during a debate, 'You stupid foul-mouthed grub. Sit down and shut up, you fat pig.

You fraud. You disgraceful, disgusting fraud.' The speaker of the house promptly intervened, saying, 'The prime minister must withdraw those unparliamentary remarks.' Keating retorted, 'Of course I will not withdraw them. "Disgusting" is not unparliamentary, you clown.' Keating's favourite method of keeping his cabinet ministers in check was to remind them at the conclusion of every meeting, 'I'm sticking to you like shit to a blanket.' And when former Australian Prime Minister Robert Gordon Menzies was addressing a disorderly crowd, a heckler called out to him about the 7 per cent unemployment rate. Menzies' response was, 'I assume when you say 7 per cent, you must be referring to your own IQ level.'

In England, Liberal Democrat MP Vince Cable's recent remark that Gordon Brown had gone from being 'Stalin to Mr Bean' had them rolling in the aisles in Westminster. But perhaps the greatest era of the political insult was the Victorian age, when Gladstone and Disraeli used to get down and dirty with the bare-knuckle verbal battery. 'You have not a single redeeming defect,' said Disraeli to his rival. And, better still, when asked once to distinguish between a misfortune and a calamity, he explained, 'If Gladstone fell into the Thames, it would be a misfortune. If anybody pulled him out, it would be a calamity.'

But the UK heavyweight champion is surely our old friend Mr Churchill, who was to grouchiness what Michelangelo was to art. 'A sheep in sheep's clothing,' was his famous verdict on Clement Attlee, who, he added, was 'a modest man with much to be modest about'. Bernard Shaw once sent Churchill two tickets to the opening night of his new play, with a note saying, 'Bring a friend, if you have one.' Churchill promptly returned the tickets with a note which read, 'Can't be there first night. Will be there second night, if there is one.' Later, there was Sir Edward Heath, who on being asked why Mrs Thatcher so disliked him, gave a shrug, and replied, 'I am not a doctor.' Or Jonathan Aitken on Mrs Thatcher's ignorance of the Middle

East, 'She thinks Sinai is the plural of sinus.' Indeed, Margaret Thatcher attracted more rudeness than perhaps any other politician of her era. 'When she speaks without thinking, she says what she thinks,' muttered Lord St John of Fawsley, while Clement Freud called her 'Attila the Hen'.

In other countries, too, the political insult is frequently deployed. Italy's Romano Prodi said of Silvio Berlusconi, 'The prime minister clings to statistics the way a drunkard clings to lamp posts, not for illumination but to keep him standing up.' And in America, they're no slouches when it comes to political grumpiness. Ross Perot once described Vice-President Dan Quayle as 'an empty suit that goes to funerals and plays golf' and said that looking into his eyes was 'like gazing through a window into an empty blue sky'. Even those nice Canadian politicians have had their moments of huffiness. Pierre Trudeau once paused during a parliamentary speech to remark, 'I see the honourable member opposite disagrees. I can hear him shaking his head.'

And history provides many examples of unkind bantering among politicos. Lord Sandwich, the womanising gambler after whom your lunchtime snack is named, once lost an expensive game of cards. He drawled to the winner, 'Sir, you will die of a pox or on the gallows.' The winner retorted, 'That will depend on whether I embrace your principles or your mistress.'

But the Nobel Prize for crabby political malice surely must go to the Australian MP Fred Daly, who once remarked, 'Half the honourable gentlemen on the other side of the house are clearly halfwits.' On being ordered to retract, he immediately responded, 'Of course I retract. Half the honourable gentlemen on the other side of the house *aren't* halfwits.'

Against such a background, I think we should warmly congratulate Mr Cowen on being quite so even-tempered and cheerful. He's not the sultan of surl. He's a pussycat really. Just a great big lump of Irish male softness, waiting to be given a hug.

The Immaculate
Conception and Me
10 December 2008

One of my earliest December memories is the kindergarten Christmas play when I was four. The story was set on Christmas Eve. Santee was ready to hit the skies with Rudolph, but the weatherman had gone on strike so there was no snow. (No Met Éireann meteorologist this weatherman, but a moody wizard who manufactured the weather from his headquarters at the South Pole.) I played him with the gusto of a High-Babies Daniel Day-Lewis. Yeah, I drank that Santee's milkshake!

A girl called Niamh was my wife, the weatherwoman. But it wasn't a marriage made in heaven. The plot required that she often hold my hand. Fine; but Niamh had the runniest nose in all Dun Laoghaire, which she persisted in wiping with the same hand that she employed to clutch my own. I draw a veil over the specifics. But let's just say, Niamh and I were bonded by more than love.

Reverend Mother gave me a beard made of cotton wool, and a crêpe-paper smock with spangles glued onto it. The effect was Alvin Stardust meets Osama Bin Laden. Why a nun in 1970s Ireland would have had a false beard, I don't know, and I'm not entirely sure that I want to. The spangles were improvised from the foil tops of milk bottles. The reindeers wore beige tea-towels and were profoundly convincing. Some had cardboard hats with antlers crayoned onto them; the more committed would vigorously attempt reindeer noises. Since few in the greater Dun Laoghaire area had heard a reindeer, creative improvisation was practised. I remember a classmate informing me with the despotic certainty possessed by toddlers that a reindeer sounded 'exactly like a bat'. But alas, I hadn't heard a bat either.

One morning at rehearsal, a confrontation erupted between the shepherds and the Holy Family. A shepherd had called the Virgin Mary a rude name. She had responded with an upper-cut to the chin. Hell broke loose. Never had I witnessed such a mêlée. There were fists; boots; bits of manger being brandished. (I recall seeing Saint Joseph bawl at the Bethlehem innkeeper 'You're CLAIMED', and reflecting that the history of Christianity might well have turned out somewhat differently had the real Saint Joseph tried this approach.) In the scuffle, one of the Wise Men got sent home for spitting at an Archangel and snapping a leg off Baby Jesus. Baby Jesus was played by Roddy, my lovely eldest sister Eimear's most prized dolly. He had eyes that looked at you crossways, and was devoid of genitalia, so there was enough on his mind already without assaulting him. But I remember the Baby Jesus being hurled across the class-room, before being used to bludgeon one of Santee's elves while she was sat upon by Our Blessed Lady. It's an image that kinda stays with you, somehow. Since then, I've regarded Christmas as a contact sport. Forget decking the halls. Deck a shepherd instead.

December, in my childhood, was a difficult month anyway, for a reason I remember almost every time I enter a church these days, which doesn't happen as often as it used to back then. For it was on the eighth of December, in 1966, that the younger of my two sisters was born. It's a date that used to see the beginnings of Christmas in Ireland, in the days before we decided it had to start in late August. Country people would come to Dublin to do their shopping for the season, and the lights, such as they were, would be switched on. That date is also the feast of the Immaculate Conception, a day of obligation for Catholics. And since my mother was in hospital, having given birth that very morning, it was my beloved and devout grandmother and my wonderful father who took upon themselves the duty of taking my three-year-old self to Mass. The church was packed – it was a different time in Ireland – and we arrived late and stood in the back with many others. When the time came for Communion, my father and grandmother took it in turns to hold me while each of them approached the crowded altar to receive it. I began to feel left-out. And I didn't like that feeling. And anyone who was in Glasthule Church, on that December day in 1966, may still remember what happened. During the fervently reverent silence that descended immediately following, the priest approached the tabernacle and piously opened it, replacing the chalice and bowing his head. My three-year-old mouth opened and out came the blood-curdling shriek, 'He's lockin' it all away! And I didn't get any!'

It was the beginning of a difficult relationship with Catholicism generally, and I often think it goes back to that moment. As for the beautiful baby who had been born to our family that morning, perhaps few would have expected that one day she would record a song called 'Nothing Compares 2 U', which would enter people's memories with such beauty and power. Certainly there is possibility in the air, a little magic in December. And no amount of tinsel and gaudiness and noise can ever truly crush it out.

Pontius Pilate as an Old Man in France
17 December 2008

For years after his crucifixion, I did not think of him.
Preoccupied, sand-blown, by what came next.
My demotion, relocation – I'm not sure of the term.
Latin is subtle. My decentralisation.

They say he was born at the close of the year.
His followers I mean; they rumour of him still.
The fools do not realise a wintertime child
Is always unlucky, will be forgotten in the end.

I missed Palestine for a while. The girls
There were beautiful. But what matters that
At the death of a career? Thirty years'
Service rinsed away in a hot moment.

My wife did not come with me here. We had lost
Our cadence. And she'd never liked me much.
My touch did not content her; I was fat
By then, did not contest the divorce.

She was kind to our sons. I cannot gripe.
I simply wasn't the marrying type.

She lives back in Rome; a government villa
In the red loamy hills – the gardens are pleasant –
By the cedar forest close to the Via Rugalla
Where we hotly courted once. But it doesn't
Do to fix on the past. 'Time's a river,'
Wrote Heraclitus. It can't be re-crossed.
I think of her sometimes. I'll never
See her again. And my children, too, are lost.
So that really now, there is only work
To fill up the days and the sleeting nights.
I don't complain. It's worthy of remark
How exiles always have limited rights.
She ignores my sometime letters. Perhaps it is best.
When a marriage has died, it is wiser laid to rest…

And the natives, these Gauls – they could be worse.
My soldiers report that they are obedient, clean,
Understand what is expected. Of course
They do not love us, because they have seen
Our capability, know we are strict,
But a *modus vivendi* has been reached
By now: I demand that any edict
Be totally observed – but if approached
I can be reasonable, will give ear
To a case. They already know they're crushed.
No point in humiliation when fear
Is enough. It is folly to grind them.
Better to promulgate bright future days,
The bad years of liberty long behind them.

I am safe in most of the city when I walk at night –
(Caesar, in Rome, could you boast half as much?)
I crucify few, show discretion, reduce taxes,
Torture but rarely, water-board their thieves.
My administration has brought peace, they are not hungry
Any more. And yet – it is strange – they look

At me resentfully, like crocodiles
Up to their snouts in some famished swamp.
Guile in the glances of their children too;
The patient serenity of their hatred.

I rise in the dark, attempt lyrics, odes,
The scratch of my nib on the lamb-skin vellum.
The dawn-lit rite damps down my sleepless thoughts,
This desk a kind of raft to which I grip;
Its inks and quills; the serpents of its scrolls;
Its small bust of Caesar; its map of Judea.

And he comes to me, then. In the night,
Like a ghost. In this last cold month
Of the year, he always comes.
The season of his birth, so his followers whisper,
When the glister of the ice makes the lake
A place of dangers, and the snow wolves
Haunt the bins of the city.

I sense him in mist, in steam, in the frost
That glitters dead cornfields in wintertime.
In rainstorms, in hail, in the bowl in which I wash,
In the water I shave with, the ice in my wine.
I taste him in the empty and snow-muffled squares,
In the spittle of my mouth, in my blood when I am cut;
In the strange tears I weep, in my sweat when I dread
The Via Doloroso of an empty bed.

And my thirst is a dredger, my cud a cake of salt,
Unquenchable nights in the wringing, ruined sheets
That shackle my limbs. Is it now my fault
I granted the abasement you appeared to seek?
I bathe in him, drink him – can never be free.
Gods – *Gods* – you have abandoned me.

I see him in snowfields, the slow thaw of his victory
Dripping from icicles; I crunch him in puddles.
My bread tastes of perspiration, my wine of blood;
He flakes in my palm when a hailstone smacks my skin.
'Leave me,' I mumble, 'for pity, let me be –'
And my bodyguards believe I am speaking to them.

All those years I did not think of him. Hardly at all.
Would never grant him anchor in the Tiber of the mind;
For I did as duty needed. *I followed my orders.*
A problem needs solutions. Are you crazy? Blind?
Then run to your vagrant! See if he heals.
'Forgiveness'? 'Mercy'? These are words for little girls.
'Give your coat to your brother'? 'Help the frail'? 'Love the
    poor'?
Political correctness gone mad; nothing more.

He was a misfit who heard voices;
A prisoner; an itinerant;
A butt of jokes; a baby; not a man of the world.
A tramp born in a pigsty, in the reeking filth and cold.
He will soon be forgotten. And I will grow old.
And they will see I did my duty,
A beautiful thing.
And they will honour *me* then,
In the closing of the year,
When water freezes over,
Until snowdrops appear
And cows are led from dark stables,
Stupefied by sunlight.
And my hands will again be clean
As winter.

The Problem with Obama
7 January 2009

Kinda hard for a bard to know what to do
Now George Bush is goin'; me career could be through.
Got a bootful of blues and I'm feelin' melodrama –
Cos there's nothing that rhymes with –'Barack Obama'.

What a time for a rhymer and it's drivin' me insane
Cos I can't contrive rhymin's for the Presidential name
And I'm sayin' all me prayers to the Dali Lama
Cos I can't think of anything rhymes with 'Obama'.

In the midst of all elation, the frustration increases,
And I'm fecked since he's elected and I'm fallin' fast to pieces
And Michelle's about as lovely as all three of Bananarama
But her surname's a tough one. Cos nothin' rhymes with
    Obama.

What a great First Lady, and there's gonna be less of
All the nonsense of the past, and it's good and progressive.
Two little girls as pretty as inverted commas,
They're a fine first family – they're called the Obamas.

And if we said it 'Obomma' like they do in the States
It'd make me life calma and me rhymin' sound great

But it's causin me trouble and it's causin me trauma
Cos there's nothin in the whole world rhymes with Obama.

He's a smooth clever dude, he's a feller called Barack an'
He'll soon be the leader of all folks American.
He's fast on his feet and he's full of new thinkin'
He's a bit James Brown, a bit Abraham Lincoln.

He lived in Honolulu, where Elvis once thundered,
I'd say 'Aloha' on the blower if I only had his number,
Cos he's groovy as a surfboard, he's ready to go,
Cool as Captain Steve McGarrett in *Hawaii Five-O*.

Deh-deh-deh-deh DUH deh – that's how the theme-tune
    went.
Hope they play at the moment he becomes the President,
And I'd write him up an anthem but God help me, Momma,
I just can't come up with anything rhymes with Obomma.

Me thinking cap is on and I've been searchin' through the
    dictionary
Leafin' through the reference books both factual and fictionary.
Me teacher used to say to me *A Sheosaimh, ná bí dána.*
Ach níl fhios agam an rím atá ar Yankee Uachtarána.

'All Kinds of Everything', a ditty by Dana,
The Buena Vista Social Club they hail from Havana.
And Daniel O'Donnell prefers to be in Buncrana,
But it's curses writin' verses about – Barack Obama...

From the halls of Montezuma to the homes of Donegal,
We'll be spreadin' subtle rumours that he comes from
    Moneygall.
Oh he's Offaly's finest, a bit of a smoothie.
Biffo's charismatic cousin but he duzzen be as moody.

Say what you like and you can call it a scandal,
But I can't come up with anything rhymes with his handle,
Called him all sorts of names cos he opposed Iraq,
Yeah, they told a lot of porkies 'bout that feller called Barack.
As for me, I'm burnin' incense to Vishnu and Rama,
For the life of me, there's nothin' that rhymes with Obama.

Gerard Manley Hopkins was a great one for the rhymin',
With his lines alliteratin' and his vowels nicely chimin'.
But if faced with 'Obama', he'd be losin' his poise as
He tried to find some similarly soundin' noises.
Here in Ireland sure it's easy, sure there's never any trouble,
Fianna Fáil rhymes with Dáil, rhymes with property bubble,
We're a nation of poets all wise and amusin'
And we never met a metaphor we didn't love usin'.

For the famous Seamus Heaney, 'hope and history rhyme',
Well it's more than can be uttered at the present hard time.
He's an Illinoisan senator, it's certainly annoyin'
That his name is hard to rhyme, and it means I'm not
    enjoyin'
The great anticipation, on the fun there's an embargo,
Till I think of something rhymes with that feller from
    Chicargo,
Cos Palin rhymed with failin' and McCain rhymed with
    pain.
But Barack don't rhyme with nothin' and it's causin' me some
    strain!

You might think you got problems what with downturn and
    recession;
I ain't sayin' you don't, but this is givin' me depression,
We're surrounded by ineptitude and bankers and liars
But there's tougher times coming for us versifiers.
And it's makin' me breathless and it's makin' me pant:

He kept sayin', 'Yes We Can.' But no we bloody can't
Find anything decent that rhymes with his name!
I don't think of something soon, I'm outta of the poetry
    game!

And I've travelled all the world from Ballybunion to Bahama,
And I've paced the floor all night in my best pajama.
But in all the linguistical panorama
I'm fecked if there's anything rhymes with Obama.

But maybe that's his point: don't imagine it, be it.
The world is right in front of you. You just have to see it.

Farewell to President Bush
16 January 2009

Dear George,

A little note just to say how much we're all going to miss you. To a remarkably broad coalition, you proved a dauntless adversary: the international banking system, American house owners, the United States' car industry – you ruined them all. You did more to destroy the capitalist system than Marx and Che Guevara put together. But to comedians you were the gift that kept on giving. I don't know how they're going to manage without you.

You were much admired by leading right-wing conservatives, the kind of down-home, God-fearing, Christian folk who regard a pyramid of naked Iraqis as par for the course but want to ban *Harry Potter* novels in case they corrupt our children. And for your services to the English language, you surely deserve a Pulitzer. 'Our enemies are innovative and resourceful,' you once said. 'They never stop thinking about new ways to harm our country and our people, and neither do we.' And speaking about Hurricane Katrina, you provided inspiring leadership by saying, 'The good news is... out of this chaos is going to come a fantastic Gulf Coast, like it was before. Out of the rubbles of Trent Lott's house... he's lost his entire house... there's going to be a fantastic house. And I'm looking forward to sitting on the porch.'

Well, George, you're finally heading directly towards that porch. Which probably means you're going to end up in the garage. And let's hope you enjoy it.

I was in New York a couple of weeks ago, the great city in which I once lived, and one night I found myself watching the television. And there you were again, George, like a guardian angel. It was an old clip but I was happy to see it again.

You were attending a rally at Kansas University when a student asked if you had seen the movie *Brokeback Mountain*, a film about the love affair between two cowboys. I hesitate to call you a horny-handed son of Texas, but you can see why the student would have been interested in your reaction. To his enquiry, you did your weasel-in-the-headlights gape before plunging into the depths of an opinion, 'I hadn't seen it... I would be glad to talk about ranching... but I haven't seen the movie... I've heard about it... I hope you go... you know... heh-heh... I hope you go back to the ranch and the farm is what I was going to say... I hadn't seen it.'

Ranching? *Brokeback Mountain*, a film about 'ranching'? Was this some new erotic euphemism that had not been brought to my attention? Were the young people of the world approaching one another in nightclubs and saying, 'Any chance of a good ranching? Ah, go on. I won't tell anyone.' No, it was only the latest of those eerie eruptions we might call the George Bush mind-burp.

Leaving aside the likelihood that you had ever seen a film that did not contain the words 'Porky's' or 'Revenge' in its title, and could not be enjoyed while pelting a buddy with nuts, I felt for you, George, poor ditz up there all alone. Having to answer. Like, a question. With everyone. Listening. Such moments were best watched through the grid of the fingers. We could almost hear the brain-cogs shear.

First love fades. It's an old and painful story, George. The affection many of us once felt for your wonderful homeland you did a heck of a lot to obliterate. But I remember an earlier era in my life, when America still seemed a place of endless possibility. It doesn't seem that now, at least not to me, but a remarkable new president is about to take office and perhaps the fondness and respect so many of us once felt for your country will be rekindled again, as I hope.

I leave the last words to the central character in a book of mine called *Redemption Falls*, the Irish immigrant General James Con O'Keeffe, who writes to his son, in 1866: 'Tell any pitiable bigot who crosses your path that a black man will be elected President of these United States one day, and when that day dawns, that beautiful day, this nation will be released into the greatness of its promise and will shine as the lighthouse of civilisation.'

I wrote that sentence in September 2005, in the New York Public Library on 42nd Street and Fifth Avenue, and as I walked home to my family that evening, through the operatically noisy streets of Manhattan, I remember thinking it could never come true. But not even you, George, could put out all the lights. Happy retirement. Not a moment too soon.

Is the Taoiseach Speaking English?
28 January 2009

People have remarked from time to time on the Taoiseach's unusual approach to language. For example, he used the word 'internalise' not so long ago when talking of Ireland's economic difficulties. The Irish people have not 'sufficiently internalised' the crisis, he moodily alleged. Lesser mortals, such as you and I, might have said 'thought about' or 'considered'. But it isn't fair to criticise the Taoiseach for the manner in which he speaks English. Because he isn't. He's speaking Biffish.

Biffish is one of the most ancient languages of these islands – the Biffish Isles – along with Scots Gallic, Welsh, McCreevish and Ahernish. Mr Cowen speaks it perfectly, as how would he not, and he descended from a medieval clan of monastic druids who probably invented it in the first place. It is the perfect language for the delivery of bad economic news and the occasional pithy – indeed biffy – remark.

Biffish, like all the great languages, has its ancient literary treasures. The *Táin Bó Bhiffo*, *The Flight of the Wild Biffos*, *The Biffos of Lir*, *The Annals of the Four Biffos*, and the rousingly heroic tale of brave Cu Cullen and his ministerial brother Martin. And who could forget that wonderful saga *Fiche Bliain in Fás (On a Fantastic Expense Account)*? These treasures offered our people sustenance when times of great hardship and hunger began – round about June 2008, to be precise. Furthermore, like every other antique tongue, Biffish has its treasury of beautiful folk song. Many of these ballads have been translated, of course, some by William Biffter Yeats and other scholars. And several have been covered by that fine singer Brian Cowen himself – or 'The Fury Brother' as I prefer to call him. Yes, he often appears on the BBC – and I don't have to tell you what *that* stands for. Who could forget the Taoiseach's own unplugged renderings from the back of a lorry of such heartwarming patriotic classics as 'Wrap the Buckpass Round Me Boys', 'The Road to God Knows Where (But Probably Bankruptcy)' and 'The Night Before Enda Kenny Was Stretched'. Then there is the 'Caoineadh na dTrí Mhuire' (The Lament of the Three Marys: Hanafin, Harney and Coughlan) There is 'Beidh Repossession Amárach i gContae an Chláir'. And there is that heartbreakingly tragic lament in honour of everyone's favourite minister, 'Willie Beag O'Dea, A Stóirín'. (The noble Beethoven himself adapted this melody for his touching and world-famous Bifth Symphony.)

Oh and how do you do, me Willie O'Dea,
And you speaking the Biffish much betther than me.
And Limerick's a lady, or so I'm advised,
If so she's a lady you've… internalised.
And you manglin' the language and vexin' the verbs
As though you've been smokin' some verboten herbs
And your cara from Clara's in similar strain
For he does it again and again and AGAIN.
Did they cut back the wages? Do they have the odd rages?
Did they say we're in crisis and tightening belts?
And the thing that's been makin' me tense is
That they've twelve grand a year in expeh-heh-henses.

And all throughout the Biffish Empire, microbiffologists study the ancient tongue, a language of great subtlety and beauty.

'Cutback' in English, in Biffish is 'readjustment'. The phrase 'government falling to pieces before our very eyes', in Biffish is 'wide-ranging cabinet discussion'. And the phrase 'parliamentary colleagues' has a vivid equivalent in Biffish, often used by Tánaiste Mary Coughlan, a great lover of the *cúpla focal*.

So next time you hear the Taoiseach employing what seem to you to be unusual expressions, don't blame *him* – blame yourself for not understanding. Like everything else that's wrong with the country, it's all your fault, not his. And remember: if you must sing – sing a Biffish song. Now, I'm off to internalise my dinner.

An Amazing Invention
4 February 2009

Recently I read an article in the *New York Times*. It seems Sony have produced an electronic portable screen onto which the entire text of a novel can be downloaded. And the fine people at Amazon have manufactured their own reading device, the Kindle, with a screen 'so paper-like, it demands to be read'. What'll they think of next?

I find these cutting-edge technological developments fascinating, of course, but a while ago I came across one even more astonishing innovation which I would like to recommend to readers. It's cheaply produced, made of entirely recyclable materials, user-friendly in almost any situation you care to imagine – even in the bath. It requires no recharging or wireless connections. It's called 'the book'. It's widely available. And it's even more paper-like than the Kindle.

The other night, my eight-year-old son asked me if I thought a time machine would be invented within my lifetime. It was nice to be able to tell him that the time machine was actually invented several centuries ago by that clever man Mr Gutenberg. For the book can transport you to all sorts of time zones and virtual realities, to distant planets, magical worlds, to anywhere you'd like to go. The territory of the novel, from the form's first appearance, has been vast, capacious and daring. The shipwreck, the riot, the revolution, the storm, the knights charging windmills, the madwoman in the attic, the children of the ghetto, the pickpockets of London, the explorer who finds himself in a land of little people, the *Wuthering Heights*, the depths. Through these territories, and many others, has gone wandering the storyteller, with only words as a lamp. He has seen the hunchback in the cathedral, and Huckleberry Finn, Madame Bovary and Count Dracula and Leopold Bloom. *Paddy Clarke Ha Ha Ha* and *The Secret Scripture*. What a pantheon, what a party, what a multitude of selves. The novel has the capacity to describe the drama of life as no other art form can do. The original virtual reality, it downloads more quickly than broadband, and its effects, as we know, are more widespread.

It's also the form that captures most affectingly what it's like to be a human being. We carry the past and the future as we go. We drag anchors that are attached to us – indeed we sometimes cling to them. The very essence of the human is to experience time in this way. In addition, we carry the pasts of those people around us, and frequently, also, their futures, which we embody, because we ourselves are part of that future, and will be part of our loved ones' pasts. Only the novel can describe what that's like.

And when we look at some of the oldest things any culture possesses, we see the modes of storytelling everywhere. The Greek myths, the Celtic sagas, the legends of vanished societies. And what is the Bible, that stupendous work of storytelling, if not a kind of jigsaw novel? Four separate accounts of the life of its hero! Angels! Talking serpents! Dead men walking! 'In the beginning was the Word,' the scripture tells us. But perhaps, in the beginning, was the story.

And consider those fantastic words at the end of the gospel of John. 'And there are many more wonders that Jesus did, the which, if they should be written every one, I think the whole of the world could not contain the books that should be written.' How I love the childlike innocence of that beautiful line. It connects us with the author across the millennia. We know exactly how he felt.

The world is stranger than we can hope to understand – to picture it, to imagine it, is immediately to make a puzzle. Human existence is so mysterious, a Rubik's Cube we can't solve, no matter how many times we turn the squares. I like a novel that feels as though you can walk into it, look around, touch the walls, the way we walk into a piece of great music, like Handel's *Messiah* or The Beatles' 'A Day in the Life'. These are structures we want to experience again: one visit is not enough. I want the potholes of a novel, the bumps, the flaws, the cracks in the ceiling, the draughts. I don't want it to be smooth; I want to see the textures. I want fiction with friction, jaggedness, juice. I want the words to rub together so the sparks fly in my face. And I can say with the great French writer, Anatole Broyard, 'The more I like a book, the more slowly I read it.' This spontaneous talking-back to a book is one of the things that make reading so valuable.

Ugliness is so widespread and profitable and catching-on that if you could buy stocks in it you'd be a billionaire. There is a property crisis, we are told, but not an ugliness crisis. Invasions are justified on the basis of non-existent weapons, torture is called liberation, the hangman a hero, and everything Orwell told us has turned out to be true. Only his date of *1984* was wrong. Language is debased on an everyday basis, often by being made too smooth. The best readers, as the American novelist Philip Roth once remarked, 'come to fiction to be free of everything that is not fiction.' But that beautiful remark is not entirely accurate. The best readers come to fiction because of the paradox it offers. To know briefly what it is to transcend the self, and to imagine briefly what it is to be someone else, is to come to know more profoundly what it is to be yourself. I'm telling you, this is magic and it works.

It's available in your local bookstore, for less than the cost of a round of drinks. So do yourself a favour. Dive in.

A Birthday Letter
to my Stepmother
18 February 2009

Dear Viola,

It can't be easy being anyone's stepmother. From our earliest childhood, the stepmother peoples our fairytales – a woman portrayed almost invariably as wicked, brimming with resentments and cruelties.

There are days when I find it hard to be a good father to my own children. To be a parent to anyone else's seems unimaginable. But that was what you were, and it wasn't always easy. Another woman's frightened children tumbled in and out of your life. We were accepted, helped, minded, reassured. I'm not saying you were a saint. You were something more decent than that. A woman trying to do her best for people who needed her. A woman who would never break a promise.

In caring for a household which, at times, contained eight children, you witnessed plenty of ups and downs. You saw love stories conducted over a telephone at which a queue used to form. The bill must have been the equivalent of a small country's national debt. How many broken hearts did you soothe? How many tales of woe did you endure? You were not given to easy mottos or cheap advice, but I remember you once telling me something that remains with me still: always act with courage when love is at stake. When you're disappointed, be brave. And if you have to disappoint, be braver. Love is not sentiment, the easily repeated nothing; it is commitment and selflessness and patience. It is the acknowledgement, as Iris Murdoch so beautifully wrote, that another human being is real. We don't always remember this fact when we're thinking about the children in our lives. But you and my father did.

Ireland is a country murderously besotted with its myths. In the frightened and obedient society in which I grew up, there was still the widespread idea that a family had one definition: two people who have never been married to anyone else, happily married now, with children they always wanted, probably with a dog and never a disagreement, the picture of contentment personified. Nobody is ever hurt. No feelings have been crushed. No hopes have been trampled. Everything worked out. No one has baggage. Children are always angelic. The good have been rewarded with happiness. The fact that there were so very many of us who did not belong to such a family was invariably and continuously forgotten. Those of us who were children of separated couples felt we were the only people in the world to whom this had ever happened. That's the way it was. I don't think I exaggerate. Couples who had separated must have often felt the same way. But, to me, you embodied a truth which has become part of my thinking: that below all the propaganda and phoneyness and lies, there are quieter and very powerful solidarities that arise between people for the most important reason of all – because they should. We're a country full of carers of various kinds, minding the sick, the fragile, the vulnerable, those who need us. There are families we are born into and there are often families we choose, which don't fit the categories, the dictionary definitions. There is no destiny waiting for us, no preordained path. It is rather that those we meet and care for become that destiny. It is only a matter of recognising them.

I don't know that you'd put it like that, or if you ever thought about it much. Probably you were too busy loving us to analyse. But I see now that you made a decision that you would always do your best to stand by us, never leave when things got tough. And when they did get tough, as from time to time they did, I still never saw you break a promise or heard you tell me a lie. Blood may be thicker than water, but we make our own wine. It's the greatest lesson of being a stepson.

This week sees an important birthday for you and I send you my loving thanks, for your wisdom, your gentleness and solidarity. Like my father, you are uncomfortable with being praised, and would always very much rather no fuss was made at all. You like quietness, no atmospheres; things running along in peace. I've known you half your life. You've known me three quarters of mine. Like any other human being, I contain my mother and my father, and theirs, and theirs, all the way into the past, and I am fortunate in having come to see the beauty of everyone who made me. But I don't think I could have done that, had it not been for knowing you. So I consider myself blessed and honoured that you were one of the people who made me. Sometimes it's better to have had two mothers.

Ode to Lent
25 February 2009

Lent is arriving, we're all self-depriving,
We're giving up ciggies and candies and booze.
And it's sackcloth and ashes; it's teeth making gnashes,
It's weeping and wailing when we turn on the news.

It's a strange dream or trip; we're condemned to some kip
Where the landlord oppresses by rules all unwritten.
We seem to be tenants, we're all doin' penance
For sins only some had the fun of committin'.

The circles are golden, the centre's not holdin',
And chancer financiers of various sorts
Are under enquiry, I'm bound for The Priory,
You'd wonder if anyone's bound for the courts?

I once was a feaster but my diary says Easter
Is forty long days of denial away.
We'll be walking the wilderness, plagued by bad builder-ness,
Property billionaires learning to pray.

George Lee's gettin' gloomier, trousers are roomier,
Belts have been tightened, we're Bertie Aherned.
There's a cross on our forehead, the money's been borrah'd
And nobody knows if it's bein' returned.

You and me bought a bank, and I'd just like to thank
Messers Cowen and Lenihan, making the bids
For the sensible mission and wise acquisition
Of billions of debt on behalf of our kids.

Who needs chocolate bunnies when all the bank's money's
Been given for purchasing shares in itself?
Let the country go begging while some are nest-egging,
And what could be better for spiritual health?

And it's said the recession'll fill the confessional,
Sinners in jeeps speedin' up to the chapel an'
Pious orations, resistin' temptations,
Self-mortifications now spring does be dapplin'.

Contrition's gone popular, donnin' the scapular,
Cuttin' your pay to a million or two.
But the hairshirt don't itch when it's stitched for the rich,
And you've mates in high places to iron it for you.

We'll be giving up cookies, deserting the bookies,
Swearing off drink, giving alms to the poor,
Laying off rudeness and thoughts of low lewdness,
And turning our minds from all matters impure

And defining new goals for the sake of our souls,
And the bank may be bust – but Thank God it's our own.
And there's no point in cryin', the fellers called Brian
Are dyin' to help us confess and atone.

Ashes on brows, not much cash, many rows,
And the assets of Anglo? Dunno where they went.
And I'm feeling some rancour to end up a banker
When the money's all gone. Cos it's all been
Lent.

A Word I Like
4 March 2009

If there's one thing I like, it's that lovely word 'like'. Like, I don't just like *like* it. I *love* it like. Like, there something about 'like' that just gets me, like, excited. It's like it reminds me how wonderful is the English language, like, with these hundreds and thousands, like *millions* of words, like liken, likelihood, likely, likeability. And what I *really* like, LIKE, is how the American sitcom is teaching us to like, *like* using the word 'like' in, like, these totally likeable new ways, like.

I'm like SO full of liking when I hear, like, young Irish people, like, talking, like that, like. I like it. It's like, likeable. In fact I don't just like, *like* it, I SO like it. It's like words just SO like fail me, like. It's like do, ray, me, fa, SO, like fabulous like, and it's only rock and roll like, but I like it, like.

Like, the other night I'm at home like, with the wife like, who I like like, like I don't just like *like* her, I *love* her, like. And we're having like a conversation like, like two people talking, like. And I was like, 'Likely, it SO looks like rain, like,' and she was like, 'Yeah, like it does, like.' And *I'm* like, 'Do you like it, when people say like, like?' and *she's* like, 'Like what like, like *that*, like?' And I'm like 'Exactly', and she's like, 'Don't mind like, it's SO like a matter for *them*, like. As you reap shall you sew like, like the Bible once had it. Like, the BIBLE, for God's sake.' Like that, like.

And I'm like, 'You don't find it, like, annoying?'

You know what she says to me?

'What are you like?'

And I'm like, '*I* dunno. What AM I like?'

And she's like, 'Oh leave it, whatever, whatever...'

And I'm like, 'I don't like that much. What are YOU like, more like.'

And she's like, 'Don't be like that to ME, like', and I'M like, 'To YOU, LIKE,' and she's like, 'ME LIKE YOU LIKE ME LIKE YOU, LIKE,' and now we're getting, like, divorced.

It's like I'm becoming like a grumpy old man, like, one of those miserable, whingeing, hard-to-*like* fellows who do be appearing now and again on the telly like. They're SO like complaining, like *lighten* up like, for God's sake, like say it like you *mean* it, like yeah? I mean what are they LIKE, like? Do you know what I mean, like? Like what are they actually LIKE, like?

'Do you know what I mean?' That's another one now like. Likewise. Another little, like, *expression* they like, *like*, like. It's like my friend Luke like. He's a locksmith in Liffey Street. Terrible man for 'Do you know what I mean?' Yes, I know what you mean, Luke, like, why are you like CONSTANTLY saying 'Do you know what I mean, like?' But do you KNOW what I mean, like, DO YOU? Yes, I SO know what you mean, Luke, like it's OBVIOUS what you mean like, *you're asking me if I know what you mean, like.*

No, I'm not! I'm only, like, saying 'do you know what I mean, like?' It's just something I like to SAY like. I obviously wasn't asking you if you KNOW what I MEAN like. Like I'm assuming that's totally *obvious*, like.

Whatever? Whatever. That's like *a comma* now, like. Word 'whatever'. Do you know what I mean, like? 'Whatever.' People saying things in inverted 'whatevers'. Like share and share alike, like. Whatever. If you like, like. What happened to, like, *liking the language, like*? To saying what you MEAN like? Do you know what I mean like? Whatever.

Like I'm as bad myself, like. No I really, really am, like. Do you know what I mean? I SO am. I don't like it but it's true, like. It's like *infectious*. I'm SO as bad. No I'm WAY so as bad. Next time I meet anyone who, like, doesn't like say 'like', like, I'm SO gonna like take a picture of them with my camera. It's a Leica. Well I *say* it's a Leica but it isn't like, a *Leica*, it's more that it's LIKE a Leica, like. Do you know what I mean, like? Like if you put my camera down beside a Leica like, you'd say they were very alike, like.

It just seems a bit lacklustre, like. That way of talking. And if we could say what we MEAN, like. Not that that's what I mean. But we'd all be a lot more – I dunno. Do you know what I mean, like? Maybe you do. Sure anyway. Whatever. Good luck, like.

Ode to Saint Patrick
11 March 2009

Hail glorious, Saint Patrick,
Back in four thirty-two
You were tearin' round Erin
With conversion to do.
No, not sterling to euros
But the version devout.
If you're comin' next week
Would you smuggle us out?

Hail glorious, Saint Patrick.
When I were a lad
The parade was pathetic,
The floats fairly sad,
And the only attraction
For boys adolescent –
The American colleens
In miniskirts fluorescent.

Oh they seemed so romantic.
Their cheeks they were dimpled.
Their grins orthodontic.
Their thighs was goose pimpled.
The sousaphones blared,
The high kickers were keen.

Their makeup was orange.
Their knickers was green.

Oh, Saint Patrick's heroic!
Saint Patrick's the bold!
And Saint Patrick's athletic
Or so I've been told.
And for Lá Fhéile Pádraig
It's about-to-arrive-time
And I'm hopin' to heaven
He's listenin' to *Drivetime*.

I've a bone for to pluck, pal,
Sweet saint of our nation,
We're sunk in the muck, pal,
We're feelin' deflation.
We've bottomed our dollars,
We're tusslin' and tiffin'
And the Island of Scholars
Has become… Inishbiffen.

Three leaves on the shamrock,
The harp shall be plucked.
To be totally honest,
We're totally… *bocht*.
It's a *focal as Gaeilge*
Much beloved by Peig Sayers,
O ochón 's ochón… for me AIB shares.

Hail glorious, Saint Patrick,
The cabinet's fled.
The government jet is so easily led
In the chilly month of March when it's hard to pay the gas
But they're working hard for Ireland up above in Business
 Class.

Hail glorious, Saint Patrick
In episcopal rig-out.
We're a fiscal bad risk,
We could do with a dig-out.
If the patron of Bertie's auld gaff is your friend,
Please request of Saint Luke if he's shekels to lend?

Hail glorious, Saint Patrick
There'll be jiggin' and reelin'
And prayin' and strayin' and standin' and kneelin'
The fact is, in practice, we're banjaxed and busted
And the Land of the Shamrock has been… readjusted.

Hail glorious Saint Patrick,
We owe half-a-trillion,
O musher and crusher of creatures reptilian,
But you left one or two in position substantial
On heavenly bonus in boardrooms financial.

Hail glorious, Saint Patrick,
We're seekin' some closure,
There's buckos could do with a belt of your crozier.
It's all right for some I could mention for sure.
The Leinster House lovelies with pension secure.

Hail Glorious, Saint Patrick
The blight of the heathen!
We could do with a bit of your best intercedin'.
So look down in thy love, O you scourge of the snake,
On Erin's green valleys. *And give us a break!*

Why I Need Therapy
18 March 2009

It would be terribly unfair to compare Homer Simpson with the Taoiseach. One is a large, surly grump who likes a few beers and is rarely in control of the catastrophes unfolding around him. And the other, of course, is yellow. Yet the recent featuring of Ireland in an episode of *The Simpsons* would give you a certain pause for thought. It is hardly a surprise that America's favourite dysfunctional family has roots in our own sweet soil. And they're only the latest Irish-American characters to appear perpetually in the grip of neurosis.

Like many people, I've been enjoying the great Gabriel Byrne's performance as a New York psychotherapist in the award-winning drama *In Treatment*. And, oddly, it has been raising a haunting memory of the moment I first realised I needed therapy myself. Even more oddly, that moment involved Gabriel Byrne and New York. I'm beginning to feel I'm fictional.

One night in that city, I was attending the theatre with my wife. Gabriel Byrne was the star of the play, *A Touch of the Poet* by the greatest Irish-American writer, Eugene O'Neill. It's a story about an Irishman who is seldom far from rage, who blows his top more violently than Vesuvius. I had broken my ankle earlier that week. I was uncomfortable, in pain and tired. As the play came to an end and Gabriel Byrne gave his bow, I turned to the people beside me and asked politely if they would allow us to leave. But they didn't. I was 'disrespecting the actors', they told me. I would have to wait until the house lights came up.

'You don't understand,' I said. 'See, I have a broken ankle. I just want to get out before the crowd.'

'No,' said my neighbours. 'You gotta wait your turn.'

Something strange began to happen. As I repeated my request and it was repeatedly declined, a combination of physical pain and emotional irritation began to take hold of my senses.

'You're not listening to me,' I said.

'That's right, we're not.'

Well, I'm sorry to say, I lost it. I swore. I blasphemed. Soon I was ranting. I profaned. I cursed. I insulted. I uttered words I didn't know I knew, terms too horrendous to repeat, offered suggestions that could only have been taken up by a contortionist. By now, the stage was empty and the lights were on, but the one inside my head was flashing red.

People in the seats around me were staring, aghast. A little old lady was backing away from me smiling, as though I were a psychopath who would have to be indulged a little while longer before uniformed persons arrived with electric cattle prods or a blowpipe containing a tranquilising dart.

My antagonists said nothing – I think they were too shocked. Their silence poured petrol on my hatred. They were *cowards*, I bawled at them. They were brigands, bounders, bowsies and bollixes. Finally, they got up to leave and I hobbled out after them. I was howling as I pursued them through the theatre's lobby and, yes, even out to the street.

Attempting dignified silence, they joined the taxi queue. I limped up to them and resumed my harangue. Their parentage, their appearances, their imagined bedroom proclivities – nothing was safe from my raging scorn. A crowd began to gather as I continued my invective, my anger growing fiercer as it stoked itself. Some of them began uttering low cries of encouragement or possibly ironic cheers. By now, I was shrieking like a banshee on steroids. I think they thought I was part of the play.

It was then that I began to realise something dark and terrible: that I was *enjoying myself, shouting at these people who had wronged me* and that such a chance for righteous indignation might never come again. These small-time tyrants became everyone who had ever offended me. And now it was payback time.

I stabbed the air with my finger. I sneered. I mocked. I exaggerated my hurt feelings, the seriousness of my injury. A recording of my bellowings, in order to be made fit for broadcast, would include so many censoring bleeps that it would sound like something frightening being conveyed in Morse code. I threatened that I would put one of my crutches to a purpose unimagined by orthopaedic medicine. It was then that I passed some terrible point of rage-fuelled self-pity beyond which no civilised person should go.

'*I am a sick man,*' I howled. '*Look at me! Are you proud? Don't you think I've suffered enough?*'

'*Yeah!*' called the crowd. 'Give the poor guy a break! Shame on you people! Booo!'

At this point, they set off on foot, still without a word to me, through the heaving throngs on 42nd Street. But, not to be denied the crescendo of my vengeance, I tottered on my crutches in their wake. By now, to my deepest shame, I was challenging them to stand and fight – this middle-aged man who looked like a suburban dentist and his middle-aged bespectacled wife. My own wife was threatening that she would abandon me to the night if I didn't desist immediately. With a final fanfare of F-words, I allowed myself to be led away. I deserved her disapproval. I had behaved disgracefully.

It was a pity to see a play, we agreed in the taxi, that depicted Irish males as emotionally illiterate, only capable of expressing hurt feelings by behaving like idiots. Eugene O'Neill may have been a great writer. But he did not really understand us. The bleeping bleep.

A Broken Hallelujah
1 April 2009

I suspect that like many parents my most memorable Christmas was the one following the birth of our first child. We had been living in London for some years and that's where the lad was born. But when he was a few months old we returned to live in Dublin, arriving at the start of Christmas week, 2000. The plan had been for my wife and the baby to fly, and I would take our rusting decrepit car on the ferry. But in all the excitement and exhausted happiness and clutter of new parenthood, we left it too late to book a flight and there wasn't a seat to be had.

Thus I remember driving across England in that cold, late December, the last of the twentieth century, the last of a millennium, through fog and sleet and ice-glazed scenery, the wipers relentlessly fighting the grists of hail, and the crackle of the banjaxed radio. The car was older than our relationship, indeed practically on the scrap-heap, and at some point someone had spilled a pint of milk on the floor, which made the interior smell like Satan's halitosis. But you couldn't open the window – literally couldn't, in the case of one of the windows – because being face-whipped by a hailstorm as you're driving past Stoke isn't anyone's idea of air-conditioning. I had actually tried to sell the jalopy in London as a prelude to re-immigration, telling the dealer it had been valued at two and a half grand. He took it out for a brief test-drive before handing me back the keys. 'Fackin' key-ring's worf more than the car,' he said.

My wife was in the back, with a toaster on her lap, a portable telly beneath her feet, and her pockets full of spoons and forks. In my memory, she was wearing almost every exterior garment she possessed (a) because it was so cold, and (b) because we couldn't afford another suitcase. I had entrusted her with the really important things in my life, i.e. my Patti Smith and Clash records, and in my memory these were balanced on top of her head, in the manner of a Bedouin woman carrying a water-jar from an oasis, but in fact she was holding them in her frostbitten fingers, whose tips were turning a fetching shade of blue. Under many layers of clothing I had on my favourite T-shirt, an item purchased in revolutionary Nicaragua in 1985, the T-shirt having lasted longer than the revolution. Oh yeah – the baby was there too, strapped into a safety seat, but a safety seat whose workings neither of us had full confidence we understood because sadly we don't have a degree in Advanced Mechanical Engineering. While into the crock's boot had been packed the remainder of our worldly goods, total value about nine quid fifty.

I was full of mixed feelings about coming back to live in Ireland. Some of the happiest years of my life had been spent in London. I had met my wife there, had many friends and colleagues there, and had always felt strangely at home there, as I think many Irish people do. So why were we going to Dublin? I wasn't quite sure. As our car sputtered across England, my wife started telling me that it was all my idea, whereas I, countering brilliantly, said it had been all her idea. At some point we had an argument and I didn't speak to her for an hour. Well, I didn't like to interrupt her. As anyone who has ever undertaken that drive knows well, it's plain sailing through the English midlands, where things like motorways and electric lighting have been heard of, but when you cross the border in Wales, the roads start to narrow and snake, and what looks on a map as though it might take you ten minutes can end up taking you forty years. But rural Wales is of course a scenically attractive place, if you don't mind hearing 'Duelling Banjos' strike up in your head now and again. I was coughing and spluttering as a result of a bad cold, but it did make my attempts to pronounce those Welsh place-names beginning with two *Ls* as enjoyable as they were memorably phlegmy. We made it to Holyhead just as they closed the barriers. We were literally the last car allowed to board the ship, and if we hadn't had a baby with us I'm not sure the security guards would have taken pity. I had to do an awful lot of bleating and looking piteous and vulnerable, and as this was before Bertie Ahern's famous interview with Brian Dobson, it was hard to think of someone whose Oliver Twist-demeanour and facial expressions it might be useful to imitate.

It was the midnight sailing, and we rocked across the Irish Sea. It was a dreadful night, the worst crossing I've ever known. Through all of it, the little one slept soundly in a carry-cot on the floor of the lounge. Around us ranted the mobs of beer-fuelled émigrés, roaring, carousing, slapping one another on the back, singing carols with obscene or facetious new lyrics, and trying to garrotte one another with lengths of tinsel. It was like being at a re-enactment of a nineteenth-century *Punch* caricature of Irish people enjoying themselves at a funeral. There were rebel-yells and mawkish choruses, screechings, cursings, birdie-songs and boogieing and brandying. That shining pearl of Shane McGowan's genius, 'Fairytale of New York' was sung so oft and so badly that I came to hate it with a passion. I don't exaggerate when I tell you that to this very day, I immediately switch off the radio when it comes on. Every time a massive wave hit the ship, we seemed to rise a hundred feet in the air before crashing back down again with the implacable viciousness of a hanging judge's gavel. The gnash of glasses breaking. The moans of en-masse vomming. I couldn't believe the baby was so tolerant of the punk-rock ambience, and if I had never loved him before, which I had, very much, I think I bonded with him that night in some fundamental way. Here was a kid who could sleep through 'The Fields of Athenry'. Our Dozol bill would always be low.

By six in the morning the party had ended, mainly because

most of the celebrants were by now unconscious. Closer to dawn, the baby was still sleeping, comatose as a student, and his mum asked me to get her a bottle of water. After I'd done that, I remember asking her if she wanted to go out and get some air on the deck. She didn't really want to but she suggested I step out myself if I liked.

Everything was calm. It was a cold, clear morning. I don't think I had ever seen a sky that had so many stars, and certainly I never have since. You felt you could touch them, stir them around. There was an unearthliness about the beauty and the stillness. I walked the decks for a while. People were gathered here and there. And as I rounded the stern of the ship, there was an elderly couple who were sharing a flask of tea and listening to classical music on a radio. I don't know if I can convey to you the strange beauty of that scene: being that far out at sea, in the dark and the cold, with haunting music being played on a radio. I stood near them for a while. I think I was smoking. And what happened next, I'll never forget.

A piece of music they recognised came on. And I recognised it too. They turned it up a little and poured themselves another cup of tea. It was an extract from Handel's *Messiah*. You probably know it – you'll have heard it now and again. But you've likely never heard it in the circumstances I describe. The choir began to sing. And the old couple hummed along. And I found I could hardly move.

For unto us,
A child is born.
Unto us,
A son is given.

Now, I should tell you that I am not the kind of feller who easily cries. But when I heard those simple, beautiful words, it was hard to remember that. I stood in the dark and tried hard not to weep. Dawn began to come on. The sky turned red and gold. The ship was by now approaching Dun Laoghaire, the town where I grew up. I could actually see the pier where my pals and I used to hang out on summer evenings, the stretch of coastline at Sandycove, near where I kissed and was kissed for the first time, the steeples and the shopping centre, and Killiney Hill in the distance, its obelisk silhouetted against an impossibly scarlet dawn. I had a son. I was a father. I felt flooded with joy, as though everything in my life finally meant something.

I was coming home with my wife and our child. I couldn't believe the happiness. I felt we could face absolutely anything; we'd face it together. It was like a Christmas present from fate; that's how I felt about it anyway. But in another way it was nothing at all, just a moment in a life. It was a radio on a ship a few days before Christmas, among drunks and dreamers, in the darkness. 'A broken hallelujah,' Leonard Cohen might have said. But maybe that's the best kind of all.

Afterword
Old Suitcase with Contents:
No Offer Refused

I

The opened suitcase asked a short reprieve.
Before you junk me, touch what I enclose:
A boy, a girl, a scorched Midsummer's Eve.
Lost keys. A humid kiss. A book-bleached rose
In the pages of a paperback *Catcher in the Rye*.
A tape of Dylan, hoarse with lover's pain.
(… 'I laid on a dune… and looked at the sky'…)
He wanted her as rivers want the rain.
A night-tryst in the park. The burning gorse
Reflecting in the windows on the road.
They thought the houses burning, glimpsed the force
Of what it was they wanted, were afraid.
I close said the suitcase – I wrinkle, grown older;
But the flames in those windows still writhe, still smoulder.

II

Dalkey Island sulks; a bald Empress in a huff,
Her rubbled chapel and her tumbled port
Grown treeless now, where ancient winds rebuff

Bleak seals and rained-on goats, a ruined fort.
The suitcase dreams itself washed-up, beached;
An outcast lugged from a scudding yacht,
Rain-smitten, barnacled, kelped, wrack-wreathed,
Near a boy and girl kissing on a lobster-pot.
The suitcase gazes, dreeping in the furze:
They smell of one another and the sea-sodden peat,
Her hands inside his jacket – his in hers;
Soaked schoolbags in a tangle in the island sleet.
The current is fierce; pebbles crashing in the Sound;
The boy is long adrift, already long drowned.

III

This I saw said the suitcase. But I close what I contain.
Torn diaries. Old phone-bills. The tide-chart of a parting.
A card sent one Christmas. A wedding invitation.
I was stowed upside a closet in a dust-thick nook,
Hasped; clasped; unmentioned too long.
And I dreamed of some depth where the seaweed lives
And blue rumours of sunlight drift down to bless
Rusted buckles, cracked hinges, my sundered catches,
My secret combinations, my zips, my patches,
The pouches where an old letter might yet be asleep,
Swapped photos of their children.
I can live in the deep,
Closable like an oyster in the storm-blown seas,
But I know what is in me. A small, dark pearl
That grew from the grit in the sleep-crusted eyes
Of a waterfronting boy and a coast-town girl.

IV

I roost on my wardrobe, near the spider-webbed rafter
Where I slumber, old baggage, and my closeted contents:

Maps of island warrens; mildewed gatherings of novels,
And other nights, too, when I was unwisely undone,
The riptide churning like a sting.
Fingertips on faces, on the silk of an abdomen.
This too is within me, but I keep myself shut,
For my locks would burst like berries if I fumbled towards
      that.
I tense my slackened straps, turn my handle to the wall.
I need not be taken down every day – or at all.
My lining is torn. I am cluttered, dented.
A gaffer-taped rip down one seam of my hide.
I buckle when I open. I forget what I cost.
I am an orphanage.
I am property lost.

V

I console the gold flames in a window at midnight;
Crib-notes on The Sonnet; an unspooled cassette.
A shell. A quartz pebble. A poem attempted.
A Moving Hearts ticket. A comb. Divorced buttons.
These inhabit me now. I enfold them still.
And I, the rattle-bag, bunked in the murk,
Clutch-sack, salvage, I do not kiss and tell.
I accept my compartment. I do not need much.
With noisy, wanted children, my parents' mizzled thoughts
Must jumble like cross-tides.
I suppose they lost touch.
Or they share a locked cargo, a stowed, precious ache;
Like a snow-globe they treasure but can seldom bear to shake.
Then press down my lid. Thread these worn, untracked zips.
Close me to the silence of kneading mouths.
Only spare me a berth in your hold – nothing more.
For those nights can still shake me when the sea-storms roar.